# East-West Montage

# East-West Montage

## Reflections on Asian Bodies in Diaspora

Sheng-mei Ma

University of Hawai'i Press ★ Honolulu

12  11  10  09  08  07   6  5  4  3  2  1

**Library of Congress Cataloging-in-Publication Data**
Ma, Sheng-mei.
  East-West montage : reflections on Asian bodies in diaspora /
Sheng-mei Ma.
    p.  cm.
  Includes bibliographical references and index.
  ISBN 978-0-8248-3181-3 (pbk. : alk. paper)
  1.  Asian diaspora.   2.  East and West.   3.  Motion pictures—Asia.
4.  American literature—Asian American authors—History and
criticism.   I.  Title.
  DS13.M3 2007
  305.895—dc22

                                              2007018637

Designed by Lucille C. Aono

Printed by Edwards Brothers, Inc.

*To Lien and Roan*
my captive audience
my harshest critics

# Contents

Intercut on Asian Magic

Intercut on Asian Deceased

# Acknowledgments

An IRGP grant from Michigan State University gave me precious release time in the fall of 2004 to draft this book, followed by a book subvention grant from the College of Arts and Letters and an initiative fund from the Department of English at MSU. I am indebted to my university, the college, and the department for the generous support.

Portions or drafts of chapters have appeared in the following journals and books. I thank the editors and publishers for permissions to reprint revisions of "Camp Scatology," from *VERB 3*, no. 2 (2006): 1–27; "Kung Fu Films in Diaspora," from *Masculinities and Hong Kong Cinema*, edited by Laikwan Pang and Day Wong, pp. 101–118 (Hong Kong: University of Hong Kong Press, 2005); "Tradition and/of Bastards in the Korean Wave," from *Korea Journal* 46, no. 3 (Autumn 2006): 132–153 (abstract added by journal); "Rodgers and Hammerstein's 'Chopsticks' Musicals," from *Literature/Film Quarterly* 31, no. 1 (2003): 17–26; "The Nine Lives of *Blackhawk's* Oriental," from *International Journal of Comic Art* 3, no. 1 (Spring 2001): 120–148; "Hmong Refugee's Death Fugue," from *Hmong Studies Journal* 6 (2005): 1–36; "The Fad(k)ing of the 0.5 Generation," from *National Taiwan University (NTU) Studies in Language and Literature* 15 (June 2006): 63–86.

With this book published on an island that is itself an East-West Montage, I have come almost home, another island further to the west, or rather, to the east.

# Establishing Shots

## East-West Montage

Approximately twelve hours lies between Eastern Standard Time and East Asian Time, between, say, New York and Beijing. West and East are, literally, night and day apart. Yet Rudyard Kipling was dead wrong when he wrote that "East is East, and West is West, and never the twain shall meet." Over and over again in this book, the "twain" are crosscut in adjacent filmic "shots." Rather than imposing a comparative paradigm, this book insists on a montage-like complementarity of East and West, as it reads the Asian diaspora—cultural expressions in literature and film by and about people of Asian descent, primarily on both shores of the Pacific Ocean—at cultural intersections. Indeed, even the concept of montage arises out of an East-West montage, namely, the Chinese ideograms inspiring Sergei Eisenstein in his theorizing about intercuts in the 1920s. Chinese ideograms, of course, have served as the impetus for many Western modernists to flee their phonetic, logo-, and phallocentric system. Nonreaders of Chinese—Freud, Eisenstein, Barthes, Derrida, and others—have interpreted pictographs most "creatively,"[1] leading either to radiant, mutual awakenings or to appalling distortions. Foucauldian knowledge/power aside, however, advances come at times from misunderstandings, as scientific discoveries resulting from experimental errors illustrate. In that spirit, inspired by my half-knowledge of the West and, in particular, of Eisenstein's theory of montage, which is, in turn, inspired by his half-knowledge of Chinese and Japanese hieroglyphs, this book freeze-frames what I call an "East-West montage," the "flash[es] of lightning," in Ezra Pound and Ernest Fenollosa's term, from clashes between East and West ("The Chinese Written Character as a Medium for Poetry" 1920, p. 366).

Given that the abstract collectivities of East and West cannot be placed side by side filmically, I deploy the word "montage" metaphorically. As figures of speech, East and West are montaged, which, in the simplest sense, signifies the filmic technique of one shot cutting to an implicitly connected shot to create a synthetic perception that is neither the first nor the second shot. Leaping from image to image, the viewer's consciousness concludes the dialectics of montage by synthesizing imaginatively, associationally.[2] Optical and auditory stimulations to the senses are to be translated into intellectual perception and emotional affect, which shape a wide range of physical responses: tense muscles, sweating, increased heartbeat, laughter, tears, and so forth. Montage, a mechanical technique tracing back to its French root of "machine assembly,"[3] performs a metaphorical function much like clipped, condensed poetic language. On-screen images, sperm and egg, as it were, await their birth off-screen inside the viewer's head. Montage shots, therefore, point beyond the shot. Oftentimes, East-West montage not only brings together logically and explicitly related moments but also total opposites such as day and night, reason and irrationality, life and death.

In "Beyond the Shot" (1929), Eisenstein, a Russian filmmaker, himself dubiously situated between East and West, draws from Chinese writing to explicate montage, in particular, "the second category of hieroglyphs—the *huei-i*, or 'copulative,'" in which the copulation

> of two hieroglyphs of the simplest series is regarded not as their sum total but as their product, i.e. as a value of another dimension, another degree: each taken separately corresponds to an object but their combination corresponds to a *concept*. The representation of two 'representable' objects achieves the representation of something that cannot be graphically represented. (p. 139)

So far so good. Eisenstein then proceeds to give examples of such Chinese and Japanese hieroglyphs, which expose the airy, fanciful nature of his musings:

> a dog and a mouth mean "to bark"
> a mouth and a baby mean "to scream"
> a mouth and a bird mean "to sing"
> a knife and a heart mean "sorrow," and so on.
> But—this is montage!! (p. 139)

Some of these constructions are half right, others plain wrong. "A mouth and a baby" *(ying)* mean birds chirping or a human sobbing, the sense deriving not from a baby's cry, but from the pronunciation of the word "baby" *(ying)*. As such, "a mouth and a baby" is not a copulative but a pictophonetic *(xingsheng—* the first category of Chinese words) character, where one element, the mouth, points to the meaning and the other element to the pronunciation. On the other hand, "a knife and a heart" mean "endure, tolerate, forbear." Sorrow is implied as well as a whole array of emotions, such as rage, hate, even love. Despite Eisenstein's double exclamation marks over his awakening, this and many other passages read embarrassingly like contemporary Western bodies tattooed with Oriental gibberish. Innocence is indeed bliss, as willful misreading liberates Eisenstein to speculate boldly. Eisenstein engages in a double montage or montage with montage in "Beyond the Shot." Microcosmically, each alleged Oriental character splits into parts that jointly produce a linguistic sum larger than the parts. Macrocosmically, the alleged Orient—Oriental characters, haiku imagism, Noh dramaturgy—becomes the second shot the West cuts to in order to achieve a transubstantiation, a qualitative change of the West.

As a methodology and a narrative style rarely interrogated, East-West montage engineers not only modern filmmaking but modernity itself. If modernity is characterized by the Enlightenment spirit of reason, epitomized by Descartes' "I think, therefore I am," then it constructs itself, unthinkingly, vis-à-vis an "unthinking" Other plagued by irrationality. This egotistic Enlightenment is but the descendant of the Western tradition. The Greco-Roman-Judaic-Christian "civilization" has always evolved side by side with Persian, Egyptian, and Near Eastern "barbarism." In *The Odyssey,* sweet and total resignation is offered by Lotus Eaters, who live ten days' journey south of the island of Kythera in what appears to be North Africa. Greek tragedy frequently casts an Oriental chorus. Dionysus in Euripides' *The Bacchae* returns to wreak havoc in his native Thebes with a chorus of frenzied "Asiatic" maenads. Oedipus is enthroned after solving the Sphinx's riddle—the Sphinx *is* Egypt. In the Hebraic context, Moses leads the Israelites out of Pharaoh's Egypt. Freud, tortuously, attributes the cataclysmic genesis of monotheism to an Egyptian named Moses from the court of Akhenaten (*Moses and Monotheism* 1939). And, of course, the magi's Persian accents would perhaps fail to raise any eyebrows in the crossroads of Bethlehem. Many key texts in Western modernity inherit this image of a schizophrenic Asia that is at once stagnant and barbaric. Adam Smith, in *The Wealth of Nations* (1776) sees China as "stand[ing] still" (p. 175). Hegel expounds on the "stasis" of China: "Early do we see China advancing to the condition it is found at this day...every change is excluded, and the fixedness of a character which recurs perpetually" (*Lectures on the Philosophy of History* 1892–1896, p. 121). Max Weber finds the East lacking in rationality, illustrated by "deficiencies" in science, historiography, art and "rational harmonious music," and numerous other fields, which silhouette the virtues of Protestant capitalism in *The Protestant Ethic and the Spirit of Capitalism* (1904–1905, p. 14).

Critiquing yet also deploying this division of East and West, this book treats them as fluid terms. The West herein refers to the sphere of influence exerted by the Greco-Roman-Judaic-Christian Western European and North American cultures, an influence that is well-nigh global. The East refers to the

Far East or East Asia dominated by Confucian-Buddhist-Taoist traditions, which is often joined in the Western mind by Arab tropes associated with the Near East. East and West are actually no more problematic than "America," a term often taken to mean the United States, while in fact it covers North, Central, and South America. So too with the term "United States." Seemingly well-defined in terms of the geographical boundary of the fifty states, the United States extends its power overseas to remote corners of the world. Domestically, the U.S. empire contains "foreign bodies," some of whom are second-class citizens due to race, ethnicity, sexual orientation, immigration status, and other factors. And this is no more problematic than the distinction between man and woman, a dividing line complicated by homosexuality and by gender and transgender issues. Granted the controversial nature of East-West dichotomies, they remain powerful codes of difference with far-reaching social consequences, as do pairs such as "America and Asia" or "man and woman."

Across this divide, Western intercuts to the East from the classical to the modern era have relied heavily on the power of association rather than on reason, claims of the Enlightenment notwithstanding. In extreme cases in literature, these montages are incidental and haphazard, offering either a springboard to the writer's own story or a deus ex machina to close the writer's otherwise inconclusive story. W. Somerset Maugham's epigraph in *The Razor's Edge* (1944), a quotation from the *Katha-Upanishad* that includes the novel's title, has little to do with the story itself.[4] And T. S. Eliot concludes *The Waste Land* (1922) with Sanskrit chants. Both examples resemble jump cuts that ought to jolt our sensibility due to the inherent incongruity of the "shots." Given the facile juxtapositions of East and West, Eliot et al. are, nonetheless, attempting to transcend the quandary of modernity. The methodological expediency does not cancel out the psychological urgency. Political incorrectness conceals innermost human desires. To return to Eisenstein for illustration: on the dubious foundation of Chinese pictographs, Eisenstein advocates in the 1920s and 1930s a new kind of film that destroys "the dualism of the spheres of 'emotion' and 'reason,'" restoring "to science its sensuality. To the intellectual process its fire and passion" ("Perspectives" 1929, p. 158). Eisenstein calls for "ecstasy" as the ultimate pathos produced by cinema and art, "a state of transport," in David Bordwell's exegesis, "getting carried away ... a process whereby the concreteness of prelogical thought obliterates distinctions between part and whole, self and other" (*The Cinema of Eisenstein* 1993, p. 194). Eisenstein's mystical turn evokes, among others, M. Bakhtin's celebration of the carnivalesque, Georges Bataille's acephalic "nonknowledge" and "emptiness of intelligent questions,"[5] and Max Horkheimer and Theodor

Adorno's thesis in *Dialectics of Enlightenment* (1944): "Myth is already enlightenment; and enlightenment reverts to mythology" (p. xvi).

To be consistent with its dialectical nature, a book on East-West montage should not stop at analyzing the failings of montage; it needs to suggest the potentials, as this "Establishing Shots" attempts to do, cutting back and forth between the Asian diaspora and the Christian West. Missteps, like Alice falling down a rabbit hole, open onto another system, so long as we keep in mind the power imbalance fueling misrepresentations in the first place. Wedding the Enlightenment with myth, the scholarly with the poetic, in fact, resists the tyranny of rationalism unleashed by the Enlightenment. As such, the poetic title and subtitle to this scholarly book foreground the hybridity of the project as one wedged between East and West, light and shadow, modernities and traditions, bodies and their reflections. Three concepts—"montage," "reflections," and "Asian bodies in diaspora"—enable me to pursue what is essentially an intangible, lyrical project of reading the elusive Asian diaspora at the montage-like intersections of East-West cultures. The "reflections" of my subtitle refer both to thoughts on "Asian bodies in diaspora" and to images flitting across those bodies, both to idea and flesh, both to abstraction and "embodied" affect. The formulation "Asian *bodies* in diaspora" preempts "Asian diaspora," a fashionable academic catch-all term that "manages" migrancy in globalization and submerges individual agency within a collectivized concept;[6] it lays emphasis on *bodies*, the site of physical sensations and emotions that respond to being diasporic—eyes filled with tears, for instance.

These two kinds of reflection—theorizing and personally experiencing—are complementary, but they are polarized by the rational mind, with the personal strain routinely exorcized from scholarship. A book utilizing the methodology of montage does not allow a one-sided study of affect in the abstract; the poetic impulse comes to enrich and deepen the scholarly. Indeed, the poetic must be a party to any investigation into diaspora, a state of human existence characterized as much by rational decisions for mobility as by feelings of loss, nostalgia, and ambivalence. Because of this sensibility poised between the head and the heart, readers should not expect the nonemotional, dry monotone typical of scholarly works. Rather, a wide repertoire of emotions, from melancholic to ecstatic, from melodramatic to manic, emerges in these pages. Occasionally personal by academic standards, this account uses individual affect to sharpen the subject at hand: East-West montage, which remains very much a personal issue to an Asian in diaspora like myself. The marriage of scholarship and poetry is most evident when rational argument has run its course toward the end of each chapter as well as toward the end of the book. In lieu of a synthetic recap for closure, as the old scholarly habit decrees, language at "land's end" begins to fray, succeeded by poetic fragments, open-ended, eliciting questions rather than foreclosing debates. Like music taking leave of lyrics and moving into pure sound, human reason climaxes into utterances beyond prose.[7]

"Asian bodies in diaspora," by definition, masks a fissure—a montage, if you will—between body and mind. The body languishing in diaspora, the mind longs for the construct of home. The body exists spatially, yet the formless mind rushes to and fro temporally. The more alienated the body feels from its surroundings, the more prone is the mind to effect an escape through time.[8] Even the diasporic subject's attempt to recreate, spatially, a familiar, home-like environment through, for example, interior decoration within an ethnic ghetto aims to trick time, retrieving wreckages of a "previous incarnation" amidst a Western metropolis. We kill time by fantasy—daydreaming, entertainment, even substance abuse. It is ironic that time always kills us in the end. Since there is no escape, the mind finds itself locked in a bigger prison than the physical one for the body. This bleak prospect only intensifies the gap between the trapped body and the escapist mind, aggravating the "double whammy" of Asian bodies in diaspora, alien bodies whose differences potentially repel the host mainstream culture, on the one hand, and bodies attracted to similar Asian bodies across an ocean and the International Date Line, on the other. To better understand this schizophrenic montage, let us contextualize the Asian diaspora with other disciplines, including Asian American studies, which have consistently suppressed the montage I have been suggesting.

## The Asian Diaspora is Homesick!

Enjoying immense academic currency on the threshold of the twenty-first century, the term "diaspora" traces its origin to the body of Jews dispersed to the four corners of the world after the Babylonian captivity. Contemporary scholars have increasingly used the term to point to the strewing of a racial, ethnic, cultural group across the globe. Paul Gilroy's *Black Atlantic* (1993), for instance, deals with black culture on both sides of the Atlantic Ocean, coalescing ethnic and postcolonial studies to examine African, Caribbean, and African American literatures. Similarly, Paul Julian Smith's *The Body Hispanic* (1989) yokes Spanish and Spanish American texts together. Yet to actual "bodies in diaspora," diaspora is less a conceptualized collective experience than a personal, visceral feeling. To truly comprehend the intensity of emotions associated with diaspora—to grasp what can be likened to an amphibian's existence on the borderland between water and land—we need to look at a diasporic archetype such as Lot's nameless wife in Genesis, a backward glance that is a crosscut to the Judaic-Christian West. Rather than Jana Evans Braziel and Anita Mannur's choice of Janus, "whose gaze is simultaneously directed both forward and backward" (*Theorizing Diaspora* 2003, p. 9), Lot's wife is a far more appropriate trope for diaspora because of her insistence on "looking back." Lot's wife helps us understand why so many pillars of salt dot the landscape of the Asian diaspora, manifesting paradoxical affects of loss and repossession, betrayal and life-affirmation, feminine nostalgia and masculine proscription. Only through the punishment inflicted on Lot's wife can we begin to grapple with the general conscious reluctance to dwell in homesickness and the subconscious urge to do so.

To appease the sinners bent upon sodomizing the two angels, Lot offers his two daughters for gang rape. God's messengers then advise the righteous Lot to flee with his family from the "fire and brimstone" about to befall Sodom and Gomorrah. Despite a strict warning not to do so, Lot's wife "looks back from behind him [Lot] and is turned into a pillar of salt" (King James version of the Bible). In "Looking Back at Lot's Wife" (1994), Rebecca Goldstein sees "conflict between the demands of transcendence and the backward pull of love and accidental attachment" (p. 8). Far from accidental, the look back is necessitated, indeed preordained, by nostalgia, a desire to repossess in one's pupils and mind's eye the home that is lost, the home that is being annihilated by God's wrath.

Sodom is condemned and marked for "demolition" partly as a result of sodomy, which violates masculinity rather than femininity, making the reluctance of Lot's wife to leave more psychologically compelling. Forced into exile, she is destined to endless sorrow in the form of salty tears. Her punishment for transgressing God's command is, in fact, a fitting metaphor for her post-Sodom days; becoming a pillar of salt is both punitive and descriptive. As Lot's wife drags herself away, tears pour from her eyes, water and salt exuding, shriveling her into an empty shell, crusted with crystals of bereavement. Like words from the mouth and perspiration from the pores, tears are both in and out of the body, salt being part of and independent of the body. Tears do more than register physical sensations and mental longings; they confess them to the world. The body remembers, whatever the mind forbids. Why does God not incinerate her with "fire and brimstone," reducing her to unrecognizable ashes, just like the city? Why does God leave behind this weird landmark except to intimate a divine ambivalence? After all, salt is distilled from seawater, the source of all life, and in turn sustains life. Loss causes grief, yet it is the essence of life.

Upon observing someone's shock or horror at a certain sight, we tend to turn to that direction and see for ourselves. The example of Lot's wife, however, tells us to resist this human instinct. Had Lot not looked at (or looked back at) his wife, how did he know that she had turned into a pillar of salt? The King James version of the Bible places his wife behind Lot; the Revised English Bible remains mum on their relative positions. Does the Lot of the King James version walk backwards to find out what happened, or does he keep walking, holding back his tears? In any case, the pillar of salt serves as an interdiction, masculine and divine, against the human tendency and the body's urge to look back in mourning. A dubious sign, the phallic pillar congeals countless drops of "womanly" tears. Lot's and even God's hidden desire to look back themselves is projected onto the ambiguity of female transgression.

After Lot and his two daughters escape and hide in the cave, the daughters conspire to make their father intoxicated enough so that they can ensure the continuation of the tribe through incest. The mother's loss of Sodom extends into the daughters' loss of their mother. To compensate for the maternal loss, the daughters become their mother, the abominable sin securing a future for the family. The bloodline thus stays pure, within itself. The incest can also be taken as the daughters' ultimate revenge against Lot and his God for casting them out in the city and for casting the mother away altogether. Gender and power lie at the heart of this Genesis story. To stave off sodomy that makes "women" out of angels and hence God, Lot's women are sacrificed, "feminine" instincts—the mother's tearful nostalgia and the daughters' primal whole-ness—censored, albeit deconstructively. Lot's wife's looking back is repeated by her daughters and remains a foundational flashback, a repetition compulsion, of God's. He must have been as homesick as the Asian diaspora!

The Asian diaspora contains within itself this tension between the matrilineage of loss and mourning shared by Lot's women and the masculine impulse of a forward thrust. Such tension permeates even the debate over disciplinary origin, a chicken-or-egg dispute over which comes first—Asian Diaspora or Asian American studies. This debate masks a turf war: does Asian Diaspora studies encompass Asian America studies, or is the latter a stand-alone field within American studies? Let us first look back at Asian American studies. Ever since the late 1960s, Asian American literature and studies have mapped out their identity via a two-pronged approach: defining Asian Americans as opposed to mainstream Americans as well as to Asians; con-structing Asian American studies within U.S. institutions of higher education as qualitatively variant from area studies on Asia. Rather than issuing from Asian studies, Asian American studies presents itself as self-made. The Asian American focus has been more on the "here and now" than "over there in the past," more on political activism and ethnic struggle than sorrowful nostalgia. The emphasis is squarely placed on the second word in "Asian American."

Asian American productions testify to this. The very first anthology of Asian American writings, *Aiiieeeee!* (1974), announces in the preface a distinctly "Asian American sensibility" that unites American-born writers of Asian extraction. Maxine Hong Kingston concurs in her pioneering Asian American novel, *The Woman Warrior* (1976), which seeks to lay to rest Chinese haunting in hope of "claiming America." Even a postcolonial émigré writer such as Bharati Mukherjee perpetuates the American myth of individualism and emancipation, unencumbered by the Indian past. Asian American scholars largely agree with these views. Contesting the critical fixation on the generation gap, particularly between the immigrant and American-born generation, Lisa Lowe, in *Immigrant Acts* (1996), advances a horizontal alliance among divergent ethnic groups and conscious "strategic essentializing" on the part of Asian Americans. Sau-ling Cynthia Wong, in "Denationalization Reconsidered" (1995), chides the "denationalizing" trend in Asian American scholarship, which allegedly dilutes the civil rights commitment to racial equality by ushering in transnationalism and globalization. Yen Le Espiritu, in *Asian American Panethnicity* (1992), calls for pan-Asian identity, a contingency plan in critical race theory to consolidate power. Occasionally, Asian American scholars point out the problematics and even hypocrisy of politics over poetics. Viet Thanh Nguyen in *Race and Resistance* (2002), for instance, draws from Asian American preference for the politically correct Sui Sin Far over her younger sister Onoto Watana to demonstrate ideological rigidity and blindness in the face of the highly complicated texts by Watana.

Nguyen may have touched a raw nerve, but this nerve has always been there, under the "banana yellow" skin. To rebuff banana mentality (yellow outside but white inside), or in Frantz Fanon's terms, a "minority complex," Asian Americans have consistently privileged sentiments of a militant kind and gravitated toward stereotypically masculine over feminine emotions, or mental discipline over the senses. The objective of this choice is, of course, self-empowerment. Because looking back in nostalgia threatens to sap, presumably, the manly, combative spirit by giving in to physical yearnings, it is regularly shunned. Even in Amy Tan's melodrama, the suffering of Chinese immigrant mothers is rarely presented for its own sake; it is indulged in to formulaically invigorate Asian American daughters. Yet the masculine masks contradictory "feminine" emotions; the mind cannot manifest itself without the body, and, as Lot's wife illustrates, an erect penis may weep as well. Looking forward is always looking back.

Among these Asian American writers and scholars, fashioning self-identity invariably begins with gestures toward loss. Kingston's Asian American woman warrior rides on the shoulders of the Chinese legend of Fa Mu Lan.

Kingston grounds ethnic female repression in the First World on an exotic "homeland," where rural Cantonese villagers ruthlessly raid against a scapegoated "No Name Woman." The self-transformation in Mukherjee's *Jasmine* (1989) similarly opens with a brutal yet mystical India. Whether U.S.-born Chinese American or Indian-born "Brahmin,"[9] both novelists resort to Asia, which they have purportedly forgone, to compose their American talk-stories. Frank Chin's Chinatown cowboy is likewise inspired by the Chinese god of war, Guan Gung, and other male role models from such pan-Asian sources as *The Romance of the Three Kingdoms* and *Chushingura*. Even Lowe and Wong betray nostalgia for the 1960s, their sentiment of loss couched in Marxist and ethnic discourse. Both literature and criticism steal a look back to assemble an Asian American identity against the backdrop of Asian and Asian immigrant discourse. Such backward glancing is but human, as all cultural expressions concern, to some extent, the past, except perhaps prophesy, which may still be based on the past. A case in point: the clichéd future dystopia in sci-fi films never fails to hark back to the utopia of the Golden Age, even the Garden of Eden.

The cultural space Asian Americans have repeatedly carved out recalls Gloria Anzaldua's "borderlands," a forbidding place to inhabit. The origin of such an ethnic beachhead lies, however, beyond narrowly defined Asian American experience: only out of sheer necessity would "foreign bodies"— Asian immigrants—endure the unrelenting waves and scorching sun to reach this shore. Once arrived, moreover, the immigrant is an amphibian trapped between water and land, euphemistically belonging to both but possibly to neither. Even the little plot of sand under their feet is subject to erosion by the tide, the wind, the host culture's footsteps, and forces far greater than a puny amphibian. That territory has to be negotiated and reconstituted at any given time. The amphibian's precarious life turns, nevertheless, into an object of admiration for the more secure existence on land and in water. Amphibians on the beach are the new clothes the privileged, mainstream or ethnic, cannot help trying on in this global village. One such donning of immigrant identity is distinctly Asian American.

From this beachhead, generations of American-born Asians have ventured inland. Now earthbound, with degenerated gills and fins, Asian Americans find themselves paradoxically lulled by dreams of absence—the ancestral ocean. These watery dreams of Asian ghosts stem from the ambivalent Asian American psyche, for hauntings, by definition, mean that we can not or will not let go of the ghosts. Asian Americans move from the literal borderland on the beach to a psychological one between the American culture to which they wish to belong and an Asian body they would rather, in some cases, shed. To depict their liminal existence between America and Asia, Asian Americans often resort to a dream state between sleep and wakefulness populated by otherworldly apparitions who look like themselves.

Despite dubious entanglements with an ancestral past, the academic discipline of Asian American studies places the focus on the here and now, but in recent years this unspoken rule has been challenged by the rise of Asian Diaspora studies. To borrow from Mandarin, Asian Diaspora studies is an amorphous *sibuxiang* (four unlike, or unlike anything else), bearing certain resemblance to its next of kin: area studies on Asia in the West and their attendant Orientalism, which mushroomed in the post World War II era to "Know Thy Enemy"; postcolonialism that rode the wave of worldwide decolonization and academic radicalization; Asian American studies born out of the tumultuous sixties and the ethnic community's maturing; Pacific Rim studies closely associated with the rise and fall of the Four Mini-Dragons in the eighties; and globalization and transnationalism, the dominant forces of our time. Yet Asian Diaspora studies is, in the image of Homi Bhabha's mimic man, "not quite" any of the above. Asian Diaspora studies repudiates the Orientalist legacy of area studies, while enriched by the Asian cultures and languages they provide; it expands from the postcolonial scope of the Near East and South Asia; it outgrows the boundaries of U.S.-centric Asian American studies; it strives to outlive the four "geckos"; and it interrogates the neoimperialist streak in globalizing forces as well as postmodernist potentials.

As a *sibuxiang,* it is nothing. Because it is nothing, it can be anything. Through an outsider's relative disinterestedness, Asian Diaspora studies can help its cousins by interrogating, to the "right" (pun intended), conservative Asia's fetish of modernization and Westernization and, to the "left," the exclusivity of Asian American identity politics. To achieve this two-way critique, Asian Diaspora studies must be free to reflect on affects of both body and mind. This is paramount if Asian Diaspora studies is to succeed, for "diaspora" means scattering and decentering, which lends itself as a basis for interdisciplinary, cross-cultural projects in this era of globalization. Yet its strength of hybridity risks the charge that it lacks focus. That Asian Diaspora studies can serve to bridge various constituencies in area, ethnic, postcolonial, and other studies suggests the danger that it has no institutional constituents of its own. Its amorphousness can provide a powerful critical, methodological tool, one that does not require scholars' voluntary identification with diaspora. At its worst, diaspora slips into becoming an academic buzzword, a catch-all word, no different from ethnic, postcolonial, or global (*Theorizing Diaspora* 2003, p. 3). Unlike the Jewish diaspora, the Asian diaspora does not have the unifying foci of Judaism and anti-Semitism. Unlike the African diaspora, the

Asian diaspora does not have the unifying foci of colonialism and slavery. To settle for a Sartrean definition—that Asians in diaspora are those whom the society views as such—is to give up agency altogether. To accrue self-identity, the Asian diaspora needs to reflect on its physical and visceral feelings and to think critically about its bodies, individual and collective, in diaspora. The mind and the body, as well as rationality and affect, zero in on the same sensation of "homesickness," feeling sick for the home that is lost or never owned and feeling sick at home, the host country's here and now that disavows Asians in diaspora. Nostalgic rediscovery implicit in Asian studies is wedded to political activism implicit in Asian American studies.

Surely, Asian Diaspora studies does not have to invent itself in a vacuum. It can borrow, for instance, from China studies. Asian Diaspora studies ought not return to C. T. Hsia's sentimentality in "obsession with China," nor should it accept indiscriminately David Wang's hip "flirtations with China."[10] Rather, it draws from both positions, while limited by neither and informed by recent theories of globalization, diaspora, and transnationalism. Hsia's melancholia and mourning and that of an early generation are balanced by the upbeat, playful, even veiled messianic tone inherent in the contemporary emphasis on fluidity, flexibility, and hybridity. Pairs like Hsia and Wang can be found in other fields as well. Cross-breeding not only them but across disciplines offers new critical angles for the twenty-first century. This endeavor is most urgent since Lot's wife still haunts us: the elements continue to dissolve the pillar into the earth, and her tears percolate through various Asian bodies in diaspora.

## Body Parts

The book is divided into seven intercuts, each dwelling on one specific body part or physical attribute that is shared by a large number of people of Asian descent, across national and geographical boundaries within the overarching framework of East and West. This focus on the human body is necessitated by the fact that, Norman O. Brown attests, "we are nothing but body," which "the child knows consciously, and the adult unconsciously" (*Life Against Death* 1959, p. 293). This ceases to be a purely philosophical concept in the Asian diaspora, where the immigrants or first-generation Asian Americans—"big eaters" out of "Necessity"—must maintain physical well-being before the second-generation "treat-lovers" may move into a lifestyle of "Extravagance" (Sau-ling Wong's *Reading Asian American Literature* 1993). To elucidate the Asian diasporic condition, therefore, this book crosscuts on "Asian Anus," "Asian Penis," "Asian Dubbing," "the Korean Wave," "Body Oriental," "Asian Magic," and "Asian Deceased," each section consisting of a pair of chapters, mirroring yet counterpointing shots filled with irreconcilable tension. That some chapters in the same section threaten to pull apart altogether only highlights the genuine experience of diaspora, which is constantly on the edge, about to fall apart. Echoing the biblical beginning and end—the seven days in Genesis and the "seven churches of Asia" awaiting doomsday in the Book of Revelation—these seven intercuts intimate an entirety as they roam the Asian body from the lower body ("Anus," "Penis"), to the throat and mouth ("Dubbing"), to the Korean stars' fetishized faces ("the Korean Wave"), then drawing back for a full view of the "Body Oriental" and its "Magic" aura, and finally a close-up on the ashes and dust of what remains ("Asian Deceased").

"Asian Anus" explores things Asian that the West treats as the most abject and suppressed in order, paradoxically, for the West to enlighten itself. "Asian Penis" analyzes tropes of power in kung fu and swordplay films as well as their disappearance in the midst of globalization. "Asian Dubbing" zooms in on the separation of the Asian body and voice (mind) in fictions about Maoist China in English and in Japanese anime. "The Korean Wave" probes into conflicts between traditions and modernity in the phenomenon sweeping across Asia, Asian diasporic communities, and even mainstream American culture. "Body Oriental" illustrates the deployment of racial stereotypes in popular musicals and comics. "Asian Magic" is bestowed upon Asian bodies in diaspora—immigrants and the Dalai Lama—by Asian American discourse and by Hollywood. "Asian Deceased" concludes with a requiem for the Hmong refugees and Chinese retirees in the United States. From the stridency of earlier intercuts to the elegy of the later ones, this book strikes a balance between body politic and the body that feels. For sections that appear to be racially and ethnically defined, their purchase on diaspora is still self-evident. Although having originated in South Korea, the Korean Wave has grown to be not only pan-Asian in the twenty-first century, but part of global cinema. With specific groups such as the Hmong and Chinese retirees, their "death fugue" or fad(k)ing stems from their diasporic experiences. A metaphorical reading of East-West montage veers toward a metonymic one, as Asian bodies disintegrate into bits and pieces upon impact with diaspora, each shard intimating the whole. These seven intercuts then fade out to Finis, and, as in a movie theater, to lights and a new beginning.

# Intercut on Asian Anus

# 1 Anal Apocalypse

## On the W/Hole of Asia and the Christian West

> The *solar annulus* is the intact anus of her body at eighteen years to which nothing sufficiently blinding can be compared except the sun, even though the *anus* is the *night*.
> —Georges Bataille, *The Solar Anus*

## The Rear End

Of the human body, the anus is the part most shunned. By contrast, the face is the most privileged and public body part. The two are intimately entwined, of course, as the mouth is the entry point to the digestive system and the anus the exit point.[1] If either hole malfunctions, not only the other suffers but the whole body. With regard to Nature's digestive system, the anus may well be its entry point and the mouth its exit. Far from existing alone, the human digestive system complements the ecosystem. The mouth appears more presentable as it serves multiple functions other than food consumption, whereas the anus serves primarily one—defecation. As orifices, both the mouth and the anus are potentially transgressive in erasing the boundaries between the outside and the inside, acquiring, as a result, a sexual, erotic tenor, since sexuality has always been the trope for two bodies to merge into one, be it two lovers, mother and fetus, or the Immaculate Conception between Virgin Mary and the Holy Spirit. As bodily counterpoints, the anus and the surrounding buttocks resemble the mouth and surrounding face; the buttocks are the hidden face, its center so secreted away in the gluteal cleft that Adam and Eve forgot to cover it with fig leaves. Shame applies to frontal nudity in Christian iconography, not to the backside, which has been stricken from consciousness except in Christian revulsion against the Devil. Norman O. Brown writes: "The climax of the ritual of the Witches Sabbath was to kiss the Devil's posteriors or a facial mask attached to the Devil's posteriors" (*Life Against Death*

1959, p. 207). Takeshi Kitano's *Dolls* (2002) highlights this hidden face when a mad woman imagines a satyr-like male wearing a mask on his buttocks. A rare moment in contemporary visual and performing arts,[2] in which the least expressive, most veiled body part is showcased in a tracking close-up, Kitano unwittingly evokes Christian excommunication. After all, shunning decrees that a Christian community turn its back, often literally, to the sinner. But is it the community members' backs or is it their buttocks that are turned? The cheeks (in slang) below the back wink at the sinner, communal refuse expelled from the members' anuses.

The hole in the face issues ethereal commands that escape the body and the earth to commence the light of Genesis, the star of the Nativity, Christ's magic healing, and John's Book of Revelation. God's mouth that commands light turns into the alien magi's mouths that herald Christ and then into Christ's mouth that heals lepers and finally into John's mouth that prophesizes the endgame. These incorporeal ascensions are tied, corporeally, to the hole in the ass that is a mute, except when passing gas, and is empty and worthless, except for passing body waste. Although one hole baldfacedly proclaims a future that devours all differences and the other shamefacedly vacates all that is left of the differences, they are the two ends of human bowels or Nature's bowels. Contrary to conventional wisdom, however, the upper hole often mouths more garbage than wisdom, while the lower hole, to scramble Freud with Jack and the Beanstalk, lays golden eggs.[3] In view of the brevity of an individual's being and the eternity of her non-being, humans resemble more what we have laid than what we have said, with one exception. Obscenities relocate lower-body functions to the upper body, to the mouth and the middle finger specifically.

The quarternal prophetic revelations mentioned above—the four bangs inaugurating the Old and the New Testament, the miracles performed by the Messiah, and the coming of the end—veil their unseemly opposites. To the Christian West, the construct of Asia is a recurring trope for alienness, repressed like the body part associated with anality, against which Christian apocalypse comes to pass. The half-knowledge or zero knowledge of the East frees the Christian West from rational constraints to proclaim its single, totalizing vision. The anal hole that is Asia is made to discharge, repeatedly, messianic revelations of a transcendent whole. By calling attention to the anus as an essential part of the human body, this chapter bridges Asia and the Christian West like the rear end and the front end in a West-centric world view. This brings geopolitics to bear on sociological and theological insights that crystallize in Mary Douglas's dictum that dirt is matter out of place (*Purity and Danger* 1966, pp. 35–36). Nothing is in essence filthy, polluting, or tabooed, a designation that points rather to transgressiveness that no longer obeys established boundaries. James Aho in *The Orifice as Sacrificial Site* (2002) laments that Douglas's Catholic prudery has prevented her theory from developing to its natural end, which is what I have come to call the paradox of W/Hole: "What exactly is it about the anus and feces…that induce a feeling of unease, dis-ease? It is, simply, that they are *limmode* [unclean]. They occupy ambiguous, transitional statuses.…They are other things in the geography of the lived body, passages and districts of otherness, holy holes" (p. 23), sites of "numinosity, sacredness" (p. 21), yet forever tainted by the Janus-faced *sacre*, for both sacred and damned, both awe-inspiring and abominable.

Julia Kristeva rhapsodizes over this duality in *Powers of Horror* (1982): "It is no longer I who expel, I is expelled.…The corpse, seen without God and outside of science, is the utmost of abjection. It is death infecting life. Abject. It is something rejected from which one does not part.…It is thus not lack of cleanliness or health that causes abjection but what disturbs identity, system, order. What does not respect borders, positions, rules. The in-between, the ambiguous, the composite" (p. 4). Even Kristeva's style is in-between scholarly prose and mystical chant, with clipped, abstruse sentence fragments, relying on poetic metaphors and associations rather than logical argument. More a welling-forth of emotions than a lucid, measured argument, Kristeva deploys poetry within and outside of the system of scholarly inquiry to launch a critique of that system.

Kristeva's in-between-ness encapsulates the pun of W/Hole, or as one of the subheadings in her book illustrates, "AS ABJECTION—SO THE SACRED" (p. 17). Kristeva contends that abjection "persists as *exclusion* or taboo (dietary or other) in monotheistic religions…but drifts over to more secondary forms such as *transgression* (of the Law).…It finally encounters, with Christian sin, a dialectic elaboration, as it becomes integrated in the Christian Word a threatening otherness—but always nameable, always totalizable" (p. 17). The mystery of W/Hole, however, lies in the fact that without the suppression of abjection or anality, there would not be sacredness. The Christian Word so valorized originates from the body, which is a corpse on borrowed time. The human corpse is abhorrent because it transgresses against the boundary of the living. Yet human excrement bears an eerie resemblance to the corpse, because excreta, whether in, being ejected from, or out of our body, is waste, which our entire body will eventually become. In Norman O. Brown's well-turned phrase: "The nonbodily excreta of the body, which are at the same time the dead matter produced by the body, and which incorporate the body's daily dying" (*Life Against Death* 1959, p. 294). The body part most closely linked to feces is, of course, the anus. A taboo then forms around the trinity of feces, death, and anus.

But the anus and feces are located in the neighborhood of erogenous zone, if not in the zone itself; reproductive organs—vagina and penis—live right next door.[4] Sexuality and life are centimeters away, anatomically and psychologically, from God's Law that forbids sexuality and death. Neighbor to the anus on the back side is the coccyx, the stump, according to Darwin, left behind as our ancestors shed their tails. Anality, a metonym for waste and death, is flanked by procreation and pleasure in front and by ancestry and shame in back. Within this framework of the paradox of W/Hole, the fact that, in most Western texts, the anus undergoes a Freudian displacement onto the negligible and censored other—Kristevian abjection, biblical magi, South Seas leprosy, opium den in Western metropolis, and film noir's China-town—need not dishearten us. Viewed as pornographic smut, the anus never manifests itself, except veiled in the undesirability of the abject, the abhorrent, the abysmal—to sum up, the anal. Like a fetish, such a physical and mental state disavows the specific body part, the hole that brings on, uncannily, a sweeping cataclysm.

Destruction of the old and creation of the new, the apocalyptic Genesis arrives enshrined in light, the rising of the sun in the East. Yet the dawn shining forth and retiring darkness are equally *rooted* in darkness. The new day in the West pivots on the night in the East. At the opening of the New Testament, "the astrologers from the east" inquire: "Where is the new-born king of the Jews? We observed the rising of his star, and we have come to pay him homage" (Matt. 2:2). While the East is the direction of the sunrise and the opening of a new era, the East brings a star instead. The sun or fire worship in Zoroastrianism turns into its priests'—the magi's—star-gazing. It is striking how the pivotal yet obscure magi—synecdoche of the Orient or the non-West, the Siamese twins of Near East and Far East in our time—call forth the apocalyptic vision. Since no one but the magi see the star, there is no way to verify the astrological phenomenon. In fact, the magi *are* the star that proclaims the coming of the Messiah, shining briefly before drifting into the night sky of oblivion. The Bible minimizes the magi's role—they make only an apocalyptic cameo appearance—but in fact they are the first apostles, in attendance at the manger, alongside Mary and Joseph.

Based on the number of gifts they bear, the magi are traditionally represented as three, hence a shadow Trinity. The miracle initiated, if not incarnated, by the magi is immediately transferred to Christ. The apocalyptic vision presupposes the erasure of the East: its absence and unfathomability. The East is epigraphic: although the magi and their seeds—Nietzsche's Zarathustra, Hesse's Siddhartha, Duras's Cholon lover and Hiroshima, Pound's Confucius,

Eliot's Hinduism, Yeats's Noh, Coppola's Vietnam, to name just a few prominent ones—effect earth-shaking self-awakenings in the West, they vanish as soon as they materialize or are straight away dropped after being quoted. An epigraph turns out to be an epitaph; what precedes a text resembles what is left behind after one's demise—an inscription on a tombstone. The simultaneous birth and death of the East, mirroring Nativity in the dead of winter, leads us to rewrite Edward Said's Orientalism as Orientalia, so that it is associated with genitalia that bring forth life via a birth canal, at once a miracle and a trauma that no human consciousness can ever recall.

Asian, alien, and anal establish a kinship if we read the Bible in conjunction with Freud. Retreating into obscurity, the shadow Trinity leaves in its wake nonperishable gold and the intangible Oriental fragrances of frankincense and myrrh. A sense of déjà vu links God's gift of the child Jesus with the gifts from the East, all deposited at a foul-smelling stable. In Freudian terms of sexual development, these gifts signal both, in the phallic stage, the boy's golden phallus—evolving into the fetish of money and power—hiding two testicles and, in the anal stage, the faecal stick with the accompanying odor ("On the Transformation of Instincts with Special Reference to Anal Erotism" 1916, p. 169). Christ's golden phallus and Freudian faecal stick provide two paradigms—in fact, one and the same—for anal apocalypse. On the one hand, Asia signifies, metaphorically, an inspiring totality of nothing, legitimizing, among other things, modernist enlightenment. On the other, Asia secretes itself, metonymically, in sites such as opium dens and Chinatowns, holes in the cities of the West that open up to reveal nightmarish hallucinations otherwise unavailable. The golden phallus is ultimately fake idolatry; the faecal stick gives us an afterimage of the human body.

The third apocalypse occurs as Christ displays his power by means of the body of the infirm, the leprous, the dead, and, ultimately, as the first-born from the dead (John 1:5). While the magi proclaim the sanctity of the newborn Christ in one single line in the Bible, the epileptic, the sick, the crazed, the blind, the lepers, and the dead come forth repeatedly in the New Testament to substantiate Christ's power. "And now a leper approached him, bowed before him, and said, 'Sir, If only you will, you can make me clean.' Jesus stretched out his hand, and touched him, saying, 'I will; be clean.' And his leprosy was cured immediately" (Matt. 8:1–3). Christ also informs ten lepers to show themselves to the priests and "they were cleansed." Only one returns to thank Christ and Christ praises him: "Thy faith hath made thee whole [both healthy and one with the Lord]" (Luke 17:11–19). As leprosy denotes a decomposing body, one increasingly close to trash, it has long been, in Susan Sontag's view, a metaphor as much for physical filth in general as for spiritual decay; both are linked to the excretory organ, the anus. In the Middle Ages, leprosy was regarded as God's curse. By the time it appears in Jack London's primitivist noble savage "Koolau the Leper," leprosy is called the Chinese disease, an allegedly tropical disease spreading from the Orient to Hawai'i, the doorstep to the West. W. Somerset Maugham, in *The Moon and Sixpence* (1919), portrays his Gauguin-like painter in the South Seas at long last achieving his vision of beatitude, which he paints on the interior of his hut after he is disfigured and blinded by leprosy. In Tahiti, the painter has found himself, both the sacred, awe-inspiring art of his house of pleasure and his putrid, deformed body—with horny feet resembling animalistic hooves and a lion's face. Lois-Ann Yamanaka's *Blu's Hanging* (1997) embodies the self-abjection of Hawai'i's Japanese Americans via a leper family mired in a fetal-fecal universe, which the son Blu transcends through angelic hymn-singing. Out of a narrative style fraught with litter and detritus, Yamanaka kneads such Christian symbols as the Lord's Prayer and Christ's stigmata. The doggy motel in the basement where Blu and his siblings, abused themselves, work frantically to save the dogs resembles a uterus, where feces and dogfood intermingle. Maimed by leprosy from the East, London's, Maugham's, and Yamanaka's characters conjoin the leprous, the fecal, and the divine. Their characters redeem themselves by means of soldiery, painting, and singing. Dialectically, only those social lepers who have fallen into the anal abyss can enter Christian heaven.

The fourth apocalypse closes the New Testatment when the schizophrenic disciple John rants against fornicators and sinners from "the seven churches of Asia" [the seven churches refer to those in the Roman province of Asia in today's Asia Minor], a number echoing the seven days of creation in Genesis. While biblical exegeses have largely taken the seven churches of Asia as one Church of Christ,[5] some scholars have noted the geographical division, intimating that the binarism between Christianity and Asian deviation paves the way for John's prophecies. Colin Hemer's *The Letters to the Seven Churches of Asia in Their Local Setting* (2001) studies the seven churches in terms of their locations. Richard Bauckham contends, in *The Theology of the Book of Revelation* (1993), that John addresses "specific churches as *representative* of *all* the churches," hence uniting the consensus of one church and the specificity in the Book of Revelation (p. 16). The number seven, to Bauckham, represents completeness. While suggesting at an early point that the churches are a "contemporary allusion" to "the threat of invasion from the Parthian Empire," Bauckham proceeds to elucidate John's message vis-à-vis Roman oppression (p. 19). Whether Parthian heathens or Roman tyranny, the fact remains that John would not be John without the schizophrenic symptoms of the fallen churches of Asia, the Beast, the harlot of Babylon, and a slew of dark imageries.

The quarternity of Genesis, the magi, Christ's miracles, and John implicates the Other in various ways. This paradox of apocalypse lies in the fact that the inherent self-transcendence posits a denial of one's own system, which is possible only if one assumes a position outside that system. In the Middle Ages, that bird's-eye view comes from God. In the post-Enlightenment era, when God has been pronounced dead, the external vantage point is consistently ceded to the non-West, such as the role assigned to the Median prophet Zoroaster (c. 628–551 B.C.) by Nietzsche in *Thus Spake Zarathustra* (1892). An apt analogy for the outside-the-system viewpoint is perspective in Western art: the optical illusion of depth in Western painting depends as much on the human eye that renders objects increasingly diminutive at a distance as on a vanishing point beyond the ken of the eye. The eye that launches perspective can be usurped as the raison d'être by the point of convergence withdrawing from the eye. The eye and the imagined infinity, *in cahoots*, create perspective. The apocalyptic in the West, therefore, perennially issues from an intercourse of East and West. Although the apocalyptic promises a state of being incomprehensible to human faculties, that vantage point from beyond the West invariably entails discursive quotations of the Other—God or the East, God *as* the East, God *as* shit, to quote Freud's analysis of the obsessional neurosis of "anal erotism."[6] Freud lays the groundwork for the bird's-eye view to lapse into, shall we say, the dog's-eye view, or the anal-eye view.[7]

Like Freudian eros and thanatos, like Yeats's line that "love has pitched his mansion in the place of excrement," the apocalyptic and the anal are situated side by side. Jung would view this yoking of opposites as constituting a totality, "the One": "One, as the first numeral, is unity. But it is also '*the* unity,' the One, All-Oneness, individuality and non-duality—not a numeral, but a philosophical concept, an archetype and attribute of God, the monad" (*Memories* 1963, p. 310). Drawing from Lacan and Derrida, Rey Chow argues against Jungian mystical unity: "The desire to begin from the origin—from the first as it were—is thus haunted by the inherent duplicity of its own articulation: the figure of 1, even as it is being invoked as a way to clear the past, inevitably derives its meaning from that past. 1 is always already a *reiteration*, which makes sense only in the supplementarity of 1+" ("Nostalgia of the New Wave" 2001, p. 231). Moving backwards, however, "1" becomes "1-," which diminishes steadily toward "zero." Midway, "1" becomes "one half" before reaching "zero." As a consequence, the One or the entirety already presumes the suppression of contrasting halves, each of which further breaks down into more miniscule pairs. Should the unity of the One begin to crumble, its two halves instantly revert back to unknown abysses, dark holes. Yet even the whole, taken in totality that has dissolved the differences between two halves, remains a mystical, oceanic void, a hole variously called Yahweh, Buddha, Allah, and other names. What is viewed by believers as the One is the nonbelievers' No-One. One person's apocalypse looks to another like anal retentiveness. This unending dialectics resembles computer language, in which two numbers, zero and one, representing negative and positive, infinitely switch and compute within a split second. The Wachowski brothers' anime- and *Matrix*-inspired film *Animatrix* (2003) contains a tale of a war between humans and robots. The robots finally retreat to a homeland called 01 situated in the Bible Land as seen from a satellite photograph. The homecoming to the cradle of Western civilization is undertaken by computers, which intuitively grasp the meaning of anal apocalypse, or the paradox of W/Hole.

Computer instincts are shared by a host of Western thinkers and writers. A thread of modernism derives from the discursive emptying of the East to make way for the modernist apocalypse. Asia becomes a symbolic golden phallus, a godsend for modernists trying to break away from the Western tradition. In "Beyond the Shot," Eisenstein explicates a theory of montage based on his whimsical understanding of Chinese and Japanese written scripts, which he regards as interchangeable look-alikes. Awed by the stylization of Beijing Opera as performed by Mei Lanfang in Moscow in 1935, Bertolt Brecht lays, in "Alienation Effects in Chinese Acting" (1964), the foundation for epic theater. In *About Chinese Women* (1974), Kristeva projects into the inscrutable Chinese women alternatives, such as matrilinearity and pre-Oedipal language, to First-World feminism. Roland Barthes, in *Empire of Signs* (1970), lets loose altogether such childish regressiveness, transferring his thirst for an antithesis to the West onto a universe of signs he labels Japan. In every instance, Asia crouches—silent, abject—a dark night awaiting the lightning of Western epiphany to strike. Even for the stellar Mei Lanfang, his role impersonating female parts renders his performance ambivalent and transgressive to Western eyes. Ironically, while attempting to restore dignity to the Orientalized Other, these Western intellectuals subjugate Asia to the exact formula of reification that they accuse the West of committing.

Such a golden phallus is already a hologram of a faecal stick. To demonstrate, we need only turn to Freud's patricidal son, Jung, who blends Eastern mysticism with psychoanalysis. In his seminal "Synchronicity" (1952), Jung advances a theory beyond the logic of cause and effect. He argues that apparent coincidences in life are connected acausally or rhizoidally in the web of the collective unconscious. Jung attributes the inspiration for synchronicity to an Eastern source—a bug that reminds him of the Egyptian scarab. He develops his theory from a "coincidence" of a patient relating a dream of a "golden scarab" just as Jung notices a gentle tapping on the window. This turns out to be "a flying insect" that is "the nearest analogy to a golden scarab that one finds in our latitudes, a scarabaeid beetle, the common rose-chafer *(Cetonia aurata)*" (*The Essential Jung* 1983, pp. 339–340). Jung sees the two events informing each other. The scarab, or dung, beetle is an ancient Egyptian symbol of the sun or rebirth. The ancient Egyptians believed that the sun rose out of nothingness in an act of spontaneous self-creation described as *kheper* ("to come into being"). The dung beetle pushing a ball of dung resembles Ra, the Sun-God, moving across the sky. Since the beetles lay their eggs in the ball, young beetles emerge as if rejuvenating themselves (Stephen Quirke, *The Cult of Ra* 2001). Jung thus foretells his patient's eventual breakthrough from her animus—a woman's masculine principle—of Cartesian philosophy and rationality (*The Essential Jung* 1983, p. 341). Yet the patient merely moves from one kind of patriarchy to another, from Cartesian philosophy to Jungian synchronicity. The break-in performed by the beetle may well stand for Jung's invasion into the patient's psychic defenses; she is remade by Jung. The claim of self-creation on the part of the patient self-destructs not only because of the shadow cast by the Creator Jung but because of the necessity of the beetle analogy. The discourse articulating a new European Self relies on an ancient Egyptian Other that takes the form, in Western eyes, of a repellent insect. Jung continues this flight to Eastern imagos, to originary sources that are deified and demonized, apocalyptic and abysmal, throughout his career.

Rather than discovering synchronicity, Jung may have chanced upon the archetype of the dark sun or solar anus, which is pivotal to the occult and which had obsessed Jung. Jung has written a perfect gloss not only for Shakespeare's famous passage on Cleopatra's barge but for any astral vehicle bearing the unidentifiable, or UFO, a subject of Jung's ruminations in his last days.

> The barge she sat in, like a burnished throne,
> Burned on the water. The poop was beaten gold,
> Purple the sail, and so perfumed that
> The wind were lovesick with them…
> …For her own person,
> It beggared all description. She did lie

In her pavilion, cloth of gold tissue,
Oer picturing that Venus where we see
The fancy outwork nature.
(*The Tragedy of Antony and Cleopatra*, Act II, Scene ii,
ll.196–199, 202–206)

A hardened soldier, the speaker, Enobarbus, offers uncharacteristic praise of the Egyptian queen, who remains, nonetheless, a void as she is never described. Cleopatra's golden barge approaches like the blinding sun, a scarab beetle rolling a ball of dung. Cleopatra is an empty sign, presenting a synaesthetic extravaganza, the sensorial minutiae of the exterior blocking all access to the interior. In Yamanaka's controversial *Blu's Hanging*, the "solar anus" resides in the incestuous and pedophiliac Uncle Paulo, who sodomizes Blu in his car with the license plate "Da Sun."[8] Yamanaka's urine- and feces-splattered fictional universe is regressive, infantile, the exact opposite to Cleopatra's "burnished throne." Yet golden dung points away from the matter to the spirit, a mystical turn shared by psychoanalysis and art.

## The Opium Den

Anal apocalypse is the euphemism for apocalyptic anus, or Bataille's erotic-mystical "solar anus." One avatar of the apocalyptic anus, both attractive and repulsive, is the opium den found in Anglo-American "body politic" from the English Romantics of the late eighteenth century to films of the twentieth century. In the lineage of this neurotic Western imaginary, the opium den, shrouded by a whole array of Orientalist images, is where non-Western races congregate to practice their abhorrent yet strangely titillating rituals. While the word den already implies an animal hideout, an opium den resembles a beastly uterus, from which either the newborn emerges or monstrosity is spawned. The ambiguity of these sites disgorging new life or debilitating death maps out the extremities of affects, celestial and hellish, otherwise inaccessible to a Western sensibility. The opium den's shadowy, lowly existence represents the bottom, from which a flailing, drowning West can finally rebound. Without the anal hole of the opium den, the West is unlikely to achieve its blissful ecstasy.

This opiate obsession reflects, historically, one of the first substantial encounters between East and West, namely, the colonial exploitation of opium, a narcotic allegedly originating in Turkey, then cultivated by British India (the East India Company), shipped through the Malay archipelago and Hong Kong (via the taipan of Jardine Matheson Company, among other traders),[9] and marketed in China. Two opium wars (1839–1842, 1856–1860) were waged by England to enforce the trade. Arabs, Indians, turbaned lascars,[10] and pigtailed Chinese are dots figuratively connected by the elusive opium smoke. Given that the West invades the East with gunboats and infects it with an addictive drug, opium is ironically transformed into an "Oriental Narcotic," invasive, infectious, and addictive, threatening the well-being of the West's body. Invariably, one witnesses in the opium den nightmarish Oriental accoutrements, most prominently the addicts' Chinese pigtail and Arabic turban, through which Asians of the Far East and Muslims of the Near East are conjoined, creating a conglomerate non-West that entraps the West, oftentimes embodied by a white woman. The West routinely splits itself, schizophrenically, into the weaker, feminine half intoxicated by opium and into the stronger, masculine half, which interdicts opium use and comes to the women's rescue.

The West's paranoia about Oriental sin reveals its obsession with the tabooed and forbidden. Opium, when inhaled, provides a conduit for the Orient to snake into the body of the West, so that the two flow together and become one, however ephemeral the interpenetration may be. Although literature and art cannot convey the euphoric sensation induced by opium, the representation of opium-smoking hints at its lulling effect. Given the laborious process of opium-smoking,[11] the user depends upon the assistance of another person—consistently an Oriental.[12] Western addicts consent to self-abdication in the posture of lying down to receive Oriental servants' offering, by which the masters are irredeemably enslaved. As users in an opium den inhale and drift into semi-consciousness, they share the proverbial "communal bed,"[13] hence erasing the hierarchy of race, class, and gender that is the bedrock of imperialism.

Anal apocalypse enlightened the English Romantic poet Coleridge, who, in 1797 or 1798, composed his laudanum—alcohol spiked with opium—reverie "Kubla Khan," a poem marked by polarized images of Kubla Khan's pleasure-dome: the marriage of "sunny dome" and "caves of ice," of paradise and hell. The Orientals who inhabit the site are undifferentiated, with Mongolians morphing into an Abyssinian (Ethiopian) maid singing of Mount Abora. In *Confessions of an English Opium-Eater* (1821), Thomas De Quincey punctuates both sections—"The Pleasures of Opium" and "The Pains of Opium"—with the serendipitous appearances of Orientals. A Malay traveler materializes abruptly in the Pleasures section to be given opium by De Quincey, who is subsequently plagued by anxiety. This Malay is said to be "fastened afterwards upon my [De Quincey's] dreams, and brought other Malays with him worse than himself, that ran a-muck at me" (p. 316). The sentence confuses dream and reality so much that hallucinations of Malays running amuck manifest the author's subconscious fear over his own addiction. This anxiety foreshadows withdrawal symptoms in the later section, culminating in the May 1818 fragment of chaotic and grotesque Oriental imageries. Compressed into a single hysterical vision are "antediluvian" Chinese, all tropical flora and fauna, Indian Vishnu and Seeva, and Egyptian Isis and Osiris. The addict externalizes demons of opiate within his own body as multiple haunting images from the East. To escape, he "ran into pagodas: and was fixed, for centuries, at the summit, or in secret rooms; I was the idol; I was the priest; I was worshipped; I was sacrificed" (pp. 333–334). Yet the utter "spread" of summit and secret rooms, of God's grace and damnation, signals the duality of W/Hole.

Victorian and subsequent novels continue to shock or even climax by means of anal apocalypse. Charles Dickens's unfinished *The Mystery of Edwin Drood* (1870) opens with the villain Jasper's opium-induced drowsiness. He mistakes a bedpost for a "spike" for "the impaling of a horde of Turkish robbers," followed by Orientalist fantasies in which "cymbals clash, and the Sultan goes by to his palace in long procession" (p. 1). Jasper awakens to find himself in the company of "a Chinaman, a lascar, and a haggard woman" on a communal bed at a London opium den. The haggard, presumably Caucasian woman "has opium-smoked herself into a strange likeness of the Chinaman." Seeking to satiate the same need for opium as the woman, and sharing the same bed, Jasper appears to have been contaminated by the evil of the Orient. The 1870 cover design to this murder mystery features a "Chinaman" with a long queue and a Muslim in turban at the bottom corners. Reclining in what appears to be a stupor, the pair are smoking opium and, above their smoke, scenes of crime unfold. Evil is shown to have originated from below, from alien lowlifes and their depraved habits.

Oscar Wilde's fin-de-siècle Gothic *The Picture of Dorian Gray* (1891) builds suspense toward the eventual visit to the opium den, a devolution foreshadowed by a "Chinese box" containing either opium or hashish and the overall Oriental décor of the dwellings (p. 1). Gray's life of sin reaches its nadir when he frequents an opium den inhabited by Malays:

> The door opened quietly, and he went in without saying a word to
> the squat misshapen figure that flattened itself into the shadow as
> he passed. . . . [He] entered a long, low room which looked as if it had
> once been a third-rate dancing saloon. Shrill flaring gas-jets, dulled
> and distorted in the fly-blown mirrors that faced them, were ranged
> round the walls. Greasy reflectors of ribbed tin backed them, making

quivering discs of light. The floor was covered with ochre-coloured sawdust, trampled here and there into mud, and stained with dark rings of spilt liquor. Some Malays were crouching by a little charcoal stove playing with bone counters, and showing their white teeth as they chattered . . . by the tawdrily-painted bar that ran across one complete side stood two haggard women mocking an old man who was brushing the sleeves of his coat with an expression of disgust. He thinks he's got red ants on him, laughed one of them, as Dorian passed by. The man looked at her in terror, and began to whimper. (p. 178)

A hellish sunken space, the den is dimly lit, the source of light, "dulled and distorted in the fly-blown mirrors . . . [and in] Greasy reflectors of ribbed tin," rendering the place ghastly and grotesque. Flyblows infesting the den are larvae of blowflies that feed on food or rotting flesh. Evil eats up the opium-eaters, body and mind, the imagery of contamination spreading from pests to the entire "uterus" marked by and producing waste. Except for Dorian Gray, the addicts have no individuality; they are identified only by their profession, age, or gender. Female addicts lose maternal compassion altogether as they mock an old man who imagines that red ants from hell are upon him. The English-speaking addicts are apparently all white as opposed to the Malays, who seem so at ease in the opium den that they carry on with their business as usual. Since Malays are the sole group identified by race, that group, in effect, comes to characterize every addict; a woman's crooked smile is "like a Malay crease" (p. 189). Strewn across the common bed, addicts lose their humanity, trapped "in what strange heaven they were suffering, and what dull hells were teaching them the secret of some new joy" (p. 188). Heaven and hell switch places in Nirvana Opiate, ecstasy and agony intertwined.

A number of Western writers and filmmakers have unwittingly problematized the discourse on the opium den, making the externalization of evil ambivalent. Sir Arthur Conan Doyle's detective story "The Man with the Twisted Lip" revolves around the mysterious disappearance of one Neville St. Clair, who is last seen at an opium den in the East End of London. This opium den is a hotbed of crime and deception, complete with a trapdoor, a lascar manager, a Malay attendant, and cavernous space "terraced with wooden berths, like the forecastle of an emigrant ship" (p. 260). Aliens and their practices run aground in the East End slum, and both Sherlock Holmes and Dr. Watson visit the den in order to resurrect fellow Englishmen who have fallen. But the white crusade is not without treachery of its own: Holmes disguises himself as an opium-smoker; St. Clair, contrary to his name, turns out to make a living in the guise of a beggar with the twisted lip. Based in the den, St. Clair ventures out daily to collect charity. The reversal of Oriental fraud and Occidental authenticity extends to the lascar manager, whom St. Clair has entrusted with his secret and who never betrays it. The final twist in this story of the twisted lip lies in Holmes, who is himself addicted to cocaine and who solves the mystery by taking on, as it were, an Eastern mentality. Contemplating the case throughout the night, Holmes reclines on "a sort of Eastern divan" constructed with pillows and cushions (p. 271).

Similar indeterminacy over opium dens is at the heart of W. Somerset Maugham's *The Razor's Edge* (1943), in which the protagonist Larry's struggle between body and soul reaches an epiphany of sorts in India, when he witnesses sunrise. The low counterpoint in the story is when Sophie, Larry's intended, revels in an opium den:

> Hakim's an Algerian and he can always get you opium if you've got the dough to pay for it. He was quite a friend of mine. He'll get you anything you want, a boy, a man, a woman or a nigger. He always has half a dozen Algerians on tap. I spent three days there. I don't know how many men I didn't have. (p. 174)

The Orient is made to emanate both Indian spirituality and Algerian debauchery. Although Maugham explicitly celebrates the baseness Larry discovers in a coal mine as well as loftiness at a Benedictine monastery, broad-mindedness applies to masculine characters only. The misogynist representation of Sophie and other women in Maugham suggests repressed homosexuality. Every novel from Maugham's prolific career centers on a conventional heterosexual romance that unfailingly comes to a tragic end due to female lust like Sophie's.

At odds are not only desires of the flesh and yearnings of the soul, Maugham's homosexuality and a heterosexual culture, but also Maugham the fiction writer and Maugham the reporter. Maugham's travelogue, *On A Chinese Screen* (1935), contains a one-page journalistic report on "The Opium Den." Maugham opens with typical stage representations of the revolting yet alluring opium den. But halfway through the piece, Maugham begins to describe a firsthand experience he has had at such a site. Instead of a low and squalid den, Maugham climbs *up* to a room "neat," "brightly lit," where in one cubicle an elderly gentleman

> was quietly reading a newspaper, with his long pipe by his side. In another two coolies were lying, with a pipe between them ... and they

smiled at me in a friendly way. One of them offered me a smoke. In a third four men squatted over a chess-board, and a little further on a man was dandling a baby (the inscrutable Oriental has a passion for children) while the baby's mother, whom I took to be the landlord's wife, a plump, pleasant-faced woman, watched him with a broad smile on her lips. It was a cheerful spot, comfortable, home-like, and cozy. It reminded me somewhat of the little intimate beer-houses of Berlin where the tired working man could go in the evening and spend a peaceful hour. Fiction is stranger than fact. (pp. 50–51)

This personal encounter with a homey opium den and its congenial guests notwithstanding, Maugham resorts, two decades later, to the opium abyss to sharpen the razor's edge on which humans balance. The leisured, intimate atmosphere, the idealistic, classless community, the wide range of humanity of different ages, professions, and gender, the healthy, pleasant woman, and, the kinship between the den and the West, or Berlin to be exact, totally vanish, so much so that one wonders if "The Opium Den" is a piece of fiction as well, where Maugham constructs an idyllic Other, a rare un-Maughamian loving woman to boot, a utopia with the slight blemish of the cliché of "inscrutable Oriental."

## Film Noir's Chinatown

In cinematic representations, the opium den never fails to be located inside Chinatown. As a recess hidden from public view, the opium den becomes the core not only of Chinatown but of the Orient, where Oriental fetishes continue to insinuate both depravity and rapture. The long queues of earlier years are updated to skull caps in D. W. Griffith's silent film classic *Broken Blossoms*. The "Yellow Man" from China degenerates at an opium den in London's Limehouse district. Among his fellow addicts are Western-dressed, Caucasian-looking women, compatriots with loose Tang dress and absurdly huge skull caps, and a dark-skinned male wearing a white turban. The intertitle points to a medley of races in the opium den: "Chinese, Malays, Lascars, where the Orient squats at the portals of the West." The Yellow Man's apparel, especially his skull cap, and the Muslim's turban stand out as powerful racial markers. The subhuman, bestial quality of Orientals is inherent in the posture of squatting. In a long career that overlaps with Griffith's, the German filmmaker Josef von Sternberg made a series of Orientalist films that included *Morocco* (1930), *The Shanghai Express* (1932), *The Shanghai Gesture* (1941), and *Macao* (1952). *The Shanghai Gesture* was adapted from John Colton's 1926 play. The opium addiction is excised from the play, and only the protagonist's highly suggestive name, Poppy, remains.

The opium den, forever implying Oriental sin, fuels the yellow peril. Against the chiaroscuro of light and darkness, a touch of yellow, after Orson Welles's *A Touch of Evil* (1959), threatens to discolor the genre of film noir in the 1940s and 1950s, as filmic self-reflexivity redirects evil inward. Cinematographically, the yellow perilism in film noir is manifest in abundant reflections in mirrors, windows, glasses, water, and photographs, yet the projection of evil onto an Other is undercut by the very nature of reflections. Evil ultimately boomerangs right back in such noir classics as *The Big Sleep* (Raymond Chandler's novel in 1939 and Howard Hawks's film in the 1940s) and *Farewell, My Lovely* (Chandler's novel in 1940 and Edward Dmytryk's film *Murder, My Sweet* in 1944).

Chandler's *The Big Sleep* was turned into a Howard Hawks film, with a script cowritten by William Faulkner. (I refer primarily to Hawks's 1945 prerelease version of *The Big Sleep* rather than the 1946 version in circulation.) Oriental themes in the 1945 version revolve around one Arthur Gwynn Geiger, a porn shop owner, photographer of smut, blackmailer, homosexual, and supplier of laudanum. In the original novel, Geiger appears to be a yellowface character. The décor of Geiger's studio or boudoir is in the style of chinoiserie, its walls "decked out with strips of Chinese embroidery and Chinese and Japanese prints. Geiger wears Chinese slippers ... and the upper part of him wore a Chinese embroidered coat" (p. 23). Geiger himself has a "fat face, Charlie Chan moustache, thick soft neck. Soft all over. ... His left eye is glass" (pp. 18–19). Effeminate, clownish, and perverse, Geiger sports a fake eye and has a homosexual assistant and lover with the female-sounding first name of Carol. Not only Geiger's "house of sin" but his exterior appearance belongs squarely to chinoiserie: from interior decoration to Geiger's body. Inside Geiger's typical American house are rooms with enigmatic Oriental ornaments. Behind Geiger's respectable bookstore for rare books is a shop filled with pornographic materials. Living within the body of an apparently white male is an Orientalized queer.

Into Geiger's domain comes Carmen Sternwood, Philip Marlowe's client. She is a stock character, the fallen white woman, so tainted by Oriental sins that she takes laudanum into her body, and to pay for it she poses nude for Geiger. Instead of posing in the nude with only "a pair of long jade earrings," as she does in Chandler's original, the 1945 film visualizes Carmen, for obvious reasons, clothed in vaguely Chinese dress. While the original is titillatingly salacious, the film achieves similar effect via Carmen's dark, silky dress, with its sinuous, glittering Oriental design. In Chandler's book, Carmen takes the pose of "an Egyptian goddess.... The dark slate color of the iris had devoured the pupil. They were mad eyes" (p. 22). Carmen is in a trance, suspended between willing partnership and hypnotic enslavement, between white desirability and Egyptian insentience, to be photographed by a camera hidden in a totem pole (yet another association with dark primitivism). She is but one of film noir's femmes fatales, fallen white women under the spell of an insidious Orient. Her transgression lies in blurring the boundary between East and West, allowing the inside (her body, affiliation, culture) and the outside to be miscegenetically woven together. The Orient, source of all evil, corrupts Geiger, then Carmen, and threatens to infect the universe of film noir; the Orient is not only infectious and addictive, but it has already taken over part of the West. Granted that Geiger is bumped off early in the story, the first murder as a matter of fact, his house of sin remains the center of crime and mystery, in which a dead body vanishes and then materializes, and to which Marlowe is obliged to return again and again.

Even if the trope of the opium den is eventually excised from the film noir, Chinatown as a discursive lacuna continues to haunt detective and Western rationality. In Orson Welles's *The Lady from Shanghai* (1948), only the final one-eighth of the film is set in Chinatown and its psychic extension. The film closes when the heavily drugged protagonist O'Hara, played by Welles, eludes the law by stumbling into a Beijing Opera house, where the story is brought to a crescendo of unintelligibility by way of a cacophony of gongs, drums, and shrill singing. The five minutes of Chinatown's street scene and Beijing Opera serve to depict O'Hara not only fleeing the law but also taking leave of his senses, the basis of rationality. Ray Pratt, in *Projecting Paranoia* (2001), observes that the climax of *The Lady from Shanghai* is set "in San Francisco's Chinatown, moving from an incomprehensible Chinese opera there directly into the acclaimed funhouse mirrors sequence, thereby adding a further dimension of inscrutability" (p. 117). Indeed, when O'Hara comes to, he finds himself trapped inside a crazy house at an amusement park, which culminates the sensory disorientation of the Chinatown sequence. No longer drugged, O'Hara's unstable mental state continues to be expressionistically projected onto the gadgets at the crazy house, particularly the magic mirror maze. It is here that the showdown with O'Hara's clients, the Bannisters, takes place. The couple attempt to kill each other amidst the multiple mirrors, but only after shattering all their reflections do they succeed. The crazy house, epitomizing the irrational and insane, is accessed through Chinatown, the entryway into the Orient. Although the mirror maze perpetuates the Oriental myth, Welles subconsciously debunks it by the Bannisters' self-reflections therein. Just as the mirrors merely reflect the onlooker, Chinatown exteriorizes what lies deep within the Western Self.

Consistent with the generic fallen white woman, Evelyn Mulwray in Roman Polanski's neo-noir *Chinatown* (1974) is tainted by her association with the Orient, in this case, with Chinatown. Evelyn is played by Faye Dunaway with exotically shaved eyebrows and vaguely Eurasian features. The Mulwray mansion is maintained by a troop of Asian servants—butler, maid, chauffeur, and gardener. All these Orientals are comically stiff, their performance swinging between that of aloof automatons and of frantic clowns.[14] Although they seem peripheral to the plot, these Asians channel the action to the climax. Without her loyal Chinese chauffer and butler, for instance, the white lady would not be able to find temporary refuge in Chinatown. Without the setting of Chinatown, Welles and Polanski would not be able to find a vehicle in which to encapsulate their dark visions. More to the point, the pidgin refrain of Evelyn's Asian gardener—"Vely bad for glass!" ("Very bad for the grass!")—concerning the salt water in the miniature pond of the Mulwray estate unlocks the entire mystery: the unscrupulous Noah Cross (played by John Huston), Evelyn's father-fucker,[15] has secretly diverted water during a drought. Evelyn's husband, Hollis Mulwray, objected and was drowned in this pond (briny water is found in his lungs). Cross's broken bifocals also lie at the bottom of the pond, possibly shaken loose as he struggled to kill Hollis.

Glasses may improve eyesight, but they give away the murder. With one unwitting mispronunciation ("glass" for "grass") from a negligible extra, the detective Jake Gittes (played by Jack Nicholson) perceives his own blindness in missing the evidence right next to the Mulwray mansion. The Oriental gardener, totally suppressed and hardly remembered, performs only one function: to retrieve the glasses from the pond and to hand them over to Gittes, respectfully, with both hands. Without his one line and his one act, the film would be hard put to proceed. Not to mince words, the gardener in his pidgin enlightens Gittes, whose epiphany strikes as he parrots, with a contemptuous snicker, the Oriental tongue. Polanski intends the key word to echo a multitude of images: glasses in water, reflections of reflections, and lost vision found and lost again when Evelyn Mulwray is shot in the eye.[16] Polanski's *Chinatown* provides a displacement of Noah Cross's Original Sin of incest onto the Oriental Other, a black hole where evil lurks. This hole is the exit wound that makes a bloody pulp of Faye Dunaway's left eye; this hole is the concluding exhortation, "Forget it, Jake! It's Chinatown." In Noah Cross country—a Los Angeles living off his water supply and a Christendom corrupted by the Original Sin—one's evil is twice removed, relegated to abject Chinatown and then forgotten. One of the most memorable taglines in film history, this advice to Jake makes certain that Chinatown and Asia will register in Western consciousness only by virtue of its erasure, in the exact manner that the body veils its own waste.

Despite the assertion of totality, anal apocalypse is strictly confined to the Christian West that evacuates Asia for its own epistemological rupture. The logical and sensible corollary would be to ask if Asia, under siege of Western modernity, has responded in kind and put the Christian West to similar use. Illogically, nonsensically, though, the human body begins to notice the barely audible voice coming from below or behind: "Having defecated this life, the undead reaches up in the last gasp for toilet paper. There is none, no one, zero one."

# 2 Camp Scatology

## A Comparative Study of Body (as) Waste in Japanese American Literature

Suspected as enemy aliens following the surprise attack against Pearl Harbor on December 7, 1941, 120,000 Japanese Americans and 21,000 Japanese Canadians were rounded up and incarcerated in internment camps in the western part of North America.[1] These internees were caught between West and East: their Eastern ancestry clashed with a paranoid, racist West. As memoir and fiction, internment narratives have colored a large number of Japanese American writings concerned with their ghettoization, alienation, and abjection during the war as well as after it. Historically, Japanese Americans were treated as undesirable waste to be expelled from the American body into internment camps, a collective trauma manifested here as "camp scatology," or the body (as) waste. In such classics on the internment as Joy Kogawa's *Obasan* (1981) and John Okada's *No-No Boy* (1957), the Japanese American body is but body waste, as it is irreparably tainted by rejection and shame. The body is feces, "foreign matter" to be extruded. Such imagery should not be taken as Kogawa's or Okada's "eccentric" poetic metaphor for Japanese American subjectivity, for what happened was a case of extremity in the human condition, during the time of World War II. To highlight the unique Japanese American predicament, one that precariously inhabits the fissure between East and West, the opening section of this chapter, "Existential Puke, Jap Shit, Mao's Manure," compares Japanese American camp scatology to two other types of camp from the West and the East. The second section, "Amputee," gives a metonymic spin to the thesis of "body (as) waste," where missing or ineffectual body parts—waste matter literally—document in their disuse the internment. This section also contrasts Japanese American amputees with Western and Eastern counterparts. While physical deformity has been deployed in literature as a sign of evil (the lame Richard III) or of divine power (blind prophet Tiresias), disabilities in Japanese American texts, as self-representations, differ from their misshapen predecessors. Body mutilation is not *imagined* as in

Shakespeare and Sophocles, but *experienced* in Kogawa and other Japanese American texts. A comparative project, this chapter juxtaposes three strands of texts and three sensibilities on undesirable bodies and body functions, connecting West, East, and their borderland, Asian America.[2]

Research on the Japanese American internment experience has shed considerable light on that collective trauma from the perspective of history, sociology, anthropology, psychology, but this chapter examines it from the angle of affect. It considers the emotions of internees, which stand out in sharp contrast to Western and Eastern "shadows." We can do this most appropriately by analyzing literature, where the intangible and, indeed, mysterious human emotions are richly portrayed, unlike the writings of the social sciences, which are dominated by empirical, quantifiable evidence. For instance, in "Children of Inmates" (2000) Yasuko Takezawa tellingly opts to explore "effects" rather than "affects." Although her entire essay hints at the emotions of shame and guilt, she concludes with only a single articulated instance: "One Sansei said that, to the Nisei, camp means 'shame,' and to the Sansei, it means 'guilt'" (p. 312). This endeavor picks up from where Takezawa and other eminent social scientists left off.[3]

## Existential Puke, Jap Shit, Mao's Manure

Philosophically, wartime and postwar European existentialists lived in a camp called life, which nauseated them to the extent of "puking." Racially, "Japs" in America during World War II were expelled to cesspools of camps. Ideologically, intellectuals in Maoist China were sent down to the countryside and detained in "cow sheds," their wasted years likened by themselves to night soil to fertilize the "motherland." Unlike the existentialist's philosophically based camp or the Japanese Americans' race-based camp, however, Maoist reeducation camps can be set up anywhere.

Anatomically, existential puke is associated with stomach acid, Jap shit with "crap" from the bowels, and Mao's manure with the earth's aroma that suggests the cycle of life. Retching takes place in the upper body, involving organs principally above diaphragm (despite the fact that stomach lies below diaphragm), that muscular membrane separating abdominal and thoracic cavities. The mouth, esophagus, diaphragm, and stomach are key in respiratory and digestive functions. Since breathing, eating, drinking, and speaking sustain life, "heaving" acquires more "stature" by virtue of its association with these essential functions. The mouth, in particular, is primarily for talking and eating and only rarely as the conduit of vomit. At times we have to induce vomiting by sticking a finger down the throat. Existentialists seize upon this body function of vomiting to express their revolt against an absurd and meaningless world. Alienated in life and repelled by life, existentialists will a gagging response in order to reject the world that enters the body in the form of food and drink. Sartre projects this inner sensation to the outside in *Nausea* (1938): Nausea "spreads at the bottom of the viscous puddle, at the bottom of *our* time" (p. 21). The "viscous puddle" is thick, resistant to flow, like acid reflux or stomach indigestion. Half-heartedly making love to a woman, the protagonist in Sartre's *Nausea* experiences a vision of a monstrous, repugnant public park, the manifestation of her private parts. Intimacy in private degenerates into abomination in public:

> I let my arm run along the woman's thigh and suddenly saw a small garden with low, wide trees on which immense hairy leaves were hanging. Ants were running everywhere, centipedes and ringworm. There were even more horrible animals: their bodies were made from a slice of toast, the kind you put under roast pigeons; they walked sideways with legs like a crab. The larger leaves were black with beasts. Behind the cactus and the Barbary fig trees, the Velleda of the public park pointed a finger at her sex. 'This park smells of vomit,' I shouted. (p. 59)

Nightmarish, grotesque insects and animals sicken the narrator. "Barbary" points as much to a geographical region as it hints at barbarism. It is rather typical of existentialism that sexuality elicits in characters not orgasmic ejaculation but oral retching. Sexuality is not the only intense human activity that induces vomit. Even the momentous, life-and-death decision in Albert Camus' *The Stranger* (1942) affects the narrator accused of murder in the same way: "The futility of what was happening here seemed to take me by the throat, I felt like vomiting" (p. 132). The narrator is eventually sentenced to decapitation, the ultimate form of estrangement from one's own body and human life.

Not all Japanese American narratives related to internment resort to Jap shit. John Okada, writing under the influence of existentialism in 1957, favors the metaphor of puke in *No-No Boy*. When the No-No boy protagonist, Ichiro, returns to Seattle after imprisonment as a result of his refusal to serve in the military, he is greeted by a Japanese American veteran's contempt and "a mouthful of sputum" (p. 4). Not only are the veteran and the outside world repelled by Ichiro, but Ichiro is repelled by the world and by himself. Coming home to his clean bedroom makes him feel like "puking" (p. 7). Whereas "color-blind" European existentialists eject the world regardless of race, the persecuted Japanese American minority has internalized self-loathing, which manifests itself as parricidal, fratricidal, and suicidal impulses. Nearly all the saviors in Okada's novel inhabit mainstream culture: white employers offer Ichiro positions despite his prison record; his friend Kenji's loving family behave like a middle-class white family, including the broad-shouldered father, who drinks beer and enjoys baseball games; Kenji's lover Emi "on loan" to Ichiro is a woman whose "long legs were strong and shapely like a white woman's" (p. 83).

In contrast to existentialists' upper-body, voluntary puke, Jap shit, echoing how Japanese Americans were viewed after Pearl Harbor, is decidedly lower-body and involuntary. Defecating, which occurs below the diaphragm, is associated more with sinking, animalistic impulses than with rising, "ethereal" ones like breathing. Bowel movements are instinctual urges centered on the abdomen; they are less subject to personal will. And unlike the mouth, the anus has one principal function—to defecate. The orifice involved in the specific activity comes to "gentrify" or "vulgarize" that activity. While retching is not a welcome occurrence, it is at least acceptable in polite society. But defecating, in literary texts, is relegated to passing references to the senile, the pathological, the coprophiliac—except in Japanese American internment narratives. The American mainstream society exorcises the ethnic minority as if it were excrement, which becomes a pivotal symbol for Japanese American self-representation. As opposed to Sartrean, "viscous" nausea, "crap" proceeds from the "viscera" or intestines, and it is "visceral" or intensely emotional. Beyond the double entendre of abdominal and searing for "visceral," the word "crap" also carries the Freudian polarities of feces and gold, of worthless nonsense and a gambler's sudden fortune from a crap game.[4]

Milton Murayama's *All I Asking for Is My Body* (1975) concludes on this duality of "crap." The life in Murayama's Japanese camp on a Hawaiian sugar cane plantation is one of misery and debt. Crap or waste aptly glosses the plantation laborers' struggle:

> The camp, I realized then, was planned and built around its sewage system. The half dozen rows of underground concrete ditches, two feet wide and three feet deep, ran from the highest slope of camp into the concrete irrigation ditch on the lower perimeter of camp. An outhouse built over the sewage ditch had two pairs of back-to-back toilets and serviced four houses. Shit too was organized according to the plantation pyramid. Mr. Nelson was top shit on the highest slope, then there were Portuguese, Spanish, and *nisei lunas* with their indoor toilets which flushed into the same ditches, then Japanese Camp, and Filipino Camp. (p. 96)

In a sociological diagram of capitalism, Mr. Nelson, the plantation owner, "shits" on everyone else figuratively. Although this is not an internment camp, the disenfranchised narrator has intuitively appropriated camp scatology to represent their conditions. Murayama chooses to end his insightful critique of camp scatology with wish-fulfillment: the protagonist Kiyoshi Oyama joins the military, wins at a crap camp in the barracks, and thus is able to repay the family debt. Personal and family liberation are achieved in a single stroke of luck brought about through assimilation: Kiyoshi answers the call for wartime mobilization, and the Oyamas freed from generations of debt going back to the 1923 Tokyo earthquake and the Japanese tradition of dutiful sons. As Kiyoshi celebrates, "I've made my bail money out of this prison of filial piety and family unity" (p. 102). Only someone who has endured a prolonged prison term can see through the prison's stone walls to analyze the sewage system, the crap flowing through which provides the escape/escapist route. A Japanese American imagines an exit out of Japanese suffering via an American fortune.

Murayama's analysis of things excretory at the plantation camp foreshadows Japanese American internment narratives. Most such writings open with a description of the camp layout, particularly the latrines. The refrain on abominable latrines vividly testifies to the loss of privacy and dignity. Jeanne Wakatsuki Houston's *Farewell to Manzanar* (1973) is a favorite reading about the internment for a younger audience. Terrible sanitary conditions cause the famous "Manzanar runs" or diarrhea. Houston describes "the smell of [the women's latrine] spoiled what little appetite we had. Outside, men were working in an open trench, up to their knees in muck. . . . Inside, the floor was covered with excrement, and all twelve bowls were erupting like a row of tiny volcanoes" (p. 22). In the wide-open latrine, women often improvise with cardboard boxes to have some privacy. In *Citizen 13660* (1946), an internment narrative with illustrations, Mine Okubo remembers the washroom, shower, and latrine in the same breath, with a specific reference to the poor, stagnant sewage system and the stench. Mitsuye Yamada's rendition of similar experiences is "In the Outhouse" from *Camp Notes and Other Poems* (1976):

> Our collective wastebin
> Where the air sticks
> In my craw
> Burns my eyes
> I have this place to hide
> The excreta and
> The blood which

Do not flush down
Nor seep away.

They pile up
Fill the earth.

I am drowning.

In three stanzas with three, increasingly clipped sentences, the poet moves from a well-wrought description to a short, instinctive cry. The humiliation of the camp experience dehumanizes the narrator to the extent that her throat becomes a "craw," a bird's crop or an animal's stomach. The last line pointedly concludes that the internee is drowning, as of the moment of her writing and our reading, in "the excreta / and the blood" of historical memory.

A text that focuses squarely on an internment awash in excrement is *Obasan* (1981) by Joy Kogawa, a Japanese Canadian whose poetic, lyrical style entwines with the prosaic factuality of trauma, whose voice battles silence.[5] It is in *Obasan*, chock full of images and metaphors, that one finds the best evidence of how the internment is represented through feces, animals and insects, and amputation. The narrator is Naomi Nakane, a child survivor of wartime relocation from Vancouver to the Canadian interior. In her Aunt Emily's diary entry, written in a documentary prose that persists in disrupting Naomi's poetic voice, internees are relegated to animal stalls, having been expelled like feces: "The stall was the former home of a pair of stallions. . . . The whole place is impregnated with the smell of ancient manure. Every other day it's swept with chloride of lime or something but you can't disguise horse smells, cows, sheep, pig, rabbit, and ghost smells . . . . The toilets are just a sheet-metal trough and up till now they didn't have partitions or seats" (p. 97). Aunt Emily likens "removees" to "billygoats and nannygoats and kids—all the scapegoats to appease the blindness" (p. 88). A British Columbia newspaper runs the headline that "They are a stench in the nostrils of the people of Canada," justifying the evacuation to "cesspools," "flushed out of Vancouver. Like dung drops" (p. 118). When Obasan finally arrives, along with Naomi and her older brother Stephen, at the relocation site, she finds a shed filled with "cow manure" (p. 121).

The overwhelming imagery of excrement culminates in a kitten's drowning in the outhouse and an albino girl's groundless accusation against Naomi. Naomi's denial triggers a typical children's repartee, the innocence and silliness of which accentuates the horror of the kitten's weakening mewing for days:

"You threw my kitten down there," she says.

...

"I didn't do it," I say.
"You did too."
"I didn't."
"Did."
"Didn't."

The albino stands for the Euro-Canadian whites, genetically "deformed" on the exterior and filled with suspicion and hate. Naomi's accuser has not only committed the heinous crime of dumping Naomi and her like into Canada's cesspool but blames the victim for the crime. The kitten's fate blends with Naomi's hospital nightmare after a near-drowning:

> It all becomes part of my hospital dream. The kitten cries day after day, not quite dead, unable to climb out and trapped in the outhouse. The maggots are crawling in its eyes and mouth. Its fur is covered in slime and feces. Chickens with their heads half off flap and swing upside-down in mid-air. The baby in the dream has fried-egg eyes and his excrement is soft and yellow as corn mush. His head is covered with an oatmeal scab, under which his scalp is a wet wound. (p. 158)

Regressing to a fetal state, Naomi confuses what is eaten and what is discharged, food and feces, life and death drives. Her self decomposes into that of the kitten, the chicken, and the baby. The chicken's decapitation and the baby's wet wound embody her own pain.

Whereas existentialists puke to express their revulsion against the world, and Japanese Americans become waste matter to be cast out of America's body politic, Mao's manure was generated by propaganda that over twenty million intellectuals should sacrifice themselves for the motherland through *xiafang* (downward transfer, or labor for reeducation in the countryside).[6] Both satirizing and echoing the propaganda, Chinese writers describe their time in the countryside, their bodies rotting into compost. Unlike internment camps, Maoist "camps" could abruptly proliferate and anyone could turn into a *niu-guei sheshen* (cow demon, snake spirit). Neighborhood sheds instantly become makeshift "cow sheds" to house anyone who used to be in power. People could also be sent down to the countryside to be reeducated by peasants for years or decades. The roles of victim, victimizer, and spectator could shift abruptly. Although political censorship and continued survival in a totalitarian state shape how victims of the Cultural Revolution and other purges remember their traumas, the victims' Chinese heritage of seeking harmony and maintaining equilibrium with the collective whole contribute to the contour of their memories. In a desperate attempt to make something out of nothing, to extract hope from the bleakness of Mao's campaigns, Chinese writers share in a sense of futility through the self-image of feces, yet, paradoxically, a resigned quiescence prevails to transform that self-image into night soil.

This "alchemical" metamorphosis, however, is not available to Chen Jo-hsi in *The Execution of Mayor Yin and Other Stories from the Great Proletarian Cultural Revolution* (1979). An idealistic Taiwanese expatriate in the United States, Chen decided to respond to Chairman Mao's call for intellectuals all over the world to return and serve the motherland. Chen's seven-year ordeal at the height of the Cultural Revolution forms the basis for her collection of short stories. "Jen Hsiu-lan" depicts the title character, a persecuted rightist, drowning herself in the cesspool. To commit suicide while under strict surveillance, Jen has to pry open window bars at the toilet and get to the cesspool outside. After a long search in the vicinity, Jen's body is finally found curled up in the corner of the cesspool, which is only three feet deep. Jen had to have been resolved to die, or revulsion, "existentialist" or otherwise, would have compelled her to gag and stand up for air. A pool of human refuse seems to Jen to be the ideal resting place, for she views herself as refuse. Jen has squeezed into the corner of the cesspool to avoid detection: either shame lingers on even in death or Jen, through the finality of her act, rejects the world that has rejected her.

For every Jen who chooses suicide, there are many more who survive. The mainland Chinese novelist Zhang Xianliang intertwines, schizophrenically, suffering in Maoist China with escapist male fantasies in *Getting Used to Dying* (1991). Almost every chapter is split between two events at two sites (China and the West) at two different times. The affect of detachment that permeates the protagonist is a human coping strategy amidst catastrophes. What little there is of political persecution bears an eerie resemblance to Jen Hsiu-lan's demise. Zhang's protagonist recalls so-called survival strategies during the famines of the late 1950s and early 1960s:

> He had lived through China's Great Famine in the labor camps, and he knew well that the secretions of the body were precious. Both urine and saliva had their uses in an emergency.
>
> Also, if you did not allow yourself to shit for a long time, you could make believe that there was actually something of substance in your stomach. This allowed you to think that you were fully fed, that

you did not need, like others, to drop dead along the road. This was fully in accord with Mao's great dictum: "Turn spirit into matter."
(p. 44)

Tongue in cheek, Zhang satirizes Mao's regime in the guise of a document on survival. Body waste is retained for the illusion of a full stomach. This is reinforced subsequently: "I had been wise not to defecate just now in the toilet—the digested waste and my long intestines supplied each other with a measure of heat" (p. 48). Such intellectuals who survived famine and persecution must continue their lives, however shattered, in post-Mao China, an exigency that makes unrealistic either existentialist disdain or Japanese American–style truth-telling.

Yang Jiang's *Six Chapters from My Life "Downunder"* (1981) is perhaps the best embodiment of intellectuals' quiet suffering and power during the Mao era. Spouse to the eminent scholar Qiao Zhongshu, Yang is an essayist whose emotional restraint and elegance are almost classical. In this thin memoir recording her family's fragmentation and reeducation, Yang's minimalist style accentuates the deep well of strength within her. The recurring metaphor is human waste and its potential, which bears witness to the family's wasting away at May Seventh Cadre Schools and to the rustic setting of the countryside.[7] The intelligentsia were ordered to work as peasants and to learn from the peasants. In "Tending a Vegetable Plot," Yang Jiang describes the intellectual-peasants' efforts to produce their foodstuffs. To grow vegetables, they must have a source of fertilizer; therefore, they erect a roadside toilet to collect from passersby. Yang elaborates on the construction of the toilet, her details perfect evidence of how intellectuals embrace labor, only to have it usurped by the peasants:

> We erected five wooden posts—one for each corner and an additional one on the side where the door would go—then made walls out of woven sorghum stalks, and that took care of the enclosure. Inside we buried a large earthen compost basin; in front of that we dug two shallow holes into which we fitted bricks for footrests. That completed our toilet. The only thing we needed now was some sort of curtain for the door. . . . We settled on the smooth core of sorghum stalks from which we had stripped the outer layer; we then wove them closely and neatly together with hempen cord, resulting in as lovely a door curtain as one could imagine. (p. 34)

The intellectuals are naïve indeed to assume that the aesthetically conceived and privacy-oriented outhouse will encourage deposit of night soil from passersby, who steal from the toilet rather than "bank their gold" (*huangjin* ["yellow gold" in Mandarin] refers both to gold and feces). Discharge from the Cadre School being, shall we say, "intellectual property," is rumored to be "the best around" (p. 35), i.e., superior to the peasant's.

In "Quickie," Yang remembers what would be the equivalent of a "pet" dog at the Cadre School. But first, Yang Jiang shares her daughter's experience in the countryside:

> A baby who slept on the same earthen *kang* had had a bowel movement right on the bed mat, which my flustered daughter tried to clean up with a handful of toilet paper. One of the village women ran up and rebuked her over wasting not only the toilet paper but the excrement as well. Then she called out, 'Wu—lu lu lu lu', after which a dog came rushing in, jumped up onto the *kang,* and began licking at the mess, licking it all clean, including the baby's buttocks. (p. 53)

In the impoverished rural areas, the baby's stool feeds the family dog. Life is indeed a cycle, where all are interlocked, even cleanliness and filth, what is consumed and what is conserved. The essay closes with the elderly couple wondering what had happened to the dog Quickie. In response to her husband's speculation, "Maybe she's already been eaten and is now nothing more than a pile of manure," Yang gently disagrees: "Well, maybe she has, and maybe she's a mother by now, eating manure to stay alive and having one litter of puppies after another..." (p. 65). The dignity of life arises amidst shame and indigence. Her confirmation of life balances his hard-edged, almost naturalistic dismissal.

Yang Jiang accepts waste as part of Nature's recycling in a preindustrial nation caught in convulsive campaigns that are both anti-Nature, causing famine and starvation, and anti-human nature, causing a *De*-Cultural Revolution. Yang's clinging to notions of the cycle of life testifies to her quiet heroism. Her attitude of taking manure for granted contrasts sharply, however, with the magical qualities attributed to excreta in Asia. Bodily discharge from High Lamas and venerable Buddhist monks is believed to carry healing power, and there was, among some, a highly unconventional health practice in Asia of drinking one's own urine. Such ritualization of urine manifests itself in Zhang Yimou's *Red Sorghum* (1987) when the vengeful protagonist urinates into huge jars of new wine in an apparent effort to ruin them, only to add the "magic touch" of a chemical reaction that results in the best wine ever made. This plot twist foreshadows, in an explicitly Freudian fashion, the protagonist's eventual insemination of the female winery owner.

## Amputee

Body (as) waste in Japanese American internment narratives takes a met-onymic turn when body parts are severed or rendered dysfunctional—dilapi-dated extremities laid waste. While Western literature is replete with physically handicapped characters, such "deformity" is consistently perceived by the eyes of normalcy, and rarely by those of the "deformed." As Disabilities studies has contended in recent decades, physical and psychological disabilities signify as much the Other or the non-Self as possibilities that may occur for Everyman. Deformities in literature are, therefore, projections of either the author's or the culture's anxiety. By contrast, Japanese American texts attest to mutila-tions imposed from without, by history and society.

Since perhaps the most celebrated historical amputee in the Anglo-American world may be Admiral Lord Horatio Nelson, it is not surprising that his literary "crew" turns out to be sailors as well: Captain Ahab, Long John Silver, and Captain Hook. They compensate for their disabilities with prostheses—an ivory leg, a wood peg, and an iron hook, respectively—the artificial limb being made of nonhuman material that possesses its possessor so much so that he becomes the first generation of cyborg. In subsequent sci-fi imaginary fims such as *Six Million Dollar Man, Robocop,* and *Terminator,* the foreign matter or machine absorbed into the truncated human body offers superhuman, at times demonic, power. However, even such "enabling" dis-abilities carry a stigma, which goes back to the lame and deformed Richard III in Shakespeare and even further back to more ancient "scapegoats," as René Girard analyzes it.[8]

The opening monologue of *Richard III* amounts to a confession prior to the crime, as though what one character refers to as "thou dreadful minister of the Devil" is born with Original Sin by virtue of the fact that he is born deformed:

> I, that am curtailed of this fair proportion,
> Cheated of feature by dissembling nature,
> Deformed, unfinished, sent before my time
> In this breathing world, scarce half made up,
> And that so lamely and unfashionable
> That dogs bark at me as I halt by them.
>     (Act. I, Scene I, ll. 18–23)

A sorry imitation of a human, Richard III's "physical difference" suggests "debilitating deformity."[9] Resemblance to nature and human is marred by its inherent dissemblance, which becomes an outward sign of the duplicitous inner nature of characters with disabilities. Lameness evokes corruption and usurpation, although it is reiterated as a comic, light-hearted leitmotif in children's and young adult literature.

The one-legged Long John Silver in Robert Louis Stevenson's *Treasure Island* (1883) pretends to be a "clean and pleasant-tempered landlord," happily without a sailor's mouth, in order to go on the treasure hunt. The wooden leg belies Silver's nice language and accommodating manners. While every pirate in *Treasure Island* carries on his person some sort of Cain's mark—facial scar or blindness—Silver's conspicuous handicap does not stamp him with Richard III's malice. Rather, it humanizes Silver with an endearing flaw. By the same token, J. M. Barrie's *Peter Pan* (1904) attributes to Captain Hook's metal prosthesis incipiently mechanical or sci-fi robotic, animalistic, and insect overtones, all of which are nonhuman characteristics. Hook's crocodile "familiar" attends him like an animal spirit after a taste of his arm; his primitive, animal side haunts him since it already claims part of him. (This parallels Peter Pan and his "firefly" or fairy familiar, Tinker Bell.) Since the metal hook is a synecdoche for Captain Hook, his anxiety comes to be most keenly felt *there:* "it made his iron claw twitch, and at night it disturbed him like an insect" (p. 125). His "iron claw" is not only metallic and animalistic but resembles a pestering insect in his sleep. Subconsciously, the hook takes on a form even lower than animals.

In reconstructing their camp experiences, Japanese American internees join the ranks of amputees, deploying, in an eerily consistent manner, the metonymy of amputation or "phantom limb pain" to denote loss and emptiness. The internment festers into a hollow, gnawing wound that rots rather than heals. Unlike their Western literary predecessors of Captain Ahab and company, Japanese American protagonists have no prostheses or ineffective ones. In Okada's *No-No Boy,* Ichiro the despised No-No boy is posed against the decorated veteran Kenji, whose compliance has cost him a leg, a persistently decomposing stump that eventually kills him. Kenji's contradictory description of his pain encapsulates not only Ichiro's dilemma but the Japanese American community's: "Not having it doesn't hurt. But it hurts where it ought to be." Rationally, one accepts the fact of amputation, but the physical absence coexists with the presence of phantom limb. Pain is hardly contained by prosthesis; instead, it erodes the entire being. It is not a state of loss with which Kenji must come to terms, but a gradual losing. Nor will the losing ever come to a close, since Ichiro must live with the loss of Kenji as well as his own identity, and we as a society must live with the injustice of internment. Such is perhaps the ultimate meaning of "phantom pain": the loss of one's limb or part of oneself is irreplaceable, leading to perpetual mourning.

Although not an amputee like Kenji, Stephen in Kogawa's *Obasan* depends on a crutch because he has not received proper medical care for his leg injury during the internment. Arriving at their first relocation site, the shed made of "cow manure," the limping Stephen takes out his pent-up frustrations on the butterflies:

> Stephen whacks his crutch into the grasses, scattering the butterflies. Each wing bears two round circles of gold and when the pairs are spread, they are infant eyes, staring up at us bodiless and unblinking. I stare back as Stephen tramples and slashes, hopping deeper and deeper into the tall grasses, swinging his crutch like a scythe. Within moments, the ground and grasses are quivering with maimed and dismembered butterflies. The ones that are safe are airborne and a few have reached the heights of trees.
>
> "They're bad," Stephen says as he wades through the weeds. "They eat holes in your clothes."
>
> His crutch clears a wide path...as he continues his crusade....Some brambles and vines are clinging to his pant leg and one butterfly he cannot see is hovering above his head. (pp. 122–123)

Having been crippled, Stephen now shifts from a victim to a persecutor. The crutch of powerlessness turns into the scythe of Death. Once he becomes aware that Naomi is watching him, he justifies his violence with a lame excuse. By blurring butterflies with moths, Stephen adopts the Canadian rationale of equating Japanese Canadians with "Japs." The multiple gaze at the crime scene is intriguing. Naomi stares at Stephen being stared at by the butterflies' "infant eyes." Stephen is not only one-legged but blind: he cannot see the lone butterfly above him. These gazes link the children with butterflies. Stephen is the maimed butterflies and butterfly-killer. Naomi is the maimed butterflies, is implicated in the crime as a bystander, and hopes to transcend or re-envision the carnage through airborne, fleeting beauty. Be it a high-angle shot from the butterfly's infant eyes, a long shot from a child narrator, or the novel's tone of restraint from the passage of time, distance enables Naomi-Kogawa to come to terms with the internment. Victimized Japanese Canadians blame themselves for acquiescence, yet they also bear witness to their suffering.

Much like scatology in *Obasan*, internment as amputation is initially articulated in the battle cries of Aunt Emily, the Word Warrior:

> "We're gluing our tongues back on....It takes a while for the nerves to grow back." (p. 36)

"You have to remember.... You are your history. If you cut any of it off you're an amputee.... Denial is gangrene." (p. 50)

Propelled by Aunt Emily's force, Naomi parallels her childhood molestation by her white neighbor Old Man Gower and the communal persecution by Canada. Foreshadowing the sexual abuse, Naomi recounts a nightmare that blends her private shame with collective pain. "Three beautiful oriental women lay naked in the muddy road," and as one of the women tries to offer her body to survive, she is rewarded by soldiers' rifle shots: "The first shots were aimed at the toes of the women, the second at their feet. A few inches from the body, the first woman's right foot lay like a solid wooden boot neatly severed above" (p. 61). Thus the theme of amputation is introduced in the novel.

Summoning the courage to confront her memory of Old Man Gower's sexual assault, Naomi establishes the tension between silence and voice throughout her adult life: "If I speak, I will split open and spill out. To be whole and safe I must hide in the foliage, odourless as a newborn fawn. But already the lie grows like a horn, and unfurled fiddlehead fist, through the soft fontanelle of my four-year-old mind" (p. 63). The alliteration of "f," with the repeated puffs of air, fractures the façade of a holistic entity. What are supposed to be symbols of innocence, "soft fontanelle" and "unfurled fiddlehead," turn grotesque like a satyr's horn. Similar to the magic of the butterfly's momentary transcendence as it is being slaughtered, Kogawa's smithery of words reaches a new height when the pain is most intense. With an imagination rivaling Yeats's when "Crazy Jane Talks with the Bishop" yokes together "fair" and "foul," "sole" and "soul," "hole" and "whole,"[10] Kogawa associates three words—"saw," "sew," and "sow"—in the finale of her recall of Old Man Gower's abuse. "My legs are being sawn in half" (p. 65). Only something sawn in half can be sewn back up. Likewise, sowing seeds or rejuvenation entails ploughing or breaking the land. The molested Naomi has low, sow-like self-esteem that serves as the pig bed in which molten metal is solidified into re-enforced alloy. Amputation proliferates in the fact that even her Japanese doll, her doppelganger gift from her absent mother, has legs "dislocated and she cannot stand on her own" (p. 115), and that her pet frog propels itself on one good leg to prey upon crippled insects (p. 207).

Phantom pain over war and internment is passed on, transethnically, to David Guterson's *Snow Falling on Cedars* (1995). A feat of empathetic imagining, despite stereotypes of samurai reserve and exotic Oriental beauty, Guterson locates the core of his generic hybrid—murder mystery, courtroom drama, seafaring tale, nature writing, regionalism, war narrative, and ethnic trauma narrative—in hollowness: the white protagonist Ishmael's "phantom limb," which feels "as if the arm were *there* again but half-numb"; the loss of his Japanese American lover Hatsue; the emptying of Japanese from San Piedro Island during the war; the hollow cedar where Ishmael and Hatsue had their trysts; the strawberry fields the Japanese farmers should have owned; the darkness within the island bigot's mind; the snowstorm that incapacitates the island. The liberal guilt that prompts Ishmael's defense of Japanese Americans finds a trope in "phantom limb," the void within Japanese American consciousness transferred now to mainstream American.

By contrast, the Chinese tradition pays scant attention to disabled amputees. Lu Tieguai, a cripple with a crutch, is a member of the Eight Immortals in folk belief, and Zhang Che's *One-Armed Swordsman* (1967) has initiated a slew of Hong Kong *wuxia pian* (swordplay films) with disabled fighters. Concurrently, Japan produces films featuring Zatoichi, the blind samurai. In recent years, the Korean television drama that has been sweeping across Asia and Asian diasporic communities favors sightlessness as a melodramatic tearjerker. But other than these scattered instances, Asian culture does not seem to register amputation in its midst. Even in representations of disabilities, the cultural stress on a harmonious whole, whether body politic or human body, leads to the deployment of blindness, deafness, muteness, insanity, and retardation rather than amputation. Since this essay explores the darkness and the unpalatability of camp scatology, it is fitting to end with this blind spot in East Asian culture, a repressed brokenness. A comparative project yields insights not only about different cultural configurations but also about the absence of any configuration at all. The consciousness raised by Disabilities studies in the West in recent decades, which makes possible the critical focus on amputees, has yet to materialize on the other side of the Pacific Ocean.

# Intercut on Asian Penis

# 3 Brush and Blade in East-West Cultures

## Global Phallus, Colonial Acephalus

## Unsheathe

The apparently contradictory pairs in the chapter title have blood ties that go back to the nineteenth century. These cultural opposites, after the initial shock and revulsion of colonialism, begin to attract each other, driven by the urge to be one: East and West, brush and blade, the literary and the martial, head and headlessness. In the West, nineteenth- and early twentieth-century colonial loathing of the Orient gradually gives way to high-modernist and postmodernist idolization; the demonic, dehumanizing non-West metamorphoses over time into a dream-self. Whereas Conrad, Forster, Maugham, and Orwell—all implicated in colonialist ideology to various extent—project irrationality and acephalic violence onto non-Western cultures, their initial shock evolves into a phallic sign of empowerment in contemporary Hollywood and independent cinema. Nearly a century ago, novelists dreaded the blade of wrath in the hands of the colonized. Today's filmmakers circulate to a receptive global market the ideal oneness of the poetic and the manic, a notion borrowed from the East. Yet the diametrically opposed sensibilities spring from the same root of Orientalism. A colonialist attempt to inflate and to lose itself, Orientalism has formulaically polarized the West's "shadow" into the aesthetic and the abominable: geisha and samurai, chrysanthemum and the sword,[1] Madame Butterfly and Dragon Lady, Charlie Chan and Fu Manchu, castrated celestial and the Yellow Peril. The binarism renders each of its attributes indispensable to the other.

When high modernists inherit the Orientalist legacy, dialectic clashes often come in the metaphor of thunder, whose abruptness and raw force embody a conceptual cataclysm that destroys and enlightens. Thus, in the flash of the Montashigi blade as it is unsheathed,[2] in the shock of Kali's bloody tongue,[3] modernists and avant-gardists such as Yeats and Bataille intuit an apocalyptic vision.[4] Modern, secular, and "scientific," the West transfers its need for myth and magic to the phantasmagoric Orient. Accordingly, in literature, Pound borrows from what he believes to be Chinese ideograms a medium to inaugurate modernist poetry, alleging that Chinese sentence structure gives the desired *"transference of power"* like "a flash of lightning…between two terms, a cloud and the earth" ("The Chinese Written Character as a Medium for Poetry" 1920, p. 366). Imagistically, Pound weds two disparate, intangible realms: language and nature, half-understood Chinese writing and modernism in the making. Pound closes his essay with three Chinese ideograms, "sun," "rise," and "East," all of which, in his split-word analysis, come to pictorialize their meaning. "East" is taken to visualize the sun amidst trees, hence sunrise in the East. Not only the language of the East but the East itself becomes the rock on which modernist poetry is founded. Likewise, the drought of Eliot's *The Waste Land* ends in an Oriental epilogue, as "What the Thunder Said" pronounces *"datta," "dayadhvam," "damyata"* (give, sympathize, control). In both Pound and Eliot, high modernists are speaking in tongues, and unintelligible Oriental tongues at that, to usher in a new era. The brush is the blade of annihilation and creation.

These cultural opposites attract because East and West share the same "blood," only it has been forced apart schizophrenically. Science and logic favor the analytical over the synthetical, a preference conducive to the maintenance of boundary and power. One particular duo is implied by "brush and blade": the name and the named. While blade betokens violence, the naming of violence through the sword's classical, elegant nomenclature—King Arthur's Excalibur; *Crouching Tiger, Hidden Dragon*'s Qingming sword; or *Kill Bill*'s Hattori Hanzo sword—effects a sublimation. Bloodshed and death, which are, ultimately, what is being named, retreat in the chain of signification, abstracted first as the named sword, then as the name of the sword, a proper name in foreign words without dictionary definition, whose linguistic elusiveness intimates wonder and mystery

Blood is the missing link between brush and blade as well as the true signified; it alludes to both the physical and the spiritual, both the body's essential fluid and the essence of "race," "nation," and "spirit." Rather than a fifty-fifty split between human biology and human mind, "blood," in its role as the Holy Spirit to a Trinity with brush and blade, privileges the unseen, the veiled, and the spiritual over the materialistic. In both the films and literature discussed here, the master narrative dictates that only by sacrificing physical blood can one attain its spiritual counterpart. Although these texts on brush and blade are written in invisible blood, as it were, the fact that brush enjoys "top billing"—preceding blade—demonstrates the belief that the spirit is superior and gives meaning to matter. Philosophically, Nietzsche's Oriental Superman Zarathustra admonishes us in this fashion: "Write in blood," a ritual of self-sacrifice that elevates the human drama of bloodletting by the sword.[5] The proverb, "the Pen is mightier than the Sword," serves a similar function to rein in and euphemize human aggression. In the Old Testament, the Word, the Voice from the Burning Bush, and the Unnameable "I am" take precedence over idols and images. Derrida labels this Greco-Judaic-Christian tradition "logocentrism" that valorizes the Word. This age-long belief in brush over blade runs counter to the human history of unrelenting war and struggle. Louis Althusser's idea of ideological interpellation of individuals as subjects ("Ideology and the Ideological State Apparatuses" 1971) helps explain why traces of blood are missing in these tales jointly written by brush and blade. Ironically, whereas these tales laud spiritual triumphalism, their very existence must be understood in a materialistic framework. Swordplay films elegizing sacrifice, in our present day, aim to cash in at the box office. Market-driven colonialism, a century ago, breathed life into the nationhood and masculinity in Conrad and his colleagues. Consistent with this ironic veiling, blood courses through the subheading of this chapter: the "Global Phallus" requires blood for erection; the "Colonial Acephalus" spews blood from the severed neck.

In Freudian psychoanalysis, the sword is a phallic fetish, whose power is acknowledged and disavowed at once, and whose potential stems from the originary trauma of a boy's inference that his mother has been castrated. The copulation of brush and blade constitutes a fetish of power as well, in the Lacanian nexus of signs. Lacan argues that rather than a one-to-one correspondence between the signifier and the signified, the signifier acquires meaning through its connection with other signifiers. The structure of language creates the effect of signification. A word no longer points to the thing, but to other words. Instead of the Freudian Patriarch suggested by the word "father," Lacan coins the term "Name-of-the-Father" to underline his idea of linguistic self-reflexiveness. Lacan proceeds in "The Signification of the Phallus" (1977) to analyze the phallus as a sign: the phallus "can play its role [of signifier] only when veiled, that is to say, as itself a sign of the latency with which any signifiable is struck" (p. 288). The more obscure the phallus, the more it is vested with transformative possibilities. In fact, since its debut in Freud's psychoanalysis, the penis has been an absent presence, or a present absence.[6] The sword is a perfect phallic symbol not only because of its aggressiveness but also because of its occludedness—it is encased in a scabbard, untainted by the blood it has shed, the erection of the penis implied. Layers of veiling come to be crystallized, not in "Name-of-the-Father," but in "Name-of-the-Sword." The Name-of-the-Sword, in turn, sets off a signifying effect, the center of which is the absence of the object, a void behind the name. The phallic sword can also be taken to figure, in Bataille's *Death and Sensuality* (1962), as both an instrument of love or eroticism and an instrument of death. Yoking together seemingly unrelated spheres, all these thinkers, Pound and Eliot included, manifest a shared desire to grasp, in a single stroke of wedding antitheses, the totality, or oneness, of things. In essence, these theorists are in search of a systemic explanation that is constructed by human speech but goes beyond it in a way evoking the so-called "oceanic feeling" in mysticism.[7] They are after the unnameable, like the vowel-less, unpronounceable YHWH of Judaism or "You-Know-Who" in Harry Potter.

Standing on its head, this tale on brush and blade comes out backwards, from contemporary postmodernist rave flashing back to colonial horror, from global cinema's fetishization of Orient to emergent modernity's fixation on primitivism. A welding of the literary and the martial, the phallic fetish in contemporary films grows out of last century's primitivist irrationality so dreaded by colonialists and celebrated by avant-gardists. The "head" on the screen that sprouts from the headlessness of a century ago is not a head; it is a phallic brush that carves. On the other hand, the state of headlessness erupts from state-run, institutionally calibrated colonial policies; a blunt blade cuts just as deep.

## The Phallic Brush of Globality/Postmodernity

At one entrance to the Bronze Exhibit Hall in Beijing's Forbidden City stands a Shaoyu sword dating from the late Spring-Autumn period (652–476 B.C.). As if made of steel, the blade shines after 2,500 years. Like a silent spell, twenty ancient characters are inscribed in gold down the middle of the blade on either side. The blade and the words cut through time, creating an aura of power, where violence and culture—even grace—are immanent. Arising out of the Asian dialectical philosophy of yin and yang, of *wen* and *wu* (the literary and the martial), the calligraphic brush and the sword have long defined masculine empowerment in Asian culture and, more recently, in Asian films. The adage *"litouzhibei"* (strength penetrating to the back of the paper) compliments calligraphy in the metaphor of swordsmanship, namely, the force of the brush goes through rice paper in the same manner that a sword penetrates its target. *Li* (strength) alludes not so much to muscle strength as to *qi* (breath or inner strength), thereby elevating the calligrapher beyond the physical world. The precursor to Chinese swordplay films, *wuxia xiaoshuo* (novels of chivalry), frequently juxtaposes the book and the sword, as does Jin Yung, the leading contemporary practitioner of this genre, in *Shujian enchou ji (The chronicle of book and sword, favor and hate)*. In the West, heroic feats must also be retold artistically. Achilles and Odysseus are indebted to Homer, the hero with the pen; *Beowulf* and *Sir Gawain and the Green Knight* owe the existence of their exploits to anonymous Old English and Middle English bards; the symbolic loss of swords of Antony, Othello, and others depends on Shakespeare's poetry; Don Quixote with his makeshift lance requires a Cervantes.

The contemporary medium crystallizing the union of sword and art is global cinema. As the world shrinks in the vein of David Harvey's time-space compression (*The Condition of Modernity* 1989), filmmakers omnivorize various warrior traditions, Western and Eastern, for the late capitalist market. Dominated by the post-Fordist circulation of capital, information, and images, television and cinema are key players in today's globalization. Reality is increasingly interwoven with what Jean Baudrillard terms hyperreal simulacra (*Simulacra and Simulation* 1994). In this "infinite sea of images" and "information overload" (Besser, "Internet to Information Superhighway" 1995, p. 69) drift commodities and, perhaps, subjectivities that are "memory-less" (Perry, *Hyperreality and Global Culture* 1998) and "affectless," "depthless" (Jameson, *Postmodernism* 1991, pp. 9–10). Drawing from the aura of various heroic traditions for profit-making, global cinema routinely flattens these traditions until they become a "funhouse of hyper-real media images and . . . of floating signifiers in the postmodern carnival" (Cvetkovich and Kellner, *Articulating the Global and the Local* 1997, p. 11). But let us return for a brief moment to Old Asia, the source of this global film style, before the coming of the barbarians.

Asian swordplay films at their best resemble the brush that traces the way of the sword, ideographic stroke copying the stroke of the blade. The samurai leader in Akira Kurosawa's classic *Seven Samurai* (1954) wields a sword during battle; subsequently, he picks up the brush to cross out enemy kills and strategize against the remaining bandits. In Lo Wei's Hong Kong swordplay classic *Wuhu tulong* (*Five tigers killing a dragon* or *Brothers five,* 1970), one of the heroes fights with a pointed metal brush. Not surprisingly, he happens to be the group's tactician. A recent barbarized example of this style is Zhang Yimou's *Hero* (2002), which repeatedly aestheticizes violence through calligraphy: one of the protagonists, Canjian (Broken Sword, as he is called, after the half-sword he uses), persists in his writing of *"jian"* (sword) while arrows fly around him; with his sword, he even composes two gigantic characters *tianxia* (under the sun, or in the world) in the desert sand. The episodes of composition are captured in slow-motion, body and brush/blade synchronized in a dance. The finale arrives when the First Emperor of Qin turns his back on the assassin to contemplate a hanging scroll with the single character, *jian.* Invariably, the action sequences in *Hero* consist of a counterpoint of stasis and dynamism, prolonged shots of stillness magnifying the explosions of move-ment.[8] *Jing* and *dong* (quietism and motion), or *wen* and *wu,* work like day and night, each issuing from and pregnant with the other.

Complementarity lodges itself in the "dramaturgy" as well: scenes of vio-lence unfold through the *naming* of violence. A shower of deadly arrows is literalized by the written word *jian* and by the writing of it. Fundamentally opposite activities, writing and fighting, accentuate each other, the former's stillness, persistently the focal point of the camera, anchoring the latter's movement. Even during fight scenes, characters keep a stoic, expression-less, dispassionate façade with downcast eyes, as if the core of self is removed from and coolly observes the fighting self. Moreover, at least two fights—at the chess house and on the lake—are conducted in the contestants' minds, with their eyes closed, their bodies frozen, the imagined battles proceeding in black-and-white and in slow-motion stunts. That brush receives higher regard than blade in this swordplay film manifests itself in the narrative structure as well. The Rashomon-like versions of the assassination attempt are not arrayed horizontally, as varying angles and possibilities, but vertically, from human greed and deception to sacrifice and undying love. Unequivocally superior, the brush also prevails in that the "words" or calligraphy of Zhao survives beyond Qin's military might and the obliteration of the state of Zhao.

The second key scene of *naming* of violence is shot on location amidst the barren beauty of Xinjiang. To dissuade the swordsman Nameless from assas-sinating the emperor of Qin, Canjian renders *tianxia* (the world) in the desert sand, not so much to urge Nameless to forgive as to remind him of the great-ness that resides in the emperor's ambition. Sparing the emperor's life means that he will eventually seize the vast territories prophesized in *tianxia* and found the Chinese empire, which continues to the present day geographically and conceptually. Qin's control, however, exacts an extreme form of violence historically called *fenshu kengru* (burning books and burying scholars alive) and *shutongwen chetongkuei* (one written script, one width for carts). Differ-ences in terms of written scripts, ideas, and lifestyles are suppressed in the rhe-torical magnanimity of *tianxia,* simultaneously an imperial self-inflation and an odious ethnocentrism. In the film's closing moments, the emperor confides to the assassin that he will conquer a *da—da—de jiangtu* (vast—vast—terri-tory), sweeping his right arm in an arc, his mouth opened wide to utter *"da,"* his face tense with aspiration and disdain, as if swallowing the entire space. In the name of "the world," carnage is perpetrated and then absorbed into the oblivion of history.

The film concludes as the emperor, "enlightened" by his meditation on the scroll of Sword, grasps the true meaning of *sa* (to kill), which is *bu sa* (to not kill). Utilizing four-word proverbs in pseudo-classical Chinese, the language chosen to underscore the faraway time period, the emperor explicates the three levels of swordsmanship: *renjianheyi* (the swordsman and the sword are one); *shouzhongwujian, xinzhongyujian* (no sword in the hand, the sword in the mind), which kills with the mythical *qi*, or breath, of the sword; and *shouzhongwujian, xinzhongwujian* (no sword in the hand, no sword in the mind), which refrains from killing altogether. Zhang Yimou appears to sanction peace, yet ends his film with the assassin's death in a swarm of arrows. The emperor's Zen-like awakening fails to apply to politics, the order of execution given under the pressure of the court. The true awakening is the assassin's in sparing the emperor and sacrificing himself. Brush and its attendant values— peace and spirit—are eulogized through filmmaking, but somehow defused by it; even the elegant, pithy four-word proverbs are soon buried under the excessive, kitschy special effect of violence. Throughout *Hero* (2002), Zhang manifests an Althussian interpellation of Chinese nationalism and global cinema's commercialization, reflecting China's emergence as a superpower and his personal quest for financial success, name recognition, and perhaps an Oscar.[9] The string of China's top tourist attractions shot on location gives the impression that this film is a collection of picture postcards or a scrapbook, relishing in Zhang's aestheticism rather than venturing beyond the material world. Repeatedly, Zhang dwells obsessively on *his* blade, or trademark cinematography, in the heavy-handed artistry and exuberant color schemes, now coupled with mind-boggling special effects. Zhang's recent swordplay films, including *House of the Flying Daggers* (2004), are so derivative of Ang Lee's *Crouching Tiger, Hidden Dragon* (2000) in soundtrack and visuals that they are symptomatic of an auteur-to-be lapsing into recycling rather than innovating. Take, for instance, the subject of brush and blade. Zhang Ziyi in *Crouching Tiger* gives away her swordswoman identity when her brushstrokes reveal hidden strength. Originally meant to give the blade's heroism a spiritual dimension, Zhang Yimou blows up the twins in such an extravaganza of special effects and cinematography that it unwittingly parodies the swordplay genre. While Zhang Yimou resorts to traditional Chinese thinking in "dialectic concepts" (Li Zhilin, "On the Dual Nature" 1991, p. 246) when the emperor infers "to not kill" from "to kill," the filmmaker evinces a similar dialectical reversal: from his early career of well-wrought art-house products to recent global-cinema commodities.[10]

Zhang Yimou's assassin, Nameless (yet another typical Chinese inversion), confesses to the emperor that his special move is *shibu yisha* (ten step, one kill), named after his accurate coup de grace within a ten-step circumference. Here, Zhang continues the swordplay and kung fu film convention of "naming the move," a particular form of the counterpoint of brush and blade. In action sequences, a specific martial skill is routinely named and even described before or during its execution. Such metanarrative moments contain not only action but self-referentiality to action, not only violence but a reading of it, which defuses violence. Predating Judith Butler's performativity and devoid of the stringent level of self-reflexivity, this tradition of performance has been dubbed by Brecht as the "alienation effect" utilizing defamiliarization.[11] For example, Stephen Chow's comical *Kung Fu Hustle* (2004) narrates and displays a number of famous kung fu techniques, all of which having been constructed discursively within the long history of Hong Kong cinema: Double-Ringed Arms, Yang Family Spear, Lioness's Roar, Toad Kung Fu, climaxing with the most potent of all, Buddha's Palm, a deus ex machina to claim final victory. Even the supposedly unique Buddha's Palm reprises other films, such as Tsui Hark's *Once Upon a Time in China* series (1991–1993).

Given the Western tradition of heroes and bards,[12] Hollywood and independent filmmakers of the last decade or so—Jim Jarmusch's *Ghost Dog* (1999), Edward Zwick's *The Last Samurai* (2003), and Quentin Tarantino's *Kill Bill I* and *II* (2003, 2005)—have looked eastward to appropriate the kinship of brush and blade. A benign form of Orientalism that projects more longing than loathing onto Asia, these filmmakers nevertheless rehearse much familiar Oriental discourse. Admittedly, Asians perpetuate their own myth, such as in Stephen Chow's naming of the kung fu moves and in Zhang Yimou's increasingly unabashed self-Orientalization, yet it appears that the farther away filmmakers are situated geographically and culturally vis-à-vis the subject of brush and blade, the more prone they are to stylization and stereotypes, i.e., repetition of an Orientalist repertoire. Figuratively, Western filmmakers who have never acquired calligraphic skills are destined to paint the Orient in broad strokes. Jarmusch et al., as a consequence, name elements of an Orient far more denuded than Chow's or Zhang's, while performing it—the samurai's seppuku, the geisha's tea ceremony, the Shaolin long staff, Drunken Boxing (via Jackie and Neo), and so forth. When it comes to brush and blade, the difference between Asian and non-Asian practitioners is one in degree, not in kind. Hence, the action of the black samurai *Ghost Dog* in the urban ghetto is interrupted, commented on, and foreshadowed by intertitles, all quotations from the eighteenth-century *Hagakure: The Book of the Samurai*.[13] *The Last Samurai* opens with Japan's genesis as God's blade is steeped in the ocean, followed by the single character of "samurai," and the voiceover saying "honor," all banal Oriental tropes to deify the tragic samurai heroes of modern times. The opening credits to *Kill Bill* show kanji (the Japanese version of Chinese ideograms) cut horizontally by a sword, with blood dripping down from the wound. This appears to be a spin-off from a still in *The Matrix* where Neo and other characters appear against a backdrop of green vertical Japanese words and numbers.

This nostalgia for heroes with swords at a time of politicians with nuclear footballs is intriguing.[14] Now that the "blade" is "dead," the "brush" of film-making and cultural representation tries frantically to keep the memory of its partner alive. The tragic beauty of individual heroism fits with swords more than guns, guns more than machine guns, and machine guns more than bombs, for the simple reason that the valor and honor of one-to-one combat becomes progressively impossible in remote-controlled warfare with indiscriminate killing and massive casualties. Many swordplay classics mourn the outdated-ness of swords: every samurai killed in *Seven Samurai* dies from a gun shot; the battle in Kurosawa's *Kagemusha* (*The Shadow Warrior* 1980) is decided by musket volleys that ruthlessly cut down the charging cavalry; *Once Upon a Time in China I* concludes with a kung fu master's death by bullets. That the moviegoing public exhibits such an anachronistic taste for swords bespeaks a suppressed anxiety over (post)modernity, one that seeks relief in equally far-fetched scenarios of a samurai "retainer" Ghost Dog; of an American Civil War veteran Algren, played by the narcissistic Tom Cruise, training Japanese soldiers in firearms use; and of an over-the-top revenge saga that culminates in the killing of Bill. While Jarmusch and Tarantino, with their independent and art-house sensibility, tweak the Eastern swordplay genre through irony, parody, pastiche, and montage, Cruise revitalizes a vintage Orientalism of the kind James Clavell perpetrates in his two-volume *Shogun* (1975).

Cruise's title gives away the white man's imagination. Like *The Last of the Mohicans* (1992) and *Dances with Wolves* (1990), *The Last Samurai* is so named to project the romantic tragic glow associated with extinction and self-alienation. In the name of the demise of the samurai lineage, Cruise recycles mainstream masculinist fancy over the obliteration of a racial other—Mohican braves, the Wild West, or Japanese samurai. Tinged with white liberal guilt, all these texts adopt the point of view of a lone white male, deeply dis-satisfied with his own culture, who ventures into an alien land and gradually identifies with it. The films alleviate the neurosis over past violence against Native Americans and over the American imperialist thrust into Asia in the wake of Commodore Perry; what the blade has done to the racial Other, the brush tries to undo. Yet the cathartic cleansing requires sacrificial blood, the reinscription of Orientalist discursive violence. The linguistic and cultural labyrinth of the Orient turns out to be a well-rehearsed style; the Orient is predictably fetishized, while remaining, forever, beyond grasp.

Granted, Zhang Yimou generates the quasi-spiritualism of the swordsman by using Chinese calligraphy and wordplay, yet for Western filmmakers, this more or less literal "brush," a system of representations between language and culture shared by Chinese on and off the screen, becomes radically defamiliarizing. Indeed, white protagonists in *The Last Samurai* and *Kill Bill* subject themselves as much to a punishing martial apprenticeship as to a linguistic and cultural disorientation, as much to the mastery of blade as to that of brush, in order to achieve the skills necessary for redemption. The training of Cruise's Algren in swordsmanship is predicated on his acquisition of the Japanese language, culture, and mindset. And that mindset, similar to the emperor of Qin's "to not kill" or Neo's "no spoon," turns out to be "no mind," the term perhaps coming from D. T. Suzuki's *The Zen Doctrine of No-Mind* (1949). Once Algren lets go, entering into a state of egolessness, he draws a tie in sparring and, subsequently, disposes of a fair number of opponents. The 1960s Zen cult continues in this magical dissolving of technical, linguistic, cultural, and conceptual barriers by turning mental faculties—rationality in particular—on its head. Seemingly a self-effacement in the immersion into the Other's philosophy, Cruise's, Kevin Costner's, and the Wakowskis' Christ-like protagonist remains quintessentially Western within the messianic narrative. The no-mind oceanic feeling intimates a Christian divinity in yellowface, disguised as an Oriental trope.

On a more secular level, Algren moves from his captivity by samurai in an agrarian setting to becoming a disciple of *bushido,* the way of the samurai. His tale of "gone native," like those of his fellow white men Mistah Kurtz and Lord Jim, is in fact a tale of "gone Orientalist." Surely more conscientious than Puccini's ugly American Pinkerton, Algren, nevertheless, is next of kin to Clavell's Blackthorne, the English pilot stranded in shogunate Japan. While Clavell's male fantasy over a heathen paradise has been cut to a kiss and a shot of bare shoulder against long black hair, Cruise, nonetheless, follows the same Orientalist recipe. Death-wish runs amuck in Clavell's hierarchical Japan, with the samurai mantra of "take my head" or "slit my belly," offered whenever honor is in danger. Algren exhibits similar proclivity as he, kneeling and kowtowing, beseeches the Japanese emperor to grant him permission to end his life. Awkward phrases such as "so sorry," "karma," or "pillowing" (lovemaking) punctuate Clavell's thousand pages with numbing regularity, a speech defect that Algren picks up when he apologizes, "So sorry." Although linguistic stereotypes occur in Tarantino and Jarmusch as well, such as Bill's "Aso" and Ghost Dog's "I'm your retain-a," they are somehow redeemed by the former's playful, sarcastic delivery and by the black accent of the latter. Both filmmakers reinvent visual and auditory clichés. One such moment is Ghost

Dog's hilarious flourish of his gun before reholstering, as if he were sheathing a long samurai sword. By contrast, both Clavell and Cruise construct romantic stories, which are but glosses of a stylized Japan. The pivotal ritual in the array of stylized actions is seppuku, which is both the end of life and the height of aestheticism. A clash of Freudian eros and thanatos, Clavell's death poem amidst falling cherry blossoms, in effect, concludes *The Last Samurai*.

Seppuku is self-disembowelment that should properly end with a second's beheading of the samurai. The rite of beheading, whether linked to seppuku or not, veers the thesis—of the "oneness" of brush and blade, Self and Other, the name and the named—toward the next section, "Colonial Acephalus," but not quite, since all the examples of actual beheading are squarely contemporary, despite being anachronistic in outlook. Clavell's novel teems with severed heads; Cruise obscures the decapitation behind a tree trunk; Tarantino's *Kill Bill* overdoes and parodies the headless gore, on the one hand, and minimizes and contains it, on the other, in the "scalping" of Lucy Liu's O-Ren Ishii. A Japanese culture aficionado, Lian Hearn opens *Across the Nightingale Floor* (2002), first of her Otori trilogy, with a beheading and repeats it on numerous occasions. While it is certainly not limited to Orientalist discourse, Kurosawa's *Ran* (1992) interweaves actual beheading into King Lear's "losing his head"; the same motif runs through Hayao Miyazaki's anime. *Princess Mononoke* (1997) culminates in the sacrilegious beheading of a god-like Nature Spirit, which is avenged by the head of a divine dog biting off the offender's arm. *Spirited Away* (2001) counts three muttering, jumping heads among the evil witch's familiars.[15] Considering the difficulty of severing a neck with bullets, all beheadings are carried out by swords, except for that of the supernatural creature in *Princess Mononoke*.

Decapitation means the truncation of head and body, the seats of reason and heart. Symbolically, it severs the two fundamental traits of humanity. With the corpse in two parts, death is exposed in all its rawness, without any of the semblance of life countenanced by an intact body. As such, decapitation has been banned in most civilized countries as cruel and barbaric. In *Kill Bill*, however, the hyperbolic beheadings, with blood gushing out, are carnivalesque, celebrating Jamesonian pastiche and flatness as well as postmodern schizophrenia. In the Lacanian-Jamesonian sense of schizophrenia, beheading exteriorizes the disrupted "signifying chain," where "the interlocking syntagmatic series of signifiers which constitutes an utterance or a meaning" (Jameson, *Postmodernism* 1991, p. 26) is superseded by a cacophony of images and sounds. The whole "revenge" genre, to which *Kill Bill* belongs, consists of cause and effect, violence and its reaction. But between what is metaphorically head and body, a schizophrenic wedge intrudes. Instead of the human response of horror and grief, the audience "sees through" this cartoonish, fake violence. The sensory overload in Tarantino, particularly the excessive, culturally hybridized fight scenes, indexes psychic discontiguousness, but with a sense of post-Kafka ease. An angel of vengeance seeks to marshal violence even greater than the enemy's, consequently becoming the enemy. This is self-evident after the first revenge in *Kill Bill*: Uma Thurman's Bride turns to find her victimizer/victim's daughter staring at her dead mother. The Bride comforts the little girl by saying, "When you grow up, if you still feel raw about this, come and find me," thus foreshadowing cycles of violence, for the Bride will have a daughter of her own at the end of the film. Any existential anxiety over the switching of Self and Other, one of the clinical definitions of schizophrenia, is shrouded in the rush of nostalgic presentness. Schizophrenia becomes Tarantino, who is so keenly aware of the division that he capitalizes on it. Hence, the Bride embarks on a preposterous quest for a sword across the Pacific, at the same time poking fun at the banalities of the martial arts genre. Tarantino's own quest for Asian filmic style receives its share of self-scrutiny. The somewhat rough-hewn, fraying nature of *Kill Bill* calls attention to the many mélanges as incomplete cultural and psychological links. From its opening "Acknowledgements," montaged citations of East and West characterize *Kill Bill*. The logo of the Shaw Brothers' Hong Kong film studio is followed by the blurred inside of a pistol barrel typical of the 1970s Bond movies, each image accompanied by its respective soundtrack. While "Acknowledgements" keep image and sound intact as a unit, the subsequent film often montages, in Eisenstein's fashion, the visual and the auditory so jarringly that it flaunts incongruous collage in each frame. A bloodbath with samurai swords is accompanied by a spaghetti Western soundtrack; a black-and-white shot of a doorway against a bleak American Southwest landscape is disturbed not by whistle but a Chinese flute.

The cast exhibits this insouciant schizophrenia as well. Oriental characters are routinely split: the victim O-Ren grows up to be an assassin; the giggling schoolgirl Go-Go thrusts a phallic sword into a pedophile; the comical, bantering sushi bar chef metamorphoses into the solemn Hattori Hanzo swordmaker; the raving chief of Crazy 88 with a Kato mask and shaved head becomes the kung fu master Pai Mei, with a white beard and long robe.[16] Caucasian characters go through similar transformations: Michael Parks plays the Texas sheriff and the Latin American pimp; The Bride moves from a vegetative state to becoming an avenger, assisted by the Hanzo sword and her sadomasochistic apprenticeship under Pai Mei. All these narrative movements take the characters inexorably toward the blade, not only owning the Hanzo sword and Pai Mei's Five-Point-Palm Exploding-Heart technique, but becoming the named themselves. The name and the named coalesce. Although these film stars' long silence, until *Kill Bill,* evokes a sense of wistfulness, nostalgia is infused with Tarantino's stylistic jouissance, rendering depthless all the intervening years for Sonny Chiba, Gordon Liu, and Michael Parks. The violence of time resembles the violence of the fetish sword; both wrinkles and blood are seen and forgotten. Hence, the ludicrously named Five-Point-Palm Exploding-Heart technique endears the memory of Pai Mei, despite all his Zen master cruelty, including clichéd blows to the novice's head to induce sudden enlightenment. Tarantino even lightens up the foulness of racial stereotype and transgressive murder: Pai Mei is poisoned by his disciple when he consumes his favorite fish head.

## The Acephalic Rush of Coloniality/Modernity

Grisly beheadings by Asians has turned comedic, Bakhtinian in the postmodern Tarantino. Tarantino's dubious, "trans-cultured pearl" would not have come to pass without centuries of discomfort over the irritating sandgrain of a primitive Orient, one that undergirds colonial expansionism and modernization's pursuit of happiness in terms of raw materials, labor, and market. Coloniality and modernity collaborate in Conrad, Forster, Maugham, and Orwell, locating what is opposite to Western progressiveness in native characters and mobs, caught in a state of fury. The brutal blade of imperialism is transferred by the brush of fiction-making onto native brutes' headlessness. Projecting their own violence onto the Other, colonialists have resorted to stereotypes of inhumanity that Homi Bhabha analyzes in *Nation and Narration* (1990). Such stereotypes used as partial justification for imperialism include cannibalism, head-hunting, and decapitation. Nicholas Daly in *Literature, Technology, and Modernity, 1860–2000* (2004) takes as one mark of the beginning of modern Europe the banning of public executions (p. 4). As Western modernity defines itself against the "acephalic rush" of the colonized, modernism is inspired by the alterity of African sculpture, Oriental ideogram, and various non-Western traditions. To extend the argument that Matei Calinescu makes in *Five Faces of Modernity* (1987), the abysmal colonized in colonialist texts is but the shadow to the apocalyptic Other in modernist and avant-gardist texts.

Banishing executions and even tortures in their midst, modern Westerners travel abroad to view and document them. A case in point: *The Face of China As Seen by Photographs and Travelers, 1860–1912* (1978) includes at least three photographs of beheading and torture. One photograph from about 1860 catches the moment when the machete is poised in the air, before slashing down, the victim bound and kneeling, his neck stretched forward as the executioner's assistant pulls on his hair queue. The most curious part about this photograph is that the spectators are gazing at the photographer, not the victim. Evidently, the camera has a greater appeal than the execution. The real show takes place not with the machete but with the camera. In the war-torn, poverty-stricken mid-nineteenth century, the Chinese were only too familiar with the blade, but the new props—the camera and later the shadow magic of motion picture—offer a diversion. By shooting the Chinese Other's violence, this foreign "brush" or art-making veils and transposes the brutality of gunboat diplomacy. Nonetheless, from the perspective of the photographer and viewers of the photograph, Chinese savagery lies in the public spectacle as well as in the public's indifference. Western reception is characterized by distancing, i.e., no conscious identification with the spectators occurs.

For Chinese intellectuals trained in the art of the brush, this detachment from public executions by the sword amidst colonialism is out of the question. Under the onslaught of Western modernity, Chinese tradition symbolized by the calligraphic transcription of classical poetry is to be supplanted by translation of Western literature in *paihua wen* (vernacular Chinese), by the introduction of Mr. De and Mr. Sai (Democracy and Science), and by a myriad of literary activities which, in essence, seek to transform the effete, castrated brush into a revolutionary blade. This tendency to promote sociopolitical reforms through literature eventually lapses into Chairman Mao's agitprop.[17] Surely not as blatant as subsequent communist propaganda, the famous story of how Lu Xun (1881–1936) became a founder of modern Chinese literature portends the changing dynamics of traditional brush and modern blade, the twins bonded by blood or beheading. In the Preface to his first collection of short stories, *Call to Arms* (Beijing Foreign Languages Press's militarization of the Chinese original *Na Han* or *To Cry Out*), Lu Xun confides that he abandoned medical studies in Japan after having viewed the decapitation of an alleged Chinese spy:

> This was during the Russo-Japanese War, so there were many war films, and I had to join in the clapping and cheering in the lecture hall along with the other students. It was a long time since I had seen any compatriots, but one day I saw a film showing some Chinese, one of whom was bound, while many others stood around him. They were all strong fellows but appeared completely apathetic. According to the commentary, the one with his hands bound was a spy working for the Russians, who was to have his head cut off by the Japanese military....
>
> Before the term was over I had left for Tokyo, because after this film I felt that medical science was not so important after all. The

people of a weak and backward country, however strong and healthy they may be, can only serve to be made examples of, or to witness such futile spectacles.... The most important thing, therefore, was to change their spirit, and since at that time I felt that literature was the best means to this end, I determined to promote a literary movement. (pp. 2–3)

Lu Xun goes on to publish a magazine entitled *Xin Sheng (New life)*. Its spiritual intent is to rejuvenate the readers. Rey Chow analyzes this episode at the outset of her *Primitive Passion* (1995) to establish the inextricability of modernity and visuality. Lu Xun's shock, Chow contends, is caused not only by the heartless decapitation but by the medium of film. Naturally, the shock of film is taken very differently by Lu Xun's Japanese classmates "clapping and cheering." Granted the Japanese point of view in the production of the film, how the product is received is determined by the recipient's subjectivity: racial pride for the applauding Japanese; shame and outrage for the lone Chinese among them. Furthermore, Lu Xun's response derives from the fact that he sees both Chinese on the screen and Japanese off the screen. His dual perspective and double consciousness lead him to be equally repelled by the Chinese spectators' apathy and the Japanese audience's heartlessness. The Chinese identity prompts him to "cry out, in an iron house," the metaphor that gives the collection of stories its title.

With the common motif of beheading, Lu Xun and Lao She (1899–1966) try to move to action their sleeping compatriots in the "subcolonial" iron house. Lu Xun's memorable portrait of his contemporaries, "The True Story of Ah Q" (1922), concludes with the execution of the abject protagonist. Ah Q likens the spectators to "swarming after him like ants" and wolves (p. 111). After his death by shooting, "most people were dissatisfied, because a shooting was not such a fine spectacle as a decapitation" (p. 112). Likewise, the execution of a conniving intellectual, Yuan Ming, occurs toward the end of Lao She's *Rickshaw* (1936–1937). The predatory crowd laments that "execution by firing squad seems too simple. People love to listen to tales of execution by slicing, beheading, flaying, and burying alive" (p. 241). Lao She's narrative voice even predicts that

if one morning they [the masses] had the power in their hands, any man among them could do as Chang Hsien-chung did in 1630: have the inhabitants of a city butchered and then order the women's breasts and feet to be cut off and piled into two heaps. That's what they'd enjoy doing. (pp. 241–242)

Bestiality taints China's past and present, crystallized in the dismemberment of the human body. In the early decades of the twentieth century, Lu Xun, Lao She, and many other Chinese intellectuals tried to reanimate the torn body of their motherland through literature and leftist politics. Finding China a foreign land, Western writers of the time wielded their brush not out of a double consciousness, but out of self-denial—distancing themselves from the reality of colonialism by means of scenes of native passion, such as revolt and beheading. If the Foreign Languages Press in Beijing has retroactively mobilized Lu Xun's short story collection in the service of the Party, imperialist writings, even among the most conscientious, such as George Orwell, are marked by an absence of empathy for the natives.

In colonialist novels, native violence perennially lurks beneath colonial rule; a state of headlessness threatens. Although set in Africa, Joseph Conrad's quintessentially colonialist *Heart of Darkness* (1902) manifests the paradox of power and its anxiety, echoed in E. M. Forster's Marabar Caves (*A Passage to India* 1924), W. Somerset Maugham's cholera-infected Mei-tan-fu in the Chinese interior (*The Painted Veil* 1925), Orwell's Burmese revolt (*Burmese Days* 1934), and others. The colonized—Lu Xun and Lao She—not only give the "last words" to executions, thus having blood spilled beyond their texts, but also portray the participants as irredeemably bloodthirsty. The colonialists' brush, by contrast, tames the violence within the discourse. This taming lies partly in self-mocking caricature; native wrath as well as English control are tinged with buffoonery. The disorientation English heroes undergo amidst native mobs never takes hold. Even in a crowd incensed by racist snobbery, the tense atmosphere is soon replaced by farce. For instance, Orwell's protagonist, Flory,

> pushed his way into the crowd and was immediately swallowed up
> like the others. A sea of bodies closed in upon him and flung him
> from side to side, bumping his ribs and choking him with their
> animal heat. He struggled onwards with an almost dreamlike feeling,
> so absurd and unreal was the situation. The whole riot had been
> ludicrous from the start. (pp. 251–252)

The horror of being cannibalized inside the belly of a beast ("animal heat") is quickly relegated to a nightmare, "dreamlike" and insubstantial.

In addition, the refrain of English reserve and reason throughout colonialist novels serves to rein in what is viewed as indigenous hysteria. One of Maugham's favorite motifs in a colonial setting is adultery committed out of boredom and loneliness. When his protagonists' liaison is exposed in *The Painted Veil*, the male culprit appeals for calmness: "no good losing our heads," and "keep our heads" (pp. 72–73). Similar voices advising discretion occur in Forster's *Passage to India* following the alleged sexual assault inside the Marabar Caves. The last resort of rationality is ultimately self-deceiving, for it keeps up appearances, while ignoring true causes. In Maugham, the colony and the colonized provide the illusion that the expatriates are no longer bound by British mores, leading to infidelity in stories set in Malaya and other exotic locales and even to incestuous love in "The Book-Bag." Maugham's protagonists invariably expel the consciousness of transgression onto the natives. The idiot hydrocephalic girl haunts the adulteress Kitty Lane in *The Painted Veil* because she is Kitty's Chinese alter ego, the misshapen head taunting Kitty's, ravishingly beautiful yet already ravished inside.

Should native violence prove to be overly infectious, as when Flory commits suicide in *Burmese Days*, the loss of the "English" head is transposed in this story to Flo, Flory's dog and "diminutive," since his familiar embodies all his subhuman degradation: the facial, Cain-like birthmark; the proposition of marriage even if the wife-to-be refrains forever from intimacy. Summoned by her master, Flo

> crawled very slowly towards his feet, flat on her belly, whining, her
> head down as though afraid to look at him. When she was a yard away
> he fired, blowing her skull to fragments.
> Her shattered brain looked like red velvet. Was that what he would
> look like? The heart, then, not the head. (pp. 280–281)

Flory prefers broken-heartedness to headlessness. The twin deaths further bear out how colonialism suppresses its dark undercurrent: hubris versus self-doubt; the man with a gun versus the bitch with no head; romantic suicide versus mangled, acephalic mirror-image.

In principle, however, deranged fanaticism is attributed to the natives. Rare exceptions to this stereotype are in the other Orientalist extreme—mythic and idealized Orient. Forster concludes *A Passage to India* with a Hindu saint's severed head. Urged by his mother to "free prisoners," the saint

> took a sword and went up to the fort. He unlocked a door, and the
> prisoners streamed out...but the police were too much annoyed
> and cut off the young man's head. Ignoring its absence, he made
> his way over the rocks that separate the fort and the town, killing
> policemen as he went, and he fell outside his mother's house, having
> accomplished her orders. Consequently there are two shrines to him
> to-day—that of the Head above, and that of the Body below.
> (pp. 295–296)

The reference dangles between a timeless allegory of emancipation with the opening of "long before" and what appears to be an anticolonist fighting against policemen and the "fort." A schizophrenic split between the two shrines near the fort above and the town below, between the sacrifice of insurrection and the return to mother(land), this separation de facto beatifies the saint, granting him life after death.

Forster's is far from the only mythic touch of headlessness. The most infamous are, of course, the heads on Kurtz's stakes in *Heart of Darkness*—"black, dried, sunken, with closed eyelids" (p. 107). Even Kurtz's name, "'short' in German" (p. 111), epitomizes the headless body "gone native" as well as castration. The name thus veils the named. Another pair of namings emerges when out of sympathy for the bereaved, the narrator changes Kurtz's last words—"The horror! The horror!"—to the name of Kurtz's Intended. If Kurtz indeed rips the "veil...during that supreme moment of complete knowledge" (p. 130), his cry then points to the truth of human love and sentimentality. The name of the Intended and the vision of horror merge into one: love may be cruel; beheading merciful. Francis Ford Coppola's *Apocalypse Now* (1979), a filmic adaptation of *Heart of Darkness* in the context of the neocolonial Vietnam War, elaborates on the theme of headlessness. Kurtz, played by Marlon Brando, narrates his rude awakening to the secret of victory. He recalls, in fragmentary jump cuts under strategic lighting, a scene of atrocity in which the Vietcong cut off the arms of all the village children recently inoculated by the Americans. Looking up, his head turned in a bizarre 90-degree angle, Kurtz blurts out, "And I remember, I was shot with a diamond bullet right through my forehead," pointing to the spot between his brows, his third eye, "the genius, the will, the moral...to kill without judgment." The ambiguity of primordial instinct coupled with iron discipline becomes Kurtz's driving force. The allusion to diamond underscores the duality of Coppola's Kurtz. The Diamond Sutra in Buddhism aims to enlighten; alchemy and the occult have intuitively grasped the value of diamond as "black light," pure carbon, which also constitutes its "dark cousins," coal and graphite.[18] The hardest rock, diamond shears through everything, like delirious epiphanies annihilating human pretension, civilization's trappings, but also rationality. Hit between the eyes by a magic bullet (solution) or silver bullet (doom), Kurtz dies to be reborn as the executioner and sacrificial lamb. In the finale, Kurtz raids and decapitates Willard's (played by Martin Sheen) American comrade, whose severed head propels Willard into the insanity of carrying out his mission. He kills Kurtz, the assassination mixed with intercuts to the village sacrifice of a water buffalo by hacking it through the neck.

Among others, Calinescu has argued that modernity exhibits multiplicities, including the apparent opposites of kitsch and avant-garde. Accordingly, the (neo)colonial banality of native irrationality is a close kin to the avant-gardist valorization of acephalus. A family resemblance exists, after all, among Forster's Marabar echo and headless saint, Conrad's and Coppola's heart of darkness and light, and, lastly, Georges Bataille. At first blush, the short-lived avant-garde secret society that Bataille headed on the eve of World War II—Acephale—does not seem overly connected with the East, except through occasional references to the Hindu deity Kali. In his introduction to *Encyclopaedia Acephalica*, Alistair Brotchie describes Acephale as a cult bent upon a-theology, a Nietzschean destruction of God to create a counterreligion. Acephale members would meet in the darkness of night "on a marshy soil, in the center of a forest . . . [where ] stands a tree struck by lightning. One can recognize in this tree the mute presence of that which has assumed the name of Acephale, expressed here by these arms without a head" (qtd. in intro. p. 15). Truncated by lightning, the tree symbolizes the sudden, violent jolt of awakening and decimation. Andre Masson drew the cover design of a headless man for the first issue of *Acephale* in June 1936. Of this design, Masson wrote:

I saw him immediately as headless. . . . [The head] finds itself displaced to the sex, which it masks with a 'death's head'. Now, the arms? Automatically, one hand (the left!) flourishes a dagger, which the other kneads a blazing heart (a heart that does not belong to the Crucified, but to our master Dionysus). . . . The pectorals starred according to whim. . . . The empty container [stomach] will be the receptacle for the Labyrinth that elsewhere had become our rallying sign. (qtd. in Brotchie's Intro., p. 12)

Bataille, in "The Sacred Conspiracy," analyzed the same drawing:

Man has escaped from his head just as the condemned man has escaped from his prison, he has found beyond himself not God, who is prohibition against crime, but a being who is unaware of prohibition. Beyond what I am, I meet a being who makes me laugh because he is headless; this fills me with dread because he is made of innocence and crime; he holds a steel weapon in his left hand, flames like those of a Sacred Heart in his right . . . his stomach is the labyrinth in which he has lost himself, loses me with him, and in which I discover myself as him, in other words as a monster. (*Visions of Excess* 1985, p. 181)

Fleeing from the prison-house of reason and moral, human beings, argued Acephalians in the Nietzschean style, approach the paradoxical oneness of things: comic violence, innocent crime, sword and heart, the head that is the sex, the Self that is the Other. By the power vested in their brush for drawing and writing, they invoke a conceptual holocaust to demolish the status quo. Although Acephale as an organization dissolved with the onset of the war, Bataille's vision of headlessness as counterculture persisted until the end and in the last pages of his final work lies an Oriental closure.

*The Tears of Eros* (1961) traces how sensuality and death, aestheticism and violence, or brush and blade in the present lingo, are intertwined in Western art history, starting from prehistoric archaeological finds to Greco-Roman Dionysian antiquity and to Christian paintings, including two biblical decapitations—Salome and John, Judith and Holofernes. What is essentially an inquiry concerning Western sculptures and paintings concludes, quizzically, with four photographs of "Voodoo Sacrifice" and five photographs of "Chinese Torture," an Oriental epilogue to recapitulate a lifelong heretical conviction, an apocalyptic finish in the vein of Pound's sunrise or Eliot's thunder. Nonetheless, the distancing throughout *The Tears of Eros* by means of the media of paintbrush and chisel devolves into the shock of documentary photographs. While the voodoo shaman is smeared with blood, covered with feathers, and, in one picture, holds a goat's head, these photographs are nowhere near as gruesome as what follows. "Chinese Torture" records a 1905 execution of death by a thousand cuts. Surrounded by spectators reminiscent of Lu Xun's and Lao She's crowds, a naked man is being sawed piece by piece on his breasts, his arms, and his legs. The photographs are laid out around the margins of facing pages to graphically illustrate the fracturing of the human body. One picture in fact crops its neighboring image, accentuating the process of rending. Not only is the victim's body being rent, but the human mind as well, as Bataille confesses to his sadomasochistic obsession with these images. Through torture and pain akin to religious sacrifice, Bataille annihilates reason in the attempt to reach divine ecstasy. Such an explosive, iconoclastic theory arises from, uncannily, hearsay: "I have been told that in order to prolong the torture, opium is administered to the condemned man. [Georges] Dumas insists upon the ecstatic appearance of the victim's expression. There is, of course, something undeniable in his expression, no doubt due at least in part to the opium" (p. 205). Allegedly drugged and insensate, the victim is taken to be hallucinating. The fact that Bataille would conclude with "Chinese Torture" suggests that the Orient *is* the opium, doubly inducing euphoria and a cessation to Western level-headedness. Citing his source, Dumas's *Traite de Psychologie* (1923), Bataille divorces the man's face (head) from his body, based on a perceived rapturous expression despite the mutilated body. Bataille discursively decapitates his victim. True, the condemned man looks up to the sky, with almost longing, no contorted muscles or screams, yet it remains ironic for someone who has championed "no head" throughout his career to round it off on the strength of countenance-reading. Granted that passion and blood are forever conjoined in Bataille, granted that he immerses himself imaginatively in native violence, Bataille, unlike his imperialist contemporaries, nevertheless, ruthlessly inscribes spirituality onto a Chinese body. Just as Nietzsche commands in the voice of the Median prophet Zarathustra, Bataille's text in blood is someone else's blood.

## Last Words

A true warrior—Christ nailed to the Cross or the apple-peddling snake nailed to the ground—inhabits crazed calm, controlled madness, a still center to the vortex of violence. Even when the head is cut off, the sword broken, the body stays convulsed, spewing life.

# 4 Kung Fu Films in Diaspora
## Death of Bamboo Hero

In our global village, scholarly attention has increasingly turned to Hong Kong kung fu films, exported to the world via Tsui Hark (Xu Ke), Jackie Chan (Cheng Long), Jet Li (Li Lianjie), Yuen Wo-Ping (Yuan Heping), and others. In the past decade or so, two strains in writings on what I term "Hongllywood" films have emerged: in the first, film Orientalists see in Hong Kong cinema a cultural alternative to mainstream Western productions; in the second, film nostalgics analyze the Chinese/transnational identity being constructed on celluloid. At their worst, these writings simply degenerate into fanzine plot summaries or the fetishization of celebrities. At their best, however, they map out not only an engaging art form specific to Hong Kong but also point to its global reach. Mostly of non-Chinese descent, the first clan yearns for a non-Self, an essentialized entity that was never part of Westernness. Mostly of Chinese descent, the second clan yearns for the "lost" Self, an essentialized entity imagined to be part of Chineseness. The former is tinged with fresh-eyed, exotic longing, the latter with tired wistfulness. I belong decidedly with film nostalgics. In view of the nostalgic nature of Hong Kong kung fu films, as contended by Hector Rodriguez and others, I am apparently not alone in this.[1]

But first, a disclaimer about the opening focus on Hong Kong: at least two of the filmmakers analyzed here are based partially in Taiwan—King Hu (Hu Jinquan) and Ang Lee (Li An). The fight scene in the bamboo grove in Hu's *A Touch of Zen (Xia nu,* 1969) was filmed in central Taiwan; Lee, himself from Taiwan, shot most of *Crouching Tiger, Hidden Dragon (Wohu canglong,* 2000) on location in China. In addition, Taiwanese and overseas capital and the market play as pivotal a role in the filmmaking process as does the felt need for an essentialized Chineseness amongst people of Chinese ancestry in diaspora.[2] Rather, I take Hong Kong more as the epicenter than a confined geographical area for the nostalgia industry on Chineseness. Now that Hong Kong has returned to, as they say, "the embrace of the Motherland," I see an even greater need to grant the island its due as the core for the network of celluloid fantasies.

Consequently, this essay explores the stylization of Chineseness in the trope of kung fu masters, particularly at the moment when they—or their shadows—relocate across time and space to Southern California. As the trope of martial arts continues to wed masculinity with power within the context of global market, the traditional "bamboo-like gentleman hero" has fallen out of favor. But before exploring that, we need to sort out the intricacies of *wuxia pian* (swordplay films) and kung fu films (using primarily fists and legs) in the evolution of Hong Kong cinema. The dominance of *wuxia pian* gave way to kung fu in the early 1970s, but the two never truly parted company, as Jackie Chan's (Cheng Long) modern action thrillers continue to thrive on props and stunts, drawing from both traditions. Their merger is not surprising, in view of Hong Kong films' complex fountainheads—*wuxia xiaoshuo* (novels of chivalry), Beijing Opera, Chinese *wushu* (martial arts or kung fu), and even Hollywood's gun-toting action heroes and special effects. All these cultural strands contribute to the visual spectacle that is kung fu, which can be simulated as much by Jet Li, a martial artist, as by Jackie Chan and Michelle Yeoh (Yang Ziqiong), a Beijing Opera trainee and a modern dance student, respectively.[3] Hence, references to "kung fu films" in this chapter also allude to *wuxia pian*. Despite the difference in fighting styles, the two genres closely resemble each other in terms of their historical settings and escapism. The removal from the present makes possible the self-empowering fantasies. Action thrillers associated with names such as John Woo (Wu Yusen), Chow Yun-Fat (Zhou Runfa), and Jet Li project identical, a-historical longing forward, into a postmodern or futuristic setting, where gun-slinging, car-chasing, multiple explosions, and consciousness- and form-altering are justified by the same kind of distance from the here and now. Mutating in response to the global market, action thrillers in diaspora have skillfully cloned themselves, replacements for the casualty list I bemoan in these pages. I intend to study kung fu's afterlife at some future date.

## A Casualty of Three

As kung fu films migrate from Hong Kong's Chinese cultural context to Hollywood's global marketability, creating the hybrid subgenre of Hongllywood films, kung fu's "Chineseness" is stylized to bring it more in line with consumer preferences. Granted that Chineseness has always been stylized, even in Mainland Chinese or Hong Kong films, it takes on shared characteristics in Hongllywood "bastards." In this stylization, certain filmic elements, which

I call "casualties," are suppressed in accordance with martial metaphors inherent in this genre. Given the inevitable changes in the history of filmmaking, this chapter may be taken as a requiem of sorts, for disappearance or even extinction signals vulnerability, ill-adaptability. Specifically, I bear witness to a casualty of three. In terms of film sets, the once-ubiquitous bamboo is gone; in terms of fighting, the traditional kung fu and Beijing Opera forms and tableaux are replaced by special effects stunts, cinematography, editing, and computer wizardry; and in terms of body exudation, the extravagance of blood, *qi* (breath), and traditional sentiments like *yi* (camaraderie) are excised. This trinity of setting, stunts, and exudation, I contend, are the composites of any particular fight scene, the "essence" of the masculinist kung fu genre. The "bamboo-like gentleman hero" was one who possessed all three: the revered qualities of bamboo, exceptional fighting skills, and traditional values.

To illustrate the first component, imagine yourself a film editor working on the rushes in the editing room. You can freeze a fight scene and digitally erase the fighters, thus directing attention to the set and props. In this process, bamboo emerges as one of the favorite sets and props; it frequently transforms itself from part of the static set to a dynamic prop, even into one of the hero's weapons. A pioneer kung fu film, King Hu's *Come Drink with Me* (*Da zui xia*, 1965) creates a *zui xia* or drunken master wielding a bamboo staff as both a weapon and an emblematic scepter over his gang of beggars. Similarly, the protagonist in Lau Kar-Leung (Liu Jialiang)'s *36th Chamber of Shaolin* (*Shaolin sanshiliu fang*, 1978) chances upon a new weapon concept, a prototype of *nunchaku* (numchucks), when he toys with a broken yet still attached bamboo stem. Bamboo, a fixture of Hong Kong kung fu films, is completely cut from Hongllywood productions.

Let us put back in the frame the fighters, the intended focal point of any martial arts sequence. We soon discover, however, that the choreography of fighting has undergone drastic changes. Hollywood places far more emphasis on stunts than on traditional kung fu punches and kicks and Beijing Opera tableaux. However supple and acrobatic, however elaborate the footwork and martial arts forms, the repertoire of the body is limited in comparison with that of the high-tech dream factory. In place of the longish takes from a single camera in early films such as *36th Chamber of Shaolin* and Jet Li's *The Shaolin Temple (Shaolin si)* (dir. Zhang Xinyan, 1979), now multiple cameras, brief shots, cinematographic innovation, constructive editing, and special effects have come to dominate Hong Kong films, as is evident in Tsui Hark's oeuvre. I count John Woo's aesthetics of bullets and explosives among "stunts" as well, for the simple reason that the next area, on body exudation, entails *immediate, direct* issuing of substance from the human body rather than by means of guns or machines. By the same token, *anqi* (secret or concealed weapons like darts) in *wuxia pian* belongs among "stunts" as well. The often-used reverse playing of a flying dart sequence in kung fu films testifies to *anqi*'s "technical" origin.

The last area, body exudation, includes all that that issues, *without mediation*, from a fighter's body—body liquids like blood (especially the kind that spews forth profusely from the mouth), vomit, sweat; body parts in certain grotesque, sadomasochistic cases such as Zhang Che's *One-Armed Swordsman* (*Dubi dao*, 1967); sounds emanating from the body, such as heavy breathing, grunts, moans, cries, last gasps, cracking bones and skulls, cackles, and variations of what I have come to regard as quintessentially Chinese performance of mirth. This final item is intriguing: a Chinese kung fu laugh consists of a series of near-detached units similar in tone but in decreasing volume and intensity, each utterance punctuated by a slight pause, enough to give the laugh the appearance of a sentence of monosyllables like Mandarin and Cantonese. How one laughs, I submit, is determined by the language one speaks; a monosyllabic tongue engenders monosyllabic laughs. The most memorable duet in merriment is the sonorous, deep-throated "Hah Hah Hah," signifying contentment or exultation and the shrill, semi-insidious "Heh Heh Heh." Conceivably, this stylization of laughs stems from Beijing Opera performances of Zhong and Jian, loyal and traitorous characters, respectively. To illustrate the likely origin of these stylized laughs in film, we recall Tsui Hark's *Peking Opera Blues* (*Dao ma dan* 1986), where the opening and concluding credits roll over the image and distinctly "monosyllabic" laughter of a Beijing Opera warrior with painted face.

In addition to body sounds, the typical kung fu soundtrack encompasses loud, oftentimes discordant music; the abrasive, aspirative contact noise of punching and kicking; and, of course, the ridiculous, side-splittingly funny dubbing into English. The formulaic performance of *qigong* (kung fu with *qi* or breath) is yet another kind of body exudation that never fails to send Western audiences into uncontrollable giggles. What appears to be "supernatural" transmission of one character's energy through his or her palms into another ailing character is so unscientific and eccentric that it has come to confirm all the stereotypes Westerners harbor about the backward Orient. Yet in recent sci-fi films, *qigong* seems suddenly plausible and even respectable, judging from the showdown between Yoda and Count Dooku in *Star Wars: Episode II—Attack of the Clones* (dir. George Lucas, 2002). There they hurl colossal stone pillars at each other with *qi* or energy emitted from their bare palms.

Western audience's taunting of the extravagance of kung fu exudation aside, fight scenes are the key to kung fu's popularity in Hollywood, so long as they are properly repackaged. The secret of success for martial arts choreographers like Yuen Wo-Ping lies in the fact that kung fu—to borrow Maxine Hong Kingston's concluding sentence in *The Woman Warrior* (1976)—"translated well." Primitive grunts, sounds of smashing into human flesh, and the metallic clanks of swords are not dialogue, and so present a minimal obstacle to moviegoers from another linguistic system. Indeed, such prelingual articulations of fight scenes, including the whooshing of bullets, deafening explosions, and the shattering of glass in a vintage John Woo film, vie with English as the lingua franca of global cinema. The balletic choreography of kung fu requires miniscule linguistic and cultural proficiencies for it to be appreciated in much the same manner that the dance numbers of musicals are appreciated. But as it is translated, many of the culture-specific subtleties are lost. Bamboo is but one example.

First of all, we look at the set, or the disappearance of bamboo from kung fu films. Bamboo has been cut from the film because it does not "translate well." The United States is a country without bamboo, so the rich symbolism inherent in bamboo in kung fu films would be entirely lost on American audience. Indeed, there is an American Bamboo Society (ABS) formed in 1979, which became incorporated in the state of California in 1981. Today it has over 1,300 members living throughout the United States and in thirty-nine other countries. The ABS issues a magazine bimonthly and a journal irregularly. In 2001, there were ABS chapters in Southern California, Northern California, Texas, the Northeast, Florida-Caribbean, Pacific Northwest, Hawai'i, the Southeast, Oregon, Louisiana–Gulf Coast, Tucson, Arizona, and Puerto Rico. It is part of an international bamboo society. But bamboo grows only in coastal areas and the large expanse of the United States knows next to nothing about the plant group, except perhaps the myth that it is tropical and invasive. The familiarity situation may be improving in certain segments of the U.S. population, however. The Freer Gallery of Art and the Arthur M. Sackler Gallery, part of the National Smithsonian Institute in Washington, D.C., feature a monthly family program called ImaginAsia, which hosted "Sacred Lotus, Symbolic Bamboo" in the summer of 2002. This program coincided nicely with "The Silk Road," the theme of the thirty-sixth Festival of American Folklife at the National Mall that was held in late June and early July of the same year. Also, among the junk mail I received recently, I discovered a United Airlines brochure promoting its Mileage Plus frequent-flyer program to China, Hong Kong, and Taiwan. Printed prominently on the envelope and the brochure was fresh-green bamboo, along with an ancient coin with Chinese script and a classical arbor with an upturned roof. Bamboo has become as recognizably Chinese as Chinese scripts and classical architecture. In fashion, bamboo has long been deployed to evoke the exotic in décor—lamp supports, teakettle handles, even printed on wallpaper. In a *New York Times* full-page ad on May 19, 2002, Banana Republic featured a line of summer products protruding from a handbag with circular bamboo handles, displayed on a tabletop made of thin strips of bamboo or rattan, a retro look of women's fashion of earlier decades. The Travel section of the Sunday *New York Times* frequently features advertisements for Jamaica in which a long bamboo raft has two Caucasian tourist-passengers seated in the rear and a dark-skinned man at the bow propelling the raft with a long bamboo pole.

In Chinese culture, bamboo is, for lack of a better word, Chineseness itself. Similar to roses in the West, bamboo permeates Chinese culture, so much so that it requires exceptional mental rigor to think of bamboo as, for instance, river cane, or tropical grass, or a "bamboo tree," as Judy Garland sings it in *Meet Me in St. Louis* (dir. Vincente Minnelli, 1944). One of the "four gentlemen" (plum, orchid, bamboo, chrysanthemum), bamboo is said to stand for probity because of its straight posture, for flexibility because of its gently swaying and graceful stem, and for humility because of its hollow inside. Beloved in Chinese painting, each part of the bamboo—its long stem with knots, its finger-like leaves, the bamboo shoots—resembles a particular brush stroke in Chinese calligraphy. Since painting and calligraphy were the domain of the traditional literati, bamboo has long been dear to the "keepers" of Chinese culture. At the other end of the cultural spectrum, a major gang in Taiwan, constituted of descendants of Mainland émigrés, is called Zhu Lian Bang (the Gang of Bamboo Union). Its leader, Chen Chi-li (Chen Qili), masterminded the 1984 assassination of Henry Liu (Jiang Nan), a San Francisco-based journalist alleged to have defamed then Taiwanese president, Chiang Ching-Kuo (Jiang Jingguo). Chen Chi-li is believed to have acted at the behest of Taiwanese government's intelligence chief.[4] With strong ties to the Guomingtang (the Nationalist Party), the Gang of Bamboo Union also feels itself exiled from China and claims the values associated with bamboo—old-fashioned loyalty and camaraderie *(zhong* and *yi)*. The practical and decorative functions of bamboo are boundless: it is used for scaffolding in construction, building materials, drying poles, broomsticks, furniture, chopsticks, calligraphy brushes, and so forth. Alas, however, bamboo's richness in Chinese culture, like a Zen koan, is untransmittable or undecodable in American culture.

Both stunts and body exudations are subject to the same tension between submission and sovereignty of the human body, a tension that runs through Chinese *wushu* (martial arts), Beijing Opera, and the early Cantonese and Mandarin kung fu films in Hong Kong. First, the body is always made to undergo rigorous training and trials tantamount to torture to obtain victory, which often verges on the spiritual rather than the merely physical; the body, with all the pain it must endure, becomes a vehicle for higher goals. The protagonist's arduous apprenticeship and later combat is predicated on a philosophy of stringent self-discipline, so much so that it appears to be "national sadomasochism" to outsiders. On the other hand, the protagonist's absolute subjection to the master seems to run counter to the ultimate lesson of self-sufficiency, for kung fu is nothing if not self-sufficiency. The physical body, its materialist extension in the form of weapons, its transcendental reserve of *qi* or spirit, and its faith in nationalism and ethnic identity constitute all the arsenal the protagonist needs to annihilate multiple enemies, at times a whole army. The abjection of blood and sweat, the grimaces of pain, come to suggest the sublimity of the mind and ideology—an Eastern version of romanticism yoking the mundane and the sublime.

Body exudation, of course, pours out of this wedding of opposites: it can be the invisible, life-giving *qi;* it can also be the vomited blood that forecasts defeat and imminent death. In the worst presentations, the former looks rather superstitious, the latter revoltingly uncouth. Given the blood, sweat, saliva, and the yells, moans, and other sounds which permeate any kung fu fight scene, a middle-class Western sensibility tends to tune it out, dismissing it as kitsch. Be that as it may, kitsch reveals much about the "home" culture that engenders it and the "host" culture that receives it. Perhaps due to the lack of scientific equipment as much as to anything else, traditional Chinese medicine and health care practice place tremendous emphasis on physical symptoms: visual examination of the patient; taking the pulse; inspecting blood, phlegm, and other secretions. An audience of Chinese descent is more receptive to the familiar episode where a diagnosis is made on the basis of a brief pulse-taking. To non-Chinese, this seems ludicrous. In addition, the discrepancy between production and reception of filmic body fluids may well stem from the two cultures' drastically different environments. An island just south of the Tropic of Cancer, Hong Kong is unremittingly hot and humid; sweating and human secretions happen as soon as we step out of an air-conditioned building or automobile. The pungent reek of perspiration wafts close by; the maps around armpits, back, and waist are a common sight on both men and women; tempers flare up—short and quick, demanding instant release, such as in kung fu's quick punches. Southeast Asia, where Cantonese emigrants were once the major market for early Hong Kong films, is even more tropical. Like lush tropical vegetation, the exuberance of body fluids as well as of human emotions comes across in the West as both exotic and excessive, both life-affirming and chaotic. In accordance with the "editing room" procedure, the following analysis of "bamboo-like gentleman hero" foregrounds the set, stunts, and body exudations whenever it is possible. In the vortex of action, however, one can not always discern the lines of separation among the trio.

## Bamboo-like Gentleman Hero

Critics have repeatedly pointed out the nostalgic quality of King Hu's oeuvre. A Beijing exile in Hong Kong, Hu draws extensively from Beijing Opera and Chinese tradition. Bordwell in *Planet Hong Kong* (2000) observes about kung fu films in general and about King Hu in particular: "The alteration of swift attack and abrupt rest is characteristic of the Asian martial arts"—a style attributed to both the martial arts and Beijing Opera, in which movements contain what are essentially tableaux of stasis (p. 224). Without doubt, Hu's action sequences and their musical accompaniment owe an enormous debt to Beijing Opera. Other stylistic borrowing from Chinese culture includes bamboo, which associates protagonists with righteousness. This bamboo lineage of the gentleman hero manifests itself in King Hu, Tsui Hark, and Ang Lee, among others.

Aesthetically framing a key fight scene halfway through Hu's classic *A Touch of Zen* (1969), bamboo comes to link human bodies with death by the sword. The central duel takes place in a bamboo grove, as the protagonists are overwhelmed by their enemies. On the run, the protagonists cut down numerous bamboo, and their enemies do the same, apparently in an effort to "clear" the battleground. Yet the heroine abruptly doubles back and performs a flying stunt, alighting on top of a bamboo branch before hurling herself down to slash her opponent, a move made possible by the earlier clearing. Similar to bamboo felled by steel, the heroine reverses the fortunes of war when she turns the bamboo's fragility into flexibility. Faced with swords or adversity, human bodies are not unlike bamboos, bending temporarily but bouncing back in the end. Hu further ties bamboo to an essentialized Chinese rectitude in that the protagonists are being persecuted by the Ming emperor's chief eunuch. Nationalist paranoia intertwines with castration anxiety.[5]

Compared with today's swordplay films, Hu's action sequence here appears rudimentary, overly static by the standards of MTV and Tsui Hark: fighters freeze in preparation for the next move; swords lock in awkward, arm-wrestling stalemates. Mediocre fights are, nonetheless, enlivened by a beautiful set, by what Bordwell describes as "constructive editing,"[6] and by the soundtrack. Fragmentary, elliptic shots of leaping to the top of a bamboo stem and falling from it are woven together by the soundtrack's crescendo of bodies whooshing through air while traditional Chinese musical instruments play. The scene rounds off perfectly when the male protagonist (played by Bai Ying), exhausted and spent, resheathes his sword at the very instant the music falls silent.

While Hu sets his film long before the presence of the West in China, Tsui Hark's 1990s series called *Once Upon a Time in China (Huang feihong)* locates the nationalist hero squarely in the late Qing entanglements with colonialism. An increasingly complex symbol, bamboo resurfaces in several fight scenes throughout the series. Toward the end of *OUATIC (Once Upon a Time in China* 1991), the Cantonese Wong and the northerner Yim duel in a warehouse filled with bamboo, and, more specifically, on bouncy bamboo ladders. Yim's northern kung fu of "iron robe"—a legendary *qigong*—shrouds and protects his entire body, stopping even a huge iron weight in its slide. Yet the southern kung fu practiced by the bamboo-like gentleman Wong prevails. Under the larger nationalist sentiment, the Hong Kong audience is surely gratified by the outcome of this north-south rivalry. Ever so calm and with a faint smile, Wong readies himself for any attack in an open-armed, welcoming stance, in contrast to Yim's teeth-gnashing, animalistic rage. Wong does not seem even to breathe any harder throughout the fight. The battle is further "ritualized" by the Wong Fei-hong (Huang Feihong) theme music that has accompanied the hero, invariably played by Kwan Tak-Hing (Guan Dexing) in the ninety-nine films since the 1950s. By contrast, Yim issues bestial yells. Viewers turning on closed captions are immediately aware of Yim's battle cry, rendered in hilarious English as "EEE-YAH!" or "HEY-YAH!" Toward the end of their fight, Yim's disheveled hair, cut loose by his own *anqi* (a knife hidden at the tip of his queue), links him with barbarians according to Confucian ethos. Indeed, Yim's iron robe, steel-like moves, and *anqi* liken him to a West of modern weaponry. To drive that home, Yim collaborates with a gang that collaborates with Americans in smuggling coolies and women to the United States. Although blinded by his ambition to reign supreme in kung fu, Yim is not the arch-villain. His disciple, played by Yuan Biao, in fact defeats the American henchman on the slave ship and practically lynches him on the mast. Witnessing Yim being cut down by a volley of musket fire, the disciple cries out "Master!" in effect acknowledging both Yim and Wong. Yim's ultimately benign nature is brought out by his dying words. Lying in a pool of blood, he cautions Wong, "You can't fight guns with kung fu," clearly evoking the history of gunboat diplomacy and Western imperialism in late Qing. Once again, however, Wong exhibits Hu-style trickstery when he kills the American villain with a musket bullet finger-flicked like a traditional *anqi*. As resilient as bamboo, Chinese kung fu wins when it integrates Western technology.

As Hong Kong goes Hollywood and high-tech, the filmic imagery of bamboo is replaced by a more generalized, contemporary code of flexibility and resourcefulness. For instance, at the end of the sci-fi Kato-esque *Black Mask (Heixia)* (dir. Daniel Lee, 1996), Jet Li destroys his enemy by flinging not a marble-shaped bullet, but a computer disk. The final showdown of Jet Li with his demonic antagonist takes place in an underground chamber. The gloomy set appears to be vaguely post-holocaust, with bouncy boards over a pool of water conducting electric current. Once stripped of their postmodernist trappings—computers, electric cables, guns—the set resembles the rickety bamboo ladders from the 1991 *OUATIC*. The slashed electric cables spewing forth sparks are wielded much like the "cloth" whip in *Once Upon a Time in China II* (*OUATIC II* 1992).

Bamboo serves both as set and prop in *OUATIC II*. The finale comes as a corrupt Qing official (played by Donnie Yen) and Wong confront each other in a warehouse full of bamboo racks and baskets. Subsequently, Wong and his disciple are cornered in a narrow, dead-end alley. Donnie Yen's weapons associate him not only with Yim, but with the West. Yen tries to gun down Wong and his disciple in the warehouse and, in the alley, he twists a length of bed sheet, turning it perversely into a steel-like whip with his *qigong*. Although Wong is vulnerable, his weapon—a splintered bamboo pole—is made to prevail yet again. As Yen tightens the steel-like whip around Wong's neck, his cracked bamboo pole enables Wong to cut through the cloth and, with a single fiber sticking out of his pole, Wong slashes Yen's throat. In slow-motion, a stunned Yen picks the fiber out of his throat and first a thin line of blood oozes out and then the wound explodes. Blood spurting from Yen's throat brings his violent end. By contrast, bloodletting via the normal orifice—the mouth—is less deadly: Wong's disciple survives despite the copious blood he coughed up when he was whipped earlier.

Like Hong Kong itself, Tsui Hark is a cultural crossroads: born in Vietnam, trained in U.S. film schools, and based in Hong Kong, he is restlessly innovative and unabashedly commercial.[7] Tsui Hark adroitly manipulates nationalist sentiment in his *OUATIC* saga, varying the antagonists against the constant of Wong's heroism, or giving the appearance of difference in what is essentially a banal formula. *OUATIC* pits the hero against Western imperialism in the form of an American slave ship, while *OUATIC II* locates the antagonists in the nativist White Lotus rebellion. The U.S. consulate in *OUATIC II* provides a sanctuary for founding father Sun Yat-sen (Sun Chongshan) and hence supports the struggle to overthrow the Qing dynasty: Americans are now the good guys. *OUATIC III* casts Russians, complemented by native thugs, as the evil forces. Taken in totality, the *OUATIC* series demonstrates that a Chinese-speaking audience accepts the shifting alliances with foreign powers and, more importantly, that racial/ethnic consciousness grows in conjunction with conflicts and interactions. *OUATIC III* closes with a lion dance contest vying for a ball on top of a bamboo dome. Despite the extravagance and "bang" (literally, of gongs and cymbals), despite the loaded "Chinese" symbols of bamboo and lion dance, the scene proves to be an anti-climactic "whimper" to the trilogy.

Ang Lee's *Crouching Tiger, Hidden Dragon* is a belated tribute to *wuxia pian;* it revisits the sets and symbols of bamboo, but with unprecedented sexual tension. Based *very* loosely on the fourth part of Wang Dulu's magnum opus, the five-part *wuxia xiaoshuo* (novels of chivalry) *The Crane and the Steel (Hetie wubu qu),* Lee's *Crouching Tiger* makes a number of major changes to Wang's plot. The narrative perspective is no longer that of Liu Taibao, a second-rate martial artist with all the foibles of Everyman. Wang's focus on the young lovers, Jen (Yu Jiaolong) and Lo (Luo Xiaohu), played by Zhang Ziyi and Chang Chen in the movie, is balanced by Ang Lee with an older pair of lovers, Yu Shu-Lien (Yu Xiulian) and Li Mu-Bai, played by Michelle Yeoh and Chow Yun-Fat. To bring out the film's theme fully, passion and eroticism mark the young lovers' relationship, in contrast to their suppression by the older pair. Characterization and plot are similarly revised to intensify sexual transgression, especially with respect to the alleged affair between Li's master, Southern Crane (Jiang-nan He), and the witch-like Jade Fox (Yu Huli). Lee also magnifies Wang's Taoist tendencies, making the film more consonant with contemporary New Age or alternative culture.

Like many novels in this genre, the story revolves around a precious sword, Qingming (Green Destiny, but literally "Bright and Obscure," a yin/yang Taoist union).[8] Because its Chinese name is so suggestive, I elect to use the Chinese version in the following discussion. First of all, the sword is a phallic symbol; the exceptional aggressiveness of Qingming manifests in its effortless shearing of every other weapon. A patriarchal heirloom, Qingming has been passed down by Southern Crane to Li Mu-Bai. That Jen seeks to steal and possess Qingming shows female subversion of patriarchy, an attempt no different from that of Jade Fox, Jen's "master," who, decades earlier, had tried in vain to gain access to the martial arts secrets of Wudang Pai (the Taoist counterpart to the Buddhist Shaolin) by giving Southern Crane the pleasure of her body. It is worth noting that a Wudang master has violated his vow of celibacy while hypocritically upholding the Wudang interdiction against passing on its martial arts, and hence power, to women. Another way of thinking about the "obscure" or suppressed history of the sword is to reflect on the blood it has shed, not only the virginal blood of the young Jade Fox but that of its enemies, all traceless now in the brightness of the sword.

While Li Mu-Bai appears to be on the verge of changing the Wudang tradition and taking Jen as his apprentice, he remains staunchly traditional in his resolve to kill Jade Fox and avenge his master. Moreover, his interest in Jen is not entirely professional. A master-disciple relationship across the gender line can be characterized by mastery and submission in such a way that it becomes fraught with sexual longing and repression. A heterosexual bonding is no longer "containable" by the family paradigm of filial piety and devotion. After all, the genesis for action lies in Li's unrequited love for Yu Shu-Lien, with whom he has maintained a platonic relationship out of respect for her dead fiancé and his sworn brother. Li's discontent is so powerful that he decides to *chuguan* (terminate or come out of retreat). The retreat being the avenue to transcendence of the secular world, Li wishes to embrace, rather than abandon, human passion. And yet his love for Shu-Lien is derailed once he comes across Jen, the thief of his masculinity. As if counterpointing Jen's desire to usurp male power, Li subliminally satiates his sexual drive toward a younger, more attractive Jen by pursuing and subjugating her. The erotic entanglement between Li and Jen is buried under the two explicit pairings—Jen and Lo, and Shu-Lien and Li. Another hidden secret of Qingming—the mutual attraction between Li and Jen—is a reprise of their respective masters' transgression. Whereas no film critic has mentioned the jealousy and tension in the triangular relationship between Li, Shu-Lien, and Jen, it is readily apparent if we closely examine Shu-Lien's anxiety and Li and Jen's interaction, both of which take place very close to or amidst bamboo. Ang Lee transforms bamboo from King Hu's aesthetic object and Tsui Hark's utilitarian function into an "objective correlative" for human desires.[9]

During the brief confession of love between Li and Shu-Lien at a roadside rest stop, bamboo provides an idyllic backdrop through the geometric wall opening. The couple's teacups are carved from bamboo stems as well. Asking Shu-Lien to be patient, Li fails to initiate an escape from the prison of human constructs (like the rest stop) and of social obligations to the dead. So close to the bamboo grove, the pair cannot bring themselves to venture into Nature and their love. Instead, Li follows Jen into a much wilder bamboo grove later in the film. This turn of events is foreshadowed by Shu-Lien's anxiety over Jen as a potential rival. In their duel, Shu-Lien proves to be a far superior swordswoman, yet Jen's Qingming sword cuts through all her weapons. Comparing this fight with those in Hu's *A Touch of Zen*, one perceives that martial arts choreography has come a long way. Multiple camera angles, quick editing, acrobatic moves and stunts, and Tan Dun's Academy Award-winning soundtrack capture the action in an exhilarating flow. A brief skirmish involves a medium shot of the two women, followed by a shot from above, then another from behind one character as if seen through her eyes and highlighting her opponent, then its reverse as seen through her opponent's eyes, and so forth. Ang Lee is nonetheless pacing this sequence with the time-honored kung fu film counterpoint of dynamics and stasis. Pauses exist in the action, like inhalations, before one launches into another round of combat. Better still, such caesuras lie between exhalation and inhalation, a momentary voidness where life is suspended in uncertainty, making the continued life all the more precious.

One of these caesuras arrives when Jen complacently runs her fingers over the blade that has rendered all of Shu-Lien's weapons useless. Shu-Lien shouts almost in hysteria: "Don't touch it! That's Li Mu-Bai's sword!" "Come and get it if you can!" dares Jen, in a battle of words over control of Li's manhood. Shu-Lien's shout is out of character, for otherwise she manifests a composed, resolute demeanor throughout, in contrast to Jen's breathlessness and flustered look. (Zhang Ziyi's acting involves a great deal of heavy panting.) In fact, there is a note of desperation in Shu-Lien's warning. Instinctively, she feels insecure. Halfway through the film, Shu-Lien comments on Li's interest in Jen: "I know she'll intrigue you," a somewhat misleading translation of the line in Mandarin, "I know you'll be suspicious." The English subtitle intentionally heightens the sexual innuendo. When Li does give chase to Jen, the matronly servant Wu Ma comforts the injured Shu-Lien that perhaps "Li Mu-Bai can do it [kill Jen]." Shu-Lien's worried and doubtful look in response bespeaks her suspicion of an emotional entanglement between Li and Jen.

Into the bamboo grove go Jen and Li. The two alight on waving bamboo stems, thanks to wirework.[10] Unbeknownst to the Godfather of human sexuality, Sigmund Freud, bamboo is phallic, as visualized by Ang Lee's cinematography. Bamboo bends and stays soft at one moment, then straightens, erect, the next. The drama of submission unfolds as a power play, the hypnotic eroticism written on Jen's youthful and almost translucent face as it flows across in slow motion. Bamboo leaves and Jen's long black hair cast shadows like a veil over her face to accentuate the mystery of desire. With her supine posture and her facial longing captured in a high-angle close-up, with her near-perfect face occasionally occluded and completely controlled in the frame, this aesthetic gaze at Jen is launched from Li's and the audience's dominating point of view. As Jen's bamboo swings back to loom over Li, he suddenly kicks it, and Jen falls down, and thus, in effect, Li denies Jen any position of power. This is the first of Jen's three falls, all of which have to do with loss, with Jen crashing down from dizzying ecstasy.

Li finally corners Jen on a boulder by a pool. In a classic Wudang move, Li points two fingers at Jen's forehead and subdues her. She nearly faints under the magnetic power. What Li accomplishes in that fleeting moment is the transmission of *xinjue* (heart secret, a psychic and spiritual empathy and identification between master and disciple), a kind of mystical body emission involving, I imagine, *qi*. But Jen's "little death," in Bataille's term,[11] when touched between the eyebrows seems a consummation of the erotic arousal started back on the bamboo stalks. Jen gives in, promising that "If you can get the sword back in three moves, I'll follow you." The phrase *wo jiu gen ni zou* (I'll follow you) brings to mind the misogynist Chinese proverb, "Follow the chicken if you marry a chicken; follow the dog if you marry a dog." Directly stealing the sword in an underhanded move, Li commands Jen to *ba shi* or *pa shi*, translated as "kneel." Jen, for good reason, is unwilling to capitulate. Li then hurls Qingming into the pond, claiming that the sword is of no consequence now that she is his disciple. Jen initiates the second fall in the film: she dives in to retrieve the sword and is rescued by Jade Fox. The crisis of submission to masculinity is averted, only by a return to matriarchal oppression.

Li's cry of *ba shi* or *pa shi* is so poorly articulated that this critical turning point becomes a bewildering lacuna. This is not only because Chow Yun-Fat's voice tends to be indistinctly high-pitched whenever he gets emotional but because, more fundamentally, his Mandarin is shaky. The initial reaction to the film shared by many Mandarin speakers is that Chow's and Michelle Yeoh's delivery of lines in Mandarin is so monotonous and stilted that it severely mars the film. (Chang Chen's is not much better by northern Chinese standards.) But for global cinema and the film festivals around the world that Ang Lee targets, the discomfort of native speakers matters very little. Non-Chinese moviegoers are unlikely to notice the flatness of emotion in Chow's and Yeoh's voices. Moreover, in view of the tradition of dubbing Hong Kong films for non-Cantonese speaking markets, performers have long been regarded as bodies and faces divorced from "authentic" voices—humans reduced to visual spectacles with no simultaneous dialogue and thus no interiority. As far as global audience is concerned, Chow and Yeoh may just as well be pantomiming throughout the film. For that matter, the English subtitles clearly package the product for the West. In addition to the examples of sexual tension I have already alluded to, subtitles are often simplifications to accommodate the West. One case in point is the northwestern province of Xinjiang, translated as "the West" to evoke the American West and the genre of Westerns.

In pursuit of Jade Fox, Li moves from his territory, the phallic bamboo grove, into her territory, a dark, rain-soaked, womb-like cave. (The mouth of the cave is reminiscent of an underexposed picture of Georgia O'Keeffe's vaginal orchid.) Li enters the cave and finds a drugged Jen trying to rouse herself in a shallow pool. Jen turns to Li, her flimsy blouse so drenched that it hugs her breasts and protruding nipples. "Is it the sword or me you want?" offers Jen, subconsciously tearing open her blouse. The scene borders on foreplay. Li, supposedly one ethical rung above his philandering master, remains unmoved and paternalistic. Li then proceeds to revive Jen with *qi* transmitted through his palms into her back. At this juncture, Li and Jen are caught red-handed by Shu-Lien, who has tailed Jade Fox back to the cave. Shu-Lien is momentarily taken aback, but quickly recovers when she realizes the lurking danger. Yet that fleeting moment of suspicion of the pair's subterranean "liaison" is intriguing. Shu-Lien is the only "witness" to Li and Jen's repressed eros, from the theft of Li's "penis," to the stroking of it during the heroines' fight, to the actual physical touch of the "lovers" in the cave. Li touches two women in this film: he caresses Shu-Lien in the rest stop and kisses her before he dies; he touches Jen on her forehead and, during the resuscitation, on her shoulder blades. Ang Lee fine-tunes these scenes so that they hover somewhere between classic heroism and decency on the one hand, and Freudian clashes of thanatos and eros on the other.

Carnal desire also intertwines with death in the form of Jade Fox's *anqi*, poisoned needles propelled from her cudgel. One needle finds its way into Li's neck and his bloodstream, a masculine penetration delivering death. The duality of Qingming—its manifest and latent drives, its masculinity and femininity, its love and hate, its attraction and repulsion—self-destructs in a suicidal bloodbath. Ang Lee manages to pack one more ambiguity into this double death scene. Li kills Jade Fox before his own demise. No blood spews forth from Jade Fox, which is quite atypical of the gruesome endings most kung fu villains suffer. On the contrary, Jade Fox confesses that her real target is Jen, who harbors true poison because as an eight-year-old apprentice she decided to withhold the subtleties of the Wudang martial arts manual from her illiterate master. This well-founded indictment implicates Southern Crane, who also withheld secrets, Li Mu-Bai, who avenges Southern Crane, and the entire institution of martial arts. Jade Fox articulates, in crisp, couplet-like Mandarin, the theme of paradox in *Crouching Tiger*: "Jen, my only family, my only enemy." Likewise, Jade Fox and Li destroy each other, members of an illegitimate family sired by Southern Crane.

Following Li's last wish, Jen travels to the mountains of the Wudang Monastery. She reunites with her young lover Lo for one night and, early next morning, has Lo repeat the Xinjiang legend that one who has "a faithful heart" can survive a fall from the top of the mountain—"*xin cheng ze lin.*" As abrupt as in a dream sequence, Jen jumps off the cliff, to the music of Yo Yo Ma's (Ma Youyou) elegiac cello. This is Jen's third and final fall. In religious terms, it suggests the leap of faith necessary for taking the vow to enter Wudang and leaving the secular world and Lo. But the profound sadness in this fall recalls the pattern of her prior falls from the height of the bamboo, into the deep pool, and now through the clouds, all for the specific loss of Li Mu-Bai: the first time an anticlimax to the orgiastic play with Li; the second time in search of Li's phallus; the third time in mourning for Li himself. To read the leap literally, Jen is jumping to her own death, which demonstrates her total surrender to Li and his last words. For his part, Li, refusing to save his last breath to elevate himself and reach eternity, as Shu-Lien counsels in tears, instead confesses his thwarted love for her. Rather than the enlightenment Taoists strive for, Li chooses human love, as ephemeral as it is. Now bereaved, Jen dies of her own unrequited love. Her love-making with Lo the night before may well be a last farewell, but the shot of a grief-stricken Jen, with a blank stare past her lover's shoulder, does not divulge whom she fantasizes herself having sex with—Lo or Li or both.[12] Nor does Ang Lee foreclose the ambiguity of her leap. Even if it is actually a suicide, Jen's airborne suspension acquires a mythic dimension. Posited on romantic longings, kung fu films often locate finales in the expediency of deus ex machina, a reversal of the fortune of war through the intervention of a larger-than-life, otherworldly power. The monk savior in King Hu's *A Touch of Zen,* for instance, sacrifices himself and emits golden blood from a spot reminiscent of Christ's chest wound. The vaguely apocalyptic tone of kung fu "endgames" permeates Ang Lee's closure as well.

Ang Lee's film, however, is an anomaly amidst the trans-Pacific careers of his fellow film practitioners. Jackie Chan, John Woo, Chow Yun-Fat, and others carry various forms of their "Chineseness" into the genre of Hongllywood films. The symbolic capital of an exotic Orient begins to outweigh their early Hong Kong works, leading them to further commodify and universalize culture-specific performances for a global audience. In such contemporary, Westernized settings of post-Hong Kong films, there is no place for tropes exclusive to China. Ironically, the symbol of kung fu and the core of Chineseness—bamboo—is *bumped* from the cast or bumped *off* altogether. When bamboo returns in *Rush Hour 2* (dir. Brett Ratner, 2001), it supplies comic relief. Dangling from a bamboo scaffolding bent into an "L," Jackie Chan reassures his partner Chris Tucker: "Chinese bamboo, very strong," just before the pole breaks and they crash to the ground.

## Fade-out

"Three" in Chinese suggests multiplicity. Among the many casualties of Hong Kong kung fu films in diaspora, I have identified only those bodies recognizable to me. Perhaps you can do the same for other remains.

# Intercut on
## Asian Dubbing

# 5 De/Alienation in Diasporic Dubbing/Rubbing of Maoist China

## Dubbing and Rubbing

Who hasn't had a keen sense of estrangement when a beloved radio host with a youthful, mellifluous voice materializes into a bald, pot-bellied middle-aged man? The classic movie *Singin' in the Rain* (1952) dramatizes the inverse of this disillusionment, when the beautiful silent film actress turns out to quack rather than speak in sound films. The mismatch between body and voice, visual image and soundtrack, gives a shock to the system, catching one off guard. This is perhaps why the French filmmaker Jean Renoir was so outraged by dubbing in foreign films: "If we were living in the twelfth century..., the practitioners of dubbing would be burnt in the marketplace for heresy. Dubbing is equivalent to a belief in the duality of the soul" (*My Life and My Films* 1974, p. 106). This sentiment appears to be shared by another filmmaker Robert Bresson when he dubs dubbing "naïve barbarity" (*Notes on Cinematography* 1977, p. 25). Indeed, Westerners most often associate dubbing with foreign films of inferior quality, such as Hong Kong kung fu and action films. Deemed low-brow, mass entertainment, these films routinely redo the soundtrack for the English-speaking market. But in fact this is merely an extension of their earlier marketing strategy to non-Cantonese speakers of Chinese descent all over Southeast Asia.[1] Accordingly, dubbing serves to explain, in the audience's language, the filmic bodies. Designed to bridge the gap between body and voice, between—in dramaturgical terms—stage and theatergoer, dubbing strives to minimize any difference in lip-sync to achieve a naturalistic illusion. But the attempt to erase the discord between performers' lips and sound can eerily highlight the schizophrenic divide. Since the voice issues from inside the body or, as it were, from the mind, the dissociation widens, by corollary, to that of body and mind, even to the alienation of Self from the Other. Rather than an aberration from the supposed integration of voice and body, of mind and body, of Self and Other, dubbing epitomizes, through its inherent schizophrenia, life itself. It is difficult to accept this view in part because of the universal assumption that content and form should conform. We are taught to speak our mind, cohering words with thoughts, lest we be seen as hypocritical and Machiavellian.

Defined as the dissonance between voice (mind or Self) and body (Other), dubbing lurks in nearly every corner of life, not just in foreign films. Silent films used to be accompanied by live music. Ballet continues today to rely on music from the orchestra pit. Cartoons featuring animal characters are dubbed in human voices. When these cartoons travel overseas, the dubbing is redubbed in foreign tongues. Subtitles dub visually. The technology of DVD allows for dubbed dialogues and subtitles in various languages. Listening to radio or watching television, audiences experience disembodied voices or after-images of bodies long dead. The ideal union of body and voice raises significant questions with reruns of old television shows, especially those repackaged to put fissures under erasure. Complicit viewers contribute by ignoring the palimpsest of dubbing. Lying deep beneath Renoir's and Bresson's righteous indignation about dubbing is the filmmakers' wrath concerning human indifference to the chasm in life. Yet the duality of the soul Renoir so abhors resides in each of us. When is the last time we have had to pay for thoughts spontaneously spewed forth? Do we not always "dub" our inner thoughts for the public? Life is a long dubbing session, preferably one in which we dub ourselves rather than being dubbed by someone else.

A norm in life, not an aberration, dubbing becomes a key metaphor for understanding diasporic writings on Maoist China.[2] Under more open policies in the post-Mao era, many Chinese intellectuals, affected and even traumatized by decades of political campaigns, particularly the Cultural Revolution (1966–1976), left China for the West. As is natural with émigrés, exiles, and immigrants, they have looked backward at their native land, yet in English and French. Their subject matter—those imaginary bodies of the past—is Maoist China, both under Mao as well as post-Mao (for post-Mao China is still overshadowed by the Great Helmsman) yet these bodies converse in English and French. Maoist China has been dubbed by diasporic writers, an inevitable decision should diasporic writers wish to be read at all. It is more than just a sales issue; expatriate authors may find a detachment in an acquired language as they approach what is essentially their own past fraught with moral ambiguity. An alien tongue helps us remove ourselves from our text. This psychic maneuver on the part of expatriate Chinese authors goes in precisely the opposite direction from that experienced by Western readers, who are linguistically de-alienated from—that is, made familiar with—the alienating fictional universe of China. The trick to diasporic dubbing lies in the double-edge of De/Alienation. For this dubbing seems to have moved beyond mere linguistic mediation required in making the subject matter—an alien body—intelligible to Western readers. Not to mince words, this dubbing of body consistently turns into a rubbing of body. Faced with diasporic dubbing/rubbing of Maoist China, it seems absolutely eerie that dubbing and rubbing should so often coincide in human sexuality.

A perfect union between the bodies and minds of sex partners is a beautiful thing, if rather romanticized. That sex gurus from the *Kama Sutra* to sex therapists today teach about timing and coordination points to the urgency of synchronized love-making. But human sexuality is characterized by its infinite variety, which all seem to share the commonality of "tease," as in "striptease." Fanned by technical advances in the history of human sexuality, carnal desire is itself a tease waiting to be satisfied. The outdated industry of phone sex offers voices without bodies, while one has to do the rubbing oneself. Virtual sex through the internet comes with both image and sound, yet no corporeality. The sex industry dubs its client's rubbing, or the client rubs in sync with the dubbing. Across the chasm in space, time, and subjectivities, the desiring Self and the desired Other merge, fleetingly, through electrical and digital links, into a climactic moment of ejaculation. While remaining separate from the images and sounds, one achieves a trance-like cessation of one's alienation. Judging from the boom of cyberporn, such intercourse between Self and Other, temporary and short-lived by design, makes possible de-alienation.

In its formulation with a slash that privileges neither side, "De/Alienation" is the essence of diasporic dubbing/rubbing of Maoist China. In dubbing a potentially alienating Maoist China for Western readership, diasporic writers de-alienate the subject matter by rubbing, or sexualizing, it. Sexuality is, after all, held to be a universal human trait, one that can presumably bridge East and West. Two distinct forms of diasporic dubbing/rubbing emerge: "Aftersex," practiced by Anchee Min, Wang Ping, and Dai Sijie; and "Afterrape," practiced by Ha Jin and by Joan Chen in *Xiu Xiu* (1998). Set against a repressive totalitarian regime, Aftersex romanticizes sexuality as the core of an individualistic, humanist spirit. Min deploys lesbianism and a ménage à trois at a commune and reeducation camp, the sexual- and self-awakening verging on market-driven sensationalism in the United States, the titillating sex scenes intensified by Communist repressiveness. Wang's semi-autobiographical stories likewise dangle between poetic license and self-exhibitionism, a neurosis continued in her "scholarly" book on bound feet, *Aching for Beauty* (2000). While in Aftersex protagonists engage in sex *of* their own free will to defy collectivity, Aferrape dwells on sex *against* the protagonists' will, perpetrated by the collectivity. Politics interpellates Chinese lives so thoroughly in Ha Jin that communal rape—sexual, physical, mental, and psychological—looms above a dark, violent, primitivist world. Each in his or her own way, diasporic writer defies revolutionary Puritanism by exposing the desiring body underneath the Maoist uniform. If the premise of Aftersex is naive humanism, then Aferrape is surely anti-humanist. If Aftersex gives off the scent of romance, Afterrape reeks of violence: the lingering fragrance of love as opposed to the residual odor of blood and semen.

Both schemata are labeled "after" to underline discursive deferrals—coming after Mao, outside China, speaking with a chameleon's forked tongue, facsimile to the "real thing" from the 1970s Scar Literature to contemporary Chinese literature, stigmatized by something akin to Renoir's "duality of the soul." But just as diasporic dubbing/rubbing familiarizes Maoist China for the West, it alienates itself from Chinese discourse. A comparison with Chinese self-representation inside China or in the Chinese language bears out the highly-sexed nature of diasporic writings.[3] With the exception perhaps of Zhang Xianliang, most Chinese discourse on suffering during Maoist China—Yang Jiang, Feng Jicai, Chen Jo-hsi, Gu Hua, Bei Dao—manifests narrative lacunae, understatedness, and asexuality over those dehumanizing years. The alienation from Chinese discourse has its price, though: out of the five artists discussed in both Aftersex and Afterrape, only Dai Sijie enjoys a relationship with Chinese authorities cozy enough for him to shoot in China the filmic adaptation of *Balzac and the Little Chinese Seamstress* (2000), whereas none of Ha Jin's novels, including the award-winning *Waiting*, has been translated into Chinese; Min and Wang's stories, granted much slighter than Ha Jin's corpus, are virtually unknown; and Joan Chen was barred from entry into China after the release of her film.

## Chinese Narrative Lacunae and Asexuality

For those who have survived Mao, there is a shared urge to bear witness to the ordeal, particularly the "ten-year holocaust" of the Cultural Revolution, a posttraumatic reckoning through writing in an attempt to put shattered lives back together, if possible. This testimonial strain runs through all Chinese writings on the Maoist campaigns. From the "Scar Literature" of the late 1970s (named after Liu Xinwu's "The Wounded") to the Menglong Poetry (poetry of the obscure, or misty poetry) of Bei Dao and others, to the more substantial works of Yang Jiang, Chen Jo-hsi, Feng Jicai, and Gu Hua, Chinese writers have registered their trauma, loss, grief, resentment, and distrust within the parameters of totalitarian politics and the Chinese tradition of moderation and social accord. Hence, Liu Xinwu offers a hasty happy ending, now that—so the Party line goes—the Gang of Four had been crushed. Poetry of the Obscure, of course, veils itself in abstruse images. And the other four writers, with amazing restraint, come to terms with horrifying experiences. A key feature that unites all four appears to be a skirting of the abysmal. Gu Hua allows two months to elapse in *A Small Town Called Hibiscus* (1983), during which the heroine is "reformed," a process from which she returns as a disgraced "ghost" in the Black Five category (p. 118). Feng Jicai's "The Mao Button," in *Chrysanthemums and Other Stories* (1985), chronicles the fanatical personal cult of the Leader during the Cultural Revolution, as Feng's characters vie for the biggest and most eye-catching Mao button. The protagonist wears so big a Mao button that his jacket becomes creased, yet he accidentally steps on the button that has fallen off, an act that brings him to the brink of destruction. The novelist concludes, "There is no need to recount the details here. Suffice it to say that he recovered from his Mao-button mania and came to look upon these objects of his affection with fear and trembling" (p. 29). This evading of the worst is once again Feng Jicai's tactic in "A Letter," where an absentminded researcher undergoes six months of "struggle," the nadir of his life, which Feng merely sketches. Writing in her style of understatedness and gentle irony in *The Execution of Mayor Yin and Other Stories* (1978), Chen Jo-hsi—albeit an expatriate since 1973—is rarely given to the diasporic streak of physical obsession. This may well be due to the fact that Chen was already an established writer in Taiwan and overseas, so she did not have to cater to the English-speaking readership. Moreover, her stories came out in the right place at the right time, when Hong Kong residents and the Taiwanese were eager to peer behind the Iron, or rather, Bamboo Curtain. Chen documents family disintegration, betrayal, suspicion, and absurdity in a mild tone that paradoxically intensifies the suppressed emotions. Yang Jiang distills her three-year re-education at a May Seventh Cadre School with her husband, the eminent scholar and writer Qian Zhongshu, into a thin volume of six chapters, *Six Chapters from My Life "Downunder"* (1981). Sent to the countryside to be re-educated by peasants, leading intellectuals like Yang and Qian concern themselves with matters such as night soil and night patrol, the elderly Qian getting carbuncles on his face as if he were regaining his youth. Such are Yang's humorous, self-mocking touches that enliven the whole ordeal. Yet she also hints at the darkness in this period when she mentions, in passing, her son-in-law's suicide. Around the same time, an anonymous mound "like a huge steamed bun" is dug for a suicide at the Cadre School, the filling of the bun soon swallowed by forces of nature (p. 47). These reminiscences conclude with an allusion to a painting of "an old man with a bag slung over his back and a cane in his hand walking step by step down a mountain path directly into his own grave" (p. 49). As is typical of these writers' calm, detached style, allusions to a steamed bun and painting help objectify personal suffering and cushion the shock of painful memory. Writing alone in her nineties, Yang perfects in *Womensa (Us three)* (2003) this allusiveness into a dream-like allegory for her family saga, in which she is robbed of her husband and daughter. A rare gem in contemporary Chinese literature, *Womensa* remains untranslated, shelved by the robust Chinese translation market as a result of, perhaps, its gerontology-related subject and allegorical, essayistic, episodic style, which does not accord with the West's preference for "realistic" treatment of Maoist China.

Feng and other Chinese writers have continued to expand their output, publishing on topics other than political persecution. For example, Feng has written a historical novel about bound feet and spearheads conservation projects in Tianjin. And even when revisiting the trauma, as in *Womensa*, Yang's approach has evolved from the documentary, factual *Six Chapters* to the symbolic and the poetic. None of these writers seems as fixated on Mao's body as diasporic dubbing/rubbing does. As is the trajectory of many émigré writers, without the living organism called China, diasporic writings tend to ossify somewhat. Having no soil in which to put down roots, diasporics must grow aerial roots. Whether diasporics would repeat the pattern of ethnics and metamorphose from ethnic-specific novels (Kazuo Ishiguro's *The Pale View of Hills* [1982] and Chang-rae Lee's *Native Speaker* [1995]) to whiteface performances (Ishiguro's *The Unconsoled* [1995] and Lee's *Aloft* [2004]) remains to be seen. With the lukewarm reception of Ishiguro's and Lee's more recent novels, we may wonder whether Ha Jin will remain popular once he turns to non-Chinese themes.

Unlike Feng Jicai and others, some writers never live to tell their stories. A novelist and a playwright for the poor and the disenfranchised, Lao She (1898–1966) tried to answer the Party's call by grinding out propagandist works throughout the 1950s and 1960s. But in 1966, he was humiliated and tortured by middle-school Red Guards. The cause of his death remains a mystery. Either a suicide or homicide, his body was found in Taiping Lake just beyond Beijing's old city wall. I had been a visitor to the area in recent years,, but no matter how vigorously I was accosted by the throng of drivers in their unmotorized, two-passenger tricycles, I never found the courage to ride in one because of their antecedent, the labor-intensive rickshaw that Lao She so movingly humanized in *The Rickshaw* (1936–1937). Instead, I walked along the lake, wondering just exactly where Lao She had met his death, a lacuna in Beijing's tourist attractions and modern Chinese history. For every Lao She, however, there are scores of writers-to-be who have not only survived Mao's water cell but managed to swim across the shining sea.

## Aftersex

Constricted by our mundane lives, human beings often escape imaginatively to historic, larger-than-life moments. The more removed, fantastic, and exotic the moment, the better for assuaging private angst. The West, therefore, has long harbored a fascination with what alleges to be its opposite, Communist China—ancient, authoritarian, driven by the collective. Tales of the Cultural Revolution offer glimpses of massive catastrophe and evil believed to be absent in the First World. Readers can empathize with as well as secretly gloat over the misery that befalls the Other, elsewhere. To meet the need in Western academe, there exists, practically, a whole field on Communist China. Many specialists in this field are of Chinese descent; a number of them explicitly claim personal connection with the subject of their study. One critic of modern Chinese theater, for instance, repeatedly legitimizes her books by referring to her family's history in Beijing's theatrical world and her own involvement in the Cultural Revolution. A true heir to performativity, she has learned her parents' trade well. This case reflects that on the stage of Chinese studies in the West, certain players enact something similar to diasporic dubbing/rubbing in that the ambivalence of De/Alienation lies at the heart of such scholarship—researchers' simultaneous removal from and kinship to Maoist China; their professional disinterestedness as part of the institution of Western universities and research centers and yet their personal investment in China. The line between diasporic and compradoric being rather blurred, it would be intriguing to see this researcher—and the handful like her—launch the proverbial Communist self-criticism on diasporic novelists' dubbing/rubbing.

Any single representation of a colossal event shares certain broad outlines because individual differences tend to be erased by large social forces. Consequently, native Chinese and diasporic narratives about Maoist China share distinctly similar elements: intellectuals' wasted years in the countryside, political repression, absurdity, the frenzied cult of Mao, family fragmentation, humiliation, abjection. Under this common framework, the autobiographical and testimonial nature of Aftersex further lends credence to the writers' stories. Min provides not only specific dates to open and close *Red Azalea* (1994) but also historical figures such as Jiang Ching, or Madame Mao. It is the sexual orgy that Min and others present in the name of Maoist China that requires scrutiny.[4] Min, for instance, serves up the Orientalist staples of bound feet, effeminate men, and ultrafeminine women, every trope silhouetted sharply against totalitarianism. *Red Azalea* recounts the protagonist's bildungsroman at a re-education camp; her sexual maturing comes about by way of a ménage à trois among herself, the unit leader Yan, and Yan's male counterpart Leopard, whose role is subsequently assumed by the unnamed Supervisor, formerly a female impersonator in Beijing Opera and now confidant to Jiang Ching in the production of a model revolutionary drama. Gender indeterminacy lays the foundation for Oriental erotica. Flirting with a taboo, the protagonist makes love in a public park with the Supervisor, whose lips are "tender like a naked lichee fruit," who has a "beautiful feminine long neck," and who exudes "the smell of jasmine" (pp. 261–262). Their love-making coincides with the acts of masturbators hidden in the park, both made more transgressive and more thrilling by the danger: "The masturbators are making their move with us, struggling with a fright so deep it has blinded their inner sight. They know they will be shot if caught—so do we" (p. 264).

Min's *Katherine* (1995) follows the same pattern of ménage à trois, this time made up of Lion Head, Katherine, and Zebra Wong, the protagonist. An American language instructor, Katherine symbolizes freedom, independence, and sexuality, an Occidentalized "goddess" to spice up the self-Orientalizing soft porn (p. 179). During a preposterous scene of Lion Head and Katherine making love near a mountain path (again in public), the peeping Tom of a protagonist fuses in her imagination with the lovers: "I could feel Lion Head move inside me.... I entered Katherine through Lion Head" (p. 99). It is an episode that unwittingly mirrors Marguerite Duras's Oriental erotica in *The Lover* (1984), the female protagonist, her classmate at the convent school Helene Lagonelle, and her Indo-Chinese lover:

> I'd like to eat Helene Lagonelle's breasts as he eats mine in the room in the Chinese town where I go every night to increase my knowledge of God. I'd like to devour and be devoured by those flour-white breasts of hers.
>
> I see her as being of one flesh with the man from Cholon, but in a shining, solar, innocent present.... Helene Lagonelle is the mate of the bondsman who gives me such abstract, such harsh pleasure, the obscure man from Cholon, from China. Helene Lagonelle is from China. (p. 74)

Duras's Oriental Other—not just a male but a stereotypically effeminate Oriental male—gives birth to a trinity of sorts that brings about divine knowledge, or the oceanic feeling where Self and Other are merged. The Oriental Other turns Occidental in Katherine, yet Duras's religiosity is no longer there to grace Min's, if you will, orgiasticity. Both Orientalism and Occidentalism are driven by the need for self-expansion, be it (neo)imperialist control, liberal quest for metamorphosis, or both. Katherine does, eventually, adopt an abused mute girl from an orphanage, thus rescuing the brutalized China from the brutalizing China.

Targeting the same English-speaking market, Wang Ping's *American Visa* (1994) resembles Min's work in rendering character and place names more reader-friendly; Wang's protagonist is Sea Weed, whose sister is called Sea Cloud. This contradicts the identity politics of Western-raised, mostly U.S.-born, Asian Americans, who tend to employ foreign-sounding names for their characters as well as for their own names: Amy Tan adroitly uses Chinese names to lend an exotic flavor to her novels; Kazuo Ishiguro, Chang-rae Lee, Bharati Mukherjee, Jhumpa Lahiri have not Anglicized their names. It is chic, in the late twentieth-century multiculturalism and in the subsequent globalization, to call attention to one's Otherness, particularly if that helps sell one's book. These American ethnic writers do resemble their diasporic counterparts in the tendency to gloss unfamiliar words and terms in order not to alienate their readership overmuch. A series of interconnected stories, *American Visa* is autobiographical to the point of juvenilia about the working out of an ugly duckling's psychological complexes caused by a domineering mother and a swan of a sister, Sea Cloud. The first half, filled with stories of Sea Weed's immediate family in Shanghai, is written without much artistry. The title story, "American Visa," is heartrending in its depiction of the friction between the protagonist's two sisters, who are trying desperately to leave China and are vying for the same man, who has a foreign visa. "Fox Smell," a story about body odor, takes the art of self-exhibitionism to a new height. The scars in Sea Weed's armpits left by the surgical removal of her sweat glands and hence her odor are fetishized as an erotic turn-on by her American boyfriends, who "liked to inspect them before and after sex, licking them, squeezing out the dirt that hid between the creases" (p. 99). Synecdoche of the pain and trauma that is China itself, the scars are flaunted and displayed in English, to Americans. So, too, a myth of China as destroyer and redeemer appears in Chinese American literature, such as in Maxine Hong Kingston's *The Woman Warrior* (1976) and Amy Tan's *The Joy Luck Club* (1989). The diasporics' China mutilates as well as empowers: Wang reads into the disability of body odor the legendary beauty of Concubine Yang in the Tang dynasty and the potent Fox Spirit in folk belief. Whereas China is largely associated with disgrace and shame, the United States delivers sexual liberation. Wang's sensationalism culminates in the maternal grandmother's aerogram to Sea Weed in the United States. While Sea Weed may have developed a sailor's mouth overseas—she counters her boyfriend's slight at a Moroccan restaurant by saying, "Why don't you show Nick [their gay dinner guest] your asshole?"—it is beyond me that a Chinese grandmother would so unabashedly write about a maternal uncle: "The two prostitutes slept with him together, one sucked his penis while the other licked his balls" (p. 87). As conversant with Chinese obscenities as any male with a proper public school education, I would hazard that it is wrong to translate the grandmother's words as "sucking," in a context where it ought to be "licking" and "balls," where it should be "eggs," unless, of course, the regional dialect of Shanghai is serendipitously close to American slang. It is an utter failure in characterization when an elderly Shanghainese talks American English.

Rather than, as it were, rubbing it in, Min's and Wang's counterpart in France, Dai Sijie, offers more gentle, romantic caresses to Maoist China in *Balzac and the Little Chinese Seamstress,* in a style reminiscent of Duras's aestheticizing of her youthful prostitution to a wealthy Indo-Chinese man.[5] The French taste for chinoiserie partly encourages the setting of a premodern, pristine, rural China, removed from political turmoil, a nostalgic look backward that one finds as well in recent Chinese films such as *The Road Home* (*Hueijia de lu,* 1999), *Postman in the Mountains* (*Naren nashan nago,* 1999), *Pretty Big Feet* (*Meili de dajiao,* 2002), and *Lovers in the Sky* (*Tianshang de lianren,* 2003). Propelled by this ethos of "lighting out" of the harsh reality of modernization, Dai proceeds to turn his novel into a film shot on location in China. De/Alienation encapsulates Dai's novel and film like a Chinese box. In French and in English translation, on the one hand, Dai de-alienates the subject matter by using Balzac and the Oriental stereotype of the petite Chinese handmaiden, pleasure and beauty incarnate. On the other, to Chinese moviegoers of his film adaptation, Dai tantalizes with Occidental objects of desires in terms of Western writers, the violin and classical music, and, of course, the individual freedom and fulfillment inherent in these tropes. Dai dubs the Cultural Revolution into romantic French and English for the West, which is then redubbed in nostalgic Chinese for the Chinese. Quoting both Oriental and Occidental tropes in the novel and the film, Dai offers his audience whatever it wishes to read/see. Dai authenticates dubbing/rubbing by way of his autobiography; the fact that he was "re-educated between 1971 and 1974" is prominently displayed like a plaque in the front matter, not in the end matter, as is customary in "About the Author" in books. Riding on his success in France, Dai, as the adage goes, *yijin huanxiang* (returns to his hometown in silken robes—having achieved wealth and official distinction), a home frantically Westernizing itself in the twenty-first century. Who is dubbing and rubbing whom? Does Dai still retain the agency of a ventriloquist if the dummy of post-Mao China favors being dubbed? Will Western customers still enjoy a banal sex show in book after book if they see that autoerotic images play out in their own mind?

## Afterrape

Anchee Min and Wang Ping eroticize Maoist China, Dai Sijie romanticizes it, but Ha Jin rapes it, or rapes it back after having been raped himself. Sexual and physical assault becomes Ha Jin's central trope for the searing sense of violation inflicted upon individuals. Metaphorically speaking, two kinds of characters exist in Ha Jin's fictional China: the rapists and the raped, with interchangeable roles. While shifting roles among persecutors, bystanders, and victims characterize most native Chinese narratives on Maoist China, the practice has rarely reached Ha Jin's macabre extreme. A certain moral center is usually preserved, if not the persevering, loving protagonists in Gu Hua and Feng Jicai, then at least the rational, restrained tone of voice in Yang Jiang and Chen Jo-hsi. By contrast, Ha Jin, in a sensibility as ghastly as that of contemporary Chinese writers Mo Yan and Yu Hua, pushes the ambivalence beyond the point of no return, into a bitter universe devoid of human warmth. A few examples will suffice. "Saboteur," which opens the collection of short stories *The Bridegroom* (2000), shows how an abused, illegally detained hepatitis patient decides to indiscriminately infect the townspeople once he is released. "An Entrepreneur's Story" concludes with a nouveau riche's whim that he will sleep with his wife and mother-in-law to return the insult of their condescension while he was poor. A teacher's secret abortion and financial straits in "In the Kindergarten" leads to exploitation of her charges' labor, which the kindergartener protagonist Shaona resents. Shaona avenges herself by urinating in

> the duffel [the teacher is to bring back to home], made sure to conceal her little bottom with her skirt, and peed on the purslanes inside the bag. But she dared not empty her bladder altogether; she stopped halfway, got up, and covered the wet purslanes with dry ones.... The whole evening she was so excited that she joined the boys in playing soldier, carrying a water pistol, as though all of a sudden she had become a big girl. (*The Bridegroom* 2000, p. 53)

Feeling abandoned by her parents who now have a baby boy and betrayed by her teacher, a mother figure, Shaona subconsciously regresses to the Freudian anal stage as she employs bodily discharge as weapon to control the outside world beyond her control.[6] But fear of discovery prompts her to stop and cover up her transgression. Her urine has given the misused and bullied girl a sense of power, strengthened by the association of urine and the toy pistol shooting water.

Faced with the bleakness of his subject matter, Ha Jin exhibits a clinical, almost chilling, affectlessness. At times, this muted, dispassionate style achieves an amazing Kafka-esque effect. Readers are introduced to a disorienting universe with the opening sentence of *Waiting* (1999): "Every summer Lin Kong returned to Goose Village to divorce his wife, Shuyu" (p. 3). As matter-of-factly begun as Kafka's "When Gregor Samsa awoke one morning from unsettling dreams, he found himself changed in his bed into a monstrous vermin," the opening forces readers to confront a series of jarring situations: the narrator is married yet has been living apart from his wife; their annual reunions occur for the sole purpose of divorce; and their divorce attempts have thus far been thwarted. However, the alienating sequence is made less so by the pronounceable names of the foreign characters and place. Consistent with fellow diasporics, Ha Jin de-alienates Chinese materials through translated names and follow-up glosses for difficult terms; "a pair of Mandarin ducks" is explained, in the same breath, as "an affectionate couple" (p. 115). But diasporics seem so solicitous of the non-Chinese-speaking readership that they distance themselves from their Chinese subject matter. Having taken leave of one tyranny, diasporics submit themselves to another, the tyranny of the English language. Or perhaps Ha Jin does not so much escape from one tyranny into the other as he serves as a conduit between the two. Ha Jin thrives, after all, on a blood-curdling portrayal of Chinese tyranny, the lone threat to the U.S. superpower after the collapse of the Soviet Union. Ha Jin's rise may be partially based on U.S. paranoia over a potential contender for supremacy in the global economy, as a political system, and in other spheres.

Language serves to illustrate this point about De/Alienation that concerns dissociation and alliance in the Sino-U.S. power relationship. Whoever has grown up in frigid northeastern China (Manchuria), and has slept night after night on a warm *kang,* will almost instinctively recall with great fondness the bed as a *kang,* except Ha Jin, who gives his English-speaking readers the cold, lifeless translation "heated brick-bed." This phrase and others like it recur throughout his writing, indicating how closely tied to northern Chinese life Ha Jin's stories are yet how removed, emotionally, they are. Almost in revulsion, Ha Jin apprehends Maoist China as predatory and vile in every single one of his backward glances, yet it remains his experiential home base, without which he would not enjoy his literary success today. Creativity seems to spring from what amounts to self-loathing and self-abjection. Likewise, Ha Jin sets "A Tiger-Fighter is Hard to Find" in his native Manchurian Changbai Mountain, which is accurately rendered as Ever-White Mountain, the attachment inherent in the transliterated original name totally discarded for it would not reach an American audience. The calculated translations of the original source material, or the dubbing of the Chinese body, extends even to the name Ha Jin; the author retains his surname (Jin for gold) but adopts Ha, most probably in memory of Harbin, one of the largest cities in Manchuria, where he attended the University of Heilongjiang in the 1970s and 1980s. Indeed, Harbin, the Songhua River flowing through the city, and the city's university often feature in his stories as sites of human bondage. His pen name remembers his "hometown" almost the way a "Made in China" tag does a product: it denotes an origin, but little affection, indeed, an origin from which to flee. Ironically, Ha Jin's fame in the West is intertwined with his products "Made in China." For "Made in China" to succeed in the West, products need to satisfy consumers. Indeed, in his melodramatic language of the body, Ha Jin does resemble vintage Amy Tan. A rape victim in *Waiting* feels "[h]er heart began absorbing warmth again" (p. 194). As the news of her rape spreads, she "hated the telltale's bone marrow" (p. 196). (An accurate translation would retain "bone" but delete "marrow." Ha Jin seems bent upon deepening the emotion.) In *The Crazed* (2002), the young protagonist is so moved by his teacher's confession that it "made my gums itch" (p. 172). (An accurate translation would replace "gum" with "teeth." Here Ha Jin seems bent on conveying correct neuroscience, despite the fact that the Chinese adage does not apply to the context.) Whether faithful translation or not, Tan fans—the "Sugar Sisterhood"—would no doubt recognize this voice that entwines physical sensations with affect, hence bridging the alienating Chineseness for a white middle-class readership.[7]

Going beyond Tan's cruel Chinese men and backward China, Ha Jin dwells so obsessively on a naturalism in the primitive Third World that it both shocks and captivates the First World. In bare-bones English that reads like a translation, Ha Jin's stories focus on restricted space and characters as well as on ghastly storyline, such as the sewing up of piglets' anuses (in *Waiting*) to increase their weight for sale. The narrative perspective is routinely that of educated, often urban, intellectuals sent down to the countryside or entangled in political repression, bludgeoned by animalistic greed and primal instincts. Presented as ignorant and savage, rural China and totalitarianism offer glimpses into politically incorrect gender relationships and primitivism, so long repressed yet still craved by the advanced, democratic First World.[8] In gratuitous, repeated explosions of violence that are nearly pornographic, Ha Jin eroticizes abomination into what resembles "gang rape," perpetrated by individuals and by the society.

Wang Tingting in "Broken" (from *The Bridegroom* collection) is raped by First World standards, yet she is scapegoated and "raped" many times over by the patriarchal, Communist system of public interrogation, confession, and humiliation over her sexual activity. Pressed for details, Wang Tingting recalls her assailant's words to the effect that his wife has a "cold pussy" and his "cock...by nature it was always restless and about to fly" (p. 78). Chinese slang for penis is "bird," which is perfect for the figure of speech, if only Ha Jin were willing to subject readers to a bit of the alienation effect. But Ha Jin does not dare stylistically alienate his readers, not even a tiny bit, which contrasts sharply with the potentially disorienting subject matter. The shocking "gang rape" of Wang Tingting is muffled in rhetorical ambiguity. The actual sex organs are a taboo; male and female sex differences are there and not there, present and absent, not looked at but desired, suggested in veiled, metaphorical language. That a woman who loses her virginity is called in Chinese "broken shoes" transposes the vagina to unsightly feet associated with soil and filth. Freudian "penis envy" further hypothesizes female inadequacy and male castration anxiety based on the elusive, "behind-the-scene" phallic sign. Despite its bawdy jokes and crude language, "Broken" never actually describes a penis or vagina in so many words. Indeed, clinical, factual description of sexual organs can be found only in hard-core pornography, which, by definition, is banned, hidden from the public eye, precisely because of its obsessed gaze at the sexual organs.

In Ha Jin's dehumanizing world, male and female sexual desires clash and cancel each other out. The protagonist of "Broken" is so mousy and ignorant that when he starts to have illicit sex with an unidentified woman in the darkness of a movie theater, he cannot even follow through: "One of his knuckles rubbed her stiff kernel.... She began gasping and whining softly, so he let go of it." As for himself, he retches instead of ejaculating. Forced to confess his crime at the theater, the protagonist is led to implicate the usual suspect, Wang Tingting, who commits suicide, victim of a ruthless society. A genealogy of "castrati" runs from the protagonist in "Broken" to Lin Kong in *Waiting*, to the paralyzed "giant larva" Professor Yang in *The Crazed* (2002, p. 223), and to the mutilated, disemboweled Korean War inmates in *War Trash* (2004). Only a beast like Geng Yang in *Waiting* comes so superlatively equipped that he not only reaches orgasm inside his victim's body but triumphs in the jungle called Maoist China.

In *Waiting*, hospital colleagues Manna Wu and Lin Kong, a married man, have held back their love for eighteen years out of fear. But before their physical and psychological longings are consummated, Manna is raped in Ha Jin's graphic yet paradoxically elusive language. Phallic ambiguity blurs the center of the rape scene, in which the rapist's genital is said to resemble "a donkey's," "a rolling pin," and "a little mortar" (p. 181), the tabooed penis escaping all clinical description except in similes. Whereas the source of power remains beyond the reach of words, the body of the raped is fully controlled rhetorically:

He pulled her over on her stomach and forcefully pressed his thumb on her spine at the small of her back. The pressure nearly made her black out. Her lower body turned numb; she felt injured. He spat on his fingertips and began rubbing her anal cleft. She tried to hold her legs tight, but they felt no longer her own. (pp. 180–181)

After the rape, Geng Yang threatens yet more violence as he waves a liquor bottle: "You know, if you weren't a virgin, I would've given you this" (p. 182). Unlike the flabby impotent ones of Lin Kong and the other Chinese male characters, Geng Yang's aggressive penis projects not only the symbolic force of a beast or a weapon, but it *is* its metonym—a bottle that happens to be at hand. After his retirement from the military, Geng Yang flourishes as a businessman, news of which sends Manna Wu, who has married Lin Kong and given birth to twins, into a much delayed posttraumatic depression. That the memory of trauma overtakes Manna years later signals that she has never healed from the rape, only buried it; the assault is further aggravated by the social "rape" immediately after the rape. The so-called "date rape"—once again, Ha Jin takes the easy way out by borrowing from an American ethos a concept that is nonexistent in Manna Wu's China—goes unreported because that sort of occurrence is rarely treated as rape. In addition, Manna is shunned as a fallen woman, accused of "self-delivery" (giving herself to a man) and being "poked by a man" (p. 195). Geng Yang is introduced into the narrative during Manna Wu's unsuccessful bid to become the secretary-wife of Commissar Wei, Geng Yang's superior. Her candidacy fails because her penmanship is not up to par. Dumped onto the dehumanizing marriage market by Commissar Wei, the patriarchal "alter ego" concerned with the analysis of literature (Whitman, to be exact) and personal expression, Manna receives her final trashing through the patriarchal "id" in the form of a donkey's penis.

In the long tradition of madmen—Lu Xun, but also Dostoevsky, Gogol, and other Russian writers—the crazed in *The Crazed* is as much the individual as the society. Professor Yang collapses in a stroke under political pressure, which derives from a sexual indiscretion and miscalculation. As the book concludes with a dissident witness account of the June Fourth Tiananmen Square Massacre, it is a crazed China from which the protagonist—Professor Yang's disciple and future son-in-law—must take flight. Ha Jin refines his pseudo-documentary style in his most recent novel, *War Trash,* which takes the guise of a memoir written by a Communist Chinese veteran of the Korean War. The factual, credible voice of the protagonist, Yu Yuan, self-destructs in the opening paragraph when he reflects on his tattoo, "Fuck…U…S…," a silly conceit that is the driving force of the novel. Trapped in the liminal state of prison camps, Yu Yuan recalls, Chinese soldiers were torn between Communist diehards who clamored to be repatriated to China and pro-Nationalist "turncoats" who wished to be sent to Taiwan. The seesaw battle takes place on the inmates' body, as would-be-repatriates are tattooed, by force, with anti-Communist slogans so as to cast doubt on their patriotism and to make it impossible for them to return.[9] The protagonist is beaten unconscious and tattooed with "Fuck Communism" below his navel. How is this feat accomplished by pro-Nationalists who are represented as not having even finished elementary school? Are there U.S. "advisors" to offer consultation or even to execute the tattooing? The protagonist's Communist comrades subsequently erase certain letters to make the tattoo read "Fuck...U...S..." Of course, the whole notion of tattooing in English is so ridiculous that Ha Jin tries a pre-emptive deflection by having one character wonder "why they had used English instead of Chinese" (p. 99). The answer lies in Ha Jin himself, who carves the Chinese body to reach his English-speaking readers. Under the pretext of an authentic memoir, Ha Jin not only compromises linguistically but, more problematically, embeds flashes of his trademark style, such as the sadistic disembowelment. The pro-Nationalists' coercion at the prison camp explodes in the bloodbath of Chapter 9, "Before the Screening." The butcher Liu Tai-an first flays the skin of the victim and then disembowels him: "Blood and intestines spilled out, and a few men at the front began retching. With a sidewise slash, Liu slit his chest, then pulled out his lungs and heart, all the organs quivering with steam. He cut out the heart and skewed it with the dagger" (p. 108). English written on the Chinese body, internal organs off that body—both are bared for the consumption of English-speaking readers. In his high praise of *War Trash* in *The New York Times Book Review* on October 10, 2004, Russell Baker speaks for many readers when he appears placidly unconcerned about the fundamental question of how the "documentary" on the Korean War interweaves with the fictitious, or the memoirist-protagonist Yu Yuan with the fiction writer Ha Jin. Lauding *War Trash* as a "nearly perfect" novel, a "moral fable, timeless and universal" (pp. 8–9), Baker fails to reflect on the anachronistic nature of the title itself, or its catchy association with "white trash"! Rather than being a historical designation for Korean War veterans in China, "war trash," as we gather from Dwight Garner's interview with the author, seems to have been Ha Jin's own coinage, based on his military experience in the 1970s rather than on research about the Korean War. Asked about the "impetus" for the novel, Ha Jin recalls his fear of captivity, i.e., a soldier would rather commit suicide than return to China as a POW, who "would be treated like the dregs of society" ("Somehow I Couldn't Stop" 2004, p. 9). *War Trash* is no exception in Ha Jin's oeuvre in that his representation of Maoist China—from the book's title and its operative trope to the nightmarish scenario—is predetermined by the writer's "gothic" sensibility.[10]

Indeed, the morbid is Ha Jin's muse. Without the insulation of fiction's plot, Ha Jin's poetry showcases his penchant for the monstrous most fully. His collection of poems *Wreckage* (2001) drives home the point that, to the writer, wreckage inspires through its shock value. For good reason he is known as a novelist rather than a poet. In prosaic, nondescript lines, Ha Jin raids Chinese history for wreckages that are appalling yet salacious. "Human Pig" deals with a concubine, rendered blind, deaf, mute, with her limbs cut off, and incarcerated in an outhouse. The concluding stanza is unequivocally Ha Jin's:

> The Empress often led her guests to
> The pigpen. They'd empty
> Their bowels and bladders in there.
> Sometimes a flagon tipped,
> Wine trickled through a hole—
> Burbling on the smacking lips.

In images sickening beyond words, Ha Jin outdoes his ancestors in devising legendary tortures. As if dubbing a historical disfigurement, he coldly exploits what is utterly shameful and painful in China. His detached voice continues to take English readers through a gallery of grotesques, savoring every physical mutilation in the process of castrating eunuchs and binding the feet of young girls. Ha Jin's poetry dubs Dynastic China just as his fiction does Maoist China.

Ha Jin's fellow expatriate, the actress-turned-filmmaker Joan Chen, gives us *Xiu Xiu: The Sent Down Girl*. Its English subtitle hinges on Western knowledge of the tumultuous Cultural Revolution, during which millions of urban youths are dispatched to the countryside and remote areas for re-education. The film's Chinese title *Tianyu (Sky bath)* relies on Chinese knowledge of the Tibetan custom of spiritual cleansing by water. An innocent city girl stranded on China's Western frontier, the protagonist Xiu Xiu attempts to obtain authorization (*zhangzi* or "official seals/stamps") for her repatriation by giving freely of her body. Multiple rapes and Xiu Xiu's gradual emotional dissolution unfold in front of her "guardian," Lao Jin, a castrated Tibetan shepherd. A synecdoche of Tibet, gentle, loving Lao Jin is powerless to protect his ward: both women and minorities are raped. The film ends with their twin suicides, their bodies romantically cleansed by water and buried in snow on the ridge of a hill.

## "In my end is my beginning"[11]

Where is diasporic discourse going? Will it turn its attention to the West—the un/familiar here and now? If so, will it be accepted as part of American, French, or other national literature? Will Asian Americans and their counterparts in France and elsewhere embrace it as their own? Will the majority of the public?

Will diasporics write in their mother tongue? Will that sound like a re-dubbing of their English and other Western-language dubbing? Will the Motherland find un/intelligible the voice of her "native" sons and daughters?

Or will diasporics continue dubbing and rubbing Maoist China?

Rather than making an either-or choice, a diasporic must, by cultural and linguistic necessities, be a chameleon with a forked tongue, changing color, stalking prey. Yet a chameleon that is too glib-tongued may be slowed down by its corpulent bulk and may just spell its own end.

# Anime's Atom Dialectic

## From Trauma to Manna

**The** infinitesimal atoms clashed midair in 1945, triggering the infinitude of the mushroom cloud over not only Hiroshima but our nuclear age. Presented as simultaneously Apocalypse and Armageddon, massive cataclysms in postwar Godzilla movies and Japanese animations—those of Katsuhiro Otomo, Mamoru Oshii, and Hayao Miyazaki—are often reflected in the pupils of a child, teen, or young protagonist: the incomprehensible balanced by the inconsequential; cornucopia by destitution; the cosmic by the comic; extreme human conditions by miniaturized bugs or critter "familiars"; a "gift" from the West by legacy of ancient Japan. Inspired by the double-entendre of "atom" for both the smallest particle of matter and for the Bomb, Godzilla movies and anime, especially by Otomo and Oshii, seem to share an "atom dialectic" that yokes such binary opposites of miniature, diminutive, and subliminal that is the atomic molecule, on the one hand, and transcendent, hyperbolic, and sublime that is nothing short of the atomic apocalypse, on the other. While an atomic reaction resembles Walter Benjamin's mechanical reproduction in its predictability—thoroughly programmable, repeatable, and subject to human control—this chain reaction inexorably leads to unfathomable nuclear holocaust. Hence, an atom dialectic arises as a postwar totalizing strategy, in Jerome Shapiro's terms from *Atomic Bomb Cinema* (2002), to restore "harmony and balance" (p. 271). Shapiro's argument pays tribute to the Japanese tradition stressing order and equilibrium. Nevertheless, if one looks at such an atom dialectic askance, somewhat skeptically, Otomo's and Oshii's fixation on binarism does not so much neutralize and transcend the extremes as obliterate contingencies in between.[1] By virtue of an aesthetic and mystical superstructure, these filmmakers alchemize Western modernity, the most traumatizing of which landed in 1945, into a godsend or "manna" fallen from the sky, suppressing the politics of race, or East-West relationships, and the politics of gender, or woman-man relationships. At first blush, anime appears to resolve racial, cultural, and sexual power differentials in a futuristic dystopia (Otomo and Oshii) or utopia (Miyazaki), yet the totalizing narrative veils Japanese idolization of the West, exoticization of China, and subjugation of women.

The prevailing complaint about the convoluted plots of anime, indeed much of Asian cinema, stems from the Western insistence on a linear, logical, analytical story line. By contrast, anime by Otomo and Oshii favors a holistic, circular, and atmospheric narrative. While the West treats with suspicion, even contempt, deviation from rational, "realistic" progression, these creators of anime fantasy by and large shun "realism" as a tyranny of the head, opting instead for feelings from the heart. One "gut reaction" is anime's atom dialectic in which any existence already suggests the opposite, but in a contrapuntal rather than a contestational arrangement. Opposites abound in anime so much that one is tempted to proclaim this atom dialectic the ultimate organizing principle. The impotent adolescent in *Akira* (1988) turns messianic, yet his atomic power proves self-destructive. The identical twin witches of evil and good in Miyazaki's *Spirited Away* (2001) are cast in Western images: the West is both destroyer and savior, bringing damnation but also redemption. The horror brought on by the Other in anime is formulaically softened and absorbed, trauma metamorphosed into manna. *Ghost in the Shell* (1995 and its sequel in 2004) blurs human and machine, spirit and matter, "I" and "non-I," "eye/visual" and "non-eye/soundtrack." Blurring—say, an idealized Asian melon-seed or oval face (*guazi lian* in Mandarin) with blue-eye inlay as in an Amerasian face—calls attention to differences within its own composition. Synthesis is as much a radical departure for the future as traces of lost origins of thesis and antithesis. Since the bodies of the largely Western-looking characters in anime, particularly by Oshii, are dubbed in Japanese and then re-dubbed in English for the world market, we have to wonder whether Japanese anxieties animate Western marionettes or postmodern—indeed posthuman—anxieties animate *ukiyo-e-* and *bunraku*-inflected cyborgs. But let us return to atom dialectic, which is, in essence, montage of opposites.

The anime pattern of juxtaposing and thus resolving confrontations emerged at least as early as the postwar Godzilla movies. Some critics even trace this characteristic to traditional Japanese art.[2] Inoshiro Honda's 1956 film— later reworked by Terry Morse as *Godzilla* and starring Raymond Burr as an American journalist—concerns a prehistoric monster awakened by nuclear bombs.[3] Godzilla inaugurates its urban rampage by smashing a train, symbol of industrialization and modernity. Eyewitness-journalist Burr then describes Godzilla breaking through the last defense of Tokyo, high-voltage electric wires and transmission towers that ring the city. Not only does electricity drive modern civilization but it also constitutes a protective circle. When this circle of balance is broken, the Godzilla saga tries time and again to mend it, as Takao Okawara's *Godzilla and Mothra* (1992) demonstrates. The urge for restoration leads Okawara's film to pair evil with good with such inane regularity that it resembles a child's make-believe. Consequently, the destructive Godzilla is balanced by the good Mothra, a giant moth in the image of the traditionally venerated silkworm,[4] who is in turn balanced by the evil Battra, except that Battra turns out to be good after all since Battra originally intends to head off the millennial meteor strike against the earth. Battra then joins forces with Mothra to defeat Godzilla. The beeping insect communications between Mothra and Battra are translated for us by Earth Cosmos, miniature twin fairies resembling Tinker Bell, but with more girlish, coquettish body language, fluffy sequined dresses, hair braids twirled into buns, in-sync singing and hand gestures. A pair that are mirror images rather than opposites, their duet summons Mothra, its primal force apparently responding to the call of innocence. Mothra charges ahead to locate Earth Cosmos, annihilating a city along the way. Good turns destructive with equal ruthlessness.

There exist even the good boss (government officials) and the evil boss (a greedy capitalist and his corporation), who monitor the final showdown between the beasts. This duel takes place at Yokohama's seaside amusement park, and Godzilla is brought down by a Ferris wheel. The quintessential gadget of childhood fun defuses the downfall of this monster. Similar to the roller coaster, the Ferris wheel elevates the rider to a dizzying height, the thrill of the ride deriving from the potential horror of falling. The proximity of fear and fun lies in Godzilla as well, which constantly deflates its own horror in order to be entertaining. Its painfully slow, toy-like, lumbering gait and its radioactive light beams and fires have to look fake; the audience has to be able to "see through" the crude special effects to feel in control. Given that Godzilla is the genie unleashed by nuclear power, both Japanese and American viewers turn the trauma, past and ongoing in the global nuclear stalemate, into a joke, albeit a nervous joke endlessly circulated to veil anxiety. When it was retold by Roland Emmerich in 1998, *Godzilla* proved to be a box-office flop, even though the special effects far surpassed its Japanese predecessors. Hollywood has outdone itself; the monster is so fast and malicious that it ceases to endear.

Otomo's classic *Akira* (1988) is set in postnuclear urban ruins, where rebellious, almost nihilistic young biker gangs roam the streets. In "Akira and the Postnuclear Sublime" (1996), Freda Freidberg comments that "*Akira* was made...by and for a generation of Japanese who have no personal memory of Hiroshima and Nagasaki" (p. 92). Shapiro concurs: "*Akira* is more about the crises inherent in contemporary Japanese youth culture than what the bomb means" (*Atomic Bomb Cinema* 2002, p. 258). An assault of imagery and sound, *Akira* exemplifies the puerile drive to transcend boundaries by every means: speeding motorcycles, hallucinogenic trippin', ESP, human-machine interface or cyborgization. The zeal with which this film weds all differences to herald an apocalypse reminds us of John's Revelation as well as teenage angst turning into self-aggrandizement. An atom dialectic lurks behind the god-like Akira, whose remains preserved in test tubes include human tissue and computer chips, and behind Tetsuo, Akira incarnate, whose prosthetic arm swells up in the finale to devour Tetsuo himself. The bloated limb and body strikes one as a grotesque human body turned inside out, with organs, muscle tissue, blood vessels, and whatnot released from the prison of body to cannibalize the universe. The irony lies in the fact that just as the Self becomes the cosmos, Tetsuo—a newborn stuck in the birth canal, as it were—cries for help. Both life and death, alpha and omega, seem inherent in any apocalypse. Otomo follows the same logic by placing the three prophets, who speak with children's voices yet look like old men and women, in a nursery. These three "naughty" kids turn teddy bears into colossal Techno-Golems to intimidate Tetsuo. A mythical, rambunctious Leech Child himself,[5] Tetsuo wreaks havoc, smashing the nursery walls made of Lego blocks, and then, awash in a flood of milk, regresses to the fetal state.

If *Akira* indulges in child's play, Oshii's *Ghost in the Shell I* and *II* play with the big boys. Devoid of Otomo's sensory overload, with its restlessness and apocalyptic eruptions, Oshii's style is almost static and pensive. Oshii's sci-fi characters articulate their atomization and melancholia with intellectual reflections and citations from the Bible, Milton, and other classics, which would be downright boring for younger audiences. But this contemplative streak befits Oshii's theme of the yoking of human and machine, since the cyborg crime-fighters, Major Motoko Kusanagi and Batou, are plagued by self-doubt in their pursuit of the Puppet Master. Their physical perfection—Batou's towering, Schwarzenegger body and the Major's equally muscular yet curvaceous form—is debunked by obvious flaws. The most blatant is where their "ghosts" or souls would reside amidst prostheses, synthetic rubber, and metal exoskeleton, if all they have left of human residuals are their brains and memories.[6] After all, anime's favorite power suits—akin to a cyborg's robotic exterior—resemble the lowly insect's exoskeleton. Kinship with bugs aside, many critics have bemoaned the ill-defined "ghost" throughout these two films, but it remains beyond grasp, phantom-like, a mystery of life and death. Although powerless to unravel what is essentially the human soul, Oshii montages visual and sound to highlight the mystery.

Voice, sprung from inside the body, has long been viewed as representative of thoughts and even the human soul. In films, a voice-over, originating ex-diegetically, has often been regarded as the omniscient, god-like viewpoint. As opposed to the hypothetical oneness of body and voice—and by extension, of body and soul—Oshii calls attention to the dubbing of anime, with characters serving as "shells" whose voice or ghost is being dubbed. Often a still or slow-moving camera lingers on a character's pose, as if the mise-en-scène of a motion picture has given way to the frame of a comic book. Characters stay still, even their lips, despite the running dialogue. Oshii creates a Brechtian alienation effect by highlighting not only anime as constructed rather than authentic, but reality itself. By separating body and voice, as it is in ventriloquism, Oshii sheds light on the duplicity of human actions, the alleged "oneness" of each individual and the "wholeness" of humankind as nothing more than romantic rhetoric. When lips and words do coincide, after a silent, "virtual" conversation, they always punctuate an emotional outburst. Like a spurned lover, Batou explodes to warn the Major not to cut him off in her dive into the Puppet Master, which Batou compares to a "Double Suicide" after Chikamatsu's eighteenth-century *bunraku* play. After an elaborate account of his life, the Puppet Master, in the shape of a mutilated blonde, abruptly raises its head and proclaims: "I am a life-form born in the sea of information." Set against ventriloquist performances, these two moments jolt our consciousness because, ironically, the characters behave normally.

In addition to the general disconnect between body and voice or soul, there are two specific flaws in the heads of the two cyborgs: Batou "wears" his infrared eyes like jewelers' monocles; the nape of the Major's neck has a four-hole receptacle. This high-tech equipment allows them to operate; for instance, Batou can spot a hacker veiled in thermoptic camouflage, but he will forever see the world through a screen, a mediation aptly captured in "For now we see through a glass, darkly" (1 Cor. 13: 12). This biblical line falls, literally, from the sky during a night excursion the Major and Batou make on board a boat. Amidst stunning cinematography, they hear what Brian Ruh, in *Stray Dog of Anime* (2004), identifies as the theme song, sung in the ancient Yamato language, about a god descending from the heavens (p. 135). Biblical passage and Shinto chant join to enlighten the robots.

The epiphany occurs as the Major in the foreground becomes progressively smaller and the cityscape in the background grows progressively larger, as if there were two cameras shooting simultaneously, making the Major recede from, and the cityscape loom closer to, the audience. The dual perspectives create the effect of shrinking the Major into a looming metropolis. Her reflection leads to self-effacement. Contrary to Descartes, the Major thinks, therefore she is not. The same technique is deployed at the climax of *Ghost II,* in which the most human of the security team, Togusa, turns into a mixture of robot, Western marionette, and *bunraku* puppet, shambling toward the camera without getting visibly larger, whereas bookshelves in the background that frame the shot increase in size.

The boat ride is intercut with multiple shots of highrises along the canal. The Major looks up to find her mirror image in an office cubicle looking down at her. In display cases are mannequins with stumps for arms, an image that flashes back to the Major's "birth" or assemblage in a laboratory's "amniotic fluid" and that foreshadows the Major's mutilation at the end. With the life-less mannequins as her doppelgangers, the Major accepts the danger of "falls" from humanity in an unremitting search for self.[7] Her boat ride comes after her dive into the ocean depths, an inverse of the laboratory process, to return to the source of all life. But as Batou grimly observes, diving as a hobby is suicidal in view of the weight of a robotic body. In the opening sequence, the Major executes a free fall to shatter a fish tank, which is a mere hologram, and the head of a diplomat, which is a robot. The Major is bent upon annihilat-ing illusions, reminiscent of the Buddhist sword of wisdom, with the ultimate aim of ego elimination, which the Major accomplishes on the boat, albeit fleetingly. In the final sequence, the Major drops from a helicopter to a glass-roofed museum, and then into the Puppet Master's mind, which is the net, the sea of information. The Major's final plunge into the source culminates the leitmotif of looking back in melancholia. These stylized, prolonged sequences of head movement are always preceded by the character's stillness to intensify the subsequent action. For example, the Major pauses before turning around to look at the mutilated blonde, the host for the Puppet Master. The Major senses a kinship with the blonde, although their faces are drawn as the ideal-ized Japanese melon-seed or oval face in the shape of a teardrop as opposed to the idealized Caucasian slender face with sharp, strong jaw lines. Both, however, have blue eyes, the Major's in a lighter shade.

The stylized Western features of anime characters have received some critical attention. Commenting on Hayao Miyazaki's *Nausicaä of the Valley of the Winds* (1984), Shapiro finds the characters and locale "Slavic." The protago-nist Nausicaä has "exaggerated 'Western' features—for example, her hyper-bolic round eyes (a common feature of most anime characters), hourglass body shape that never quite looks good in kimono, and revealing short skirt," char-acteristics that make her "highly erotic and exotic" (*Atomic Bomb Cinema* 2002, p. 268). Shapiro attributes this Westernization of characters to a Japa-nese deflection of private, personal longings, since Japanese are not wont to make public confessions: "In a culture where talking openly about problems is abhorrent, one of the functions of these erotic and exotic depictions of fantastic foreign peoples and environments is a mechanism for the displacement and projection of anxieties about Japan" (pp. 268–269). Antonia Levi, in *Samurai from Outer Space* (1996), recounts her firsthand experience of querying Japanese friends about the Caucasian features of anime characters. The Japanese professed bafflement, since "[w]hat began as a portrayal of Westerners, became a distinctive style in *shojo manga* [sic]" (p. 11), its origin or original intention lost. Fans revel in these Western supermodel images; indeed, fans identify with them emotionally, without thinking about them. The Brechtian alienation effect, which compels viewers to think critically rather than to identify empathetically with images, turns out to be short-lived after the ventriloquist body. Anime fans, particularly males, repress the phantasmagoric Westernization in anime images so that they can revel in male fantasy, notwithstanding the female characters' disproportionately inflated eyes, hair, breasts, and legs.

This gender studies approach may constitute the best retort yet of Toshiya Ueno's "Techno-Orientalism." In "Techno-Orientalism and Media-Tribalism" (1999), he asserts: "If the Orient was constructed and invented by the West to build up its cultural identity, then the Techno-Orient has been invented to define the images and models of information capitalism and the information society" (p. 97).[8] Ruh refutes this, stating that rather than a Western perception of anime Techno-Orientalism, "the Japanese are responsible for the propagation of Techno-Orientalist formulations of themselves in the West," for instance, the Japanese self-image as "the Robot Kingdom" (*Stray Dog of Anime* 2004, p. 129). Ruh fails to see that the strongest evidence against Techno-Orientalism lies in anime's male fantasy that Occidentalizes female characters. In other words, the West does not formulate a new Orientalism; it is Japan that Occidentalizes itself, or specifically, its women. Restricting his critique to race and culture, Ruh even defends what is clearly sexism: "Nudity in such a context [*Ghost*'s opening scene of the Major's birth] should not be interpreted as necessarily being sexual, but rather portrays the cyborg Kusanagi as more human" (p. 133). Ruh dodges into semantics, since few humans are born with full adult breasts, erect nipples, bare buttocks and loins, all shown in close-ups, all captured by a voyeuristic camera, so low-angled that it simulates a peep up the short skirt. Ruh's appeal to the universality of humanity—a typical white male maneuver to suppress the issue of power—misses the opportunity to interrogate male stylization of females cross-culturally, which problematizes Ueno's thesis based on the demarcation of the Orient and the Occident.

Oshii's films appear to empower women, as is evidenced by the perfectly toned Major, but they are equally littered with violated female bodies, the

Major's and the blonde's severed limbs in *Ghost I* and the identical sexaroids' ripped-open bodies and faces in *Ghost II*. The Major's body never quite crosses into androgyny, as do certain, pardon the expression, flat-chested female body builders. The Major's muscles, in fact, serve as a tease to accentuate her feminine lines. Her male-inflected physique and soldier-like resolve and single-mindedness are ultimately self-destructive, however, as if female self-empowerment is doomed. She meets a tragic end when she relentlessly pursues her objective of recovering the Puppet Master. The Major leaps on top of the kidnappers' armored tank and makes a last-ditch attempt to open its hatch. In a scene punctuated by mournful music, the Major squats like a weight lifter to force open the hatch. Her muscles ripple ominously through her back and arms, until the strain tears her limbs off and wiring, metal, and rubber burst out. Her body contorts, sending her head up in what appears to be a sigh. We expect a look of shock or pain, but her face is half shielded by tinted, wrap-around goggles that suppress her individuality and humanity.[9] Viewers are drawn, instead, to the center of the frame where the intact breasts and nipples protrude amidst splinters. This pattern of kneading masculinity and eroticism together repeats in every single shot showcasing her manly strength. Shots from the back and the side capture her muscles tensing like armies of ants burrowing under the skin, yet this grotesquerie is attenuated by the beauty of the breasts and nipples in the same frame. The masculine aggressiveness—going it alone, attempting to pry open the hatch—results in self-inflicted violence. Oshii has ingeniously devised politically correct female empowerment, while undercutting it by having females undercut themselves as they overstep the limitations of femininity. The Major is shown to exhibit more brawn than brain: the Puppet Master is actually in the car underneath the tank, not in the tank, as Batou easily discovers after he rescues the Major (just another female in distress).

A mutilated nude like the blonde, the Major executes her final plunge into the Puppet Master with the help of two saviors, both male: Batou shields her brain from attack, sacrificing his left arm, and the Puppet Master, who is dubbed with a male voice, takes her in so that both can die to be reborn into a new entity. The Major questions the merger in a frail, timid, nearly shaking tone, only to be met by the Puppet Master's stern reproach that the Major is clinging onto "I," forgoing his domain that is as overwhelming as the blinding sun. Like the double perspective on the boat ride, Oshii draws from Buddhist self-effacement the transcendental vision, which is pontificated, ironically, by a superior male consciousness. In view of the master-disciple relationship, the Major's human brain, rather than the Puppet Master's "vast and limitless" net, is the vessel from which a new life form is conceived. This resembles the Immaculate Conception where the Holy Spirit's breath, or the Puppet Master's solemn voice in this case, finds a conduit or a surrogate mother in the Major.

Male fantasy of the ultimate female subjugation surfaces in *Ghost II* as well when a sexaroid, after killing several people, whispers to Batou, "Help me." Her girlish vulnerability belies the macabre exoskeleton exposed suddenly as her body and face rip apart. Pedophiliac desirability and demonic reprehensibility entwine once again in the finale. Batou and the Major, now downloaded from the Web into a sexaroid, battle hundreds of identical sexaroids, all half-finished, with plate-like torsos and limbs and the awkward gait of shy teenage girls. But bodily rawness sharpens the sensuality of their blue eyes and red lips. A Dr. Haraway—modeled after Donna Haraway, the author of "A Manifesto of Cyborgs"—points out that the sexaroid in the opening sequence is attempting suicide before being blown apart by Batou. Oshii's deployment of this politically correct aside in favor of feminized cyborgs does not detract from the repeated, though veiled, assaults on femininity in both films. And this, in turn, is linked to sexploitation in anime such as *Ninja Scroll* (*Kawajiri*, 1995) and in earlier Japanese art, such as Hokusai's and Yoshitoshi's woodblock prints and erotica. The most notorious of these, perhaps, is Hokusai's "A Pearl Diver and Two Octopuses" (1814), which features two octopuses sucking a naked woman's mouth and vagina.

The tortuous story line concludes as Batou and the Major discover that the yakuza kidnap young girls and dub their souls or ghosts into sexaroids. Unabashedly, Oshii avails himself of clichéd tropes such as the yakuza. When his films require exotic settings beyond the violent episodes justified by the yakuza, Oshii borrows as much from stereotypes of the West as from those of China long in existence in Japanese art. Many of Hokusai's woodblock prints and drawings illustrate Chinese classics and visualize Chinese characters after a fashion. As J. Hiller cautions, however, in *Hokusai* (1978): "But too much stress should not be placed on the Chinese character of his drawing...the men have exotic-looking whiskers and are accoutred in outlandish armour." Hiller concludes: "[T]he drawings are very much Hokusai and only superficially Chinese" (p. 46). Not only Oshii but almost all the films considered thus far continue this Japanese version of chinoiserie. Godzilla's attacks are often prefaced by a fleeting shot of Chinatown's proverbial arch, as in *Godzilla and Mothra*. Anime from *Akira* to *Ghost II* manage to set their action in unidentified cities suspiciously like Hong Kong or Chinatown with store signs and advertisements in Chinese.[10] Whereas cyberpunk-inspired sci-fi revolves around sets like *Blade Runner*'s Tokyo-inflected metropolis, Japanese animation exoticizes through Chinese-inflected imageries. This is yet another pair in the "atom dialectic": projecting into a future dominated by Western science and technology, anime regresses to a Japanese past, a time when Chinese influence was prominent.

Likewise, *Akira* shows in the midst of its urban ruins a store sign of "Chunghua xuan," a high-flown name for a Chinese restaurant. Sino-exoticism culminates in *Ghost II.* Not only does Chinese food, such as "Kuailai Dumpling" ("come soon" dumpling), predictably greet the viewer but two entire segments are set, not in Roland Barthes's construct called Japan, but in Oshii's construct called China.[11] Batou's residence lies in the Chinatown ghetto, where he nightly shops at the Chinese grocery store *(wan shi hua chao shi)* for canned food for his basset hound, a recurring symbol of human/cyborg alienation. Basset hounds, once valued hunting dogs because of their keen sense of smell, are reduced to pets in the urban jungle, and serve only to demonstrate that humanoids seek in vain for warmth and love in postmodern atomization. Batou who has lost the Major and the basset hound whose nose picks up the scent of canned dog food keep each other company.

As Batou and Togusa venture into an outlying city to investigate the sexaroid crime, they descend into a sequence bathed in orange and yellow tones as opposed to dark gray of the rest of the film. Their hawk-like ship lands on what appears to be a gothic cathedral with flying buttresses, yet statues of Guan Gung (Chinese god of war) rather than Christian saints stand atop the pillars. The camera pans in slow motion across a Chinese-themed parade of floats, accompanied by the theme music of the Shinto chant from *Ghost I;* we see an array of pagodas, temples, arch bridges with Chinese characters advertising Baishi Yagao (White Gentleman Toothpaste).[12] Under the canopy of classical architecture, with lavish costumes and deafening gongs and cymbals, a Beijing Opera is in progress, complete with still tableaux that complement the cessation of music. Gigantic gods and demons saunter past, played by stuntmen on stilts, a common sight in folk festivals in Hong Kong, Taiwan, and China at large. This extravaganza of Orientalism, nevertheless, shifts to kids in ghost masks scurrying into dark tunnels and sewage canals, where Batou and Togusa locate the criminal Lin. Consistent with classic Orientalism, sensory luxuriousness turns into horror, the aesthetic into the abominable. The lowlife Lin puts them on the trail of the computer hacker Kim at the Locus Solus castle. It is worth noting that both shady characters are given Chinese- or Korean-sounding names. Blending of chinoiserie and the West materializes at Kim's castle, where the stained glass is actually etched with Chinese latticework. Four-character poems in kanji are in display on the temple walls as well as projected into the air in subsequent scenes. The fact that these poems in an unfamiliar language vanish before even a native-speaker can possibly grasp their elusive meaning adds to the mystique Oshii tries to cultivate. Not only Chinese characters and images, but the Cantonese dialect contributes to exoticism: as Batou breaks into the Locus Solus vessel, the computer firewall converses in muffled Cantonese. Aside from the omnipresent Western physique of the characters' bodies and the chinoiserie-inflected scenes, one particular racial stereotype stands out. Early in *Ghost I*, a computer hacker appears darker of skin than the others, with vaguely semitic facial features. In the hacker's ruthless, indiscriminate strafing of city streets, Oshii evokes the fear of Middle Eastern Muslim terrorists. But as the hacker succumbs to the Major, his sunshades fall, revealing two Hasidic sidelocks. The atom dialectic combines even feuding parties like the stereotypical Arab terrorist and the orthodox Jew into one semitic-looking character.

To domesticate trauma into manna, anime—particularly the anime of Otomo and Oshii—becomes an omnivore of polarities. In the end, trauma is suppressed in Japan's animated fancy. That suppression persists in the anime subculture in the United States, as throngs of young American fans crowd around the anime section in bookstores. Expanding from this subculture of printed anime, film directors such as the Wachowski brothers and Quentin Tarantino have introduced anime style to the mainstream American audience. Anime-inspired, *The Matrix* trilogy borrow freely from Otomo and Oshii in terms of plot, visual effects, action sequences, and dialogue, in a manner close to Fredric Jameson's postmodern pastiche. The Wachowskis released *Animatrix* (2003), a collection of animated shorts echoing the live-action *The Matrix*. One is not sure whether *Animatrix* is a spin-off of *The Matrix*, or the other way around, for *The Matrix* can be viewed as a spin-off of anime. Like Neo, whose name is an anagram of "One" as in "The One," much cultural production revolving around anime is characterized by this simulacrum of an original idea that no longer identifies itself. The valorizing of feature films over tie-ins such as video games and toys is immediately challenged by the large number of feature films that stem from comics and anime, which may be inspired by Japanese paintings and woodblock prints. A segment in *Animatrix* entitled "Program" illustrates computer sparring programs between a samurai and his lover, who fight in settings reminiscent of Japanese classical art and even the ubiquitous bamboo groves of kung fu films.[13] The final showdown takes place precariously on the rooftop of an ancient building with geometric tiles and upcurving roof corners. This vertigo of an image comes from Yoshitoshi's 1885 woodblock print "Two Brave Men on the Roof of Horyukaku."[14]

With his signature excess of graphic violence, peppered with black humor, Tarantino's *Kill Bill I* and *II* (2003 and 2005) trade guns for samurai swords and kung fu fighting. Blessed with directorial manna from the East, Tarantino even pays tribute to anime by integrating the Japanese company Production I. G.'s seven-minute-long animated segment, "The Origin of O-Ren," into *Kill Bill I*, which consists of nineteen segments in total. Production I. G. has to its credit *Ghost in the Shell I* and *II* and many other anime. "The Origin of O-Ren" is a flashback of the Bride's. The Uma Thurman character survives the slaughter perpetrated by O-Ren and others and is about to embark upon her revenge. Production I. G. follows what I call the "atom dialectic" in yoking victim and victimizer. Inherent in the kung fu genre's archetype of vengeance, the roles of avenger and culprit keep shifting. In a voice-over, the Bride narrates nine-year-old O-Ren's trauma at witnessing the murder of her parents by a yakuza boss and his henchmen, followed by her revenge, in which she poses as a schoolgirl to gain access to the pedophile boss to kill him, and her ensuing career as a professional killer. And this circles back to the Bride's own assassin past and her imminent revenge. An unending cycle, the traumatized comes to inflict even more violence. But violence is somehow contained in the medium of animation. *Kill Bill I* earns only an R-rating as it smuggles in the Japanese yakuza bloodbaths and schoolgirl porn made world-renowned by certain manga and anime, joined perhaps by Takeshi Kitano's gangster movies.

The shock of transgression in "The Origin of O-Ren" is amplified through contrasts to the point where the contrasts merge into one. Recurring motifs echo and reinforce one another, an aesthetic of polarities set to a fugue of refrains. The child O-Ren hides under a bed to escape detection; she later exacts her revenge while hiding under the yakuza boss's bed. Earlier, her father's blood splashes out in slow motion, and her mother's blood seeps through the mattress and drips on her cheeks. Avenging her parents, O-Ren, astride the yakuza boss, executes a similar blood-letting. When O-Ren finally reaches the pinnacle of her profession, her fingernails are painted bloody red as she pulls the trigger on the rooftop. Graphic images of gushing blood, gouged eyes, and severed limbs are intensified because they are seen from the point of view of an innocent girl. Violence is counterpointed by pathos: in the comics convention of dialogue bubbles, "WHIMPER" materializes from the girl in hiding, and then her whisper of "Mommy." Here and elsewhere, Production I. G. montages seemingly contradictory images and soundtrack to heighten the dramatic effect. When O-Ren's eyes travel up the samurai sword to commit to memory the face of her father's killer—who is, by the way, never killed—the camera's pan up the length of the blood-stained sword is accompanied by spaghetti Western music. Visual and auditory incongruity arises yet again in the slaying of the pedophile. Thrusting the sword deep into the yakuza boss, who grits his teeth until they snap, the girl urges demurely, in cute, schoolgirl Japanese, "Take a good look at my face...look at my eyes...look at my mouth. Do I look familiar? Do I remind you of someone you murdered?" East and West are the ultimate pair in Tarantino's "atom dialectic"—he has a Japanese company, the martial arts choreographer Yuen Wo-Ping, Sonny Chiba, and Gordon Liu co-opted into a Hollywood production. Lucy Liu, a Chinese American who plays a mixed-race Japanese character, is a product of the West who has assumed "yellowface" rather than mainstream American roles throughout her Hollywood career. The fact that an Asian American continues to play Asian and not American roles, and in this case, a stereotype of Dragon Lady, bodes ill for racial and ethnic equality. Liu's dilemma epitomizes the politics of race, culture, and sex mentioned at the outset of this chapter. There I attributed the Caucasian physical features of anime characters to a yearning to identify with, or at least to lean on, the West. The reverse is true in the films of Tarantino, the Wachowskis, and other Western directors who have incorporated the East. Just because they utilize Asian bodies and motifs filmically does not alter the fundamental power imbalance. Furthermore, by joining the anime market, these American filmmakers contribute to the global dissemination of manna without trauma, pleasure without pain, euphoria without withdrawal—the new opiate for our millennium.

# Intercut on
## the Korean Wave

# 7   The O of Han Ju

## Those Full, (Over)Painted Lips that Dare to Confess

### Opening Credits: Korean Wave

Like wildfire since the 1990s, Han Ju or Han Chao—the Chinese name for Korean television dramas, or the Korean Wave—has swept across East Asia, Southeast Asia, and Asian diasporic communities in the United States. And I include feature-length films under the rubric of Han Ju. Through promotion by South Korean television companies and multinational contracts, many Asian countries are currently airing Han Ju as prime-time programs.[1] In the United States, Han Ju's circulation in DVD, VCD, and video formats has reached many Asian diasporics as an alternative form of entertainment beyond the American television shows. One only needs to do a random Web search on, for instance, the quintessential Han Ju, *Winter Sonata* (2002), to see how popular it has become. A concrete illustration of the genre's popularity is shown in the largest Chinese-language newspaper in circulation in the United States, *The World Journal*. The entertainment section usually contains eight pages, the front page focuses on Western, primarily American, stars, pages 2 and 3 on Taiwanese, pages 4 and 5 on Hong Kong, pages 6 and 7 on Mainland Chinese, and the last page on Japanese and Korean stars. The only pages in color are pages 1 and 8, on the Western and Japanese/Korean stars, as if they are of equal weight. Han Ju follows previous waves that have reached both sides of the Pacific Ocean, such as the Hong Kong Cantopop stars and Japanese teen idols, culminating in cross-cultural, even global phenomena. Unlike previous waves, however, Han Ju's fans are not restricted to the young; the Korean Wave cuts across cultural divides and age differences. Like fashion, it is nearly impossible to determine what exactly has driven mass psychology in these disparate areas to favor the Korean Wave. As documented in Doobo Shim's "The Rise of the Korean Media in Asia and Glocalization" (2003), the boom of the South Korean economy in recent decades as well as the support of the government and the *chaebol* (business conglomerates) have led to the production and distribution of programs; the economic and cultural ties of the Pacific basin have also no doubt played a crucial role in the Korean Wave. Beyond these external, socioeconomic factors, however, certain motifs are shared by the myriad Korean television dramas and films that appeal to East Asians and diasporic communities.

But first, I should clear up some potential objections to my analysis of Han Ju. Because I do not read Korean, I am uncertain what kind of research has been done on this television genre in its country of origin, other than what has been reported in English- and Chinese-language materials. Rather than being a liability, my approach stems from the transliterated title of the chapter—Han Ju—which makes it clear that I am examining the reverberation of this Korean drama outside of South Korea. The dual emphasis on English- and Chinese-language materials serves to bridge this phenomenon in Asia with the West, which so far has been literally untouched by this rage. This particular collective dream of Han Ju—undying romance of lovers forever young—seems to be resonant only among people of Asian descent, while mainstream American society enjoys its own modern versions of Romeo and Juliet, who are less inhibited, more egotistical than their Korean counterparts. On one side of the Pacific Ocean, from Japan to China to Southeast Asia and, in some cases, leaping across even to Latin America, there is a frenzy over not only Han Ju, but over the stars' costumes and hair styles, the program sets, and more. On the other side, total unawareness among Westerners. The gap between East and West is indeed as wide and deep as the biggest ocean on earth. Compared with Western serial dramas, Han Ju is closer to what Ien Ang calls "prime-time serials," such as *Dallas* and *Dynasty*, rather than day-time soap operas (*Watching Dallas*, 1985). Yet the characterizations of soap operas by Charlotte Brunsdon and others can be applied to Han Ju with just a slight tweaking: "the paradigmatic television genre (domestic, continuous, contemporary, episodic, repetitive, fragmented, and aural)" (*The Feminist, the Housewife, and the Soap Opera* 2000, p. 123). While largely true, the description "contemporary" needs to be negotiated. A number of Han Ju, including *Shan dao (The tao of business)*, are period pieces, set in nineteenth-century Korea.

Another pitfall is that my analysis may be a masculinist, Freudian reading of female bodies, particularly the O or hole of red lips, a reading that is imposed on a feminine narrative form as Tania Modleski's pioneering *Loving with a Vengeance* (1982) argues. Yet as I persist in contrasting Western feminist theories and Han Ju, or West and East, I see my effort as contributing to both. Indeed, the simplistic opposition of female and male needs to be fine-tuned in the presence of Asian feminist writings, such as Angel Lin, Becky Kwan, and Ming Cheung have produced in "The Dilemmas of (Modern) Working Women in (Post-)Confucianist Asia" (2004). At any rate, now that *wuxia pian* (swordplay films) have come to encompass heroines in *Crouching Tiger, Hidden Dragon* (2000) and other films, perhaps Han Ju should expand in the other direction to include male fans launching male gazes illuminated by feminist insights. It is worth noting that the best of Han Ju specializes in female self-effacement, despite the stardom of the actress playing the role. While the sex appeal of actresses is important, an aura of virginal asexuality surrounds the female lead's image. This is in sharp contrast to the display or flaunting of sexuality in U.S. serial dramas. In the following analysis of two specific scenes of lovers parting, one can see immediately the shared motif that individual desires must accommodate social responsibility and conventions.

## Scene 1: Female Repression Unbound

One particular thread stands out in Han Ju. Female repression is repeatedly unfettered in this genre, where the master narrative seems to stipulate that one climax must be a woman's confession of love for a man. However, this emotional outburst is invariably contained by rather than destabilizing to the patriarchal tradition and results in a deferment of female desire in tragedies and in patriarchal legitimization of female desire in comedies. In Asia, while the Korean woman's daring confession no doubt captivates the audience, who are burdened by the heritage of feminine passivity, it may signify less a feminist breakthrough than a subtle boost to the male ego that withholds its affection until the "weaker" sex confides first. This patriarchal interpellation in Han Ju is amazingly similar to that in Western soap operas. In *Love and Ideology in the Afternoon* (1995), Laura Mumford contends that the "paternity plot"—characters in search of their fathers—is a staple. Mumford sees this as a way to ultimately neutralize "woman-centered fantasy ... through the inevitable reestablishment of patriarchal order" (p. 95).

The best metaphor for the paradox of Han Ju's female repression and confession lies in the full, sensuous lips of the leading actress, painted and even overpainted beyond lips proper, to intimate rebelliousness or transgressiveness, even as the lipstick connotes femininity. The tiny fraction of bright, striking color taints beyond the under and the upper lip; this border-crossing verges on the indecent in the same way that bra strap or thong line does. To allow glimpses of the forbidden constitutes a flirting against taboos. This feature in Korean dramas lies at the core of its appeal to Asian female audiences as well as to the volatile Asian communities juggling tradition and modernization. Those full, (over)painted lips that dare to confess in Han Ju have been fetishized to support, simultaneously, old-fashioned femininity and boundary-crossing empowerment.

The Korean preference for full red lips diverges from that of its East Asian neighbors, who see feminine beauty in what the Chinese call *yingtao xiaozuei* (a miniature cherry-like mouth). Now, suddenly, these neighbors are drawn to the charm of full lips—sensuous as well as vocal—just at a time when South Korea itself is being "discovered." A peninsula locked between two strong states and subjected to colonization by both, Korea has historically been ignored, left to eke out a living in utter anonymity. This historical obscurity has contributed to the Korean sense of resignation in the face of suffering, which is punctuated by periodic defiance. A fatalistic acceptance of pain helps maintain the status quo, a pressure cooker that turns the masses into food for the powerful, with the safety valve releasing the excess steam of revolt. The Korean culture expressed in Han Ju retains traditional values to an amazing degree. In fact, Chua Beng Huat sees Korean society as far more intensely interpellated by Confucianist and traditional Chinese ideology than its East Asian neighbors ("Conceptualizing an East Asian Popular Culture" 2004, p. 203). As a consequence, the modernizing and even postmodernist Asian and diasporic communities nostalgically embrace Han Ju's merging of modern and traditional, of West and East, of fast-lane capitalism and timeless romanticism. Han Ju is its fans' collective dream of what they wish to be.

*Shan dao (The way of business, or The tao of business)* was an award-winning television drama in 2002. It revolves around a nineteenth-century romance between Lin, a commoner turned businessman, and Piao, the daughter of his rival. (All names are in Mandarin pronunciations as the version of *Shan dao* I watched is dubbed.)[2] The most striking of female lead Piao's facial features are her full lips that require no overpainting to suggest sensuality. Yet those "ripe" lips remain forever unkissed. The blood feud between Lin and Piao's father (father-in-law, in fact, because he adopted her when the bridegroom suddenly died, a plot twist consistent with serial dramas' recipe of paternity concern and identity change) prevents the lovers from becoming united. Contrary to the formula of romance in China and Japan, Piao is the one who confides her love *first*, but she immediately describes their love as doomed. This pattern of confession of longings followed closely by repression repeats itself: the couple stand side by side during their trysts, bow to each other on the street, cast glances across crowds. Expressions of love are instantly repressed, desire indefinitely deferred, teases never achieving consummation. The element of time in the fifty-episode *Shan dao* is crucial in lengthening and deepening the protagonists' love. Piao takes this paradox to the extreme during the climax, in episode 38, when she takes the initiative of inviting Lin to a secluded location to bid him adieu. She recalls that when she worked in the ginseng fields for her future father-in-law, a geisha passed by. Gazing into Piao's face, the geisha foretold her future in a poem: "Dreaming of a lover, / The one I miss will miss me. / Our dreams will not converge, / Perhaps only in the next life will we meet." Piao adds that she is content to pine for Lin in her dreams. The plot of serial drama unfolds in a prosaic manner, only to explode into lyricism where the action stops in favor of affect and poetry, assisted in no small measure by the theme music. When the lovers, full of sorrow and tears, fall silent, it is as if music speaks for what cannot be said. As the life-story is confided and the poem recited, the camera, naturally, dwells on Piao's tear-streaked face, echoing Laura Mulvey's insights on close-ups of the actress in *Fetishism and Curiosity* (1996): "The star close-up would hold the story in stasis, cutting her image out from the general flow of the narrative, emphasizing her function as spectacle in its own right" (p. 41).

But such a scene is as much about the expression of affect as it is about suppression. The climax of the couple's romance, this adieu occurs at the moment of the total denial of their love. Such love, rendered platonic by circumstances and remaining physically unfulfilled, intensifies the desire. In terms of a heterosexual audience, male viewers find this moving because they project themselves into Lin, to whom Piao confesses. A symptom of narcissism, male fantasy often involves the male imagining himself to be a female imagining himself. To aggrandize the male ego, the male subconsciously *becomes* a female. Female viewers, on the other hand, find the scene moving because they masochistically identify with a woman who must stifle her love at the very moment of revealing it.

Piao's sensuous lips unkissed points to her gender ambivalence. Her unrequited love and emotional vulnerability notwithstanding, she assumes a man's position in managing Sung House, one of the largest business conglomerates in Korea. Treated as the heir apparent by her father, she is not the only manly woman in *Shan dao*. Indeed, Lin's widowed mother is another. But some of Piao's most stunning performances come from her masculine façade, when she holds back her emotions when her father and colleagues discuss her lover's rival business. Repeated shots of the slight knitting of her brows, the movement of her lips, constitute minimalist expressions of her inner repression. Ultimately, Piao chooses responsibility to the business—hers as well as his—over love with Lin, a choice usually reserved for males. Her devotion to her father and the employees of Sung House is completely congruent with Lin's business motto, that businessmen accumulate not capital but "human heart" (or human affection). Likewise, the predatory capitalism that Piao's father embodies is defeated by Lin's honesty and altruism. In a capitalist world where businesses are driven by profit alone, it is ironic of *Shan dao* to anachronistically preach business ethics. How much more tragic, then, that such role models in business, with compassion for humanity, should be deprived of their heart's desire—happiness with each other—exactly because of business considerations!

*Shan dao* deviates from more popular Han Ju, such as *Winter Sonata*, in being a historical drama. This setting leads to a key difference: whereas contemporary dramas invariably locate themselves in a network with the West—the United States and Western Europe—*Shan dao*'s narrative involves Korea's immediate neighbors, China and Japan. The Qing dynasty is shown to be Korea's largest trading partner and the center of culture. Lin launches his career in Beijing due to his mastery of classical Chinese poetry and familiarity with dynastic history. A Zen-like monk foretells the three crises in Lin's life and writes out solutions to them in Chinese script. The tone of admiration for things Chinese is balanced, however, by unscrupulous Qing businessmen and marauding bandits along the border.

Almost every Han Ju has at its core a female feistiness that serves the interests of patriarchy. The long-running Han Ju entitled in Mandarin *Kan le yu kan (Watching it again and again)* features a nurse-protagonist from a modest family background, who wins the love of a prosecutor, a venerable profession in South Korea, in a rivalry with a female intern who occupies a higher rung in the hospital and social hierarchy. The 2000 film *Chunhyang* shows Chunhyang ripping apart her skirt and hanging onto her husband's steed and being dragged along the ground to keep him from leaving. Subsequently courted by a new governor in her husband's absence, Chunhyang would rather endure torture than betray her husband. As a middle-aged man with a raspy voice narrates the entire film in the style of traditional folk performance of drum-accompanied *sopyonje*, Chunhyang's screams during torture coincide with the male "voice-over," her pain and vulnerability "spliced," alloyed, and toughened by his gruffness in a Brechtian alienation effect.[3] Chunhyang has agency, in that she controls her destiny, yet she is also controlled by a male narrator. Furthermore, her agency is directed toward faithfulness to the man who chose her to be his bride. Her loyalty is finally rewarded when her husband returns as the emperor's emissary. In a globalizing East Asia, gender roles have become so destabilized that the female audience projects its yearnings onto strong women whose sacrifices support male dominance, feeling at once empowered as women and secured in tradition. In their joint paper on Korean television drama, Angel Lin and her colleagues testify to that fusion in one of their Hong Kong female interviewees, whose managerial position leads her to identify with the male manager-protagonist in the Han Ju *All About Eve*, while secretly wishing to be the vulnerable actress. Overpainted lips are most conspicuous in ghost films such as *Ghost in Love* (*Zi gui hui* or *Jaguimo* in Korean, Kwang-hoon Lee, 1998), where female ghosts wear black lipstick and eyeliner in Goth fashion. But all the female revenge and violence against men lead to two ghosts being given a new lease on life to continue their love.

## Scene 2: The (W)hole of *Winter Sonata*

The O in my chapter title refers to the roundness of full lips, but also to the circle of Asian and Asian diasporic fans. The largest following of Han Ju is undoubtedly for *Winter Sonata*. *Winter Sonata* is the second installment in Korean director Yun Seok Ho's four-season television drama: *Autumn Tale, Winter Sonata, Summer Scent,* and *Spring Waltz.* While *Summer Scent* pales in comparison, the central theme of trauma and loss runs through all of them: identity switch in *Autumn Tale;* amnesia in *Winter Sonata;* heart transplant in *Summer Scent.* The female lead in *Autumn Tale* loses her identity and upper-class family when she finds out that she was switched as a baby by accident. With its fairy-tale plot of reverse Cinderella, or the princess into the pauper, *Autumn Tale* aims to strike a chord in every audience member who as a child may have imagined being a poor orphan or, on the contrary, having been born rich. The story's greatest potential lies in the element of social class in an archetypal tale. Continuing *Autumn Tale's* motif of bereavement, the O in the chapter title acquires yet another thematic double entendre of (w)hole in *Winter Sonata:* a *hole* is left in the female lead's heart as a result of her lover's death, which she revisits out of Freud's repetition compulsion to feel, subconsciously, *whole.* Winter is a lull in the seasons, life put on hold, in hibernation. Snow erases all differences, as if it were oblivion itself. Yet the protagonists' love bursts forth in the snow when they are high school students; their first love is written in the script of the snow. While the two snowmen they sculpt by the frozen lake will melt away, their love remains steadfast like Polaris, a recurring metaphor throughout. The hole that is the winter constitutes the whole, the totality, of their love.

This fissure exists emotionally as well as sexually. A displacement of female genitalia, the young woman's lips call attention to themselves as an orifice to be filled, an American pornographic rendition of which is *Deep Throat* (1972). However, given that desire deferred is what Han Ju is all about, it is amazingly asexual compared with the flaunted sexuality of Western soaps. The actress Choi Ji Woo in *Winter Sonata* never exhibits more of her body than her angelic face and neck, which suggest virginal purity rather than carnality. Even when the lovers spend several nights together, they are never touched by the rawness of sex. (But is Asian innocence more ridiculous than Hollywood passion, with those predictable bedroom scenes?) Because Choi appears to wear dark-colored tights or stockings and long skirts throughout, and because the camera favors the top third of her body, we do not even recall what her calves look like. Chua Ben Huat likewise observes that "[t]he lead women are beautiful, of course, self-confident with very non-revealing clothes, commonly in formal office wear, showing very little explicit sexuality" ("Conceptualizing an East Asian Popular Culture" 2004, p. 218). Yet sexuality is simultaneously the subtext and the surface sign; sex appeal concentrates on the fetish of her face and, in particular, her red lips.

Anatomically, the external female genitalia, or vulva, consist of the vestibule of the vagina, clitoris, and four folds of tissue called labia majora (greater lips) and labia minora (lesser lips). In Chinese, the labia are *yin chuen,* or vaginal lips. As *yin* is also the homonym for cherry, one can see the association of a woman's cherry lips with her vaginal lips. Consciously or subconsciously, human beings superimpose mouth and lips onto the cavity of the female sexual organ and its exterior rim. The same Freudian logic suggests that those facial features that protrude or are detachable carry phallic potential: Gloucester's eyes are gouged out so he is incapacitated or castrated in *King Lear;* a nose becomes a vain military officer in Nikolai Gogol's story; Robert Arneson gives his 1984 sculpture "General Nuke" at the Hirshhorn Museum in Washington, D.C. a "phallic MX 'peacemaker' missile of a nose." Iconizing Choi's face and lips in *Winter Sonata* sublimates the sexual drive. This is implicit in Freud's "A Mythological Parallel to a Visual Obsession" (1916), where he cites an archeological terracotta image found in Asia Minor; it is "a body of a woman without head and bosom, and with a face drawn on the abdomen: the lifted clothing frames this face like a crown of hair" (pp. 153–154). While mainstream culture like Han Ju displaces sexuality onto the face, "underground" culture "sinks" the face to abdomen, lifting up the skirt or taboo to unite the upper and the lower body as one and the same, driven by the same desires. Lips and vagina must work together to satisfy sexual longing: the one can say its longing but cannot satisfy it; the other can satisfy longing but cannot say it. In Korean drama or popular culture in general, sexual yearning will remain unquenched, a tease, due to a missing mate.

The twenty-episode *Winter Sonata* opens at a provincial high school, whose routine is interrupted by a melancholic transfer student, Joon Sang (Bae Yung Joon). Joon Sang has chosen this school, where his pianist mother grew up, in the secret hope of finding his biological father, but he soon falls in love with innocent, carefree Yu Jin (Choi Ji Woo). The first two episodes focus on their first love, moments of which will repeat religiously in the following eighteen episodes, always accompanied by the theme music. The wintry scene by the lake is beautifully shot, a storehouse of sweet memories, including their first kiss. Yu Jin kisses him first, consistent with the thesis of the lips that dare to confess. Then Joon Sang suddenly dies in a traffic accident and Yu Jin mourns for the next ten years.

At age twenty-eight, a promising interior designer and architect, Yu Jin chances to work for a Ming Yeong, who has recently returned from France and who looks exactly like Joon Sang, except that his hair is dyed reddish. Ming Yeong turns out to be Joon Sang, who developed amnesia after the accident and was "implanted" with new memories via a psychiatrist's hypnotism at the behest of his mother. Yu Jin is torn between her love for Joon Sang's mirror image and her social obligation to Sang Hyuk, her childhood friend and fiancé, and to their families and friends. The seesaw battle of love results in a strained, depressed Yu Jin, whose performance borders on the catatonic, slumped in the seat, her gaze downcast, shrouded in a deathly pall, a beautiful corpse whose only "vital sign" are the tears rolling down. She is, in a way, dead at precisely the moment when Joon Sang returns from the dead. Without memories, an amnesiac is dead to his previous incarnation, so Yu Jin has to retrieve Joon Sang from the dead piece by piece, like a jigsaw puzzle, evoking one memory after another. The plot makes the formulaic paternity discovery, which causes Joon Sang to suspect he may be Yu Jin's half-brother. But deeply in love, he decides to marry Yu Jin anyway. In fact, they literally marry themselves at an empty church, defying social pressures and taboos. While the drama flirts with forbidden love, that it is a self-orchestrated wedding, and a thwarted one at that, downplays the transgressiveness. Once Yu Jin finds out about the possibility of incest, they must break up. Even when Joon Sang eventually realizes that he is Sang Hyuk's rather than Yu Jin's half-brother, he still leaves for the United States, for the aftereffects of his traffic accidents (the second of which jolted him back to his original memory) have begun to threaten his eyesight and even life. The final episode concludes, three years later, as a blind Joon Sang reunites with Yu Jin at a seaside mansion. The mansion has been built according to the miniature model she gave him as a parting gift.

As breathless as this summary sounds, it misses many twists. Nevertheless, the strength of *Winter Sonata* lies not in plot but in the atmosphere of amour created by refrains of images and soundtrack, flashbacks, and interior monologues that delay the consummation of desire and give characters layered interiority. It is hypnotic at times, maddening when overused. The story line unfolds not linearly, but in a looping, circuitous, repetitious fashion. The drama spans over ten years. The characters change their hair styles and, of course, their wardrobes, but they remain young and glamorous, close-ups revealing faces with no trace of wrinkles, not even after copious tears and sleepless nights. Never is a strand of hair out of place, even as Yu Jin hovers on the verge of the psychotic. The close-up shots of faces and head-to-shoulders produce statuesque beauty tantamount to "talking heads," crafting a deceivingly intimate, voyeuristic relationship with viewers. The fetish of face severs the body; the persistent head shots imply a loss reminiscent of lovers' loss. Viewers identify with and seem to possess the face, but they have already lost it. Dennis Porter, in "Soap Time" (1977), contends that a face in close-up is "what before the age of film only a lover or mother ever saw" (p. 786).

At the risk of exhibiting male narcissism myself, allow me to elaborate on this illusion of closeness: when Choi Ji Woo's face appears on the screen, the image enters into my brain. Do I possess Choi or am I possessed? Does she live through me or do I lose myself in her image? When my mind drifts to something else, Choi is forgotten, dead to me. When my thoughts return to Choi, she comes back alive. (Am I being rather absurd, indulging in fantasies over a woman young enough to be my daughter, hence, the incest taboo, the superego on the heels of the id? Yet the hypnotic, trance-like power images exert over the mind is irrefutable.) After a grueling marathon viewing, during which I finished the latter half of *Winter Sonata* in the wee hours one April morning, I caught myself muttering: "Joon Sang Ah!" Yu Jin's endearing address laced with sadness. So immersed or so disoriented was I that I, *in a woman's role,* called for a man. Instead of homoerotic urges, this is the essence of male narcissism in that a male conjures up a female image pining for himself. Ironically, male narcissism entails that a male takes on the voice and identity of a female; self-absorption or self-love turns out to be predicated on merging with an Other. Conventional love, after all, involves two or more people, while male narcissism turns love inward—a male Narcissus, in the guise of a woman, grows enamored with himself. Narcissism is indeed autoerotic or masturbatory, for one *plays* with oneself, without another, except in mental constructs. Deep at the heart of each fan's infatuation glows a magic lantern, from which an Other is created in one's own image. The alternative is to whisper, "Yu Jin Na," thus reminding the Narcissus of Bae Yong Joon's fleshy lips and white teeth that utter those very sounds and thus undermining the illusion of being the desired person. If Han Ju were not so exclusively about heterosexual romance, gender identification and narcissism would need to be reevaluated. Dazzled by stars that seem to shine forever, the viewer is fixated, which deserves some morbid thoughts. After we die, will the bones of Choi Ji Woo and Bae Yong Joon be prettier than mine, or yours? Which Choi and Bae last longer, the perfect faces frozen by the camera or the skulls and the ashes? But these questions seem totally irrelevant to human desires. In other words, we continue to be obsessed with beauty, its biological ephemerality masked by photographic perpetuity.

The paradox of (w)hole lies in the immediacy, yet impersonalization of close-ups. Head shot presents a part, albeit divorced from the body, that seems perfect and whole, that invites fans to form a unity with the image that is beyond reach. Such a paradox is the very definition of fetish: it is there and not there, present and absent. In Freud's male-oriented psychoanalytical theory, the phallus is the origin of fetish: boys develop an oedipal complex and castration anxiety, whereas girls are plagued by "penis envy." What Mumford sees as the "paternity plot" in soap operas plays out in Joon Sang's search for father, the missing phallus, as well as in the absence of fathers for Joon Sang and Yu Jin. The domesticity or family unity inherent in this television genre is broken, and both characters seek to fill that hole, to render it whole again. Their love runs along the same line: they formed a whole as two eighteen-year-olds, but an irreplaceable hole opens in Yu Jin's heart, as she confesses to her mother, after Joon Sang's presumed death. Joon Sang suffers from the same hole, except it lies in his head, his memory. Arguably, both Joon Sang and Yu Jin die in the traffic accident, only the hollow shells of their bodies survive. Then once the reputed father is found, the castration anxiety persists in the sin of incest and in Joon Sang's blindness as a price for that discovery.

The male occupies the limbo state of a fetish, existing physically yet psychically void. As though he were suffering from dementia or Alzheimer's, the amnesiac Joon Sang must be nursed back to his old self; Yu Jin gives him her memories, literally, one piece at a time. Whether through amnesia or sightlessness, male fantasy is consistently regressive, seeking a fetal state within the womb. Similar to the mental gymnastics of a male fantasizing a female fantasizing a male, male narcissism fashions a sense of masculine control on the basis of losing control, a sense of power on the basis of powerlessness. But male fantasy also dichotomizes woman as a menace: The pianist mother "rearranges" Joon Sang's memory in her favor, thus creating a hollow man Ming Yeong; a jealous Chae Lin manipulates the triangular relationship among Ming Yeong, Yu Jin, and Sang Hyuk in order to possess Ming Yeong; Sang Hyuk's mother is biased against her future daughter-in-law, Yu Jin. The transfusion of memories, like blood seeping out of the hole in Yu Jin's heart, culminates in the repeat of the traffic accident. The return of memory, however, means the return of the incest taboo.[4] The point where their love is restored to its pristine state is also the point where its assumed corruption forces them apart. To repossess the fetish coincides with letting it go.

Memory is closely tied to knowing. A loss is a loss only if one remembers, knows what has been lost. Choi's performance peaks when she comes to the realization that Ming Yeong is at once Ming Yeong and Joon Sang. Torn between her obligation to her fiancé, whom she does not love, and her love for Joon Sang, who is half Ming Yeong, she sinks into a catatonic, death-like state. By contrast, Bae Yong Joon's acting throughout this stage exhibits more inner confusion than grief, for he is not haunted by the past. His performance peaks only toward the end, around the second accident and the recovery of his memory. Thereupon, the roles of knowing switch. Joon Sang suffers with his "knowledge" that they may be related by blood, whereas Yu Jin is blithely happy about the prospect of marriage. Yet after a DNA test, the "knowing" about their having the same father turns out to be mis-knowing. Although characters suspect incestuous love, viewers are more secure in their knowledge that this is but a misunderstanding. It is these two levels of knowledge that provide the context for the most heart-wrenching adieu, in episode 19.

One of their last farewells—yes, they say good-bye again in the final episode—takes place at a public park. Strikingly "fresh" like a schoolgirl in a black suit and white blouse buttoned up to her neck—a color contrast repeated in her black hair and fair-skinned face, which is a thematic refrain of her purity despite traumas—Yu Jin moves the scene forward even more slowly than all the others. She inquires after Joon Sang's well-being and he echoes the greeting; she gives him the model mansion she designed, and they apologize to each other. (Next to saying the protagonists' names, apologies come in a close second for frequent speeches—this is indeed a culture of guilt and self-blame.) Consistent with the female initiatives within Han Ju, Yu Jin confesses her love first, reaffirming it as "beautiful" and "not shameful." While the pronouncement verges on the scandalous, the audience already suspects that they are not siblings, since a DNA test is being conducted unbeknownst to them. The rhetorical transgressiveness of Yu Jin's declaration is thus neutralized, defused. In crisply enunciated language, each syllable washed clean, as it were, by teardrops, she states that she will forever remember him until the day she dies and beseeches him to remember her. (Tears are essential, never excessive, always well-placed; they well forth almost at will.) He concurs. Inscribing faces in memory is one of the drama's refrains. At the time of the first traffic accident, a near-crazed Yu Jin feared that she would forget Joon Sang's face, so here, in their final adieu, is a prolonged, silent shot of Joon Sang taking to heart Yu Jin's face. The park scene proceeds as they thank each other three times in the intimate expression: "Go ma wa." The muted performance and the turn of phrasing from agony to gratitude accentuate the inner turmoil they strain to hold back. This exchange is in close-ups and a shot-reverse shot sequence. The intimacy invites viewers, depending on gender and sexual orientation, to identify with either lead. Audience members are visually solicited to carve one image in their own minds. Before the couple turn and walk in opposite directions, Yu Jin asks Joon Sang not to look back, for she does not wish either of them to have in their memory the sight of the other's receding back. Yet the shot-reverse shot as they part does just that, alternating between Yu Jin, in focus, moving toward the camera and Joon Sang, out of focus, moving away, and Joon Sang, in focus, moving toward the camera while Yu Jin moves away. The audience is given an omniscient point of view: we see not only the bereaved faces but the backs of the lovers, increasingly blurred. The audience steals several looks back, Yu Jin's interdict notwithstanding. And, in fact, their whole love has consisted of looking back to their brief time together when they were eighteen.

That *Winter Sonata* is an Asian rather than, say, an American phenomenon can be attributed to the traditional, conservative, repressed love the television drama idealizes. In the process of technological modernization and cultural Westernization, Asian countries have always harbored misgivings about the proximity of the two trends. The West is to be emulated and dreaded. The paradox manifests itself in that the lovers conduct their pure, asexual, Asian-inflected courtship in Western dress amidst bars and cafes playing Western music, including a concert at the ski resort. Two of the three "bad" women have Western ties: Joon Sang's pianist mother and Chae Lin, who returns from France. The hollow man Ming Yeong is supposed to have spent his entire life in the West. However, the West is a sanctuary as well. Joon Sang goes to New York for brain surgery, and Yu Jin consoles herself by going away to France for advanced education. Western science in the form of psychoanalytical hypnotism erases Joon Sang, but it eventually grants him the possibility of love through a DNA testing. Brain surgery heals him, except his vision—a small price of castration for coming to terms with the elusive fetishes of father and self. Indeed, even the symbol of pure, everlasting, quintessentially Korean love, Polaris, is named in a Western language. (Indeed, we have to wonder whether there is a traditional Korean name for the North Star, which may lack exotic appeal.) The story's several theme songs shift between Korean and English lines as well. Despite its appearance as being essentially Korean or Asian, *Winter Sonata* is decidedly mixed-blood, hybrid. Despite the oppositional politics one would like to read into *Winter Sonata*'s Asian rather than American success, it remains culturally collaborationist.

### Scene 3: Cosmetic Surgery

The interpellation of the West in Han Ju is most discernible in the allegedly Korean bodies. Many of the faces have full, sensuous lips that embody feminine and masculine beauty. Indeed, one reason for Han Ju's success is the casting of gorgeous actors and actresses. While these performers often enact old-fashioned loyalty and romance in modern settings, their near-perfect eyes, noses, and other body parts are, in certain cases, the product of cosmetic surgery. South Korea competes with Japan in making miracles out of plastic surgery, but the practice has spread throughout Asia. These procedures seek to recreate facial and body features largely in the image of the West—hair dyed blond or tinted reddish, double-folded eyelids, fairer skin, higher and straighter nose ridges, slim rather than round faces, taller stature. They are the most abject, self-dehumanizing "citations" of the West; individuals literally inscribe the West on their bodies. The audience, dreaming of Eastern traditions wedded to Western modernization, remains oblivious to the violence perpetrated against the Asian body and psyche—against oneself.

In *The Jew's Body* (1991), Sander Gilman has helped illuminate the history of plastic surgery by pinpointing a medical procedure on "Jewish noses" in nineteenth-century Europe, whereby Jews sought better looks, social assimilation, and economic advancement by surgically erasing their "racial marker." From its inception, cosmetic surgery has been imbued with the self-loathing of racial minorities or the disenfranchised. In post-Korean War South Korea, as a gesture toward America's ally in the deepening Cold War, the plastic surgeon D. R. Millard arrived to rehabilitate the wounded by means of plastic surgery. As David Palumbo-Liu discusses in *Asian/American* (1999), Millard took upon himself the mission to improve, surgically, the Asian look, particularly the face, in the form of changing the epicanthic folds and raising the nose ridge, which in turn would "elevate" the patient's psyche. While championing a hybrid aesthetics rather than a totally Western one, Millard initiated among South Koreans a dream of becoming physically American. Needless to say, Millard did not force patients into surgery; the Fanonian "colonization of the mind" sees to that. And today, to quote Virginia Blum in *Flesh Wounds* (2003), Asia's "wannabes," including some Han Ju fans, are already "Addicted to Surgery."

## Outtakes

In the spirit of repetition, let me reiterate: most Han Ju are way too long with too much fluff. I must confess that toward the end of these dramas, I frequently fast-forward to skip unnecessarily repetitious parts. (Or is it just to watch the scenes where the actress appears?) Since my wife and I have had to watch Han Ju after our energetic young daughter finally goes to bed, my wife often falls asleep, catching snatches of the plot when she wakes up periodically.

On the evidence, therefore, I can say that I am not being unduly sexist when I observe that the male seeks control, however futilely, the female lets go, wisely. The viewing practices of Asian diasporics in the United States diverge drastically from those explored in Western feminist studies such as Mumford's *Love and Ideology in the Afternoon* (1995) or Brundson's *The Feminist, the Housewife, and the Soap Opera* (2000). They merit a closer look. Chua Beng Huat has begun that investigation when he identifies three "audience or consumption positions" in the context of East Asian popular culture: an audience viewing "a locally produced" program; a diasporic subject viewing a program about "one's homeland"; and an audience watching an imported program ("Conceptualizing an East Asian Popular Culture" 2004, pp. 212–213).

Parenthetically, human life is but a parenthesis, marked by birth and death at either end, inserted into a text that no one can read. Perhaps this is why when the best moments of Han Ju suspend time and erase the Self, even if just for the duration of the adieus in *Shan dao* and *Winter Sonata,* one is grateful for the brief vision of timelessness and love.

# 8 Tradition and/of Bastards in the Korean Wave

**On the** threshold of the twenty-first century, the Korean Wave (Han Chao or Han Liu) represents Asia's wave of nostalgia for an essentialized tradition, as Asia plunges headlong into the ocean of modernity (aka Westernization). Global technology allows modernizing Asia to view South Korea's films and television serials, which formulaically feature romance amidst the conservative social milieu of the Confucian, patriarchal legacy. Far more than a mere escapist fantasy, the Korean Wave's melodramatic, repetitious plot captures the quotidian life and longings of its viewers. What William Rothman sees as a fundamentally Western medium of film is made to carry the Asian "core."[1] Let me hasten to add that it is difficult to generalize about the Korean Wave, which spans art-house films and the equivalent of television soap operas, contemporary and period pieces, romance and action, comedy and tragedy, sci-fi and classics. But particularly in the historical TV serials, each audience discovers a fossilized Asian-ness, a preserve, an enclave of tradition. While this trait is shared by Korean films, we are also witnessing in recent art-house and some popular films a transgressiveness that swings to the other end of the pendulum's arc, from tradition to bastardy, and this creates the dichotomy of the Korean Wave. As soaps reprise love stories by means of conventional filmic technique and stylized performances that draw from a repertoire of facial and body expressions to indicate joy, shock, annoyance, and so forth, art-house films indulge in subjects on the fringes of sensibility, among them incest (Park, dir., *Oldboy* 2003), violent entanglements, with betrayal, murder, and lesbianism (Byun, dir., *The Scarlet Letter* 2004), and forbidden romances (Jang, dir., *Everyone Has Secrets* 2004). With such a wide selection on which to project our fear and, paradoxically, our desire for a death by drowning in Western modernity, Asians—myself included as an Asian in diaspora or a(n) (un)naturalized American—drift with the Korean Wave back to an imaginary homeland, the "unmoved mover" of the Korean peninsula.

A methodological pitfall immediately manifests itself when Asia appears to be treated as a patient lying on the lounge chair, confiding its collective dream of the Korean Wave to a wannabe psychoanalyst of Asian extraction in a "white" lab coat. This approach from mass-consumed texts to culture is nothing new, of course. Peter Brooks championed the study of what he calls "the melodramatic imagination," in his book by the same name (1976), by concentrating on French melodrama of the eighteenth and nineteenth century. In melodrama, Brooks locates the "moral occult," which is "not a metaphysical system; it is rather the repository of the fragmentary and desacralized remnants of sacred myth. It bears comparison to unconscious mind, for it is a sphere of being where our most basic desires and interdictions lie" (p. 5). Brooks quotes Eric Bentley as labeling melodrama "the Naturalism of the dream life' and notes its affinities with infantile narcissism" (p. 35). Unlike Brooks and Bentley, who take a disinterested position vis-à-vis a subject created over one hundred years ago, I minimize the distance between my subject and myself: this is not so much psychoanalysis of Korean or Asian modernities as self-analysis. "Tradition and/of bastards" is a paradigm that speaks to me as much as it does to Asian fans. Although an outsider to the Korean language, I find in the Korean Wave an uncanny familiarity because of the Chinese-inflected Korean tradition, from the grand ideology of Confucian patriarchy to the more minor manifestations such as calligraphy. Of course, Asian faces and bodies are the basis of fan identification. The shock of recognition overwhelms me when I realize that on the upper left arm of Dong-kun Jang,[2] (the male lead in *Paris Lover* and *Tae guk gi* [Kang 2004]), of Hyeon-a Seong (the female lead in *Watching It Again and Again* and *The Scarlet Letter*), and indeed of quite a few others are the protuberances that indicate either smallpox or BCG (Bacille Calmette-Guerin or tuberculosis) vaccination. My bumps mark the medical practice of the 1960s in Taiwan, an inscription on the body rarely found among Americans of my generation. As there is generally not much nudity in bedroom scenes, I have no way of telling whether these Korean stars also bear two nickel-sized vaccination scars on their left hip joints and thighs. For a diasporic audience to see "celebrities" exhibiting one's own physical "defects" is a pleasant mini-epiphany.

Physical kinship aside, the cultural trajectories of Asian modernities are amazingly similar. Modernization and Westernization have almost been synonymous in the lexicons of Japan and China since the Meiji Restoration in 1868 and the Chinese May Fourth Movement of 1919. Westernization also descended upon Korea by means of the machinery of Japanese colonialism from 1910 to 1945. After a century or more of mimicking the West, the contemporary Korean Wave offers a ritual of play—outside the Western sphere of influence in work—to transport Asian and Asian diasporic audiences back to an unsullied Asian essence. The Korean Wave offers an alternative to the domination of Hollywood and Western entertainment. For transnational migrants like myself, the Korean Wave drives a wedge into American assimilation and veers toward nostalgic Asian identity, even pan-Asian solidarity. Accordingly, the Korean Wave leans toward traditional conservatism in social etiquette and gender relationships. Indeed, an insular, centripetal movement characterizes the Korean Wave. This nostalgia for the old ways comes dressed in new Western clothes, though: the set, costumes, and cityscapes marked by advanced capitalism; the soundtrack playing the ubiquitous Western piano and violin; repeated allusions to, if not partially set in, the West; and the stars' fetishized Western-looking physiques—fair skin, long legs, dyed hair.[3] Clearly the centripetal force homeward contains its centrifugal opposite Westward.

A filmic schism lies between the Korean tradition and Western modernization. Of course, Korea itself has split in two. The Korean Wave reaching the shores of China and elsewhere has in general veiled the partition of North and South Korea. Despite the fact that the aftermath of the Korean War is a recurring motif in literature, such as Heung-gil Yun's *The House of Twilight* (1989) and Sun-won Hwang's *The Book of Masks* (1989), and that a subgenre of political films, such as *Shiri* (1999), *Joint Security Area* (2000), *Double Agent* (2003), and *Tae guk gi* (2004) are enormously successful in the domestic market, the Korean Wave abroad remains adamantly silent about the divide of the North and South. The several miles euphemistically called the DMZ (the Demilitarized Zone) along the 38th Parallel is one of the most heavily armed trouble spots around the world, with patrols, watch towers, landmines, barbed wires, secret tunnels, and other unpublicized surveillance measures. Yet in romances, the sociopolitical tension is brushed aside, implied, at most, in male characters' conscription as a rite of passage for manhood and, frequently, as a melodramatic twist to bring about tear-jerking scenes of parting. Compulsory military service, along with terminal illness and overseas travel, mostly to the United States and Europe, counts as a favorite strategy to induce lovers' suffering and regret.

Given its reticence on divided Korea, the Korean Wave nevertheless lets slip a near "repetition compulsion," where "tradition" is often perpetuated or even embodied by characters who can only be described as illegitimate bastards. While bastards threaten a family's line of succession, the Korean Wave features their ultimate absorption into tradition. One possible interpretation of this is that by containing its own aberrations, the Hermit Kingdom's self-referential tradition is made more inclusive and potent. Aberrations challenge and strengthen rather than weaken tradition. Rarely iconoclastic and never anti-traditionalist, the bastards in television serials are driven by a modernist, nonconformist impulse of self-realization. They seek to rise up from their lot in life and end up marrying into the tradition, literally. The bastard characters are invariably legitimated by marriage and family acceptance, both the individual family as well as collective family of the state. Another interpretation is that tradition appears to doubt its own legitimacy, requiring a steady stream of "rehabilitated" bastards to validate itself. The former sees Korea as a tradition incorporating dissent; the latter, to borrow Zhouliu Wu's 1945 novel on the colonized Taiwan, sees Korea as an "orphan of Asia," shoved aside by bigger kids in East Asia.

A polarity exists in the Korean national character of *han* (written as *hen* for "hate" and "remorse" in Chinese). This is a concept of endless debate among scholars. JaHyun Kim Haboush finds in Korean history "narratives of the *han* (sufferings, sorrows, pains) of the Korean people" ("In Search of HISTORY in Democratic Korea" 2001, p. 190). In his otherwise insightful analysis of Kwon-Taek Im's *Sopyonje* (1993), Julian Stringer assigns *han* to a footnote where he cites Isolde Standish citing M. Shapiro making fun of *han*: "the result of injustices perpetrated by, among others, parents, friends, siblings, a colonial ruler, an occupying army, past governments, the present government, and those who in crucial moments failed to display sincerity" ("Sopyonje and the Inner Domain of National Culture" 2002, pp. 180–181). What appears to an insider to be genuine racial pain is to other scholars a running joke. The joke, nevertheless, does bring up the significance of "sincerity" or *cheng* in Korean culture. A long history of foreign colonization by China and Japan, compounded by internal strife and on-going division, has steeped the Korean consciousness in suffering and misery. *Han* is the fatalistic resignation to pain ("remorse"), punctuated by occasional outburst of rage and protest ("hate"). The Korean Wave thus swings between two contradictory emotions, between individual adherence to and rebellion against tradition, between tradition's punishment and subconscious sanction of rebels. That the Korean Wave has swept across its neighbors suggests a *han*-ing of Asia. Granted that the urban, metropolitan consumers of Korean shows are perhaps too privileged to share the anguish of Korean history, the melodramatic pull of native tradition and counterpull of Western modernity strikes a chord among Asian fans with a keen sense of being under siege.

Not only does the Korean Wave reiterate tradition *and* bastards, it, in effect, constructs a tradition *of* bastards. Both *Shan dao*[4] *(The tao of business)* and *Yi dao (The tao of medicine)* are television shows that revolve around protagonists of lowly origin caught in the hierarchy of premodern Korea. The female lead of *Shan dao*, who once worked in the ginseng fields, has now been adopted and made heiress apparent to a business conglomerate; the male lead boasts no *yangban* (aristocratic) ties other than his facility in Chinese, business skills, and a sincere heart. The spin-off, *Yi dao*, even features an illegitimate son of a concubine. In both dramas, constant references to the protagonists' humble class background render them sympathetic to modern audiences with a belief in equality. The protagonist of *Yi dao* often identifies himself as a *no* (male slave), evoking the history of slavery in premodern Korea explicated in Kichung Kim's "Unheard Voices" 2004). Another long-running television drama, *Kan le yu kan (Watching it again and again)* plays on similar characterizations. The second children of both families in *Watching* are, shall we say, bastards. Pyong Jifeng is a choreographer, almost a prodigal son in a paternal lineage that includes a doctor of traditional herbal medicine, a school principal, and a prosecutor at law, all heirs to a tradition of law and order. Zheng Yinju is an "ugly duckling" raised by her paternal grandmother and later returned to the family of her father, who have, of course, become strangers to her. While *Watching* builds its many climaxes around conflicts between tradition *and* bastards, its subtext underwrites a tradition *of* bastards. This duality of tradition and/of bastards in the Korean Wave attracts Asian audiences around the globe who find themselves ambivalently wedged between "lost" tradition and "white" modernity.

The present lowly status of these bastard characters does not bespeak a lowly origin, for all of them are inherently noble. Routinely, in the period dramas, their parents used to serve the Korean emperor at court. Framed by evildoers, the parents go into ignominious exile. The serial then follows their children's slow and painful climb back up the social ladder to the center of power occupied by the emperor. The bastards in Korean Wave television series can be male or female, young or mature, premodern or contemporary. They can be young, like the school dropout in *The Eighteen-Year-Old Bride*, who is married to the eldest grandson of a distinguished family. The only person who appreciates her talents is the traditional grandfather, who is almost "regal" in his *hanbok* (traditional clothing) and his carriage and so sagacious that he foresees his own death. They can be mature women, as in *Cheers for Women (Nuren wansuei)* and *Heaven's Match (Tianpei liangyuan)*, where female independence is celebrated in spite of age differences with younger men.

A good illustration of a contemporary, mature, male bastard is Taijun Han in *Hotelier*, who rises from bellhop to manager of a luxurious Korean hotel, only to have to resign in disgrace (temporarily) over trumped-up charges of sexual assault and to exile himself in Las Vegas. Although loved by both female protagonists—a colleague at the hotel and the daughter of a rival business mogul—he basically matchmakes on behalf of both women with his competitors. He is rewarded with loneliness presiding over a grand hotel. One of the last scenes shows him, the hotel manager, picking litter off the staircase while his beloved walks away with another man. Although it is a well-crafted serial, with an excellent script, fast-paced hotel sequences, and daring—by soaps' standards—dim lighting inside the hotel rooms to suggest the melancholy of Han and other characters, the series adamantly refuses to explore class inequity and its lifelong effect on the psyche. Plagued by inferiority, Han's suppression of love borders on self-abjection and masochism. His personality consists of "masculine" strength, which allows him to run a business and overcome episode after episode of obstacles and hostile takeover bids, and "feminine" vulnerability. His profession is, after all, service-oriented rather than mercantile raiding. The serial demurs on an exploration of Han's incongruous psyche because Han embodies *han,* the Korean sentiment of savoring one's misery and self-denial. When viewing Korean Wave productions, the "pleasure principle" resembles an urge being assuaged in the same fashion as moving from a slightly off-balanced state of being, like sexual arousal, to consummation through some measure of vigorousness and pain. Pleasure and pain are as locked together as the yin and yang on the Korean national flag.[5]

Indeed, even that which causes pain in the Korean consciousness is not instinctively demonized as the Other. Rather, it is internalized, as opposed to the Western tendency of projecting outward. The TV serial *Temptation of Eve* (also titled in Mandarin *In Love with the Anchorwoman*) is unusually gloomy because of the male character's obsession with Yingmei, a manipulative, snake-like Eve. This character's sacrifice in rescuing Yingmei from an oncoming truck engenders in Yingmei a sense of guilt and she attempts to commit suicide. She survives the drowning an amnesiac, her evil self cleansed by water, restoring her to the pristine, unsullied state as a six-year-old. It turns out that she was abandoned by her mother when she was six and abused by her alcoholic father. (Both plot twists recycle the two favorite devices of life changes in the Korean Wave—traffic accidents and amnesia.) This enacts the Korean collective unconscious of a return to prelapsarian innocence. Although populated with a constellation of adult-age performers, the Korean Wave never fails to open with or flash back to the characters' teenage years or even childhoods, which are always set in a rural, traditional Korea to create nostalgia for a lost Eden. This often entails performers in their twenties or even thirties playing high-school students engaged in puppy love. Despite all the youthful-looking stars, this remains a tired, awkward formula.

The most recent hit featuring such bastard characters is *Dae Jang Kum,* in which an orphan girl experiences the loss of her parents, who have fallen from grace due to the Machiavellian struggle inside the imperial court. Dae Jang Kum fulfills viewers' dreams in her ascent to taking charge of the imperial kitchen and finally the emperor's health (heart as well?). Through hard work and sincerity, she perfects the traditional skills of cuisine and herbal medicine. The emperor loves Dae Jang Kum so much that he does not force her into concubinage, for he has known all along of her marathon platonic love for his general Zhenghao Min. Dae Jang Kum is a part of the royal court, yet she remains apart from it, uncorrupted. The traditional Confucian value of *cheng* (sincerity, honesty, truthfulness) is repeatedly valorized, in business *(Shan dao)*, in medicine *(Yi dao)*, in cuisine and medicine *(Dae jang kum)*, and in whatever other fields the Korean Wave chooses to put on the air. The invariably long and arduous apprenticeship teaches not so much professional skills as "sincerity." Anachronistic though it may be in a fast-paced, late-capitalist Asia where TV viewers are embroiled daily in business transactions and office politics, the Korean Wave provides an after-work sanctuary where the fans live out their nostalgia for lost virtues by means of, ironically, commercial products. Desire for a sincere heart and pure love is commodified, advertised, packaged, distributed, and consumed. Such desire unfolds according to an often idiotic script, such as the frequently repeated refrain in *Dae jang kum* of "Is that so?" or "That is impossible, absolutely impossible." These phrases echo throughout the serial, serving no purpose other than to slow the story down, prolonging tension and suspense.

But what I dismiss as idiotic may be the key to the serial's Asian success. Tania Modleski's pioneering work *Loving with a Vengeance* (1982) sheds light on the alleged generic weakness of melodrama by drawing from women's studies. She quotes Marcia Kinder as stating that "the 'open-ended, slow paced, multi-climaxed' structure of soap operas is 'in tune with patterns of female sexuality'" (qtd. p. 98). Going beyond sexuality, Modleski borrows from Nancy Chodorow to link women's work at home to the melodramatic style: "The work of maintenance and reproduction is characterized by its repetitive and routine continuity, and does not involve specified sequence or progression" (qtd. p. 98). These scholars, unwittingly, shed light on the Korean Wave, since melodrama is the mainstay of the Korean Wave, TV serials and films alike. Kwon-Taek Im's groundbreaking film *Sopyonje* (1993) enjoys tremendous domestic success and continues the filmic tradition of celebrating Korean national culture via folk performances, as Frances Gateward traces it in "Youth in Crisis" (2003, p. 116). As such, the movie falls within the category of melodrama, the overseas art-house label notwithstanding. Moreover, an auteur such as Im appears to replicate, like soaps, the Korean folk art of *pansori,* and in particular the legend of Chunhyang, both in his *Sopyonje* and in *Chunhyang* (2000).

This legendary figure of female sacrifice is also the subject of the 1955 film by Kyu-hwan Yi, *Ch'unhyanjon (The story of Ch'unhyang)* (Gateward, "Youth in Crisis" 2004, p. 116). Through the singing of *pansori*, Im conducted for nearly a decade what seemed to be an unending performance of Chunhyang, a feat consistent with the aversion of most TV serials for finales. It demonstrates, as Roland Barthes has argued, "discourse's instinct for preservation."[6]

The Korean sensibility of *han* dominates *Sopyonje*, in addition to the *pansori* that the traveling troupe in the film performs. The impulsive, alcoholic Yoo-bong teaches Song-hwa and Dong-ho, both adopted, that grief is essential to the mastery of *pansori*. A comparatively raw form of art, often sung at the top of the lungs, accompanied by a drummer who echoes in yells and grunts, *pansori* comes, as it were, straight from the heart and the folk. It is an undisguised expression of emotions, its feel of spontaneity accomplished through arduous training in rote memory, delivery, and music of the oral tradition. Struggling against the onslaught of Western modernity, these performers of *pansori* are reduced to peddling ointment, the Korean version of "snake oil," on the street, and are eventually drowned out, literally, by a Western band of trumpet, horn, and accordion. Tradition and art are bumped off by modernization and commercialization. Adoptive son and apprentice drummer Dong-ho rebels against the abusive Yoo-bong and the moribund tradition he represents and runs away. Impoverished, Yoo-bong secretly blinds Song-hwa with the herbal medicine *puja* in order to bring on *han* and the perfection of her *pansori*. *Puja* from ancient Korea produces both the poison of sightlessness and the panacea to effect true vision. Dong-ho, now married and a collector of medicinal herbs for a Seoul pharmacy, searches for his adoptive family in his Western-styled windbreaker. The modernized, metropolitan Korea has nostalgically returned to the traditional, rural Korea.

The family's "reunion" unfolds in the same fashion as the climactic *pansori* piece "Simchong," which narrates how a daughter sacrifices herself to restore her father's eyesight, a parallel to Song-hwa's own suffering. The adoptive siblings sing not only to mourn their dead father but also, in a national allegory, the Fatherland, as Fredric Jameson conceives it.[7] Halfway through their farewell duet, their song and drum are gradually muted in favor of the non-diegetic theme music, consisting mostly of Western musical instruments.[8] Stringer, in "*Sopyonje* and the Inner Domain of National Culture" (2002) explores how Im suggests *imyon* (inner meaning) transcending the human body by means of non-diegetic music originating from outside the film. But Im also reinscribes a common Asian view in that true emotions move from words to silence and that the ineffable is best veiled. As Song-hwa's *pansori* fades and the Western theme music builds, Song-hwa lifts her eyes for the first time since she has entered the room and looks directly at Dong-ho as if she can see. Hers is not the blank stare of the blind, as in the latter half of the film; she sees with her heart. More specifically, their eyes appear to meet at the moment when Song-hwa cries out in her song "Aboji" (Father). Brother and sister reunite through the sorrow expressed for the *aboji* in "Simchong." The two rechannel their love, which borders on incest, to memorialize their own adoptive father. Ironically, Western theme music replaces the *pansori,* and Western filmmaking technique chronicles a vanishing Korean folk art, all in the name of valorizing tradition. Stringer dwells extensively on the artifice of the *pansori* episodes. He believes the songs mix three different female voices, but it is not readily apparent whether the three voices are featured at different times or are mixed throughout the film. Furthermore, the joyous "Chindo Arirang," sung as loud and clear from afar as nearby the camera, is the product of studio recording. Stringer concludes that "at the very moment it reveals its 'inner meaning,' p'ansori is manipulated through ideologies of editing and sound mixing" ("*Sopyonje* and the Inner Domain of National Culture" 2002, p. 177).

The shop owner who overhears their night-long concert describes their singing in erotic terms: "The words were caressing each other." The duo stop only in the predawn hours, covered with sweat, breathless, spent, as though from a bout of long-deferred, self-abandoned lovemaking. While "elevating" their transgressive amour to traditional filial piety, Im adds an ambivalent incestuous "aside" from the shop owner. Consistently, the filmmaker balances the adoptive family between tradition and taboo. When Yoo-bong blinds Song-hwa to help her gain insight into *pansori,* an old calligrapher friend wonders if it is because Yoo-bong wishes to keep Song-hwa with him. A tyrannical father, it is implied, has crippled the child not for her sake, but for his. Furthermore, the calligrapher may well have been the adoptive father to the apprentices since he asks Yoo-bong again and again to give the children to him. As a candidate for adoptive father, the calligrapher's words counter Yoo-bong's justification. The concluding scene underscores the ambiguous relationship between tradition and bastard. A blind Song-hwa is being led by a rope by a young girl (who has not appeared until this last scene) across a field in wintry snow; they walk in slow motion. This reprises earlier scenes where Yoo-bong has led Song-hwa. One is free to read this as a Korean compulsion to intensify *han*—the hopelessness of a blind woman in traditional *hanbok,* being led by a girl who is possibly her illegitimate daughter, going nowhere. Of course, the continuation of *pansori* is also implied by the presence of the young girl. Nonetheless, it is not unreasonable to speculate, as Chungmoo Choi does, that the young girl was sired by none other than Yoo-bong, which adds yet another pseudo-incestuous scenario.[9]

That the "nuclear" *pansori* family headed by Yoo-bong is constructed rather than biological only increases the challenge to the taboo of incest. Even the "extended" *pansori* family from which Yoo-bong has acquired his skills has become an outcast in mainstream modernizing Korea. As an apprentice, Yoo-bong was himself banished by his master because the master's mistress seduced Yoo-bong. Yoo-bong has to learn Chunhyang's climactic prison song from an old classmate who has degenerated into a drug addict. A circle of orphans and dubious kindred, the *pansori* families symbolize Korea's self-image torn between obsession with tradition and gnawing doubt of illegitimacy. What is countenanced as tradition often turns out to be problematic in Im's films. During a teahouse performance, an "aristocratic" guest harasses Song-hwa, coercing her to serve him drinks and to drink herself to prove her "respect for elders." Traditional respect is abused by a "bastard," who scoffs at Yoo-bong, a "peasant." The guest evokes class and social hierarchy from the Korean tradition to oppress the marginalized tradition of *pansori*. By the same token, Governor Byun uses the weight of his patriarchal and imperial authority to pressure Chunhyang into serving him as a concubine. Yet Chunhyang symbolizes the true tradition of commitment to her husband, despite torture and impending execution by the "bastard" governor.

Tradition lives forever in fear of bastards for their potential to usurp power, one form of which comes when bastards contaminate the bloodline through incest. Morally abhorrent, incest remains an ambivalent trope, perversely attractive to writers and artists from Sophocles to the Korean Wave. Elizabeth Barnes defines incest as "the impulse . . . for stasis, a refusal to circulate one's body, one's blood, even one's attention outside the sphere of one's own family" (*Incest and the Literary Imagination* 2002, p. 4). Drawing from Freud's founding myth as outlined in *Totem and Taboo* (1913), Barnes contends that after killing the patriarchal father, the sons gain power and "*access to women*" (italics in original, p. 6). In their remorse, the sons enter "into a fraternal contract that establishes 'laws,'" which include "renounce[ing] their women—the mother and sisters of the horde" (p. 6). But incest persists despite such interdiction, usually, in the West, as either "a vice of the poor" or "the prerogative of the rich" (p. 4). While incest in the form of a Freudian Oedipus complex is far too transgressive for the melodramatic Korean Wave, family structure and kinship remain so basic to the social fabric that a Korean woman calls her male lover *o-ppah* (elder brother). A common practice in many Asian cultures—the Cantonese *gaw* (elder brother) and *moi* (younger sister) between lovers—the address of "elder brother" for lover surely does not mean a proclivity for incest. Yet under the assault of foreign invasions and suffering, the Hermit Kingdom resembles a circle that has tried to stay intact, within itself, impervious to outside forces. As translated into the Korean Wave's domestic TV drama, this drive inward turns into the tease of forbidden love, usually between lovers who mistake each other for possible siblings, such as in *Winter Sonata*. Not until the "bastard" art-house film *Oldboy* does the traditional tease of incest dare to manifest itself "nakedly."

The intense lovemaking scene halfway through *Oldboy* turns out to be between father and daughter, unbeknownst at the time to the pair and the audience. The searing pain that prompts the young woman, Mido, to scream upon penetration gains new meaning after this is revealed. Ecstasy derives from sin. The film opens with the protagonist Dae-su Oh being locked up for fifteen years for an offense that is never made clear to him, hence intimating the Original Sin. In a Kafka-esque, schizophrenic state, Dae-su shifts between the extremes of dog-like servility and rage. After he breaks out of his cell and begins taking his revenge, viewers are propelled through a grotesque gallery of violence and pain, in the manner not so much of a mystery's suspense than of the horror in the Theater of Cruelty. The mastermind of Dae-su's imprisonment and incest is himself a perpetrator of incest with his sister in high school. The siblings had sinned out of irrepressible love and carnal desire, an act witnessed accidentally by Dae-su. He has spread a rumor concerning the pair, which causes the sister to commit suicide. The bereaved brother choreographs Dae-su's own unwitting incest with his daughter by manipulating their minds through hypnosis, drugs, and other devices favored in Korean melodrama. *Winter Sonata* uses these very same devices to move along its twenty episodes, which toy with pseudo-incestuous relationships. What better way to prevent devoted lovers from uniting than this abomination? In the vein of primordial Oedipus and Electra complexes, the filmmaker Chan-wook Park gives us flashes—indecent exposure perhaps—of the Hermit Kingdom's fixation on tradition and/of bastards as well as its longing for a regressive, womb-like wholesomeness. In the final bloodbath of *Oldboy*, Dae-su cuts off his tongue in exchange for Mido's innocence of her sin. They apparently continue to live in damnation, with the father-husband enduring in self-inflicted silence the everlasting curse akin to Cain's.

Over the years, my daughter, now in her early teens, has been a somewhat reluctant follower of Korean TV serials. Forced to convert from Disney animations to dubbed Korean drama in order to improve her listening comprehension of Mandarin, she, I know too well, prefers the effortless fun of Disney. Together, we have lost track of how many Korean family dramas we have watched. But a firm conviction has grown out of all these shows, which I have imparted to her regularly as life-long advice: "Never marry a Korean man!" to which she always shouts back: "I'm NOT gonna marry, EVER!" Korean actors routinely effect changes in the lives of actresses by forcibly dragging them away from cocktail parties, train stations, and airports, even weddings, through traffic and rain, even from the midst of family members or crowds of strangers. (Sang-woo Kwon is an expert on this manly show of force in *Stairway to Heaven,* which aired on Korean television in 2003–2004.) Such scenes remind me of the cartoon staple of Neanderthals dragging women away by their long hair. That such physical violence ends happily in Korean dramas reaffirms Modleski's observation that "the transformation of brutal…men into tender lovers, the insistent denial of the reality of male hostility towards women, point to ideological conflicts so profound that readers must constantly return to the same text (to texts which are virtually the same) in order to be reconvinced" (*Loving with a Vengeance* 1982, p. 111).

If mine is a stereotype of Korean masculinity, then at least one Korean American female agrees with me. In *Becoming Asian-American* (2002), Nazli Kibria quotes Michelle, a young Korean American, who vents a similar sentiment: "I always swore I would never marry an immigrant [from Korea]…. They're on top of the world, and women are second class to them" (p. 91). Conservative, even reactionary, gender relationships evidently do not diminish the attractiveness of the Korean Wave in Asia; indeed, it appears to reassures female viewers of a benevolent patriarchal modernity. By contrast, the Korean Wave subsides in the wide expanse of the Pacific Ocean before reaching North America. This is for various reasons, but gender imbalance is, I suspect, among them. As a practical matter, technology that makes possible the rapid distribution of Korean dramas in Asia makes it nearly impossible to disseminate in North America. Of the two personal VCDs of Korean films that I put on reserve for my upper-division honors seminar on "Asian Diaspora Culture" in Fall 2005, one failed to play on the university library's Sony DVD player due to a "wrong region," and the other had one entirely unreadable segment. I purchased these Korean films either in China or in New York's Chinatown and had no problem playing them on my home Apex DVD player, which is not common in the United States. The relatively inexpensive VCDs, coupled with the lax copyright laws in Asia, allows the Korean Wave to saturate one market, but these same VCDs are worthless in another market. "East is East, and West is West," chants Kipling, "and never the twain shall meet." Even as a comprador from the East tries to reach out by including the "rage" spreading across Asia and the Asian diaspora under the subject of "Asian Diaspora Culture," the West may remain blithely indifferent. I was informed by only one student that the disks were unreadable the night prior to class discussion at the end of the semester, even though the films had been on reserve throughout the semester. In Asia and the Asian diasporic communities across North America, viewers on their own initiative seek out these films and television serials for entertainment. In American mainstream culture, students dread, understandably perhaps, the drudgery of sitting through alien films with unpronounceable names and confusing plots, until the very last minute. One person's play is indeed another's work. At the conclusion of E. M. Forster's *A Passage to India* (1924), the characters Fielding and Aziz are on horseback, attempting to "hold onto each other's hands," but "the horses," "the earth," and "the sky" do not wish them to meet. West and East "swerve[d] apart" on the Indian subcontinent. In my attempt to introduce the Korean Wave to American university communities, perhaps the sea has joined the chorus of disapproval, keeping Asian technology and American "riders" on opposite shores of the Pacific—for the time being.

# Intercut on
## Body Oriental

# Rodgers and Hammerstein's "Chopsticks" Musicals

## Overture

Richard Rodgers writes, in *Musical Stages* (1975): "When I was about six, a girl named Constance Hyman, the daughter of a college friend of my father's, taught me to play 'Chopsticks' with my left hand so that it would fit the melody of any song I was trying to reproduce with my right hand" (p. 9). Throughout the brilliant joint careers of Richard Rodgers and Oscar Hammerstein II, Rodgers the composer has been true to his childhood apprenticeship, with Oriental flavor liberally sprinkling his corpus. In terms of the most memorable Rodgers and Hammerstein legacy, *The Sound of Music* (1965) and *The King and I* (1956) share the limelight,[1] musicals set, respectively, in Austria and in Siam, and both drawing from stereotypically Anglo-European versus Oriental tropes. Their corpus, which manifests predominantly Western consciousness, features one distinct Oriental period that includes *The King and I, South Pacific* (1958), and *Flower Drum Song* (1961). This "left-handed," Oriental element can hardly be viewed as an awkward appendix to their stellar achievement. Indeed, in the comical maladroitness of their Orientalist songs lies the key to the overall success of Rodgers and Hammerstein. To borrow from the metaphor of the six-year-old's piano lesson, the weaving of the left-handed "Chopsticks" into the "real" music played by the right hand is the extra stuff which enlivens otherwise mediocre compositions, just as carbonated fizz transforms ordinary sugar water into a soft drink. The ostensibly negligible Oriental ambience helps catapult each Chopsticks musical, and the careers of Rodgers and Hammerstein as well, into prominence.

The forte of Rodgers and Hammerstein is, in fact, Broadway shows rather than movies, as Rodgers explains: "Publishing songs, producing plays and writing songs for moving pictures were profitable and challenging enterprises, but Oscar and I never thought of ourselves as anything but writers for the Broadway musical theatre" (*Musical Stages* 1975, p. 237). Yet their reputation today is primarily founded on films, since live Broadway shows, thrilling as they are, vanish as soon as they are performed. My analysis, therefore, concentrates on the films. The dates given for the three Oriental musicals refer to the films, not the Broadway productions, all of which opened on stage years before their respective cinematic adaptations.

Rodgers and Hammerstein's chopsticks musicals exist in a complex web of cultural products. Each is adapted from short stories or novels, first for Broadway and subsequently for motion pictures. Anna Leonowens's two-volume autobiography, *The English Governess in the Siamese Court* (1870) and *The Romance of the Harem* (1872), record her experiences as a teacher at the Siamese court in the 1860s. Margaret Landon, who also worked in Siam as a teacher, turns the Leonowens books into *Anna and the King of Siam* (1944), a narrative "seventy-five per cent fact, and twenty-five per cent fiction based on fact" (Leonowens's self-description quoted in Elsie Weil's "Editor's Note" to the Landon book, p. ix). A black-and-white drama, *Anna and the King of Siam,* starring Rex Harrison and Irene Dunne, was released in 1946. The genius of Rodgers and Hammerstein reconstructs this film as the 1956 musical with Yul Brynner and Deborah Kerr. A 1999 version of the story, *Anna and the King,* features Chow Yun-fat and Jodie Foster as the protagonists. *South Pacific,* on the other hand, is based on several stories in James Michener's *Tales of the South Pacific* (1947), a collection that won the Pulitzer Prize the following year. The musical combines Liat, Bloody Mary, and Joe Cable from "Fo' Dolla" with Emile de Becque and Nellie Forbush from "Our Heroine" (Rodgers, *Musical Stages* 1975, pp. 258–259), merging, in effect, Oriental and Anglo-European narratives. The last of the three, *Flower Drum Song,* is adapted from C. Y. Lee's novel of the same title published in 1957. The film's genesis from a Chinese expatriate writer and its almost exclusively Asian and Asian American cast perpetuate the myth of model minority and their continued ghettoization, both themes advanced by the musical.

### Act I: English Teacher

While certain "progressive" Hollywood renditions of the encounter between East and West cast—as *Flower Drum Song* does—mostly Asian and pseudo-Asian characters, there is invariably the stock character of—for lack of a better term—the English teacher. Open-minded liberalism has its limits after all, evident in the proliferation of Western educators amongst Asians. Peter O'Toole plays the Qing emperor Pu Yi's tutor in Bernardo Bertollucci's *The Last Emperor* (1988), teaching science and the English language; Brad Pitt in Jean-Jacques Annaud's *Seven Years in Tibet* (1997) serves the same function for the teenage Dalai Lama. The shared motif of the English teacher reflects the attempt of the East to modernize itself because of imperialism. Both leaders of Eastern civilization in these films—Pu Yi and the Dalai Lama—are portrayed, quite accurately, as fascinated by science and technology, especially as embodied in objects like movie projectors and telescopes. The white teacher also helps ease moviegoers into the unfamiliar context of Asia. To examine a potentially disorienting universe is less scary if we see it through a lens similar to our own.

Hence English teachers often function as the focal point or the mediating prism of action. This stems from a deep-seated ethnocentrism, in which a foreign land acts as a blank backdrop where we can engrave virtues of the Self, or, as in Joseph Conrad's *Heart of Darkness* (1902) and Francis Ford Coppola's *Apocalypse Now* (1979), critiques of the Self. Lesser works like Rodgers and Hammerstein's chopsticks musicals manifest ethnocentrism via English teachers. All three musicals open with, in a manner of speaking, an English teacher, whose expertise takes him/her as well as the viewers into an exotic Orient. In *The King and I,* Mrs. Anna Leonowens is the quintessential English teacher, running a grammar school for the Siamese royal children, concubines, and—not to mince words—the king. Despite Brynner's imposing presence, the king remains willful, even childish, to be guided by the British governess not only in foreign correspondence but in foreign and domestic policies. Indeed, whatever grandeur Brynner's magnetism has amidst his gilded setting, his pidgin and his naiveté undercut him. Brynner's performance projects both royalty and buffoonery.

Rodgers and Hammerstein did not come up with a clownish King Mongkut all by themselves. Many of the king's farcical lines are quoted verbatim from Margaret Landon's book. The king's first line, "Who? Who? Who?" in response to Anna's unannounced entrance is drawn from Landon, as is much of the dialogue of this first audience. Similar refrains uttered by the king— "Moses, Moses, Moses" and "Etcetera, etcetera, etcetera"—are all Landon's doing to create the vocabulary and mindset of a "child" king. Rodgers and Hammerstein have conceptualized King Mongkut as a regal vaudevillian, rehabilitating Landon's "capricious and vengeful" king, who shifts between "the Oriental despot" and "the learned man of science" (*Anna and the King of Siam* 1944, p. 47). The cosmetic surgery Rodgers and Hammerstein perform on King Mongkut goes far beyond Brynner's taped eyelids; they expunge Landon's (and the Harrison film's) most egregious episode.

Among the inhumanities in Landon's account, the torture and burning of Lady Tuptim and a monk suspected of cuckolding the king stands out in its gruesomeness. Unlike Anna's previous successful interventions, for which she earns, according to Landon, the nickname of "the White Angel" (p. 173) from Bangkok's downtrodden, Anna fails in this round of rescue and is forced to witness the fiery end of the innocent pair. The Rex Harrison film showcases the burning at the stake in its trailer, a visualization of the opening caption about this "half-barbaric" country. Perhaps the abyss in Landon's version, the double executions are the dark hole that threatens to negate Anna's years of civilizing mission. An exhausted Anna begins to entertain thoughts of going home; the only thing keeping her in Siam at this point appears to be the education of the next sovereign, Prince Chulalongkorn.

Ultimately, Anna's lessons are about more than correct spelling or eating with a knife and fork.[2] She guides them in antislavery and feminist campaigns, referring constantly to Harriet Beecher Stowe's *Uncle Tom's Cabin* (1852) and equality for women.[3] Judging from the ending of *The King and I*, Anna the teacher has won, despite the setback of Tuptim's untimely death. Prince Chulalongkorn's first edict, which he issues beside a dying Brynner and an Anna bound for England, abolishes the ancient custom of kneeling and kowtowing to the king, an obeisance on hands and knees deemed henceforth uncivilized. To signal the end not only of the king's life but of old Siam, Rodgers and Hammerstein choose the most conspicuous rather than the most entrenched aspect of Siamese customs. The young prince does not announce sweeping changes, the abolition of slavery, for instance, or dissolution of the royal harem. Instead, a facile reform is declared to herald the dawn of a new era, with Anna as the surrogate mother to the young king and the spiritual leader for the future of Siam. Whether an erect posture necessarily leads to defiance of oppression is open to debate.

If Anna can make her presence felt long after she retires, evinced by Leonowens's cinematic triplets spanning five decades, then English teachers, altogether nonexistent or disguised in the other two chopsticks musicals, exert similar ideological control over Orientals. Indeed, dominance despite physical absence suggests an ultimate victory for the (neo)colonial powers personified by English teachers. The symbolic capital of the god-like West is such that its invisibility intimates omnipresence, its mere gaze from afar ensuring total submission.

*South Pacific* and *Flower Drum Song* engage English teachers for the natives or the ethnics figuratively. In *South Pacific*, U.S. Navy Lieutenant Joe Cable, on a secret mission to spy out Japanese troops on the South Sea islands, ventures into the paradise of Bali H'ai and educates the Tonkinese Liat in the ways of love. After her initial line in French, "Je parle français, un peu," Liat falls completely dumb, without a single word of dialogue other than the oohs and ahhs of a woman in love. Even during "Happy Talk," she basically pantomimes for her mother Bloody Mary's song in a pidgin so awful as to be racist. Liat surrenders herself—speech and all, like Disney's little mermaid—to Cable, who is supposed to be, among other things, her voice. The unlikely mother-daughter pair (played by Juanita Hall and France Nuyen) once again charts the polarities of Orientalist representations. Dark-skinned and overweight, Bloody Mary is a vulgar opportunist peddling native kitsch from her "vending booth," an outrigger, to American soldiers. The film's first number opens with Bloody Mary cackling drily over a human skull mounted on the outrigger's prow, cascading down which is a necklace of boar's teeth. Punctuated by the Seabees' song, Bloody Mary feigns chewing on a betel nut, then feeding it to the skull. She later displays a pitch-black shrunken skull the size of her palm. A bone through her hair bun and her wide nose complete the association with African cannibals. During Cable's subsequent visit to Bali H'ai, he is greeted by Bloody Mary, now flanked—lo and behold—by two natives with bones worn through their noses. Unlike her mother, Liat is willowy and pristine, a dream girl for any young man—except for her genes. Savagery and vulnerability are yoked together by means of an "odd couple" of mother and daughter.

Set in San Francisco's Chinatown, *Flower Drum Song* does not have any English teacher in its cast. The Asian American ghetto is presented as a universe unto itself, with little Caucasian interference. However, the English-speaking hegemony works through the Americanized Asians Linda Low and Sammy Fong to interpellate their traditionalist understudies Wang Ta and Mei Li. Even the most conservative character, Master Wang, receives stern lectures from his sister-in-law, Madame "Auntie" Liang, who attributes her knowledge of the American lifestyle and her success on the U.S. citizenship test to—who else—her (English) teachers. Juanita Hall's naturalization pales in comparison to her metamorphosis from Bloody Mary to Madame Liang, from a black Polynesian to a white Chinese. The colors are literal, since Hall's makeup in these two films creates two completely opposite skin tones.

## Act II: American Space

One of the first lessons that Anna teaches the royal children and concubines is the proper place of Siam. Finding that the Siamese map grossly exaggerates the size of Siam in contrast to its rival, Burma, Anna brings out her own world map, where Siam is a tiny speck. When her pupils reject this in dismay, she calls their attention to England, which is, in Anna's words, even smaller. What is left unsaid, of course, is that the British Empire has grown from an island to envelop the five continents. The Siamese self-image is deflated twice: first by the drastic shrinking of its domain and then by the ballooning of England despite its equally miniature size. This rude awakening is induced by space. Indeed, throughout the three chopsticks musicals, Rodgers and Hammerstein revisit over and over again the problem of space. Bruce McConachie, in "The 'Oriental' Musicals of Rodgers and Hammerstein" (1994), reads this recurring motif as a reflection of the American obsession with containment during the height of the Cold War.

In these musicals, oppression arises, invariably, in spatial terms, and cast as underdogs are Westerners, including the "Western" half within Asian American psyche in *Flower Drum Song*. All three films trace, explicitly or subliminally, conflicts over space that close, predictably, with the triumph of American liberators or American ideology. It is ironic that Westerners or the Americanized Self are purported to be under siege in Rodgers and Hammerstein at a time when the United States was expanding its sphere of influence globally, the heir apparent to the British Empire. To rationalize neoimperialism, what better way than to take on the role of a freedom fighter against great odds!

Arguably, all three musicals also resemble classic captivity narratives that use the plight of individuals to justify collective control. "A Narrative of the Captivity and Restoration of Mrs. Mary Rowlandson" (1677) records the protagonist's ordeal over nearly three months in the hands of Native Americans. The first narrative published by an Anglo-American woman on American soil, Rowlandson inspired a whole genre of captivity narratives that helped shape the stereotype of Native Americans as savages taking women and children hostage. Having established the crime against these innocents, the "collective" is now justified to rob the Native Americans of their land and herd those not killed outright onto reservations. Anna in *The King and I* and the U.S. Navy in *South Pacific* are the children of Mary Rowlandson, whose plight permits or even demands U.S. dominance. In *Flower Drum Song*, a minority's American self is said to be imprisoned by Asian tradition, while the apparent ghettoization of Chinatown is overlooked.

The dramatic tension of *The King and I* revolves initially around the king's broken promise. As Landon puts it and Deborah Kerr repeats, he was to give her "'a brick house adjoining the palace,' not within it" (Rodgers, *The King and I* 1956, p. 67). Anna's insistence on her own space stems from her understanding that she comes as a governess, not as the king's servant or, worse still, as a member of his harem, which residing in the palace implies. Yet the need for a British tutor at all suggests that, for the next generation of rulers, a Siamese education alone will be insufficient in an age of colonialism. King Mongkut, in Landon's story, actually relies on Anna's knowledge of the West to fend off foreign aggression, particularly from the French. Landon portrays the menacing gunboat diplomacy of both the French and the British, which clearly indicates that it is King Mongkut's house—his state—rather than Anna's that is threatened.

Rodgers and Hammerstein compress Landon's politics into two performances centering on space. Brynner's semi-chanted soliloquy "A Puzzlement" contemplates "Shall I join other nations in alliance?" which, he fears, may lead to annexation by strong allies. The second performance is the play arranged by Lady Tuptim, an adaptation of Stowe's novel entitled "The Small House of Uncle Thomas," to entertain European dignitaries and to impress upon them how civilized Siam has become. Musicals, of course, thrive on the device of a play within a play to introduce more songs and dances. By this device Rodgers and Hammerstein let their audience watch the banquet guests watch the play, or modern viewers in the new millennium witness the reenactment of the Cold War, which reenacts the Civil War; an embryonic U.S.-centric New World Order boasts of a pedigree back to Southeast Asia and the American South. The play of Eliza fleeing King Simon of Legree mirrors its author and narrator Tuptim's impending attempt to escape from King Mongkut's palace. Unlike Eliza, Tuptim is intercepted. Yet emancipation of all the slaves and harem females is hinted at when a defiant Anna dares King Mongkut to flog Tuptim. Brynner fails to deliver the punishment; stripped of his royal authority, he appears next on his deathbed.

Rodgers attributes the enchanting Oriental dance of "The Small House of Uncle Thomas" to the choreographer Jerome Robbins (*Musical Stages* 1975, p. 274). Frederick Nolan also praises the dance as "Jerome Robbins's balletic divertissement" (*The Sound of Their Music* 1978, p. 174). The dance derives its exotic charm from the gilded set, gorgeous costumes, the stage props, and seemingly Siamese dance movements accompanied by gongs, cymbals, and other traditional musical instruments. In a large measure, Robbins takes his inspiration from what Joan Erdman describes as "oriental dance," which since the 1920s "conjured up expectations of exotic movements, glittering costumes, flowing lines, sublime dedication, and minor mode or strangely tuned music" ("Dance Discourses" 1996, p. 288).[4]

Space and resources are at the heart of any dispute, including, of course, World War II, the setting for *South Pacific,* as well as the Cold War when the film was produced. Lieutenant Cable arrives as an emancipator of the virgin land from the Japanese and of the "virgin" Liat, who will marry no one but Cable after what appears to be one sultry evening together. As soon as he sets foot on the shore, Cable is accosted repeatedly by Bloody Mary to visit the isolated, twin-peaked island of Bali H'ai, an area off limits to naval personnel. Bloody Mary's song "Bali H'ai," shot in an orange glow produced by Panavision's tinted lenses, casts a spell on Cable. Director Joshua Logan resorts to this awful coloring whenever he wishes to create "magical," romantic moments, a tinkering with their original Broadway production that Rodgers and Hammerstein thoroughly loathed.[5] When Cable and his entourage do finally go to Bali H'ai, they are met by a motley crew of Hawaiian hula dancers, African natives adorned with bones and tusks, Asians in round, outlandish peasant hats, and Catholic nuns. This "multicultural" Eden crystallizes in Liat, a Tonkinese with Western facial features dressed in Chinese blouse with frog closings and a standing collar. Both the island and the maiden find their master in Cable.

Despite the change of scene from the wartime Bali H'ai to San Francisco's Chinatown, *Flower Drum Song* duplicates its chopsticks predecessors' concern for space, this time located in the tug-of-war between Americanization and traditionalism in ethnic consciousness. Ethnicity and race are pitted against each other; the younger generation, who have a burgeoning self-identity as an ethnic group in the United States, rebels against the older, immigrant generation, who considers Chinatown inhabitants a separate race from mainstream Americans. This is no doubt a liberal reflection of the 1960s ethos of desegregation and pride in ethnic roots. Although the ending to the film tilts somewhat toward tradition in the double marriages of the "Chinese" couple, Wang Ta and Mei Li, and of their "Americanized" counterparts, Sammy Fong and Linda Low, there is little question as to which pair commands the stage in musical performances.

Nancy Kwan, who plays Linda Low, is, of course, the star of the show, continuing the seductress role she began in *The World of Suzie Wong* (1960). The impressive heights Kwan reaches in several numbers are far superior to the static, lackluster songs of Mei Li (Miyoshi Umeki), composed perhaps by Rodgers's left hand. William Hyland, in *Richard Rodgers* (1998), depicts *Flower Drum Song* as a "clash between the Americanized lifestyle of the young Chinese and the traditions of their parents," which "allowed Rodgers to write in both a modern swing style and a pseudo-Chinese tone" (p. 244). Among the modern songs, Hyland includes Kwan's striptease "Fan Tan Fanny" and a swing number "Grant Avenue." If we broaden the swing style to count any performance denoting an immersion in American culture, then the lineup grows exponentially with Sammy Fong's "Baby, Don't Marry Me!" the dream sequence ballet involving Wang Ta, and Kwan's song of narcissism performed in front of multiple mirrors, among others. On the other hand, Hyland points out, an Asian flavor permeates Mei Li's "semi-chant 'a hundred million miracles,' which had a Chinese sound when repeated without harmonic accompaniment" (p. 244). "Chop Suey," sung by Auntie Liang, also belongs to the Asian category. The considerably slighter output from Rodgers's left hand serves primarily to lend an Orientalist slant to *Flower Drum Song*.

To make Chinatown a site of generational conflict, Rodgers and Hammerstein have altered the characterizations in C. Y. Lee's novel. Lee's universe is one of refugees from China, an immigrant enclave observed by an immigrant writer. Not only is the rigid, phlegmatic, out-of-date Mandarin, Master Wang, a Chinese expatriate, but his eldest son, Wang Ta, has yet to become an American citizen after five years in the country. Linda Tung (rechristened Linda Low by Rodgers and Hammerstein) is a former dancing girl from "Shanghai's A Hundred Happiness Dance Hall. Came to this country as a G.I. bride" (Lee, *The Flower Drum Song* 1957, p. 91). Rodgers and Hammerstein turn all the younger generation, except Mei Li, into American-born to sharpen differences between the immigrants and their children. Whether because it is inconsistent with the comical strain of their musical or because of Rodgers and Hammerstein's "classic liberalism of the 1950s and early 1960s" (Hyland, *Richard Rodgers* 1998, p. 246), the film purges from C. Y. Lee the stereotypical Tong wars, hatchet men, and the seedy side of Chinatown.

## Act III: The Mutt Teases

Mass entertainment that aspires to rise above mediocrity often finds itself resorting to titillating subject matter outside of the drab, repetitious, day-to-day human reality, but it never truly transgresses against social taboos. Therein lies the mystery of tease, the key to Rodgers and Hammerstein's phenomenal success. These two Jewish music makers intuitively knew the boundaries of race and gender; they played with public sensibility but they always played safe.[6] To illustrate, note the swift movement from comedy to romance to tragedy in *The King and I*. Comic repartee between the king and Anna ceases as they ready themselves for the waltz "Shall We Dance?" which Hyland identifies as "the only moment when there is a whiff of romance between them" (*Richard Rodgers* 1998, p. 199). A hint of hybridization emerges in the mutual attraction of the two whirling dancers with gazes locked, but the spell is soon broken by the call of duty to punish Lady Tuptim. A "pregnant moment," pun intended, intensified by the tease of miscegenation, crumbles under social constraints.

Likewise, *South Pacific* locates its double nadirs, perhaps the inverse of the twin-peaked Bali H'ai, on either side of the intermission. Each instance repeats the formula of miscegenetic tease and disillusionment, of romantic potential coming to a screeching halt. Immediately before the intermission, the Southern belle Nellie Forbush, ensign at the Navy hospital, recoils in revulsion upon discovering her French suitor Emile de Becque's two mixed-race children from his previous marriage to a Polynesian.[7] Immediately after the intermission, Cable recoils in revulsion upon being reminded by Bloody Mary that he and Liat will "have special good babies." Cable instinctively turns away from the mother and the daughter, his body language magnified by a blast of trumpets and searing tones of the violin. While Cable's response is not as hysterical as the sobbing Nellie's, the soundtrack achieves a similarly schizophrenic effect: both American protagonists are jolted out of their romances by the abhorrent crime of interbreeding or siring "mutts." The mongrel child remains only a tease in *South Pacific,* since Cable dies, and the couple most likely to bear interracial children is torn apart, while Emile survives and reunites with Nellie, both Caucasians. Emile's two mutts, like the dependent people of color of the Cold War, are destined to become the wards of a Euro-American alliance.

A mutt suggests indeterminacy on the borderland, a teasing of lines of separation. The mutt as a symbol of racial ambiguity can be applied to the crossing of gender differences as well. Nellie Forbush's vaudeville number at the Thanksgiving Follies fully exploits sexual ambiguity as a strategy of tease. To entertain "lonesome, homesick boys," Nellie cross-dresses as a sailor clown in large, baggy pants and a necktie (or necklace?) that hangs down to her knees. Nellie the sailor sings the sexually explicit "Honey Bun." Rocking her buttocks when she sings about the "br-r-r-road" part of the sailor's lover, she sends the crowd into thunderous cheers. This explosion of testosterone is dangerously close to that of a bawdy music hall, but Rodgers and Hammerstein adroitly redirect the rowdy scene and masculine aggressiveness to yet another cross-dresser on the stage, Luther Billis. A jester in a coconut brassiere and a grass skirt, Billis receives all the harassment meant for Nellie. Soldiers run on stage to fondle his bra, lift up his skirt, crawl through his legs. During Billis's belly dance, which shows the boat sketched on his midriff, someone shouts: "Billis, you got a hole in your boat," alluding to either his navel or a drive to penetrate. In a Freudian fashion, Billis is pelted by dozens of paper planes once he gets on stage. The mob's invasive urge is finally spent when a dart stings Billis's "buns." The threatened gang rape of Nellie defaults, courtesy of social taboos, to locker-room taunts of Billis; fantasies of sexual assault are transferred to light-hearted rituals of male bonding. And this is not the only occasion when Billis is feminized in relation to Nellie. His admiration for Nellie leads him to launder and iron her uniforms, while his "cottage industry" consists of weaving grass skirts for sale.[8] The finale to Nellie's performance at the Thanksgiving Follies nonetheless restores her to her feminine self, and she is joined by a dozen or so gorgeously attired Ziegfeld girls.

The Eurasian Nancy Kwan (Linda Low in *Flower Drum Song*) and France Nuyen (Liat in *South Pacific*) assume the roles of "mutt" teases; Kwan uses her sexual charm, Nuyen her girlish vulnerability. Kwan was born in Hong Kong of Anglo-Chinese parentage, Nuyen in Marseille, of Vietnamese-French parentage. Their musical performances capitalize on the inherent racial and cultural hybridity of their bodies. Kwan's swing numbers, "Fan Tan Fanny" and "Grant Avenue," take place on sumptuous Oriental sets. Preceded by "Gliding Through My Memoree," which arrays Asian American women in whiteface with various European costumes, "Fan Tan Fanny" resembles a striptease. It culminates in Kwan's simulation of the shedding of her wardrobe by suddenly folding three Chinese fans strategically placed around her body and exposing the skin-color leotard underneath. "Grant Avenue," supposedly choreographed on that very street in San Francisco's Chinatown, begins with such Orientalist banalities as gongs, obeisance to ancestors, and a flat chant on a float in a New Year procession, followed by a swing dance of the time. Even Kwan's narcissistic eulogy to feminine beauty, "I Enjoy Being a Girl," staged in front of a triptych of body-length mirrors, charms with the kaleidoscopic multiplication of a Chinese-looking tease, who metamorphoses into four images in different dresses and settings. Nuyen's Liat, by contrast, performs fewer numbers and they take advantage of less of her body. Standing in a waist-deep pond of the lush island paradise, a silent Liat puts on a finger play, her allure proceeding less from sensuality than from gullibility. In addition to presenting a similar finger play, the innocent Mei Li in *Flower Drum Song* performs also through hand gestures, as opposed to Kwan's curvaceous body language and bewitching dance routines.

Rodgers and Hammerstein employ many other "mutt" stars whose racial indeterminacy appeals to a public longing for exoticism so long as it is in keeping with white sensibility and aesthetics. Rita Moreno from Puerto Rico plays Lady Tuptim and Yul Brynner's ancestry includes, at least, Swiss-German, Mongolian, and Russian forebears.[9] Richard Rodgers offers a rather complacent comment on the multiracial cast of their musicals in *Musical Stages* (1975):

> This ethnically mixed cast [of *Flower Drum Song*] ... gave the illusion
> of being Chinese. This demonstrates one of the beautiful things
> about theatre audiences. People want to believe what they see on a
> stage. . . . Ask them to accept Ezio Pinza as a Frenchman [de Becque],
> Yul Brynner as Siamese or a heterogeneous group of actors as
> Chinese, and they are prepared to meet you nine tenths of the way
> even before the curtain goes up. (p. 295)

What is presented as the magic of theater masks an imbalanced power structure in which an ethnic minority and imposters enact white fantasies on
stage—model minority, traditional Confucianist, Dragon Lady, China doll,
childish heathens, fickle tyrant, etcetera. This kind of indiscriminate casting
long ago came under attack. As *The New Yorker* critic Kenneth Tynan put it
on December 13, 1958:

> The authors' attitude toward exotic peoples in general seems to have
> changed hardly at all since they wrote "South Pacific" and "The King
> and I." If friendly, the natives have a simple, primitive, childlike
> sweetness.... It seems to have worried neither Mr. Rodgers nor
> Mr. Hammerstein very much that the behavior of war-torn Pacific
> islanders and nineteenth-century Siamese might be slightly different
> from that of Chinese residents of present-day California. (qtd. in
> Hyland, *Richard Rodgers* 1998, p. 246)

Joseph Lam argues in a journal devoted specifically to Asian American
studies that a song like "Chop Suey" in *Flower Drum Song* can be considered Asian American music because the film's "all Asian/Asian American
cast renders the music a revealing expression of Asian American experiences"
("Embracing 'Asian American Music'" 1999, p. 53). But Auntie Liang, who
performs "Chop Suey," is played by the Hispanic Juanita Hall. It is one thing
to contend that the American "home-grown" dish of chop suey epitomizes
Asian American problematics. It is quite another to offer a simplistic solution
by eliding an "all Asian/Asian American cast" with ethnically sensitive Asian
American expression, particularly when a Hispanic passes as a yellowface who
passes, ideologically, as white American.

### Entr'acte: Oriental Numbers

Thus far I have treated Rodger and Hammerstein's musicals as a visual and
conceptual experience, leaving out the auditory part, as though we could fully
grasp a television program with the sound muted. This is obviously absurd,
and is due simply to my unfamiliarity with music. The techniques of music-
making, and, in particular, the chopsticks music from Rodgers's left hand, are
largely beyond me and, to borrow from Baudelaire, beyond a number of my
"lecteur,—mon semblable,—mon frère!" The following is merely a layman's
impressions muttered during an intermission, its next act of music analysis to
be continued, hopefully, by specialists.

The disclaimer aside, let us count the Oriental tunes from these chopsticks
musicals. Although few in number, the Oriental flavor echoes from these

specific scores to the entire soundtrack, coming alive periodically through the striking of a gong or particular refrains in the background music. Even the most Western pieces of *Flower Drum Song* usually open with a line or two of Oriental tunes and return to them regularly. Nevertheless, while a song like Sammy Fong's "Baby, Don't Marry Me!" seems to proceed in a rather monotonous tone marked by a persistent, clinging sound, the lyrics offer Mei Li the most untraditional advice, punctuated at times by rhythms of the Big Band.

Here is what Rodgers's left hand has composed: from *The King and I*, Brynner's "A Puzzlement" as well as the orchestral pieces "March of the Siamese Children" and "Small House of Uncle Thomas"; from *South Pacific*, Juanita Hall's "Bali H'ai" and "Happy Talk"; from *Flower Drum Song*, Miyoshi Umeki's "A Hundred Million Miracles." Accompanied by traditional Asian musical instruments such as gongs, drums, and cymbals, these numbers are invariably monotonal, unfluctuating for a series of beats and then abruptly jumping to a high note. These pieces render the succession of notes in a scale less than fluid, approximating a monosyllabic, singsong cadence in speech, an effect caused to a great extent by the semi-chanted delivery, in a heavy accent, of the "Oriental" performers. It is ironic that Oriental numbers in monotones are, without fail, vested with Oriental magic, be it the regal display of Siamese children, the siren song of "Bali H'ai," or the "Hundred Million Miracles" that befall an illegal alien who jumps ship. The final twist of *Flower Drum Song* occurs when Mei Li, inspired by a Mexican woman's confession on television, dissolves her marriage contract with Sammy Fong by admitting that she has entered this country illegally, saying that "my back is wet." The double happy weddings in the end are brought about by the magic touch of an alien reversing her bleak situation, a token of "A Hundred Million Miracles." Melodies from Rodgers's left hand serve as a reminder of enchantment emanating from pseudo-Oriental bodies or pseudo-Oriental reprises.

Rodgers and Hammerstein are greatly indebted to prominent predecessors like Gilbert and Sullivan, whose light operetta *The Mikado* provides a paradigm for Orientalist tunes. The characteristics of monotones, pidgin delivery, and the blending of primitivism and aesthetics mark Gilbert and Sullivan's hit songs such as "Behold the Lord High Executioner," "Three Little Maids from School Are We," "A More Humane Mikado Never Did in Japan Exist," and many more. With the decline of musicals, the virus of Oriental music has found a new host in animations for a young audience. While Disney has undone certain unsavory features from its blatantly racist past—say, "We Are Siamese, If You Please," sung by the Siamese cats in *Lady and the Tramp* (1955), and "Shanghai Hong Kong Egg Foo Yong," in *The Aristocats* (1967), many compositional traits have been passed down to *Mulan* (1998), as is evident in the protagonist's solo "You'll Bring Honor to Us All," a flat, singsong number that recycles stereotypical ideas of China. In view of the music industry's addiction to Orientalist representations, music practitioners interested in composing the next act should perhaps attend as much to orchestrating minorities and natives to sing back in their genuine voices as to demystifying extant chopsticks musicals.

# 10 The Nine Lives of *Blackhawk*'s Oriental

## Chop Chop, Wu Cheng, and Weng Chan

**What** is the point of dredging up from the lees of low-brow culture some "frivolous," "childish" comics? How can a comic possibly enlighten, or even inform us, especially a comic like *Blackhawk*—fifty-odd pages, crudely produced, selling for ten cents at its inception in 1941, seventy-five cents in 1984, and marked up to about three dollars at the end of its run in 1990? Even in its heyday, the hodgepodge, consumerist, somewhat expendable look of *Blackhawk* inspired, by traditional scholarly standards, minimal interest. Each number usually consisted of a cover page; one or two pages of advertisements for guns, ukuleles, cheap cameras, pots, typewriters, dinner sets, roller skates, and other products; two Blackhawk comic sequences of about eleven to fourteen pages each; one eight- or nine-page section of comic relief entitled "Chop Chop"; two pages of a Blackhawk story in text only; yet another Blackhawk comic of about fourteen pages; more advertisements; and, finally, one or two short comics featuring other characters.

Yet the products of popular culture surpass their counterparts in high culture by manifesting contemporary impulses in a far less inhibited, self-conscious fashion. Unfolding as part of the public discourse from World War II to the 1990s, high literary culture ordinarily suppresses or at least sugarcoats unseemly thoughts. Even when Ezra Pound, for instance, unleashed his anti-semitic tirades in *Cantos,* private correspondence, and radio broadcasts on behalf of the Mussolini government, critics such as John Harrison, in *The Reactionaries* (1966), tend to dismiss such "bad apples" in the poet's corpus. Popular culture for the masses, by stringent artistic standards, is inferior—apples as yet unripe—to "high" art. Comics are, in a manner of speaking, the doodlings or automatic writings of the U.S. collective unconscious, communicating neuroses in shockingly straightforward ways. As such, over its long life span, *Blackhawk* spoke to and for a number of generations: American GIs during World War II, cold warriors, baby boomers, and Gen-Xers. The

World War II backdrop of *Blackhawk* explains part of its staying power, as Dale Luciano correctly diagnoses for war comics: "Since both Korea and Vietnam are popularly associated with frustration and defeat, and might therefore prove unpalatable as settings for tales of war heroics, the safest bet would appear to be placing such tales in the less morally ambiguous World War II era" ("Comics Past, Comics Present" 1982, p. 54).

Even though out of the public eye for at least a decade now, the *Blackhawk* corpses rotting at the bottom of the river of time tell us wondrous tales through their pustules and odors. This salvaging focuses on the Oriental character nicknamed Chop Chop, who evolves in the 1980s into Wu Cheng and, subsequently, into Weng Chan. This Oriental character debuts as a clown and domestic. Toward the end of his Wu Cheng reincarnation in 1983–1984, he becomes a moody, impulsive, almost rebellious adolescent, whereas the Weng Chan in the late 1980s acquires the image and language of a cynical Gen-Xer. Cover not your nose, honorable readers; inhale deeply, for this autopsy releases nothing but our own poisonous gas—ignorance and racism at the heart of American culture.

Because of *Blackhawk*'s market-oriented nature, its plot and characterizations are not necessarily consistent throughout its fifty-year life span. Furthermore, an attempt at its complete publication history is hampered by the unavailability of a small number of this comic series. This comic was printed on inexpensive or even substandard paper and hence was prone to disintegration.[1] The following review is largely chronological, with particular analysis of the Oriental character. *Blackhawk* was initiated by Military Comics, and its first issue came out in August 1941. Number 43 in October 1945 was the last published by Military Comics, but *Blackhawk* continued to appear, with Modern Comics as its publisher. Hubert Crawford, in *Crawford's Encyclopedia of Comic Books* (1978), characterizes the birth of *Blackhawk* and the entire collection of Military Comics publications as "Quality's [referring to Quality Comics, a parent company for Military Comics] answer to the patriotic trend that many comic books were turning to during the early 1940s. A complete departure from superhero fantasy and the avenging masked sleuth themes that dominated the other Quality titles" (p. 58).

*Blackhawk* is about a team of daredevil pilots at the time of World War II, all but one from various occupied nations, who are united in their fight against the Nazis. Although the comic does not exactly open with a character list, or remain consistent in characterization, the members of the group gradually emerge as follows: Blackhawk, formerly Janos or Jan Prohaska, is a Polish refugee turned American; Stanislaus is from Poland; Andre from France; Chuck from America; Hendrickson from Holland (in later numbers he hails from Germany); Olaf from Sweden; and Chop Chop from China. Comics had, indeed, gone to war. In 1941 *Blackhawk* shared the spotlight with comics about other heroic figures, for every comic sequence involved the war. *Archie Atkins: Desert Scout,* for instance, combated the Nazis in the desert. A large number of the comic books deployed aviation as the center of action—aerial dogfights and Flying Fortresses having captured the public's imagination.

In view of the air domination in the Chinese theater in the early 1940s, *Blackhawk* may have been based to some extent on the feats of the Louisiana-born Claire Lee Chennault. Under the auspices of Generalissimo Chiang Kai-shek, Chennault headed the American Volunteer Group (AVG), American pilots recruited clandestinely to defend the air space of the great interior of China as well as the Burma Road, the lifeline for the great interior, against the Japanese Air Force. "Fight[ing] for pay," as Malcolm Rosholt put it, the AVG were handsomely rewarded by Chiang's Nationalist government, which did not otherwise have a reliable cadre of fighter pilots (*Flight in the China Air Space* 1984, p. 107). The covert action was necessitated by U.S. neutrality before Pearl Harbor. The AVG saw about eight months of operation and scored decisive victories against the Japanese beginning with their first battle, above the city of Kunming on December 20, 1941. Their nominally private, almost vigilante operation changed when the United States declared war. On July 4, 1942, the AVG was ordered to disband as a private force and be reorganized into the U.S. military. This did not stop Chennault from becoming a war hero, not just in China but in the United States as well; he was featured on the cover of *Time* magazine on December 6, 1943. Chennault began by flying the Hawk III aircraft. Then in the spring of 1942, his Flying Tigers were reinforced with "improved model P-40E's (Kittyhawks)" (A. Chennault, *Chennault and the Flying Tigers* 1963, p. 136). Both the title of *Blackhawk* and the frequency of China as the site of action suggests that Chennault's Flying Tigers played the role of Muse here.

Beyond the specific circumstances of war, however, the comics had a long tradition of aviation adventure strips. Robert Harvey, in *The Art of the Funnies* (1994), states: "The first of the grimly serious adventure strips were inspired by Charles Lindbergh's heroic solo flight across the Atlantic" in 1927 (p. 118). Comic strips about pilots proliferated, including *Tailspin Tommy* (1928) and *Skyroads* (1929). *Buck Rogers* extended aviation into space and heralded sci-fi comics such as *Flash Gordon*. Terry in *Terry and the Pirates* became an aviator during World War II. The lead in *Steve Canyon* was a flying ace during the Korean War. The creator of the latter two comics, Milton Caniff, in fact "became an unofficial spokesman for the Air Force" (R. Harvey, *Art of the Funnies* 1994, p. 156). Sky or space, the final frontier, as *Star Trek* described it decades later, provided the wide canvas against which heroic masculinity was delineated.

Beyond the specific circumstances of adventure comic strips, human beings have long fantasized about flight. Greek mythology gives us Daedalus and Icarus, Mercury, Pegasus, and a host of other winged creatures, a fascination with soaring through the air shared by countless other ancient cultures. Modern myth-making also enlists space, particularly in the science-fiction genre. The human longing for freedom seems symbolized by the boundless sky. However, with the exception of mythology, one is unlikely to be flying all the time. In *Blackhawk*, aerial stunts constitute periodic climaxes, but the bulk of the story takes place on land. Pilots, after all, must land to refuel their aircraft as well as themselves. So in rushes the Chinese domestic Chop Chop, who remains on the Blackhawk island—the pilots' home base—to cook, to sew, to serve, and to entertain.

In number 3 of October 1941, Chop Chop debuted. His physical appearance resembles that of the Chinese servant Connie in Milton Caniff's *Terry and the Pirates*, for he has prominent buck teeth, beady slanting eyes, protruding ears, bow legs, splayfeet, short stature, and the white gloves of a blackface minstrel.[2] Like Connie, Chop Chop's otherwise blank face exhibits an occasional grin or a frown, but more often than not he has a vacuous smile to suggest a minority happy and content with his lot. Physiologically, as we see in Figure 1, the almost squatting Chop Chop highlights the blackhawks' height and erect posture. Linguistically, the blackhawks' chorus of "Over land, over sea, we fight to make men free"—complete with musical notes—is amplified by the jumble of scribblings above Chop Chop's head, supposedly his attempt at singing along. Whenever agitated or excited, Chop Chop's verbal communication degenerates from comical pidgin to totally unintelligible quasi-Chinese ideograms. Indeed, Chop Chop appears not to belong to the same human species as the other blackhawks; he has to be led by hand like a child-monkey in Figure 1. Chop Chop is usually the butt of slapstick comedy: in number 3, for example, he breaks through a stone wall with his bare head, only to be rescued when he is grabbed by the collar and lifted into the air by Blackhawk.[3]

The blackhawks' outfits are exquisitely tailor-made. Fashionably cut, they do not recall any particular uniform worn by Allied soldiers, certainly not the U.S. armed forces. And, in fact, their uniforms are modeled, ironically, after those of Nazi officers. Eventually the blackhawk outfits evolve into blue or black double-breasted tunics with shiny brass buttons, riding pants, black knee-high boots, black belts, and yellow or red aviator scarves. The commander, Blackhawk, is distinguished from the rest by the round yellow emblem with a hawk's head on it on the front of his uniform, the yellow background

Figure 1. Chop Chop's debut in *Blackhawk*. *Blackhawk*, number 3 (October 1941).

of the patch highlighting the dark hawk's head. By contrast, Chop Chop evolves in the series to become garishly dressed: he comes to wear a yellow vest decorated with small black crosses, a red skirt, green pants and shirt sleeves, a red bow tied to his pigtail (which stands straight upwards), and red platform shoes. A red apron sticks out from under his yellow vest like the embarrassing hem of an undershirt. Compared with the blackhawks, Chop Chop is certainly the most "colorful." Over the years Chop Chop's face and skin color also gradually take on a yellowish-red hue in contrast to the lighter pigment of blackhawks.

Seemingly negligible, Chop Chop is in fact integral to *Blackhawk*. Just as we can not imagine Don Quixote without Sancho Panza, King Lear without his Fool, or Greek tragedy without comic relief, the heroism of the blackhawks hinges on their Fool's dog-like loyalty and farcical sideshow. Chop Chop and the blackhawks depend on one another; they are symbiotic and inextricable. As wartime *Blackhawk* evolved into Cold War *Blackhawk,* the kitsch of American male fantasies acquired a new urgency. The United States was now leader of the Free World, which presupposed wards, such as peoples of color from the Third World. A recurring motif, therefore, is that the Chinese "familiar," the good Oriental, seeks protection from the bad Oriental.

Number 5 in December 1941 is the first time that Chop Chop is equipped with a meat cleaver, which unfortunately fails to lend him any authority as he is immediately knocked down by a woman. Slowly, Chop Chop outgrows some of his Caniff-ite Connie image and "matures" into his ultimately pear-shaped face and body. His stereotypical facial features—buck teeth and the like—remain intact, though.

After the last number published by Military Comics in October 1945, *Blackhawk* continued to be published by Modern Comics, from number 44 in November 1945 through number 102 in October 1950. The change of name from Military to Modern Comics was probably more cosmetic than substantive, rendered inevitable by the end of the war. Indeed, the end of Military Comics roughly coincided with the dropping of atomic bombs in August 1945. In any case, both Military Comics and Modern Comics were branches of the same parent company, Quality Comics. It was and still is a common marketing strategy in comics to stagger the sale of a hot title. Certain numbers come out monthly, interspersed by others that come out quarterly, thus saturating the market and doubling the sale. Because of the popularity of *Blackhawk,* Quality Comics published it each season as well as in monthly installments.

In one quarterly issue—number 9 in winter 1944—Chop Chop wields his cleaver like a baton to conduct the chorus of blackhawks singing their famous battle cry "HAWKAAA-AAA." Even in black-and-white reproduction, Chop Chop's darker skin tone stands out against the others' fairer color. It is intriguing that Al Bryant, who drew this particular picture, turns Chop Chop's rotund body to display his stereotypical facial features, as if to reconfirm the readers' image of Orientals. Chop Chop suffers as well from obesity, with his bulging

Figure 2. Chop Chop the "conductor," with a meat cleaver for a baton. *Blackhawk,* number 9 (Winter 1944).

waistline and buttocks highlighted by the contrasting colors in his costume. Unlike the Chop Chop in 1941, who wears a hat, in 1944, as we see in Figure 2, he sports his signature erect hair braid tied with a red bow.

It may be due to the fact that Chop Chop occupies the foreground that he only comes up to Blackhawk's waist. However, number 11 in summer 1946, shown in Figure 3, makes their relative heights crystal clear. Marching in a V formation, Chop Chop walks, literally, between the blackhawks' long legs: either Chop Chop is a dwarf or the blackhawks are giants. And we also note that Chop Chop is not in step with the blackhawks, which singles him out as not quite a team member.

The Chop Chop sequence from number 10 in spring 1946 shows Chop Chop riding a rocket or oversized firecracker, yet another stock image associated with China. Chop Chop has apparently tried to entertain himself while left alone to guard the home base, wrecking havoc to create a comic interlude before the next blackhawk exploit. The Chop Chop sequence from number 12 in autumn 1946 draws deeply from racist stereotypes of Orientalism, namely, all Orientals looked alike. A mirror image of Chop Chop, the Chinese detective Kloppie Klan stems from Charlie Chan. The pidgin of "velly good likeness, no" follows the long tradition of Orientalist caricature. A great number of such twin-like Chinese characters appear in the Chop Chop sequences, giving rise to much mistaken identity and slapstick comic action. Many of

Figure 3. Chop Chop the dwarf, marching out of step. *Blackhawk*, number 11 (Summer 1946).

Figure 4. Chop Chop and Kloppie Klan. All Orientals looked alike. *Blackhawk*, number 12 (Autumn 1946).

these episodes, furthermore, are set in family businesses such as restaurants and laundries, professions responsible for holding down Chinese since the nineteenth century. Some of Chop Chop's look-alikes are in fact evil characters. The good Oriental, in the Western imagination, never strays far from his evil shadow. A funny Charlie Chan will soon team up, albeit unwittingly, with a menacing Fu Manchu. The good Oriental, under the protectorate of the blackhawks, needs to be guarded against his dark half. Figure 4 (number 12 in Autumn 1946), number 10 in Spring 1946, and many other issues display a section title "Chop Chop" in faux Chinese script—short, choppy, curving strokes pointed at one end and wide, broken-off at the other.

The slapstick nature of Chop Chop's function is readily apparent in number 29 of February 1950 when Chop Chop is kicked off a stage. A speech balloon indicates Chop Chop's interior monologue: "Velly puzzling why audience find play so comical! Me not find it funny at all!" Meanwhile the white

Figure 5. Chop Chop being kicked offstage. *Blackhawk*, number 29 (February 1950).

audience laughs in the foreground. On the one hand, Figure 5 seems to expose the charade of Chinese comic relief, giving Chop Chop some minimal reflection of his subaltern condition. On the other, even that reflective moment can be taken as charting the depth of Chop Chop's stupidity, for he has no clue as to why he has been expelled from the white arena.

The last number of *Blackhawk* that Quality Comics published was number 85 in February 1955. In the early 1950s, as described in DC Comics Senior Editor Mike Gold's letter to retailers, *Blackhawk* "was the main reason DC Comics purchased the assets of Quality Comics." DC Comics, also known at the time as National Comics, was responsible for bringing out *Blackhawk* until 1984, despite two lengthy hiatuses between number 243 (October–November 1968) and number 244 (January–February 1976) and between number 250 (January–February 1977) and number 251 (October 1982).

Immediately after DC Comics took over *Blackhawk*, Chop Chop had a face lift, liposuction, and speech therapy.[4] Just as these techniques of body alteration are unlikely to radically transform a living individual's personality, the new DC Chop Chop remained fundamentally unchanged. The "speech therapy" may have straightened out the confusion between the letters "r" and "l," but ungrammatical, awkward sentences continue to plague Chop Chop's communication. In number 119, December 1957, as Figure 6 shows, Chop Chop has shed his pig-like body, replaced by that of a young man with slicked-back hair. While Quality Comics originally justified the blackhawks' patronizing attitude toward Chop Chop on grounds of his animal or pet-like characteristics, DC Comics continued the practice for reasons of Chop Chop's apparent youth, which comes dangerously close to infantilization. Wearing the same costume, Chop Chop speaks in the same pidgin: "Will do! But nerves rattling like dragon's tail—am looking forward to end of test!" followed by "Yipes! Is miserable short circuit!" This is spoken just before Chop Chop faints and the blackhawks, in a time machine, are thrown back to the eighteenth century. Not only are Chop Chop's sentences stereotypically devoid of subjects, but the analogy of "dragon's tail" cashes in on the "trite trope" of China.[5] That native speakers of English have constructed this pidgin for

**Figure 6.** Chop Chop's new image as a young boy with slicked-back hair. *Blackhawk*, number 119 (December 1957).

the consumption of other native speakers of English seems indisputable in view of the use of "Yipes!" an exclamation few Chinese immigrants would use if taken by surprise. Chop Chop's inferior status is borne out, even after his enviable weight loss, by his different clothing, physical appearance, pidgin English, and, most of all, by the fact that he stays in the control room and does not go into the time machine. Of course, his supplementary role makes possible the blackhawks' adventure, the happy ending of which—the blackhawks restored to the modern world—would not have happened if Chop Chop did not awaken in time to reverse the time machine. Many episodes in *Blackhawk* now began to concentrate on such sci-fi themes, but even the sci-fi plots were often tangled with allusions to age-old Orientalist jokes. At the end of another successful mission, Chop Chop remarks: "Confucius say... 'He who dwells in house of evil—soon makes his home a PRISON!'" (number 134 in March 1959). Such "Confucius say" jokes are as corny as the stock image of dragons. The ideological violence the West commits against the East is hidden behind a statement allegedly made by Confucius and cited by Chop Chop, both "insiders" of Chinese culture. One's own viciousness is twice removed, so distant from oneself that one can appreciate the alleged witticism.

Under the management of DC Comics, Chop Chop's wardrobe expanded at long last. In addition to the same old clothes from 1941, Chop Chop at times bedecks himself with a "uniform" similar to that of the other blackhawks—only his outfit is a loud, flamboyant 1960s red. On several occasions, Chop Chop finds himself in a karate outfit, but even this has hints of the old apparel. What Chop Chop wears does not become a problem until around numbers 264 and 265 in November and December of 1983.

In number 230 of March 1967 (Figure 7), nineteen months before DC Comics ceased publication of *Blackhawk* for the first time, Chop Chop is dressed in bow tie, gloves, and what appears to be a swallow-tailed coat. He has been renamed Dr. Hands, alluding, of course, to his kung fu skills. When *Blackhawk* returned in 1976, it brought with it the seventies ethos, and the sex revolution succeeded in disrobing the blackhawks of their Nazi-styled uniforms, baring their chests, and including a host of scantily clad women. Number 244 in January-February 1976 (Figure 8) rechristened Chop Chop as Chopper. We can see that number 251 in October 1982 (Figure 9), after the second hiatus of five years, recycles the tableau of Figures 7 and 8 (and, to some extent, Figure 3), namely, the blackhawks charging forward in a V formation with bullets whizzing by. Yet there is a key difference. While Figures 7 and 8 feature futuristic or seventies dress, Figure 9 is decidedly a nostalgic

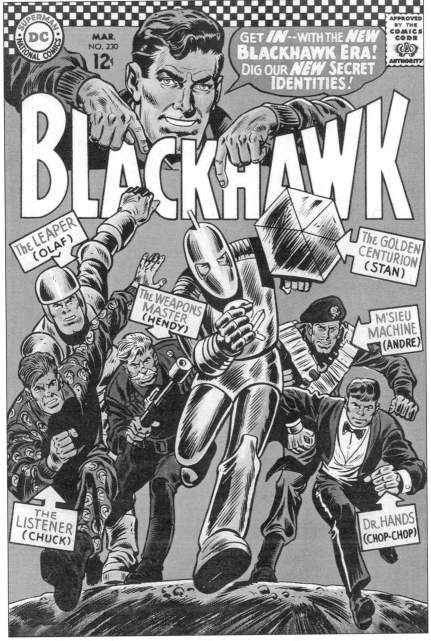

Figure 7. Chop Chop or Dr. Hands. *Blackhawk*, number 230 (March 1967).

Figure 8. Chop Chop or Chopper. *Blackhawk*, number 244 (January–February 1976).

Figure 9. Recycling the tableau of Figures 7 and 8. *Blackhawk*, number 251
(October 1982).

throwback to the original Nazi and Chop Chop costumes, including the meat cleaver.[6] Even the airplanes flying overhead have regressed to double-propeller planes of World War II vintage, whereas the 1950s and 60s *Blackhawk* preferred slick jets or more fanciful flying machines.

It appears at first glance that when Mark Evanier and Dan Spiegle revived *Blackhawk* with number 251 in 1982, they were offering nostalgic, retro depictions of Chop Chop. Not only was Chop Chop's image a reinscription of the 1940s, the 1980s revival retraced Blackhawk's European origin—the loss of his family in Poland to the Nazis. *Blackhawk* in the forties and fifties had downplayed the commander's continental background, making him a typical American. But upon closer analysis of the short-lived Evanier-Spiegle collaboration—for *Blackhawk* vanished yet again in 1984—the comic artists in fact put together one of the most fascinating episodes in the history of *Blackhawk,* especially with respect to the characterization of Chop Chop.

Echoing the tumultuous era, Evanier-Spiegle deploy stereotypical images of the Oriental fighter à la Bruce Lee of the early 1970s. Number 256 in March 1983 visualizes Chop Chop disposing of an enemy with a sidekick. Number 259 in June 1983 has Chop Chop vanquish a ninja assassin. In place of the old comic relief Chop Chop, 1980s readers witness a fighting Chop Chop, one befitting the heightened minority consciousness following the civil rights era. Another stylistic difference comes with the move from episodic to continuous strips, for Evanier-Spiegle end each number with a cliffhanger, to be continued in the following number.

Chop Chop's inner conflicts first surface in number 264 of November 1983 (Figure 10). He begins to resent clerical errands, anything that makes him less than a pilot. In number 264, Chop Chop refuses to make out a requisition for supplies. In the following number, he turns down radio detail as well as Chuck's request to mend his socks. The comic also adopts an approach that lends itself to an in-depth exploration of Chop Chop, who has heretofore been treated as a character as flat and unnuanced as his broad pancake face. While the aircraft in Figure 11, from number 264, definitely indicates a return to World War II, the comic narrative strategies are modern in terms of "window" inserts and montages adding depth to a linear story line. More significantly, Chop Chop's thought balloons permit him rare moments of "self-reflection": "They are all so good....I should feel honored to belong to such a fine team....Why do I feel like I just don't belong?" But it is worth noting that the interior monologue reveals a "sweet" and deferential Oriental behind the facade of recent belligerence. Despite the demeanor of a confrontational, even militant minority fighting for equal rights and justice, readers find once again the good old Oriental, convinced of the master race's superiority, which

Figure 10.
Chop Chop's inner conflicts, reflecting the minority struggle following the civil rights era. *Blackhawk*, number 264 (November 1983).

Figure 11. Chop Chop's thought balloons manifesting his "self-reflection." *Blackhawk*, number 264 (November 1983).

**Figure 12.** Chop Chop the kung fu master, but also the cook fighting for his identity. *Blackhawk,* number 265 (December 1983).

gives rise to Chop Chop's sense of not "belonging." Chop Chop is certainly no Black Panther, but is instead an Alex Haley minority searching for roots, eager to return to a war-torn China where he belongs. That pull allegedly felt by minorities toward the land of their roots can be read as the majority culture's subtle justification of segregation.

Number 265 in December 1983 is pivotal in pondering Chop Chop's dilemma and deserves to be closely interrogated. The cover page, Figure 12, shows an agitated Chop Chop executing a jump kick as if lashing out against his teammates, whose double-edged "innocence" appears in their simultaneous concern over "what's got into Chop-Chop?" and their disparaging call to the servant, "When's supper?" Through martial metaphors, Asian Americans since the 1960s have revolted against the subservient roles to which they have traditionally been relegated. The first blackhawk member who figures out the source of Chop Chop's discontent is the American, Chuck. Of course, a self-congratulatory ethnocentrism may have prompted this choice. Or perhaps the freckled Chuck, who appears to be so young, finds it easier to identify with Chop Chop's self-doubt. Chuck is further enlightened by a young girl, who has inquired as to why Chop Chop's outfit is different from the other blackhawks.'

Figure 13 crystallizes the core difference between the blackhawks and Chop Chop by means of intertextuality. Chuck recalls a chance encounter at a bar with an artist who has displayed his sketches of the blackhawks. The flagrantly racist depiction of the early Chop Chop is haunting, now that Chuck

**Figure 13.** Chop Chop haunted by his previous incarnation. *Blackhawk*, number 265 (December 1983).

has grasped his teammate's legitimate complaint. At this point Chop Chop requests a leave of absence to return home to fight the Japanese. Blackhawk, alerted by Chuck as to the cause of Chop Chop's recent behavior, flings a bundle containing a genuine blackhawk uniform to Chop Chop in a stoic, John Wayne gesture that veils all emotions behind a cool, macho mask. Figure 14 constitutes the best of comics in that the panels communicate with minimal dialogue. Chop Chop walks into the barracks to change into the blackhawk uniform and comes out Wu Cheng, the name he uses to identify himself in

Figure 14. Given a blackhawk uniform and renamed Wu Cheng, Chop Chop flies back to China and vanishes from *Blackhawk*. *Blackhawk*, number 265 (December 1983).

Figure 15. The blackhawks' wistful, ambiguous parting words. *Blackhawk*, number 265 (December 1983).

one of the only two speech balloons on that page. The blackhawk uniform lends him not only equal status but an individual identity. However, once Wu Cheng acquires a self-identity, he instantly evaporates from the narrative, as if a slave, once free, is no longer part of the master's story.

Figure 15, which concludes number 265, bears out this strange logic with the ambivalent moment when Wu Cheng the pilot takes off as a blackhawk, disappearing completely from *Blackhawk* for over ten subsequent numbers. Wu Cheng deviates, however, from the silent masculinist facade of the blackhawks in his parting words: "The hardest thing is to let loved ones realize that they are loved ones." The blackhawks' love, however, has arrived all crumpled up, a bundle of uniform simply thrown at him in a patronizing way. In view of the imminent end of the comic, this act of tossing the bundle may well be the cartoonists' "death-bed confession" to appease a guilty conscience over the sins committed on a monthly basis for half a century. The ambiguity comes across in Evanier-Spiegle's authorial comments in Figure 15. Mark Evanier, who wrote the dialogue, puts in a line that ironically echoes the Declaration of Independence: "And soldiers are all created equal.... And yet six men are right now feeling that the seventh is maybe a little more equal. At least, today." The very tentativeness of the tone with which this number concludes suggests an awareness that the politically correct balance may soon be disrupted, as it undoubtedly was, for Wu Cheng is "missing in action" almost throughout 1984. The awkward caterpillar of the child Chop Chop evolves into the

adolescent pupa struggling against the racist cocoon. When the grown butterfly Wu Cheng eventually bursts out in 1984, readers catch only a glimpse
as he spreads his wings, literally, at the precise moment when he recedes from
the narrative altogether.

Because the issues following number 265 in December 1983 were never
marked with exact dates, we can only surmise that they are from 1984 and
that the absence of numbers may have come about from the disarray preceding
any business failure. After Chop Chop leaves, the following issues depict the
blackhawks sabotaging the Nazi war machine in Europe. Wu Cheng does not
reappear until the last three numbers of the Evanier-Spiegle *Blackhawk*. In
number 268 of March 1984, an Oriental is pictured at the bottom left-hand
corner of the cover; the caption reads: Wu Cheng, "Chop-Chop" (China). But
elsewhere in that issue, there is no allusion to him. Again in number 269 of
April 1984, Wu Cheng is one among many faces Blackhawk dreams about.
Very much a memory or dream vision at this point in 1984, Wu Cheng's
role has been taken over somewhat by the youthful-looking Chuck. In the
last issue, number 273 in 1984, the Oriental character rises from the dead,
once again called Chop Chop. The cover queries, "Has Chop Chop returned
to the Blackhawks in time for their...Final Mission?" Number 273 contains an extensive "Detached Service Diary," which Chop Chop has recorded
during his tour of duty in China. However, Chop Chop's guest appearance
does not rescue their final mission; *Blackhawk* ceased publication after this
number.

In 1987, DC Comics breathed new life into *Blackhawk*. Under the stew-
ardship of Howard Chaykin, it came out in three installments: "Book one:
Blood Iron"; "Book two: Red Snow"; and "Book three: Iron Dreams and Bloody
Murder." Books two and three were published in 1988. In the intertextual
vein of Evanier-Spiegle, Book two refers to the Oriental member's previous
life as Chop Chop. Glossy and atmospheric, Chaykin's version of *Blackhawk*
differs greatly from its prior incarnations. Chaykin no longer relies on pen-
cil sketches and coloring, but produces his *Blackhawk* as computer-generated
graphics. The other blackhawks, including Weng Chan (the renamed Chop
Chop), retreat to the background in order to highlight Blackhawk's personal
exploits, especially with the other sex. Blackhawk is now referred to as Jan,
his given name. With few speech balloons, Chaykin's comic thrives on action,
which is further intensified by a generous use of close-ups in progression as if
in slow-motion. His characters invariably grit their teeth, grimace, frown, or
wrinkle their noses. Rarely do we find a moment devoid of extreme emotions
such as rage, depression, cynicism, and so forth. Chaykin re-tunes *Blackhawk*

**Figure 16.** Howard Chaykin's *Blackhawk*. Largely computer-generated, characters dangle between extreme emotions. Published by DC Comics, Book one (1987).

for the postmodern sensibility immured in sound bites, talk shows, and sensational news.

Figure 16 is taken from Book one of Chaykin's *Blackhawk*. The inserts of Jan, or Blackhawk, show a character dangling between anger and petrification. The operation has come under the command of Weng Chan, whose moustache fails to hide the youth's irreverent, Gen-X smirk. Weng Chan contorts his facial expression in mockery of "Janos." Jan gets his revenge in Book two when he describes the blackhawks' "youngest member...recently thrown out of at least three of the most prestigious universities in the Eastern United States" when introducing "Lieutenant Weng Chan...aka 'Chop Chop.'" We are reminded of the model minority myth in Jan's taunt about prestigious universities on the East Coast. In return, the Gen-Xer promises that "for this Chop-Chop shit...I am going to make your life a living hell—" The bantering—the back and forth of wisecracks and obscenities—between Blackhawk and what used to be his subordinates' subordinate points to a distrust of authority and an inflation of the ego characteristic of the fin de siècle as well as the start of the twenty-first century.

DC Comics brought back *Blackhawk* yet again from 1989 to 1990, initially with Martin Pasko and Rick Burchett in charge, succeeded later by Doug Moench and Rick Burchett. In addition to Weng Chan, there are two more persons of color on the team. According to number 1 in March 1989 (see Figure 17), Mairzey is from Singapore. She and Chuck marry eventually and adopt a child. Figure 18, from the same number, shows Grover Baines, the intimidating African American from Alabama. The diversity in *Blackhawk* is, however, only skin deep: the cover of the last Moench-Burchett issue exposes the underlying power differential among the races. Number 16 in August 1990, Figure 19, poses all the white members around their double-propeller aircraft. The two characters filling the bottom corners were Weng Chan and

Figure 17. Martin Pasko and Rick Burchett's *Blackhawk*. Mairzey is the secretary for the blackhawks. Published by DC Comics, number 1 (March 1989).

PERSONAL DATA

*Name:* Keng, Quan Chee, a.k.a. "Mairzey"
*Born:* 1926 Singapore
*Height:* 5'1" *Weight:* 97 lbs.
*Eyes:* Brown *Hair:* Black

HISTORY

A Malaysian National, Keng Quan Chee is the daughter of a Chinese businessman and an American missionary teacher, stationed in Singapore.

Nicknamed "Mairzey" after her favorite song, "Mairzey Dotes and Dozey Dotes," the young girl spent her early life in that city where she was also educated. Her schooling included two years at the Van der Koening Secretarial School.

Mairzey joined Blackhawk Airways in Singapore and went with them in their relocation to the U.S. in 1948. She was named Assistant Director of Ground Operations by Janos Prohaska and functioned as B.H.A.'s office manager.

The former Keng Quan Chee currently lives in the Georgetown section of the District of Columbia. ∎

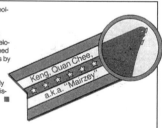

Grover Baines. The people of color—Weng Chan the mechanic, Grover Baines the radio operator—occupy, literally, the periphery, and Mairzey the secretary, is not even included in the "group picture." On the shoulders of this "support" team tower the blackhawks. Nowhere in this DC Comics version is it stated that Chan and Baines are inferior in their flying talents. They are relegated to the bottom not because they are lesser men but because they are not white men. They are lower by virtue of their race.

With "suggested for mature readers" printed on every cover of the 1989–1990 run, *Blackhawk* turns more violent and more erotic. It continues the retro look of Chaykin, but adds modern touches to it, such as angle shots, skewed panels, and zooms in on body parts. But the characters' individuality is often sacrificed in favor of action in the manner of continuous strips. The mood of these late eighties revival issues is far from hawkish. Not as patriotic

Figure 18. Introducing radio operator Grover Baines, an African American. *Blackhawk*, number 1 (March 1989).

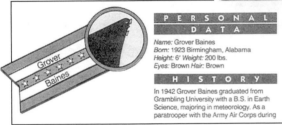

P E R S O N A L
D A T A

Name: Grover Baines
Born: 1923 Birmingham, Alabama
Height: 6' Weight: 200 lbs.
Eyes: Brown Hair: Brown

H I S T O R Y

In 1942 Grover Baines graduated from Grambling University with a B.S. in Earth Science, majoring in meteorology. As a paratrooper with the Army Air Corps during

World War II, Baines was among the most highly decorated black soldiers of that war.
After the war Baines became a licensed civil pilot and went to work for Blackhawk Airways, where he served as both pilot and expert radio operator.
Grover Baines recently was dismissed from Blackhawk Express. He resides in Westport, Connecticut. ■

Art by Tom Zuiko / Rick Magyar

Figure 19. A "group picture" of the blackhawks, with minorities on the bottom. *Blackhawk,* number 16 (August 1990).

and gung-ho as in the 1940s and 1950s, *Blackhawk* is now downright suspicious of the U.S. government, among other organizations.

The first issue of the Pasko-Burchett *Blackhawk* (March 1989) opens the action in Poland where Janos Prohaska, later Blackhawk, has lost his family to the Nazis. So in the late 1980s, Jan is faithfully modeled after the early days of *Blackhawk*. But the new version is also far more self-reflexive and postmodernist. The story interweaves various strands: the actual missions of the blackhawks, including the Weng Chan character; the misrepresentation in comics, where Chop Chop returns with his stereotypical facial features and pidgin; the "real" lives of the cartoonist, the writer, and the publisher of *Blackhawk* under the terror of a McCarthy-like Congressman Millburne. Pasko-Burchett shuttles not only between the past of Poland and the present of the blackhawks, but also between the "reality" of the blackhawks' operations and the fantasy of *Blackhawk* the comic.

As violence and sexuality have become essential in any marketing strategy of this late capitalist society, action and sex permeate this version of *Blackhawk*. A great many breathtaking aerial stunts are performed. And of course, Weng Chan punches and kicks his way through the pages. Number 4 in June 1989, Figure 20, depicts an escape attempt by Weng Chan. He has knocked

**Figure 20.** Rechristened Weng Chan, the kung fu master makes his getaway. *Blackhawk,* number 4 (June 1989).

over a casino table (chips are flying everywhere), jumped onto a counter, and is smashing through a window. The sweeping action is intensified by a close-up of Weng Chan's sweat and grimace, a moment of stillness prior to explosion. Numbers 4 through 6 are set in China, "the ol' ancestral homeland," as Weng Chan puts it. Having been parachuted into Manchuria in 1948, they are to destroy atomic bomb factories. The most important fighters turn out to be Jan (Blackhawk) and Weng Chan, who fight side by side and engage in Chaykin-esque jiving wisecracks as a sort of comic relief. Weng Chan has clearly gained in importance because he understands the language. These continuous strips are, however, littered with the awful Chinese writing of a beginner.

More than just the site for action, China proliferates metaphorically and intertextually. Many Oriental characters from other comic books are resurrected. From Milton Caniff's *Terry and the Pirates,* the Dragon Lady and the Big Stoop were recast as Sheah Chun Ryan and her henchman, Chang. Number 14 in May 1990, Figure 21, offers an excellent view of how Sheah Chun Ryan both derives from the Dragon Lady and is a modernized version of her. Part Irish and part Chinese, the red-headed agent works for the Chinese Communists. The threat posed by Sheah, embodied in her dragon tattoo and the tiger lurking not far from the place where Sheah and Blackhawk make love, increases the thrill for male autoeroticism. While Caniff decorated the Dragon

Figure 21. *Blackhawk* turns more erotic. *Blackhawk,* number 14 (May 1990).

Lady's silk blouses and cheongsams with coiling dragons, Sheah's red dragon is tattooed directly onto her body. China's logo has found its way through the clothing onto bare skin, hence intensifying exoticism/eroticism. Sheah invites an equally naked Blackhawk to "trace its [the dragon tattoo's] sinuous outline." Perhaps too X-rated in Caniff's days, this moment is all too commonplace in the sex-saturated twenty-first century. Chang is a giant, as obedient to Sheah as Big Stoop was to Terry in *Terry and the Pirates*. Both are powerful and yet both are so mangled as to be grotesque; Chang has an iron stump for his left arm and Big Stoop's tongue was cut off by the Dragon Lady.

Chop Chop has been dead for a decade now, the longest since 1941. Has he used up his nine lives? Have democracy and equality finally caught up with him, this residual of chauvinistic ethnocentrism? I think not, at least not so long as we look beyond the confines of comics and probe into films, which borrow so many characters and styles from comics. Granted that we may be free from the repugnant racism displayed in Chop Chop's whole existence, from his physical appearance to his language to his mindset, but subtle stereotypes persist. Wu Cheng and Weng Chan no longer entertain with their karate chops, but they have been replaced by Jackie Chan and Jet Li on the wide screen. Nor does the kung fu mystique entirely cancel out Chop Chop, the hapless yellow servant. As we move into the twenty-first century, the complex maneuverings of Orientalism have largely gone underground, like germs traveling through the bloodstream to other parts of American culture. Where and when will they strike next? Against Vincent Chin in Detroit? Against Hsi Lai Temple in Los Angeles in the wake of Al Gore's campaign fund-raising? Against Wen Ho Li in Los Alamos? Or can it be anywhere, against any given one of the millions of Americans of Asian ancestry, who are, after all, candidates for Chop Chop in a land of potential blackhawks?

# Intercut on
## Asian Magic

# Asian Immigrants with "Magical" Disabilities

## Oriental Tongues and Bound Feet

**Marrying** into the multiethnic, yet English-language-only American family, Asian immigrants have nominally abandoned their names/selves in favor of the Anglicized renditions/shadows. In spite of their linguistic and cultural self-disowning, Asian immigrants often find themselves the "odd man out" at the family table, bumped by their look-alike, U.S.-born and -educated Asian Americans, who feel threatened by the allegedly Johnny-come-latelies. This "sibling rivalry" can be traced back to the first collection of Asian American writings, *Aiiieeeee!* (1974), edited by Frank Chin et al., who in the Preface champions the "Asian American sensibility" shared by U.S.-born writers. In her groundbreaking Asian American fiction *The Woman Warrior* (1976), Maxine Hong Kingston agrees with Chin in her exorcism of ancestral ghosts, among others, in order to "claim America," a goal she has repeatedly pronounced in interviews and expository writings. It is noteworthy that what Chin, Kingston, and other Asian American writers and scholars are contesting is not a vibrant discourse penned by Asian immigrants born and raised elsewhere, but virtual silence. There is simply no sign of a body of Asian immigrant writings in English to challenge the supremacy of Asian American sensibility and identity. While a handful of Asian immigrants have arrived on the West coast to unsettle the real estate market with huge sums of capital, the English language and American culture present sufficient difficulty that a foreign-born Conrad figure has yet to materialize to justify Asian American defensiveness. Rather, Asian American discourse can do almost anything it wishes in its representation of Asian immigrants. This is manifestly the case if we examine the discourse from the perspective of Disability studies.

In 1990, the Americans with Disabilities Act (ADA) was passed by the Congress and signed into law by President George Bush, who stated that "some 43,000,000 Americans have one or more physical or mental disabilities, and this number is increasing as the population as a whole is growing older." These

Americans are often met with discrimination in "such critical areas as employment, housing, public accommodations, education, transportation, communication, recreation, institutionalization, health services, voting, and access to public services.... Unlike individuals who have experienced discrimination on the basis of race, color, sex, national origin, religion, or age," the Act continues to assert, "individuals who have experienced discrimination on the basis of disability have often had no legal recourse to redress such discrimination," hence giving rise to the 1990 Act in order to, among other things, "enforce the fourteenth amendment" (http://www.usdoj.gov/crt/ada/pubs/ada.txt), which guarantees privileges and immunities of citizenship, due process, and equal protection.

Despite the common association of the ADA with visible disabilities, such as people who are blind or in wheelchairs or using sign language, the 1992 National Health Interview Survey reveals that "the most frequent causes of disability in order of prevalence were back problems, heart disease, arthritis, asthma, leg or foot problems, psychiatric disorders, learning or developmental disabilities, diabetes, cancer, and cerebral vascular disease" (Fleischer and Zames, *The Disability Rights Movement* 2001, p. 93). Citing the earlier Rehabilitation Act of 1973, Lennard Davis agrees: "'Normal' people tend to think of 'the disabled' as the deaf, the blind, the orthopedically impaired, the mentally retarded ... [but] one now has to include people with invisible impairments" (*Enforcing Normalcy* 1995, p. 8). Gaining momentum from this 1990 legislative victory, Disability studies has pointed to the fluid and unstable contour of the field, one that undulates from conspicuous disabilities to less conspicuous ones. In theory, immigrants are without disabilities, for visa applications and the prospect of hardship in a strange land are enough to discourage all but the most qualified. Yet a number of immigrant (grand)parents as well as other categories of undesirables (what I call the "0.5 generation"—elderly Asian retirees who flock to U.S. metropolitan areas) may eventually turn into a "liability." With limited language and cultural skill, at times unable to drive and shop, these immigrant Americans suffer discriminations very much like the deaf, mute, and blind. It is in this spirit that I propose to reflect on the Asian immigrant, especially the immigrant (grand)parent, ranging from middle age to elderly, endowed somehow with "magical" disabilities, who repeatedly surfaces in the Asian American discourse. In such characters, debilitating traits paradoxically come to transform and empower them.

By definition, Asian immigrants exist in American culture as well as elsewhere. To give "immigrant" a sense broader than the U.S. naturalization and immigration laws, it is readily apparent that Asians travel to other parts of Asia, and, indeed, they can conceivably be *made into* a marginalized outsider—

like an immigrant—within their own country. The representations of Asian immigrants in Asian American culture can, therefore, overlap with those in Anglo-American and Asian culture. In order to highlight the magical disabilities of immigrants in a range of Chinese American and Japanese American texts, written by Maxine Hong Kingston, Amy Tan, Wakako Yamauchi, and Laurence Yep, I will first introduce a contrast in terms of self-Orientalization in Chinese/Chinese American texts written in English (by Ha Jin) and filmed for global consumption (by Zhang Yimou). While the Chinese self-Orientalization in Ha Jin and Zhang resembles Asian American fetishization of disfigured yet magical body parts, it fails to attribute agency to disabilities. Although both discourses shroud disabilities in exoticism and fetishism, Ha Jin and Zhang appear eager to launch a masculinist gaze that reifies femininity, while U.S.-born Asian American writers are prone to alchemize immigrant disabilities. On the one hand, Chinese and Chinese expatriate artists perpetuate the patriarchy symbolized by the mutilation of women's feet. On the other, Asian American gender and identity politics lead to self-empowerment by confessing to the disabilities inherent in an Asian body, yet such disabilities are vested with magical properties.

Asian American writers routinely exteriorize their own neuroses first as the disabilities of immigrants and then seek catharsis in magical transformations. The ambiguous revulsion and attraction center on specific body parts. Both alien and debilitating, Oriental tongues produce nonsensical gibberish in the English-speaking context, and bound feet signal a deformity brought about by an oppressive system no different from those that produced the chastity belt, the corset, or clitorectomy. Accordingly, enchanting Oriental tongues well forth from an Asian American anxiety of voicelessness; the fetishized bound feet shift attention away from Asian American "aberration" from the American mainstream. Like the Freudian fetish that announces and disavows a certain lack, magical disabilities acknowledge yet negate Asian American particularities. This psychoanalytical approach does not deny genuine Asian American concern for the immigrants' plight over linguistic adaptation, or Asian American outrage over the injustice of foot-binding. But intriguing issues arise if we take this literal interpretation.

While the problem of Oriental tongues is still very much with us in this globalized economy with its transnational work force, the custom of foot-binding has long been eradicated, found today only among certain elderly Chinese women. Experientially, Asian American writers may have acquaintances, or even immigrant parents, who struggle with English, but they are unlikely to have come across any actual person with bound feet in Chinatown or any Chinese metropolis accessible to tourists. One problem persists, the other is all but nonexistent. One is a living testimony of the immigrant condition, the other the afterlife of—shall we say—dead (t)issues. Both disabilities, however, enjoy equal popularity as *metaphors* among Asian Americans. By showcasing the empowerment to be gained from Oriental tongues, the authors are certainly not advocating the elimination of ESL programs for adult learners, nor are they pushing the vision of a multilingual United States. Rather, Asian American writers are trying to free themselves from entrapment by way of Houdini-type escape linguistics. Nothing short of miraculous, an Oriental tongue makes possible a *speaking in tongues,* a sort of inspired or possessed unintelligibility. Similarly, bound feet have been favored by the West as a symbol of Chinese inhumanity and patriarchy. Asian Americans inherit this attitude, but with a feminist twist, and collapse gender inequity with bound feet. Here again, Asian Americans are railing less against the historical phenomenon of foot-binding than against its metaphorical description of women's abiding pain in the here and now.

Both Oriental tongues and bound feet become fetishes in the original etymology of the word, carrying connotations of evil as well as good magical qualities. Hal Foster explicates: "The term *fetish* was first used in relation to the amulets of witches, that is, to marginal others within the culture, persecuted peasant women; then it was adopted by fifteenth-century Portuguese traders to refer to the cult objects of West Africa, that is, to alien others outside the culture, subjected tribespeople" ("The Art of Fetishism" 1993, p. 254). In Western, Asian American, and Asian representations of Oriental tongues and bound feet, fetishes operate in tandem with an Orientalist framework. They signal insider as much as outsider status; they point to empowerment as much as to disenfranchisement.

## Chinese Self-Orientalization

Eerily, bound feet, a pathological symptom of patriarchy of the nineteenth and the first half of the twentieth century, continue to haunt contemporary Chinese texts. Both Ha Jin and Zhang Yimou have responded to the English-reading market and global cinema viewers by stylizing and Orientalizing their works. Featured prominently in Ha Jin's National Book Award–winning *Waiting* (1999) is a pair of bound feet, which gradually increase in significance from an appendage of slavishness to a symbol of steadfast loyalty, the martyr-like waiting of the traditional woman in a harsh, ever-changing Maoist China. *Waiting* chronicles the long years that Lin Kong and Manna Wu, colleagues at a military hospital in northeastern China, spend waiting to be married. Before they can do that, Lin Kong must obtain the official permission to divorce his wife, Shuyu, whose undesirability is epitomized by her bound feet. Consider Shuyu's debut: "a small, withered woman...her thin arms and legs couldn't fill up her clothes, which were always baggy on her. In addition, she had bound feet" (p. 6). Wizened, dried-up inside her clothes and small feet, Shuyu inspires little passion in the husband, who married her out of respect for his parents. Hence, Shuyu stands for traditional bondage and enervating backwardness. Rhetorically, the "additional" information of bound feet simulates the limp, "tag-on" existence of bound feet in relation to the human body. That extra piece of information is simultaneously the last straw or the last word that completes the portrait of wretched Shuyu. It also constitutes the very first impression any character in the novel has of Shuyu. Upon viewing a photograph of Shuyu, Manna Wu scoffs at her feet. The hospital staff clamor to look at her bound feet, even offering money to Shuyu, which she firmly declines because, as she puts it in her rustic way, "tak[ing] off your shoes and socks is like open your pants" (p. 206), meant only for the enjoyment of one's husband. Although rendered asexual, Shuyu anachronistically holds that her sex appeal sediments in the fetish of bound feet, a substitute vagina, as it were. Shuyu is not only a victim of "feudal" practices, but she continues to believe in the perversity of human sexuality. So pitiable as to be comical, Shuyu turns out to be yet another character waiting for Lin Kong to "come home," even after their divorce. Whether out of rigid stupidity or old-fashioned commitment, Shuyu saves Manna and Lin Kong's twin baby sons with her folk remedy, and she provides a sanctuary for Lin Kong when he is in despair over his new marriage. Ha Jin paints a paradoxical picture of Shuyu and the peasant underclass: undesirable and sexually repellant on the one hand, but romantically persevering and the custodian of folk wisdom, on the other.

Catering to the West's century-old fixation on Chinese bound feet, Ha Jin's is but the first in a long list of Orientalist texts practiced by "Orientals." For instance, *The Three-Inch Golden Lotus* (1986), by the Tianjin native Feng Jicai, explores a despicable literati cult focused on mutilated bound feet in a hilarious, potentially complicitous, manner within the Chinese context.[1] Zhang Yimou was keenly aware of global tastes in cinema when he made his three "red" films. *Raise the Red Lantern* (1991) engages the foot fetish in scenes of a hypnotic foot massage, an "old custom" *(lao guiju)* as ritualistic as the preparation of bound feet for a night's entertainment of the patriarch. Zhang's transference of bound feet to foot massage is inevitable in view of the difficulty of visualizing shrunken feet: not only would special effects be required but the result could well distract from the aesthetic aura that is Zhang's trademark. Oriental tongues are much easier to perform than bound feet to duplicate, for they require no more physical representation than a stupid or blank look.[2] By contrast, bound feet, like any severe body mutilation, are too shocking or too offensive to put on film. It is ironic that a human obsession long passed and impossible to pictorialize in a naturalistic sense should occupy our imagination so fully today. Zhang solves the problem of filmic representation via displacement onto foot massages.

*Raise the Red Lantern* deals with the corrupt system of polygamy in "feudal" China. Trapped in one household are the four wives of a patriarch, referred to simply as Lao-yie (master), who is always shot from the back or the side. By never showing his face in any close-up or frontal shot, by keeping Lao-yie unnamed, faceless, and unidentified, Zhang embodies the omnipresent male hegemony. Lesser copies of Lao-yie are the male servants who light the lanterns for the master each night and who carry out the lynching of the third, adulterous wife in the roof-top room. Deviating from Su Tong's original story, Zhang has changed the location of this death from the family well in which women have traditionally committed suicide. Further revising Su Tong's story, Zhang restricts all action to a claustrophobic set within the classical architecture of the Chen compound. Even in the roof-top episode, the camera does not wander outside the family estate; the female characters are thus locked in cinematographically. Spatially, the film is set on two different planes. Under the roof, in the various living rooms for the four wives and in the dining room, are scenes in medium shots and close-ups filmed by a level, horizontal camera. By contrast, scenes of the rectangular courtyards and, especially, of the lit red lanterns, are captured through high-angle long and medium shots from the roof. While the roof allows a wider view, it focuses on framed spaces within the compound.

Female oppression is dramatized within the walls through the four wives' contestations for Lao-yie's affection, which is symbolized by his choice of companion for the night. The wives follow the family ritual of standing at the gate of their respective courtyard at sundown and waiting for the red lantern to be brought to the chosen one. Subsequently, male servants light all the red lanterns in that particular courtyard; Aunt Gao arrives to massage that wife's feet; and, at long last, Lao-yie appears in her boudoir. With minimal changes in her acting, Aunt Gao can certainly play Shuyu if Ha Jin's novel ever gets turned into a movie. With her shriveled face with missing and rotten teeth, she squats to manipulate the women's feet. Her sly grin and low position liken her to a pair of repulsive bound feet; her "trade secret" lies in how she infuses herself into the designated feet. Aunt Gao's magic consists of little hammers with which she repeatedly hits the soles of the chosen woman's feet, a sort of acupressure that, like foreplay, arouses the wife sexually. The erotic undertone abounds in the red scarf that wraps the feet during Aunt Gao's massage. In a traditional Chinese wedding, a red bridal veil shields the bride's face, only to be uncovered by the bridegroom in the nuptial bedroom, symbolizing the ripping of the hymen and the stain of the virginal blood. The covering has "slipped" from the highest point of the body to the lowest in Zhang Yimou. Hollow, with jingling bells, the hammers produce tingling sounds that can be heard throughout the entire compound. As the chosen one is increasingly stimulated, this overheard overture mocks the thirst of those who are forsaken for the night.

Given Zhang's Chinese filmic universe, "Oriental tongues" are nearly impossible to execute. Yet Zhang's linguistic stylization comes close to Asian American "spells" of Asian-language nonsense. Both seek to ritualize certain Asian phrases in an attempt to displace the realistic with the mythical. "*Diandeng chuijiao*" (lighting the lanterns; massaging the feet) is hence the euphemism for Lao-yie's sex partner. This perverted ritual shares a kinship with the bound feet erotica that Feng Jicai delineates. Lao-yie's choice first enjoys the festivity of the color red, then the privilege of ordering the menu for the following day, the attention of the servants, the pleasure of a foot massage, and, most importantly, the possibility that intercourse will permit her to bear a son. The film's protagonist, the young fourth wife played by Gong Li, comes to long for the foot massage. She acts excited whenever the hammering sounds echo in the compound. With her face inscribing desire—eyes closed, head tilted back, lips slightly open, Gong Li literally kneads her feet together, as if they itch, desire apparently spreading from her feet rather than the ordinary erogenous zones. She even asks her maid Yan'er to massage her feet, but to no avail, partly because Yan'er herself yearns for Lao-yie's sexual favors. Voyeuristic of female sexuality, Zhang depicts women's feet as a sex organ. The adulterous third mistress, the opera singer, likewise "flirts" with her lover, the family doctor, under the mah-jongg table with her foot.

## Asian American Self-Transformation

In contrast to Chinese self-Orientalization, Asian Americans routinely attribute transformative powers to their immigrant characters' disabilities. Even in Kingston's pioneering Asian American novel, *The Woman Warrior* (1976), Oriental tongues and bound feet have great significance. Kingston's protagonist undergoes body mutilations, the cutting of her frenum and the tattooing of her back. Both alien practices are to be taken figuratively rather than literally to symbolize the empowerment of the protagonist—to enable her to speak the foreign language and to fight barbarians. In a moment of reflection, the narrative voice confides that "[e]ven now China wraps double binds around my feet" (p. 57), double binds that strangle as well as strengthen. Ethnic origin incapacitates Asian American characters, yet the pain stimulates and invigorates them. Kingston opens *China Men* (1980) with an act of female revenge: taming a male and binding his feet, although it is not Tang Ao, as Kingston erroneously quotes from *Jin hua yuan (The flower in the mirror)*, but Lin Xiyang. Kingston's corpus suggests that by sharing the shame of physical disabilities, Asian Americans turn suffering into the foundation for self-liberation.

Similar to the juxtaposition of ethnic pain and ethnic pride, the Chinese and English languages are pitted against each other in Kingston to embody the protagonist's identity crisis:

> The Chinese "I" has seven strokes, intricacies. How could the American "I," assuredly wearing a hat like the Chinese, have only three strokes, the middle so straight? . . . I stared at that middle line and waited so long for its black center to resolve into tight strokes and dots that I forgot to pronounce it. The other troublesome word was "here," no strong consonant to hang on to, and so flat, when "here" is two mountainous ideographs. (*The Woman Warrior* 1976, pp. 166–167)

Confused by the two different renditions of "I" and "here," the speaker is unsure as to how to situate the self ("I") at an intersection of space and time ("here"). The two indexical terms are represented in the phonetic versus the ideographic script, while the speaker tries futilely to translate between the two. The speaker's "home-base" language, however, appears to be written in Chinese ideograms, since she awaits the English "I," straight-backed and individualistic, to transform into the complex network inherent in the seven Chinese strokes and dots, and she expects the "flat," lackluster "here" to transform into the "mountainous" Chinese equivalent, as if consonant-rich Chinese—an illusion already—would result in rock formations or jagged peaks. Kingston, of course, is playing word tricks in the manner of Pound, Eisenstein, and Barthes. Her autobiographical novel is written in English; the author has borrowed unintelligible Chinese ideograms and the attendant aestheticism of Chinese calligraphy to defamiliarize readers, achieving a sense of magic through linguistic unfathomability. While Chinese renditions of "I" and "here" are alleged to be more complicated and significant than their English counterparts, they remain a textual void to most readers, who are not Chinese-speakers. Kingston's entire book lies in this illusion of reversal of home and target languages. As is ironically true for countless second-generation Asian Americans who drift away from their "mother tongue" once they start grade school, the home language of Kingston's protagonist is the one she has forgotten, which she tries to retrieve in the current home language of English. In the Freudian sense, the protagonist fetishizes her loss, the maternal phallus of Chineseness.

In Tan's novel *The Bonesetter's Daughter* (2001), the author's formulaic co-protagonists are Ruth, whose biblical namesake implies subconscious assimilation, and LuLing, Ruth's mother, who has symptoms of Alzheimer's disease. Both characters repress their sufferings, as can be seen in Ruth's annual psychosomatic loss of voice and LuLing's dementia. Their silence harks back to the misery of LuLing's mother, Precious Auntie, in pre-Communist China. That Ruth's story repeats her mother LuLing's and LuLing's story repeats that of Precious Auntie points to the mythical. Moreover, in Precious Auntie's account of her life, the fairy-tale-style condensation renders her father and husband dead on the wedding day as well as her subsequent deformity caused by burned black resin. A matrilineage of female pain unfolds not only in terms of physical damage but in psychological hurt—Precious Auntie's life as a nursemaid to her own daughter, LuLing's immigrant awkwardness and reversal to dependency, and Ruth's childlessness and pseudo-stepmotherhood. Transformative potential, nonetheless, springs from the matriarchs' writing in Chinese, even though it is unread by and indecipherable to the daughters until too late, when the mothers are already lost—the essence of tear-jerking melodrama. Bequeathed with her mothers' life stories, the young LuLing refuses to read Precious Auntie's tale until the "maid" has slit her own throat, and American-born Ruth fails to fathom LuLing's Chinese calligraphy until LuLing has nearly lost her mind.

Consistently, Tan invests linguistic deficiencies with the miraculous. The teenage Ruth manipulates her superstitious mother by acting as a medium for Precious Auntie. Ruth's pseudo-Chinese scribblings with a chopstick in a tray of sand resembles the use of ouija board and planchette. But Ruth's child's play acquires a mysterious, spiritual sympathy, as if the dead truly speaks through her. Even in the context of China, where Chinese cannot be the exoticized script, Tan continues to fashion a mystical language for the other. With her scorched face, mouth, and vocal cords, Precious Auntie is unable to speak. She communicates instead in hand gestures and gurgling sounds, a "language of shooting stars" (*The Bonesetter's Daughter* 2001, p. 200) that only LuLing understands, and that extrasensorially, telepathically. Precious Auntie's words are all italicized to underscore their "magical otherness." At one point, LuLing reflects on her interpretive power: "Since she [Precious Auntie] could not speak and Mother could not read, when I refused to talk for her, she was left wordless, powerless" (p. 216). This self-reflexive moment comes to describe, quite aptly, Ruth's Asian American positionality, for without Ruth's interpretation for LuLing, her mother would be equally adrift in past memories. Ultimately, we can infer that Tan sees herself connecting the dots of her Asian heritage and her American identity, her genetic and adoptive parentage.

In the Japanese American canon, a similar metamorphosis occurs in Wakako Yamauchi's 1977 play "And the Soul Shall Dance" (in *Songs My Mother Taught Me* 1994). Normally, the human body dances, but when the body is bound, as the abused Issei woman Emiko's is, ritualized Japanese song and dance provides a means for the soul to escape or transcend. Such performativity of Japaneseness runs through the play, adding tragic beauty to an otherwise dreary depiction of the hardships of immigrant farmers. The play opens with a bilingual presentation of the song "Kokoro ga odoru" (And the soul shall dance). In terms of dramaturgy, Yamauchi routinely shifts from Japanese words and phrases to English translations. Conceivably, the singing of the Japanese original could be followed by its English version. While only native speakers of Japanese would benefit from the Japanese original, the bilingual version heightens readers' awareness of immigrant women's linguistic alienation, which is magically resolved in the ritual of poetry and dance.

> Red lips
> Press against a glass
> Drink the green wine
> And the soul shall dance
>
> In the dark night
> Dreams are unbearable
> Drink the green wine
> And the soul shall dance

Listening to old Japanese songs on the Victrola halfway through the play, Emiko unconsciously rises to dance, her soul echoing the music even though her body, in "drab cotton," is trapped on the edge of a desert in the American West. Her final exit from the play and perhaps from life is yet again staged with the title song and dance, Emiko now dressed in a beautiful kimono. In addition to the dance that uplifts Emiko's tragedy, the title song also transforms the character's other disability—alcoholism. This is not to say that alcoholism in women is more acceptable in Japanese culture (indeed, women frown upon her drinking in the play). However, Yamauchi achieves a Brechtian effect that dissociates the characters from their "bad" habits of consuming cheap homemade moonshine (the "green liqueur") through their performance of Japanese song and choreography that etherealizes women. Deemed disabling in English-speaking, Anglo-American culture, the Asian language and culture are presented by these Japanese Americans as the roots for spiritual ascent.

In his avant-gardist "The Big Toe," Bataille has shown us how to direct our gaze from the human head down to the big toe. He notes the irony that although "[t]he big toe is the most *human* part of the human body, in the sense that no other element of this body is as differentiated from the corresponding element of the anthropoid ape," human feet are despised for their alleged proximity to mud, baseness, darkness, evil (*Visions of Excess* 1985, p. 20). Bataille even mentions Chinese foot-binding as a sign of "sexual uneasiness": "Having atrophied the feet of women, [the Chinese] situate them at the most excessive point of deviance. The husband himself must not see the nude feet of his wife" (p. 21). Theoretically brilliant but factually erroneous, Bataille seems unaware of the foot fetish over "the three-inch golden lotus": indeed, the bound foot was looked at, sniffed, fondled, and more by men like a sex organ. Following Bataille's argument, Wang Ping, in *Aching for Beauty* (2000), likens bound feet to high-heeled shoes, such as stilettos, in that they resemble an erect penis. One might add that a ballerina standing on her toes also becomes such an androgynous phallic symbol. Consequently, bound feet yoke together paradoxes: they are both suppression and concentration of human bestiality; they substitute both for female and male genitals.

Thus moving downward in the Asian body, we stop at the bound feet, bestial hooves that, similar to Oriental tongues, lead to flights of imagination. But on the very surface, when certain Asian Americans are in need of an image for the old China, they look no further than this historical metaphor for a catchy title. While her book on the romance between a Chinese poet and her grandaunt has nothing to do with bound feet, Pang-mei Natasha Chang calls it *Western Dress and Bound Feet* (1997) to accentuate the contrast. Catherine Dai entitles her stories set in Taiwan but written in English *Bound Feet* (1992). More substantive use of bound feet appears in Laurence Yep's young adult fiction *Ribbons* (1992). *Ribbons* draws a parallel between the silk ribbons on an Asian American granddaughter's ballet shoes and the silk wrappings of her Chinese grandmother's bound feet. The generation gap is resolved only through the sharing of sorrow embodied in the mutilated feet of both parties. Western myths embodied in *The Nutcracker* and the agonizing metamorphosis in "Little Mermaid" blend with myths about Chinese bound feet, producing a magic that arises out of tremendous physical hardship. To send for the grandmother in Hong Kong, so Yep's story goes, the protagonist Robin's family must stop her ballet lessons and delay purchasing new ballet shoes for her. Unwilling to give up, Robin rehearses on the hard cement floor of the garage in toe shoes that are one size too small, which results in hammer toes. Robin's resentment is further fanned by the grandmother's favoring of her brother, the grandson, over herself.

The mutual antagonism is miraculously defused once the grandmother's secret is uncovered. Upon entering the bathroom without knocking, Robin sees that her grandmother

> tried to drop the towel over her feet, but she wasn't quick enough because I saw her bare feet for the first time. It was as if her feet were like taffy that someone had stretched out and twisted. They bent downward in a way that feet were not meant to, and her toes stuck up at odd angles, more like lumps than toes. I didn't think she had all ten either. (*Ribbons* 1992, p. 108)

Just as Bataille was wrong about the sexual practices associated with bound feet, Yep blunders as well, for the toes in a bound foot are made to bend down and inward rather than stick up "at odd angles." Anatomically, the big toe may appear to stand out or stick out but it does not stick *up,* and the rest of the toes are shriveled and hidden under the sole of the foot. Like a black hole of history, human curiosity is drawn to bound feet, but a detailed, clinical account runs counter to the very nature of a black hole. Yet the blurriness serves to attract even more attention.

An absurd change takes place in the grandmother after the bathroom scene, and she completely reforms into a fair and reasonable family elder. The story ends with Robin choosing to continue ballet, knowing that in this pursuit of beauty her hammer toes will bring excruciating pain, a decision not unlike the Little Mermaid's. Given that the grandmother is the unwitting cause of Robin's hammer toes, the story circles back to the custom of footbinding, which was always perpetrated against young girls by the women who loved them the most—mothers and grandmothers—in the hope that the girls would achieve a better match and lifelong happiness. The difference lies in the fact that Robin chooses to suffer, whereas bound feet were forced upon her grandmother and other Chinese women.

This returns us to the issue of agency inherent in Chinese self-Orientalization and Asian American self-transformation. Ha Jin and Zhang Yimou's masculinist texts prevent their female characters from developing any sovereignty, while Asian American female authors—Yep included, the author's gender notwithstanding—yearn for feminist empowerment. Nevertheless, certain groups in each discourse—Chinese women in Ha Jin and Zhang Yimou; immigrant characters in Asian American texts—are disenfranchised to effect power differentials. That disabilities such as Oriental tongues and bound feet can be represented as magical fetishes demonstrates the overwhelming discursive power of Orientalism. Yet all power contains its own deconstructive seeds, as we can see in Kingston's and Tan's flirtations with Chinese ideograms, in Ha Jin's narratological twists that take us far away from Shuyu's bound feet, and even in Zhang's schizophrenic career, which is punctuated by anti-Orientalist, neorealist films such as *The Story of Qiu Ju* (1992), *Not One Less* (1999), and *Happy Times* (2001). Given the evolution of culture, moments such as these are likely to proliferate, so much so that maybe one day they will exorcize the specter of Orientalism.

**Dalai Lama Superstar**

## Mystery and Politics in Western Films and Narratives on Tibet

### Invocation

When I was a graduate student at Indiana University (IU) in the 1980s, long before Tibetan Buddhism came into fashion in this New Age era, the first ever Tibetan stupa in the United States was being established at the outskirts of Bloomington, Indiana. The stupa was the brainchild of Thubten Norbu, professor in the Uralic-Altaic Department at IU and older brother to the Dalai Lama. My wife made and fired some of the terracotta *tsa tsa*—Buddha statues and relief images—stored inside the stupa. The Dalai Lama eventually graced Bloomington to preside over and bless the opening ceremony. We visited the stupa one day and Professor Norbu—as he was warmly known there—stopped in his work to chat with us. He joked that had he been a little bit more patient and come out a couple of years late, he would have been the Dalai Lama. Humor seems to run in His Holiness's family. With this and many other fond memories of the leading Tibetan Buddhists, readers can conclude that my title does not mean to malign the Dalai Lama, winner of the 1989 Nobel Peace Prize, but rather it suggests a charismatic celebrity idolized by the public like the superstar Andrew Lloyd Webber celebrated in his Broadway show *Jesus Christ Superstar* and in the 1973 film of the same name.

The cult of the Dalai Lama in the world, except perhaps in China, stems from his exceptionally warm, likeable, and unassuming personality, made all the more unique by his alleged identity as the Living Buddha, the reincarnation of the Awakened One. The rhetoric of such phrases as I have been using carries great affective power, in part because it points to the mystery of life that eludes us all, that lies beyond the confine of personal experience and verifiable scientific evidence. To most nonbelievers, such rhetoric is at once prophetic and superstitious. The ambivalence and the hesitancy to dismiss mystery altogether comes from the natural human longing for magic. Without this halo enveloping exotic religious faiths like Tibetan Buddhism, the Dalai Lama might have been just another Tibetan refugee in India or the West, with an open grin and a high-pitched laugh. In point of fact, he has played a decisive role in disseminating to the West a Buddhism of love and compassion, but his reputation rests more on his persona than on the person's teaching through books. The strain of abstruse philosophical Buddhist texts has not been favored by the Dalai Lama over the years, who composes easy-to-read, "how-to" books marked by commonsensical insights, honesty, and a great sense of humor. Those in search of Buddhist philosophy may be mildly disappointed by His Holiness's recent publications, penned either by himself or by others based on interviews of him, such as Howard Cutler's 1998 *The Art of Happiness*. Cutler's subtitle, *A Handbook for Living*, reveals the basic, ethical bent of the Dalai Lama's discourse. His geniality also leads him to endorse and even write forewords for a wide variety of publications on him and Tibet, including such children's books as Demi's *The Dalai Lama* (1998). A personal cult, however, is rarely built on that person's philosophical and religious exegeses. No philosopher has ever written a best-seller, which some of the Dalai Lama's recent books have been, without a doubt. This cult has inspired some of the 1990s Western films to be discussed shortly. But an overall comment on such Western discourse on Tibet is in order.

In Bernardo Bertolucci's *Little Buddha* (1993), two Tibetan monks fly from their monastery in Bhutan to Seattle in search of the reincarnation of Lama Dorje, now believed to be a Caucasian boy. Supposedly traveling northbound on Interstate Highway 5 from the Sea-Tac International Airport to downtown Seattle, their car actually moves southbound. In the car ride, a fleeting glimpse of a highway road sign before entering a tunnel confirms this. The sign says Exit 164 to Highway 90 east to Spokane and to Airport Way. Note that the exit leads to the airport, not away from it. Barring a total obliviousness to the geography of the Pacific Northwest, the filmmaker's motive for this misdirection is simple enough: only a southbound vehicle would enjoy an unobstructed view of Seattle's cityscape west of Interstate 5, including the landmark Space Needle; going northbound, the camera would have to take in the distraction of the coming traffic. Assuredly a minor miscue missed by most audiences, it nevertheless suggests a fundamental, shared feature of the Western imaginary of Tibet, perhaps also missed by most audiences. In the discursive history of Shangri-La, facts are oftentimes stretched and redirected to achieve the desired effect—escapism from the West's own quandary and wish-fulfillment of the West's sense of control. The misdirection of the car ride signals that it is not the East (Tibetan monks) coming to the West, but the West gone Oriental in search of itself. The mystery of an earthly paradise somewhere in the Himalayas bordering the Tibetan plateau and, amidst Tibetan exile, the mystery of one of its reincarnations in the heartbreakingly beautiful city of Seattle stem unequivocally from world politics at the time of the retelling of the story of Shangri-La. Mystery and politics in Western films and narratives on Tibet are Siamese twins, despite their feigned ignorance of each other. By "narratives" in the chapter title, I point to books on which such films are based, film reviews, even advertising drawing from Tibetan images. The discursive web on Tibet is interwoven through a variety of expressions—filmic, literary, popular culture. "Mystery" surrounding Western films and narratives on Tibet does not equate with the religious, although the religious plays a key role in creating this aura. "Politics" refers to the Tibet-China-West relationship as well as the East-West power structure.

This chapter proceeds to discuss the 1933 novel *Lost Horizon* by James Hilton and its filmic renditions, particularly Frank Capra's 1937 classic, in the context of utopian literature. After the "originary" texts, the chapter then focuses on the 1990s offspring: *Seven Years in Tibet* (Heinrich Harrer's autobiography in 1953 and Jean-Jacque Annaud's film in 1997), *Kundun* (Martin Scorsese's film in 1997), and *Little Buddha* (Bertolucci). This discourse revolving around Tibet is "Western" for obvious reasons: Hilton is British, Capra and Scorsese American, Bertolucci Italian, Annaud French (whose film is based on an Austrian's book). Scorsese's music soundtrack is composed by Philip Glass, an American whose career spans the Atlantic Ocean and the European continent. All these Westerners involved in the Tibetan imaginary have had previous creative and professional engagement with the East, except perhaps the insulated Americans, Capra and Scorsese. Enamored of the East as a cultural alternative, Bertolucci made *The Last Emperor* (1988), the first Western film shot inside post-Mao China, with most of its scenes set in the Forbidden City. Annaud's *L'Amant (The lover)* (1991) features the Hong Kong actor Tony Leung as the Chinaman character in Marguerite Duras's interracial romance in Indochina. In his memoir *Music by Philip Glass* (1987), Glass confesses that he is deeply influenced by Indian music, as practiced by the sitar player Ravi Shankar and his drummer. Glass's trilogy of "portrait dramas"—*Einstein on the Beach* (1975–1976), *Satyagraha* (1980), and *Akhnaten* (1983)—contains two on non-Caucasian heroes, the young Gandhi in South Africa and the Egyptian pharoah Akhnaten, said to be the first monotheist. Perhaps an intriguing Freudian slip, *Music by Philip Glass* makes no mention of Freud's controversial *Moses and Monotheism* (1939), which posits the very same thing about Akhnaten. This omission is peculiarly blatant in view of the fact that it is a memoir filled with prominent figures and boasting of the author's research work of a sort. Glass also provided the sound track for Francis Coppola's *Koyaanisqatsi* (1983) and collaborated with David Henry Hwang in *1000 Airplanes on the Roof* (1988).

Nurtured by their creators' previous endeavors on things Oriental, Western films and narratives on Tibet knead together various strains: Hilton's earlier myth of Shangri-La, the current cult of Dalai Lama, a concern for Tibetan suffering, and mystic elements associated with Tibetan Buddhism, such as reincarnation, mandalas (Carl Jung's favorite), and oracles. These elements come together to concoct, shall we say, a powerful Molotov cocktail, which finds its rag wick in politics—the Chinese occupation of Tibet since 1950. Notwithstanding the genuine, altogether altruistic, concern of the West for human rights violations committed by the Chinese in their "colony" of Tibet, the overwhelming public support, which has not yet translated into political intervention, manifests uneasiness over China's emerging role, since the collapse of the Soviet Union in 1989, as a constant irritant to American—and Western—world domination. Western anxiety of its global position lies behind the pro-Tibet and anti-China discourse. This fear of losing power is, of course, political. The pedigree of the West's self-serving apprehension goes all the way back to Hilton's Shangri-La, allegedly created by a priest from Luxembourg who is succeeded by an American diplomat, with the mission of preserving world civilization—under Euro-American masters. Lest this comment be dismissed as anti-West demagoguery, consider this: shortly after the High Lama of Shangri-La, aka Father Perrault of Luxembourg, dies, his American successor Conway "felt himself *master* of Shangri-La" (p. 146; italics mine).

## The Crash into Utopia

It is but human, in times of desperation, to dream of deliverance. Western utopian literature has traditionally reflected the longing for a miraculous release from turmoil and suffering, or a crash that lands characters right in the middle of utopia. Against the chaos of their own worlds, various writers have composed such earthly paradises: Thomas More's *Utopia* (1516), Edward Bellamy's *Looking Backward* (1888), B. F. Skinner's *Walden Two* (1948), Aldous Huxley's *Island* (1962), and many more. It is sobering, however, to reflect on the proximity of utopia and dystopia. Romantic fantasy is likely to induce its opposite—melancholy or utter disenchantment. Even Conway's first impression of Shangri-La is apocalyptic in the sense that he has reached "an end, a finality" (Hilton, *Lost Horizon* 1933, p. 49), a perfection that is also a cessation.

James Hilton's *Lost Horizon* derives from a number of such crashes, actual or impending: the plane crash in the novel ushers the characters to the foothills of Shangri-La; the Fall of the Great War scars the protagonist Conway so much that he self-identifies as "1914–1918" (p. 114); the stock market crash of 1929 rings in the Great Depression, from which one of the survivors Barnard (pseudonym of a Chalmers Bryant, Wall Street financier) tries to escape, especially from his creditors; and World War II looms on the horizon. The mystery of Shangri-La offers an exit, at least psychologically, out of the political quagmire in the West. In view of the mutual interest between China and the United States, one necessitated by the expansionist Japan of the early 1930s, Hilton's formation of Shangri-La includes Chinese and their culture. The "receptionist" lama Chang, played by Sir John Gielgud, in yellowface with taped eyes, in the 1973 production, is Chinese and the inhabitants of the valley are a "blend of Chinese and Tibetan." The "little Manchu" or "the little ivory doll" (p. 81) who takes leave of Shangri-La, only to find herself reverted back to her natural, advanced age, is Chinese. The residence for Conway and his party has a Chinese rather than Tibetan atmosphere, which pleases Conway immensely, for he has had fond memories of his decade-long residence at a station in China. In addition to a Tibetan monastery, there coexist "a Taoist and a Confucian temple" (p. 78). At times, Hilton seems downright contemptuous of Tibet and Tibetans, which explains the heavy dosage of Chineseness in the paradise. The High Lama entertains, indeed espouses, a theory of eugenics—a racial hierarchy in terms of the residents' susceptibility to his philosophical teaching and, hence, to longevity. The Nordic and Latin races of Europe occupy the top of the pyramid, followed by the Chinese and, lastly, the Tibetans (p. 110). China, however, is almost completely excised by Frank Capra in his 1937 film, since any allusion to China would remind moviegoers of the Sino-Japanese War and would distract from the transcendency Capra wishes to construct. This shift from China as part of the myth to Tibet as a distinct and separate myth heralds the 1990s eventuality where "Red" China becomes a bully to Tibet, a destroyer of Tibetan culure and faith.

The story of Shangri-La can only be aptly embodied in the genre of mystery. Hilton's novel, hence, gradually unfolds as the protagonist Conway discovers the true identity of the High Lama and the longevity of all Shangri-La inhabitants. With Conway's thrill at finding an earthly paradise, we feel that his departure from it in search of the malcontent Mallison, a subordinate in the diplomatic corps and a fellow crash survivor, is somewhat contrived. Filmmaker Capra ingeniously negates this jarring episode by recasting Mallison as Conway's young and impetuous brother in the film. Brotherly love compels Conway to leave Shangri-La to rescue the escapees, especially his brother's lover, who will in no time return to her true age. In the lover's wrinkled face outside the valley we see traces of the dystopia inherent in utopia. Citizens of Shangri-La, as Donald Lopez's 1998 book title suggests, are its prisoners.

## Tibet in the West

The section title refers both to representations of Tibet in the West and to Tibet to the west of China. Consequently, Tibet, China, and the West constitute a geopolitical and discursive triangle as intense as any emotional entanglement among humans. Of the three 1990s films on Tibet, Annaud's *Seven Years in Tibet*, starring Brad Pitt, is arguably the most popular. Loosely based on the memoir by Heinrich Harrer, an Austrian mountain climber who spent seven years in Tibet prior to the Dalai Lama's escape to India, the film freely extrapolates Harrer's book into a worn Hollywood formula to appeal to moviegoers, glossing over, uncritically, narrative fissures. One of such fissures is Harrer's Nazi or German-Austrian connection: Annaud turns the protagonist into a reluctant participant in a Nazi-orchestrated expedition to the Himalayas; furthermore, the absolute, even inhuman, silence Harrer exercises with regard to his homeland and family throughout his memoir is transformed by Annaud into remorse over leaving his pregnant wife and, subsequently, his son Rolf. Indeed, Pitt's Harrer remains tormented by his desertion of wife and unborn son, manifested in diary entries and correspondence with Europe, whereas Harrer's book contains only a few brief, vague references to his country.[1] The film closes on a note of reconciliation with Rolf; Harrer pays a parental visit to the son he has never met. Harrer's present of a music box fascinates the resentful boy, and the two begin to engage each other. That music box used to belong to the young Dalai Lama, who is portrayed, to all intents and purposes, as Harrer's son in the Potala.

Harrer the author must have regretted selling Annaud the film rights to his book. Other than an irresponsible husband and father-to-be, Harrer also proves himself to be a shady character in deceiving his fellow escapee from the British POW camp in India, Peter Aufschneiter, and in this process losing to him the Tibetan woman they both love. With Pitt's chic haircut, Gen-X irreverence, and what film critic John Anderson calls his "Zen-wear," Harrer is egotistic and self-aggrandizing. His maturing into a repentant, conscientious adult seems to coincide with his tutoring of the young Dalai Lama and with his compassion for Tibet's looming tragedy. It is implied that Buddhist detachment in the face of great adversity has an impact on the flamboyant Harrer. Similar to the irony of Capra and Bertolucci going Oriental, the West's own spiritual quest lies at the heart of Annaud's vision of Tibet.

The West's self-reflexiveness in these films ostensibly about the East recurs in the clichéd plot of Western science and technology merged with Eastern religiosity. Invariably, a fresh-eyed, upright Western teacher of language and science comes to the aid of an Eastern ruler, be it Deborah Kerr in *The King and I* (1956), Peter O'Toole in *The Last Emperor,* or Brad Pitt. True, the Dalai Lama's fascination with things Western—film projectors, telescopes, clocks, cars, and, presumably, music boxes—is legendary, verging on the unabashedly idolatrous, yet the fact that Western films forever favor this particular scenario of East meets West suggests a self-image, if only subconsciously, of Big Brotherhood. It is ironic that the all-knowing, all-seeing reincarnation of Buddha relies on a Western man of science to help him see through a telescope, watch a film projected, and hear music from a music box. In fact, the possibility of having an audience with the young Dalai is so remote in Harrer's memoir that it does not arise until the "Holy Mother" summons Harrer on page 135, more than one third into the narrative; the actual audience takes place on page 276, toward the end of the book. The relationship between the god-king and the mountaineer in the memoir never becomes as intimate and familial as the film depicts it, despite inklings of Harrer's own paternal feelings. For instance, Harrer strives to impress the young Dalai in their lessons about the West, "like many a good father who wishes to earn the respect of his son" (p. 277).

Scorsese's *Kundun* resembles a filmic biography of the Fourteenth Dalai Lama, who assisted in its completion. Based almost exclusively on documented facts from the discovery of the reincarnation to the 1959 escape, *Kundun* has the feel of a gorgeously made, aesthetic documentary, with Melissa Mathison's script and Roger Deakins's cinematography. To the credit of Scorsese and his staff, *Kundun* does not romanticize Tibet; politics and religion are shown to pollute each other. Regent Reting, whose vision leads to the discovery of the boy-king and who teaches the Dalai Lama's present-day version of Buddhism on compassion, turns out to be greedy and corrupt, demanding a great fortune for his service and staging a monastery revolt to reclaim power. The film does present the Dalai Lama's hot-tempered father in a light far more positive than does, for instance, Mary Craig's biography of his entire family (*Kundun* 1997).

The film offers glimpses of the Fourteenth Dalai at age two, five, ten, and a young adult. The *Los Angeles Times* film critic Kenneth Turan complains that "using four actors for the boy's different ages makes it difficult to identify with him. Also, having to depend on inexperienced children with varying commands of English to tell a story of holiness and belief is especially problematic" ("'Kundun' Lacks a Certain Presence" 1997, p. 6). I can not disagree with Turan more in that the four actors are, I believe, totally convincing in the context of docudrama, their English appropriately accented and their body language increasingly muted. In fact, I find the last three stages played with great flair and vigor, which is not to diminish the spontaneous performance of the spoiled two-year-old. Bertolucci uses the same child's perspective and multiple stages of growth with Pu Yi in *The Last Emperor*. In a way, this historical, chronological approach befits the epic panorama of the rise and fall of a dynasty and of a nation both filmmakers seek to delineate.

Called by Turan a "visual cornucopia," accompanied by Glass's "hypnotic" score of electronic music, *Kundun* is most memorable in those scenes interweaving mystery and politics. It opens with the search party for the reincarnation of the Thirteenth Dalai Lama. Guided by Regent Reting's vision, the search party locates the "small one-storey house with oddly-shaped guttering and turquoise tiles" (as recorded in Mary Craig's *Kundun* 1997, p. 13). Each of the two-year-old's correct choice of items belonging to the Thirteenth Dalai Lama—necklace, hand drum, begging bowl, eye glasses, and cane—has, of course, a fifty-fifty possibility of success and may appear ludicrous to non-believers. Yet we must bear in mind that this process of identification is only as "faulty" as any person looking for a lifelong mate in a sea of humanity, or as "chancy" as any given sperm out of a sea of sperms impregnating the egg, or as legendary as an Immaculate Conception.

Another node of mystery and politics revolves around the State Oracle's foretelling the Dalai Lama's ominous future due to the Chinese aggression under Mao. The Oracle appears four times in *Kundun*: the first time to caution the ten-year-old Dalai, while tenderly straightening his saffron robe; the second time to advise that the young adult Dalai be enthroned without delay; the third time to urge immediate flight from the Chinese, while dictating the route in a riddle-like prophesy; and the fourth and final time to draw the escape route right across what at the time of the prophesy is the Chinese army encampment. The Chinese subsequently relocate their position, thus demonstrating that the Oracle sees accurately into the future. The trance of the Oracle with its compelling pageantry and enigma crystallizes Tibet at its spectacular high teetering on the verge of disintegration. The brevity and perspicuity of the Oracle's clairvoyance is accentuated by his collapse in exhaustion; the vision of Tibet will soon be snuffed out by the Chinese.

Such is the lesson of Tibetan Buddhism—the impermanence of all things. A close-up of a sand painting or mandala opens the film, which transfigures into ripples of water, rays of light, forever shifting. This relentless movement is echoed in Philip Glass's electronic music. While Glass's signature synthesizers dominate the soundtrack, many scenes begin with traditional Tibetan music—low blasts of six-foot-long straight trumpets, clashes of cymbals, and chordal chanting[2]—flowing seamlessly into Glass's theme music. Glass's soundtrack is always there, barely audible at times, persistently foreboding while strangely persevering. All the visions in this film—Reting's and the Dalai Lama's—are likewise accompanied by Glass's score. These visions are the culmination of special effects and brilliant cinematography—aerial shots of a pristine mountaintop lake, tracking shots of the Dalai Lama's childhood house, aerial shots over mountains and plateaus—and editing to visualize the bloodbath about to befall the Dalai's escort and, by implication, Tibet under Chinese rule. Once again, technology in the form of soundtrack, camera skills, and special effects seeks to articulate the inexplicable; the craft of filmmaking is utilized to approximate what is essentially beyond human expression.

*Village Voice* film critic Georgia Brown calls *Little Buddha* Bertolucci's "strangest" film (1994, p. 58). A film involving parallel plots of Siddhartha reaching enlightenment and a Seattle family's spiritual pilgrimage to Bhutan is enough to elicit mixed reviews. Joe Brown finds *Little Buddha* a "botched, but beautiful, metaphysical epic" (*Washington Post,* 1994, p. 42). While calling it "only superficially superficial," Desson Howe mocks the script as "a paper-boat voyage over its [Buddhism's] surface" (*Washington Post,* 1994, p. C1). Roger Ebert, being his usual cynical self, comments that *Little Buddha* is "a slow-moving and pointless exercise" (*Chicago Sun-Times* 1994, p. 49). The point, surely known to Ebert, is Bertolucci's famous 1994 confession in *Sight and Sound* of his turn to Buddhism from "Marx and Freud" to save himself from depression once he was "deprived of the right to dream of utopias after the fall of the Wall," a turn justified by Bertolucci in terms of the centrality of man in all three systems of thought ("Bernardo Bertolucci" 1994, p. 21). The last of what Howe and others call Bertolucci's "Oriental trilogy," along with *The Last Emperor* (1988) and *The Sheltering Sky* (1990), *Little Buddha* concludes a deeply personal quest to non-Western cultures. Despite the opening disclaimer that tries to justify the film, namely, "the film is inspired by the true life stories of several children and their extraordinary voyage of discovery," which no critic seems to notice anyway, *Little Buddha*'s ending credits include a dedication "in memory of Francis Bouygues," which directs attention, instead, to Bertolucci's personal loss. Indeed, this film is about lost and found, about mourning over loss and miraculous retrieval. Whether a cooled passion for Marxism, the lulling Buddhist "opiate" of Bertolucci's, or the longing for an absent friend, elegy and the rapture of reunion lie at the heart of *Little Buddha*. Following the theme of a children's book on Siddhartha, Vittorio Storaro's cinematography shuttles between a symbiotic contrast: a blue-tinted Seattle versus an orange-tinted South Asia—ancient Nepal or present Bhutan. The blue does not signify, as various critics suggest, "cool" and "chilling" materialism; rather, it is nostalgia and melancholia. Similarly, the red-gold of South Asia is not so much "warm" as parched, hungry for deliverance.

The story begins with the belief that Lama Dorje has been reborn as a Caucasian boy, Jesse Konrad, in Seattle, to which Lama Norbu, played by Ying Ruocheng, and the search party travel from their Bhutan monastery. West-centricism—a story of Buddhist genesis told by the West, for the West, and enacted by Westerners—reveals itself in the casting of a white boy as the possible reincarnation of Lama Dorje and, of course, of Keanu Reeves as Siddhartha and later the Lord Buddha. I hasten to add, however, that Reeves's Prince Siddhartha, like the other Indian characters, speaks appropriately inflected dialogue and proper body language. For example, as his wish for a bowl to flow upstream comes true, a joyous Reeves swings his head left to right like a metronome, an accurate depiction of the Indian equivalent of pumping one's fist while shouting "Yeah."[3]

On the other hand, while Ying gives what Joe Brown believes to be a "charismatic" performance, Ying undercuts his image as "a deeply charming gentleman" (David Denby, *New York* 1994,) with the repeated unsheathings of his eye-knives and eruptions of sharp tone, reminiscent of his role as Pu Yi's warden in *The Last Emperor*. Investigating a potential Indian girl candidate as Lama Dorje's reincarnation back in Katmandu, Ying corrects an abbess in a caustic tone that the girl "was speaking Sanskrit." In the final climax of the identification ceremony among the three candidates—Jesse, Gita, the Indian girl, and Raju, the street foundling—Ying comes out of seclusion and wards off inquisitive monks with a stern wave of the arm worthy of a Red revolutionary. Ying's best moment arrives when he, in slow-motion, kneels down and kowtows to each of the three reincarnations of Lama Dorje—the body, the speech, and the mind. By so doing, Ying buries his unmonkly hostile face and achieves a high point in his performance. While Ying pays obeisance to Jesse, Jesse, in turn, kowtows to Ying. The camera freezes as the two gently touch heads inches above the ground in utter humility and Ying's voice-over narrates: "Perhaps, one day, you will find me." In view of the imminent death of Ying's Lama Norbu, this is, to all intents and purposes, his "last wish" to a successor, or predecessor. In layman's terms, reincarnation is a metaphor for lost and found, a cyclical mutual search, a wish to return betokening a love as infinite as life itself. With respect to the problematics of a Chinese actor who is also a high government official playing a Tibetan High Lama in exile, Ying's assistant monk, Champa, makes a far more convincing Tibetan. As the film opens with the tale of a goat about to be slaughtered and reborn, hence immediately setting the mythical tone, the assistant monk is called upon to imitate the goat's bleating. He gives the sound of "baaahhh," presumably onomatopoeic of the Tibetan language. Furthermore, his recitation of the Buddhist Sutra in the original language is self-assured, arising from the inner depth, somewhat different from Ying's English translation at the closing of the film.

In fact, Ying is upstaged by the character of Dean Konrad, Jesse's engineer/architect father played in a minimalist manner by Chris Isaak. Ebert criticizes Isaak's performance as "cold, closed-off," and emotionally detached, but Ebert seems to miss the point in what is also a factually erroneous review. Both Dean and Lisa (Bridget Fonda) Konrad are indeed taken by surprise by the Tibetan monks' house visit. While Lisa shrouds her confusion in feminine pleasantries, Dean looks downright rude in his John Wayne body language of nonchalance and boredom. As the monks describe their mission, Dean whispers to Lisa that he needs a scotch, and he refers to the visiting monks as "the round one" and "the square one." But Dean's evolution constitutes the subtext of this film: it is as much about Dean's own spiritual journey and rebirth as it is about the journeys of Tibetan monks, and as much about the latter half of Dean's life as it is about his son Jesse's previous life. A young, tall, and successful Dean is tempered by the suicide of his partner and by collapsing business ventures. This blow brings on a life crisis, and his journey to Bhutan as the chaperon of his son is, frankly, soul-searching for himself. Rather than Dean's taking Jesse across the globe to the great stupa of Bodhnath, the largest Buddhist shrine in Nepal and the center of Tibetan community, he is in fact *taken* there. Just like his namesake Joseph Conrad, who wrote *Heart of Darkness,* Dean ventures out only to discover what is already within. Thus, the builder who lives in the blue house in the blue city of Seattle where he has constructed impressive highrises takes leaves of the materialist realm and enters into the red-hot thirst for renewal of the soul in Bhutan. There, he mourns yet again a second death—that of Lama Norbu. Sitting close by, as if a deathwatch, counting Norbu's last breaths, Dean provides a crucial cinematic foil for the sadness of Norbu's death. According to Buddhist doctrines, the grief over death of loved ones is attenuated by the hope of their return. In addition to mourning, Tibetans await reincarnation of the deceased. In this sense, the totality of the audience's affect of "bereavement" can only be channeled by way of Dean, the sole non-Tibetan, non-Buddhist in the monastery, who bears in unalleviated sorrow Norbu's demise.[4] As such, the array of Dean's emotion ranges from mockery and revulsion over Norbu's outlandish mission to anger, sympathy, and unrelenting mourning. Without the lens provided by Dean, Western audiences would be unable to identify with the film, left adrift, unmoored in this exotic, religious parable.

Although embodying an "entry point" for Western moviegoers, Dean is not the only hinge on which the audience reception pivots. In the sequence of Siddhartha's enlightenment under the bodhi tree, Bertolucci seamlessly kneads together the realistic and the fantastic, the child's innocent perspective and the religious transcendence. Following Ying's retelling of the story in the present, the three young candidates circle around the gigantic tree in the backyard of Gita's house, witnessing on the other side the mythical scene of Siddhartha's ascendance to Buddhahood. The children crouch behind shield-like roots and stare intensely. To Bertolucci's credit, the film renders stasis and passivity exciting. After all, Reeves sitting cross-legged in meditation is not his explosive and mobile self in *Speed* (1994), nor the kung fu and Zen master in *The Matrix* (1999). What Bertolucci accomplishes is a spiritual tableau of the mind, unfolded in the temptation of Siddhartha by the five daughters of Mara, Lord of Darkness; in the strong gale from Hell which dislodges all but Siddhartha; in the legions of warriors vaporized by Siddhartha's stillness, a theme straight out of Kurosawa's *Kagemusha* (1980). Bertolucci thoroughly conjoins the story with its young listeners. As one of Mara's daughters dances flirtatiously, Gita impulsively sways to the hypnotic singing. As the powerful wind fails to ruffle Siddhartha, the children cower behind the tree. As fiery arrows transfigure into falling petals, the children revel in the shower of blossoms.

Victory, however, is only half-won. Mara, in the image of Siddhartha rising out of the reflection in water, launches a second strike not from without but from within Siddhartha's own ego. Similar to *Kundun*'s special effects in visualizing mystery, Bertolucci resorts to filmic techniques to present the moment just prior to nirvana when the doubles lock in a deathly debate:

"Architect, I have finally met you. You will not rebuild your house again."

"I am your house and you live in me."

"O Lord of my own ego. You are pure illusion. You do not exist. The earth is my witness."

While Siddhartha issues his stern rebuke to the ultimate "architect" of the illusion of life, thus circling back to Dean Konrad the builder and the contemporary, Seattle half of the film, his reproach is met with Mara's sweet, solicitous, almost temptress response. However, Siddhartha's final words are directed inward, a self-admonition that totally negates the reality of Mara, who vanishes, as he had arisen, like illusion.[5] As Siddhartha reaches enlightenment, the camera that has been roving around the bodhi tree on the heels of the three spectators now circles and hugs the Buddha, slowly elevating to capture the Buddha in a high-angle, slightly tilted shot to symbolize his soaring ascent.

The film concludes with an afterimage of Lama Nordu and his voice-over recitation of the Heart Sutra of emptiness, admittedly only the most accessible passages. The three burials of Norbu are movingly carried out by his three "finds." A snatch of a soprano's aria accompanies Gita's scattering of Norbu's ashes high in a bodhi-like tree, Raju's releasing of a wind horse near a monastery in Bhutan, and Jesse's letting go of Lama Dorje's bowl with Norbu's ashes in Seattle's Elliott Bay. The camera remains slightly above water to linger over the ebb and flow that threatens to submerge the bowl at every turn. The sunset turns the blue bay and blue city into the red-gold of the East. The contrast of colors merge; the East enters Seattle. Yet with the hypnotic rhythm of the bay, it is no longer the dry, singed orange under an unrelenting South Asian sun, but a rich, watery blue wedded to the twilight.

Compared with Annaud's and Scorsese's films that interlace mystery and contemporary politics, Bertolucci's film is profoundly personal. *Little Buddha* dwells on the possibility of redemption despite traumatic loss. With Bertolucci's personal tone in mind, I now return to the lamas' southbound vehicle on Interstate 5, where the car radio plays the country music "Everybody's wonderin' what and where they all came from." I know and can visualize the streets of Seattle. The car comes to a stop at the Konrads' hilltop house in, if memory serves, the Queen Anne Hill neighborhood north of Seattle center and the Space Needle, not far from the Lake View Cemetery where Bruce and Brandon Lee are buried side by side. If the car goes northwest from the Konrads' to land's end, Discovery Park gives you a view of the Pacific Ocean, where the beach is littered with beautiful sea-washed pebbles. To go southwest from the Konrads', cutting across downtown Seattle with its monorail, the Seattle Museum of Art, and other tourist spots, you come to Alki Beach. The tidal pools there on a wintry afternoon in 1997 hid a young moray eel the size of my three-year-old daughter's palm, so freshly green that it literally glowed. But she could not bring the eel back home; she had to leave it where she found it.

# Intercut on
## Asian Deceased

# 13  Hmong Refugee's Death Fugue

> Black milk of daybreak we drink it at sundown
> We drink it at noon in the morning we drink it at night
> We drink and we drink it
> —Paul Celan's "Death Fugue"

**Paul Celan's** Holocaust poem suffocates in the black smoke rising from the crematoriums' chimneys, shrouding inmates as well as survivors' consciousness, including daily rituals as simple as drinking milk. A disturbing parallel exists between Celan's death fugue and the Hmong's, one which mourns their loss in the Southeast Asian conflict since the 1970s. Similar to Celan's fugue, the Hmong's collective story is filled with refrains, thematic variations of demise. "I come to this foreign land, / without young brothers, without old brothers, / and the others eat, while I watch like a dog waiting for scraps" (Vang and Lewis, *Grandmother's Path, Grandfather's Way* 1990, p. 124), thus sings the Hmong woman Lee Txai in a Thai refugee camp in 1980.[1] Her self-image plummets as a result of, among other things, the wretched living conditions and the uncertainty in the camp. One would like to believe the myth that adversity comes to a miraculous end once these refugees of the Southeast Asian conflict have arrived in the United States. However, the sense of loneliness, loss, and shame becomes magnified amongst Hmong refugees relocated to the United States, as Lillian Faderman's informant, Kia Vue, laments in *I Begin My Life All Over* (1998): "Now we ride on their [the narrator's children] shoulders, through lands that are of gold, jungles that are of paradise—and yet I feel we're drowning, like many of our people who did not make it across the Mekong" (p. 174). While praising the United States as golden and paradisal, Kia Vue subconsciously associates it with the Hmong trauma of fleeing the Communists through the Southeast Asian "jungles" and crossing the Mekong River to reach Thai refugee camps in the mid-1970s. More revealingly, life in the United States is cast as a "protracted drowning." One wonders whether the refugees have indeed begun a new life—as Faderman's book title suggests—or whether they are dying a slow death, evidenced by the eerily similar testimonies of Kia Vue and a host of her compatriots. Their tales of survival are simultaneously a litany of deaths they have witnessed and a dirge for themselves. It is this collective affect out of a suspension between life and death to which I wish to lend my ears.

To attend to their death fugue, a comprehensive review of the literature on Hmong refugees is in order, from psychology, mental health, education, and journalism to sociology, anthropology, arts and crafts, and oral history. One must be exceptionally vigilant in this review of literature over the past three decades to pick out fragments of Hmong voices. As a preliterate, refugee community, Hmong experience comes to us heavily mediated by the West. Social scientists have tracked the Hmong migration pattern; health providers have researched how to tailor modern medicine to the Hmong's animistic beliefs; English as a Second Language teachers have prepared primers based on Hmong folklore. Indeed, without such conscientious effort of Western scholars and writers, the Hmong saga would be in danger of vanishing. For instance, Anne Fadiman's award-winning *The Spirit Catches You and You Fall Down* (1997) retrieved what could have become a mere statistic and wove it into a nuanced portrayal of Hmong belief and lifestyle. Fadiman elucidated the Hmong perception of "epilepsy" as *qaug dab peg,* literally "'the spirit catches you and you fall down.' The spirit referred to . . . is a soul-stealing *dab*" (p. 20). Charles Johnson laboriously compiled *Myths, Legends and Folk Tales from the Hmong of Laos* (1985), a bilingual edition of Hmong folktales that serves both as a primer of the English language for the Hmong and an introduction to Hmong culture for English-speakers. Marsha MacDowell and others collected and analyzed the Hmong story cloths on which part of this essay is based. Such works have created the framework for understanding the Hmong experience.

In accordance with the Holocaust survivor Primo Levi's reluctance to "comprehend" the Nazi genocide, I propose to venture out of the scholarly frame in order to better heed the Hmong death fugue. Levi writes in the Afterword to *Shema* (1976): "Perhaps one cannot, what is more one must not, understand, because to understand is almost to justify. Let me explain: 'understanding' a proposal or human behavior means (also etymologically) to 'contain' it, contain its author, put oneself in his place, identify with him. Now no normal man can ever identify with Hitler, Himmler, Goebbels, Eichmann, and endless others" (pp. 53–54). Levi's admonition against understanding victimizers can equally be applied to the victims, for it would be presumptuous for middle-class, First-World readers to instantly "bond" with either Levi or Hmong refugees on the basis of a good book or two. In fact, at every turn of scholarly and artistic representations of mass destructions of this kind, translation and cross-cultural negotiation inevitably take place. One element of the collective experience often falls through the cracks of various disciplinary interpretive frameworks—how victims *feel*. While researchers have played a pivotal role in preserving Hmong oral history, the elegiac, mourning quality of Hmong expression is often suppressed into a subconscious "tic" amidst the objective, professional façade of scholarship. This essay is in a way a close-up of tics, symptoms of the malaise hidden beneath the appearance of Americanization.

## Refrains in Cultural Variations

The most tragic manifestation of such "death by drowning" alluded to by Kia Vue is undoubtedly the Sudden Unexpected Nocturnal Death Syndrome (SUNDS), which in the 1970s and 1980s mysteriously struck Hmong and other Southeast Asian male refugees in their sleep. Some survivors claimed an attack by a Kingstonian "Sitting Ghost" (*The Woman Warrior* 1976, p. 81) on their chests, pressing the air out of their lungs. Western doctors could do no more than attribute the cases to cardiac arrest in otherwise perfectly healthy men, a great number of whom reported depression and ill-adjustment to the United States. One journalist has facetiously characterized the Hmong refugees' transition from Southeast Asia to the West as moving "from the Stone Age to the Space Age." Hyperbole aside, this journalist does capture the Herculean obstacles facing these new immigrants, obstacles whose psychic impact aggravates what would be termed in psychoanalysis as post-traumatic stress disorder (PTSD).

To approach the Hmong refugee experience via the concept of PTSD obfuscates a key difference between the Laotian highlanders and the Freudian model derived from Western history. The notion of trauma evolves from Freud's 1920 *Beyond the Pleasure Principle* on "war neurosis" and accident trauma to a more mystical, collective *Moses and Monotheism* (1939). Subsequent theorizations by Georges Bataille, Robert Jay Lifton, Cathy Caruth, Shoshana Felman, and others not only continue the Freudian emphasis on the unwilled, nightmarish recurrences of memory, but also point to a general state of being, one marked by melancholia over loss and irretrievability. All these emotions are shared by Hmong refugees. Yet Freud and his followers take for granted that their patients are afflicted by *post*-traumatic stress disorder, that the trauma is in the past. Two kinds of patients, for instance, figured prominently in Freud's formulation of the theory of trauma: veterans of the Great War and survivors of automobile accidents, and both groups had returned to the normal life that they were accustomed to prior to the disruptions. Drawing from a subsequent yet deciding moment in human history, one can put it this way: Holocaust survivors are haunted by memories of Auschwitz; they are no longer *in* Auschwitz. Hmong refugees, on the other hand, have difficulty putting the trauma, so to speak, behind them since they remain in the thick of a disorienting labyrinth, with its linguistic and cultural puzzles, their own heavy dependency on welfare and other social programs, homesickness and a gnawing sense of impotence, dissolution of traditional lifestyle and values, American racism and discrimination, and gradual Americanization of the younger generation.[2] Instead of *post*-traumatic stress disorder, Hmong refugees face a continuing daily ordeal in the United States, one which is much attenuated in intensity compared with what they experienced in Southeast Asia but is far more persistent now and increasingly irreconcilable, given the onset of old age and the felt diminishment of power.

Put bluntly, the terminus that is SUNDS negates the clinical efficacy of PTSD; dead patients no longer suffer from PTSD. SUNDS being the finis of these refugees' lives, one is compelled to rewind and listen again to their stories from social science studies, where the death fugue is coded into statistics and research models. Shelley Adler in "The Role of the Nightmare in Hmong Sudden Unexpected Nocturnal Death Syndrome" (1991) recaps the Hmong experience:

> The Hmong have undergone a seemingly endless series of traumatic experiences: the war in Laos, the Pathet Lao takeover and subsequent Hmong persecution (including the threat of genocide), the harrowing nighttime escapes through jungles and across the Mekong River, the hardships of refugee camps in Thailand, and finally resettlement in the United States, with not only housing, income, language, and employment concerns, but the separation of families and clans, inability to practice traditional religion, hasty conversion to Christianity, and the breakdown of the gender hierarchy, among many others. (p. 200)

This prolonged dislocation began with the Hmong entanglement in the Southeast Asian conflict. Fighting the Pathet Lao as proxy for the Central Intelligence Agency and the United States during the Vietnam War, the Hmong community sustained a casualty rate ten times higher than that of Americans who had fought in Vietnam. "It is estimated," asserts Adler, "that nearly one-third of the Laotian Hmong population lost their lives in the war" (p. 3).

Adler further elaborates the Hmong's subsequent hardships in the United States: "While difficulties involving language and employment may not be unique to Hmong immigrants, the particular combination of problems involving survivor guilt, the conflict between Hmong traditional religion and Christianity, changing generational and gender roles, and trauma-induced emotional and psychological disorders is unique to the Hmong refugee experience" (p. 135). Indeed, Mark Thompson, in "The Elusive Promise" (1986), maintains that the Hmong are one of the "ethnic groups that have fared the worst" in their adjustment to the United States (p. 46). Witnessing how the uprooting of the Hmong is compounded by their poor adjustment to the New World, Johnson comments that the Hmong face "cultural annihilation" (p. vi).

The root cause for the failure of Hmong assimilation, as Simon Fass discusses in "Innovations in the Struggle for Self-Reliance" (1986), lies in their refugee status:

> Immigrants to the United States were able to equal or surpass
> income, employment and occupational status characteristics
> of comparable Americans within 10 to 15 years of their
> arrival.... Refugees also improved their economic status with
> increasing length of residence, but progress was slower because they
> did not self-select themselves for migration. Refugee populations
> contained significant proportions of people whose motivations
> or other characteristics would not have led them to leave their
> homelands, and whose skills were not easily adapted to new cultural
> circumstances. They were at a relative disadvantage to self-selected
> migrants in terms of learning English, modifying their original skills,
> and finding out where and how those skills could be used to increase
> income. (p. 356)

Fass's argument is validated by George Scott's sociological exposition in "Migrants Without Mountains" (1986). Scott's premise is that adjustment for immigrants is "one of negotiation trade-off decision making ... in which the *benefits* accruing from a particular type and level of participation in the receiving society are weighed against the *costs* of having to modify or abandon conflicting traditional sociocultural elements" (p. ix). Hmong migration, gauged by this criteria, was doomed from the start, as Nancy Donnelly puts it in *Changing Lives of Refugee Hmong Women* (1994): "Hmong refugees do not seek new lives, they seek the same lives in a new location, and where possible they use their new opportunities to bolster preexisting social conceptions" (p. 184). Due to the great disparity between Hmong expectations and the social environment to which they came, the Hmong cannot advance economically and withdraw into their traditional culture.

Against this historical background and the medical opinion that "ventricular fibrillation" is the cause of SUNDS, Shelley Adler approaches SUNDS from the standpoint of a folklorist and links it to nightmare, or the visit of evil spirit. She quotes Stith Thompson's magisterial compilation, *Motif-Index of Folk Literature* (1958), for numerous motifs in folklore in which people die suddenly as a result of a broken heart, chagrin, grief, or even joy (p. 183). Concluding that SUNDS invariably strikes victims in a supine position, who are completely paralyzed while conscious, unable to move or cry out as an alien being presses down on them, Adler compares SUNDS with similar deaths in sleep in Filipino culture, called *bangangut*, as well as Thai and Khmu sudden deaths. The sense of a foreign body sitting on their chest is confirmed by the fact that out of Adler's sample of 118 Hmong, "74% of the informants who offered an explanation for the cause of SUNDS suggested an etiology that was directly spirit-related or involved the problem of the absence of traditional Hmong cosmology or religious practice" (p. 199). Adler contends that SUNDS usually occurs in the first two years of the victims' arrival in the United States, the period when they experience great anxiety and are the most vulnerable. The folklorist maintains that "[t]he supranormal experience traditionally known as the nightmare and familiar to the Hmong as *dab tsog* or *tsog tsuam* acts as a trigger for Hmong Sudden Unexpected Nocturnal Death Syndrome. The power of this folk belief, compounded with such factors as the trauma of war, migration, rapid acculturation, and the inability to practice traditional healing and ritual, causes cataclysmic psychological, and subsequently physiological, stress that can result in sudden unexpected deaths" (p. 197).

Christopher Hayes and Richard Kalish, in "Death-Related Experiences and Funerary Practices of the Hmong Refugee in the United States" (1987–1988), focus on the psychological aftershocks of survival: "Their escape from Laos, however, required a long march through mountainous areas and rain forests, and an eventual crossing of the Mekong River. An estimated 35 percent died during their flight from illness, drowning, starvation, jungle accidents, or Pathet Lao forces.... The Hmong seldom had time to bury their dead, who were left to rot where they fell; often the ill and wounded were also left behind" (p. 64). The authors assert that the lack of proper funeral and burial processes lead to the refugee's stress and guilt. They are afflicted with "bereavement overload": "The intensity of such bereavement might be expected to increase exponentially when the losses that follow each other in rapid succession include not only deaths, but also losses in status, possessions, familiar surroundings, and separation from loved ones" (pp. 64–65). Nor did these refugees, Hayes and Kalish believe, enjoy peace and comfort upon reaching Thai refugee camps. The authors report that "since 1983, thirty-five Hmong have died in their sleep" (p. 65).

Christopher Hayes contends, in "A Study of the Older Hmong Refugees in the United States" (1984), that the psychological problems found in the refugee camps only become enlarged once the refugees arrived in the United States—ripped apart from family members and friends, experiencing culture shock, and suffering a breakdown of traditional roles (p. 82). Maintaining that the older Hmong in the United States are bored and depressed, Hayes identifies the "stressors" on them as "loss of possessions and dependence upon public assistance" (p. 163), "loss of mobility . . . and remaining homebound," crimes against the Hmong (p. 164), and intergenerational conflict (p. 165). Observing a high level of grief and depression among older Hmong, Hayes closes ominously: "Nothing short of returning those who have died, restoring the old traditions and customs, and moving back to Laos, will eliminate the problems which many of the elders face. I have no choice but to conclude from this study that the elder Hmong have few, if any, avenues for restoring what they have lost. Besides remaining family members and a sense of their own ethnicity, the elders have little to comfort them in their old age" (p. 186). Hayes further cites a grim statistic: the Long Beach Hmong Association estimates that 90 percent of the elders in the community suffer from some form of depression (p. 164).

Statistics on the Hmong population elsewhere in the United States confirm the sobering statistic in Long Beach. Michele LaRue's "Stress and Coping of the Indochinese Refugees in a California Community" (1982) finds that in San Diego while neither the Vietnamese nor the Hmong refugees "recognized as a stress the young losing the values of the native culture and adopting the values of the American culture," LaRue's observation and further research indicate otherwise, so much so that "survivor guilt" plagues 81 percent of the Vietnamese and 90 percent of the Hmong refugees, and "helplessness" is reported by 57 percent of the Vietnamese and 65 percent of the Hmong refugees.

Attuned now to these recurring motifs in Western scholarship on the Hmong, it is time to entertain Fadiman's fancy of "splic[ing] them [the audio tapes] together" (p. ix), so that the native informants' voices may occasionally rise above those of the interpreters and the translators. Although John Tenhula's *Voices from Southeast Asia* (1991) does not identify specific Hmong interviewees, two narrators among the refugees from Laos stand out as likely candidates. Xoua Thao states in "The Sleeping People":

In America, we are away from our traditional property where we
believe our ancestors' spirits live and protect us. We are unable
to practice our religion, and the shaman says that because of this
change we have lost the protection of our ancestors and we are very
vulnerable.... But few people will talk with you about this [Sudden
Unexpected Nocturnal Death Syndrome], and if you try to talk with
them, they will not answer. To talk about it is dangerous—you could
become one of the next, the sleeping people. (p. 98)

Fear surrounds SUNDS as if it were a tribal taboo, a scourge befalling the
Hmong for their "betrayal" of the Hmong tradition.

In "A Soldier without a Country," the other possible Hmong interviewee,
Mong Pang, exhibits a deep sense of loss: "It was a good life in Laos and I miss
my country very much. I want to go back if the Communists get out. I look to
that day all of the time. We left so quickly. We just locked the door and left. We
don't know about our possessions or our house. I hope it is still there. I think
about relatives and friends" (Tenhula, *Voices from Southeast Asia* 1991, p. 128).
Mong Pang's sadness may be precipitated by the fact that while he used to be
a colonel in Laos, he now works as a janitor. The drop in social status and the
inability to recreate an illusion of homeland aggravate depression.

The most complete description of SUNDS comes from a joint study
by Joseph Tobin and Joan Friedman. In their 1983 "Spirits, Shamans, and
Nightmare Death," the authors cite extensively from their informant, Vang
Xiong of Chicago, who survived a bout of spirit possession:

The first night he [Vang Xiong] awoke suddenly, short of breath,
from a dream in which a cat was sitting on his chest. The second
night, the room suddenly grew darker, and a figure, like a large black
dog, came to his bed and sat on his chest. He could not push the dog
off and he grew quickly and dangerously short of breath. The third
night, a tall, white-skinned female spirit came into his bedroom from
the kitchen and lay on top of him. Her weight made it increasingly
difficult for him to breathe, and as he grew frantic and tried to call
out he could manage but a whisper. He attempted to turn into his
side, but found he was pinned down. After 15 minutes, the spirit left
him, and he awoke, screaming. (p. 440)

Viewing "Vang's sleeping and breathing difficulties as symptoms of the anxiety, depression, and paranoia that threaten all victims of trauma and extreme
stress" (p. 442), the authors speculate that "the Hmong [sudden] deaths may

be a form of unconscious suicide mediated by a loss of self-respect, a loss of feeling of control over one's life, and a loss of will to live in anxious circumstances" (pp. 446–447).

Upon hearing this recurring nightmare, Vang Xiong's American sponsor, a female member of the local Christian church, was taken aback, suspecting that she herself gave forth the "tall, white-skinned female spirit." Commendable in its level of cultural sensitivity and perhaps quite accurate in its diagnosis of the pressure of acculturation, this interpretation nonetheless fails to take into account the three manifestations in three consecutive nights—"a cat," "a figure, like a large black dog," and "a tall, white-skinned female spirit"—which engage in the same attempt to suffocate Vang Xiong. The spirits of the first and the third nights are easily identified, whereas that of the second night, the one that *resembles* rather than *is* a large black dog, is more amorphous. There is, of course, a contrast of colors between the black of the second night and the white skin of the third night, but the black figure is just as intimidatingly "large" as the "tall" white spirit looming above the prostrate victim. In addition to the traditionally Hmong forms of animals, the evil spirit also adopts the guise of a human female, perhaps a male reaction against the erosion of patriarchal privileges in America.[3]

From the Hmong refugee's perspective, Vang Xiong believes that he is susceptible to spirit attacks because "we didn't follow all of the mourning rituals we should have when our parents died [in Laos]" (p. 444). He escaped from the Communists with his wife and infant in 1978:

> There were 74 people in the group we fled with. We walked through the jungle for five days. We knew the Communist patrols were all around us. Many in the group demanded we leave our infant behind, that we kill her, because they feared her crying at night would give us away. We refused, and quieted her with opium. An old woman among us grew too weak to walk. Her sons took turns carrying her on their backs for three days, but finally they were forced to leave her behind, to leave her on the trail with just a bowl of rice, for the Communists were getting closer and our pace was too slow. Finally, we reached the Mekong. Several of the men in our group swam across and returned some hours later with a few small boats. We boarded the boats, and just as we got out into open water we heard shots on shore. We saw another group of perhaps 50 Hmong waiting for boats by the river bank being shot at with machine guns. Men and women and children fell to the ground. Blood was everywhere. Most, if not all, in that group were killed. (p. 444)

Note the precision of numbers. The informant remembers exactly how many people were in his group of refugees and how many survived. A strong sense of group cohesion and an emphasis on practical matters must have imprinted these numbers in his memory. "I feel I left too early but also too late." Vang Xiong proceeds to express the ambiguity of survival: "If I had known, in 1975, how bad the fighting would become in the next few years, I would have left then. But, on the other hand, when I think of my brothers and sisters and their children back in Laos I feel I should not have left at all. I will never forgive myself for leaving them" (p. 445). Such poignant grief echoes over and over again in other survivor accounts.

Chia Koua Xiong, in Tim Pfaff's *Hmong in America* (1995), reminisces that "[i]n 1982 . . . we ran out of bullets. . . . We [264 people] left Tha Vieng and departed for the Mekong River. On the way . . . the Vietnamese killed five of our people—one was my son, three were my nephews, and one was a Her family member. [We] had eaten all the food we had carried. . . . We cut bamboo to make rafts . . . [and] waited until dusk. . . . When all the people were ready, we paddled to Thailand. We arrived at Pa Sa, Thailand [sic] at 5:00 a.m. . . . Some of our people got sick. The Thai people who lived along the river brought us food. As a human being, struggling like that was the lowest life on this earth" (p. 55). The same kind of vivid details of numbers and events haunts Chia Koua Xiong, as is the nature of memories of extreme situations. Refugees' experiences are simultaneously individual and universal. Each is haunted by his or her own personal hell, but the accounts resemble one another as a result of the fact that the specific vagaries of individual experience tend to be erased in collective catastrophes. Whether escaping on foot from the north or the south, each individual is plagued by the same fear and arrives at the same river.

Another of Pfaff's informants, Houa Vue Moua, recalls his tearful departure from the refugee camp and his mother. Fearing that she will never see her son again, his mother is heartbroken, crying throughout the farewells: "So our way of leaving—from Nong Khai to Bangkok, Thailand to come to Eau Claire [Wisconsin]—was like a funeral" (p. 62). The joy of rebirth from the limbo of a camp is so muted by survivor guilt and a sense of self-betrayal that the informant conflates it with metaphors of death. Chia Koua Xiong testifies in a similar vein that life since his relocation has not improved much: "I feel bad because I have been in this country for three years and no one has taught me a word in English. My vision is getting worse. . . . I feel bad because I don't know how to drive . . . how to communicate with any Americans. . . . When I think about it I cry by myself" (p. 78).

It is fitting to conclude this section with the opening voice of Kia Vue from Faderman's book:

Coming here, I know I have become helpless. Everything I do, I just depend on my children.... [A]fter about fifteen years [in the United States], I don't even know all of my ABCs. I'm like my four-year-old girl—and she even writes her name better than I could write my name. My children laugh at me, and I laugh with them. But when I really think about it, it's not funny. It hurts a lot. It even hurts more if I think about it. (pp. 174–175)

Alienation from her children deepens Kia Vue's sense of helplessness. In the worst-case scenarios, the Hmong legacy of suffering continues into the next generation as juvenile delinquency. Faderman comments in the Gang section of her book: "The rapid proliferation of Hmong youth gangs is in large part a reaction by Hmong teens to what they perceive as their parents' social impotence in America" (p. 185). This assessment is echoed by Wendy Walker-Moffat's *The Other Side of the Asian American Success Story* (1995): "The recent rise in juvenile delinquency among Hmong adolescents suggests that the sense of security provided by the Hmong clan system no longer meets the demands of survival in American streets and schools, and that some youths are turning to their peers instead of their elders and extended family for security" (p. 98).

## Refrains in Colorful Threads

Other than written sources, another form of Hmong creativity offers corroborating evidence of the refugee's death fugue. Deriving from the more traditional *paj ntaub* ("flower cloth," a picture sewn with painstaking embroidery), Hmong story cloths of the refugee saga seem to have arisen in the Thai refugee camps and are now a staple in arts and crafts festivals in the United States. Story cloths are stylized in their narratological sequence—the fighting with Pathet Lao or Vietcong, the escape through jungles, the crossing of the Mekong River, and the arrival at Thai refugee camps—which unfold in several horizontal planes in which the refugees' zigzag route brings attention downward.[4] The tapestry is usually framed by traditional consecutive triangles or shark's-teeth designs on all four sides, which some speculate is an attempt to ward off evil spirits or serves as a mimetic representation of the peaks in the Laotian highlands.

Horrid memories, surely, need to be contained by narratological stylizations, but such containment, as illustrated in nearly all story cloths, never fails to cease at the exact moment of departure for the West. In view of the voluminous recall collected in "Refrains in Cultural Variations," it is shocking to find that Hmong refugees appear reluctant to share their American or Western experiences other than in the form of self-elegies and death wishes. A case in point: half way through Sucheng Chan's *Hmong Means Free* (1994), a telling moment occurs when Mr. Xia Shoua Fang terminates the interview abruptly, for he "did not wish to discuss his life in the United States" (p. 141). Mr. Fang has just finished narrating a horrendous tale of survival through the Laotian jungles with the Communists in pursuit, but he falls silent at the precise juncture when he is, by any standard, safe and comfortable in "the land of the free." His flight, as agonizing as it has been, is nonetheless *recalled*, whereas the present and the long, interminable future in the United States are *repressed*. It should not require a Freud's genius to see that Hmong refugees are not exactly healed by the largesse and abundance of the United States. Rather, their life-after-death is shrouded by a deafening silence on their American sojourn, a sort of death-in-life. The premature closure of Mr. Fang's account and the story cloths suggests that the voluminous recall of the Hmong escape through Southeast Asia is undertaken *so as to* repress or to counter the un-Hmong-ing in the here and now. The refugee story serves to construct Hmong identity, which appears to be fast vanishing in the West. Tales of individual survival, however, become an ironic footnote to what Charles Johnson has called "cultural annihilation."

The genesis of story cloths is usually attributed to the Thai refugee camps in the 1970s. Sally Peterson, in "From the Heart and the Mind" (1990), cites Joan Ritchie's consultant, Mrs. Chang Xiong: "I first saw story blankets in 1975, in Ban Vinai. The Hmong women wanted to make these for themselves, not to sell them. The women think about moving from one country to another country to another country. The old people worried that the young may not know. They thought, we don't have cameras, we don't have knowledge of writing stories; let us use the needle to make a memory of our customs, our history. Women gave the men the idea and asked to them [sic] to draw the pictures. Women taught the men how to sew" (p. 357). Marsha MacDowell's *Stories in Thread* (1989) provides a detailed account of the division of labor inside the camps: "Bao Lor, interviewed in Detroit by Sue Jillian, believes there are only ten men in the camps responsible for drawing story cloths; they were trained in an art program instituted by Thai personnel, and offered to men only" (p. 5). Because of the lack of art training for the masses of women sewers, the job of drawing fell on a handful of males. These drawings were then circulated in the camps as blueprints. Sewing immediately caught on since there was little else detainees could do to earn some income or, in the course of waiting for relocation, to while away time in an overcrowded camp with poor living conditions. Pfaff unequivocally asserts that at one point the

Figure 22. Yer Thor's story cloth on the Hmong refugee saga. Personal collection.

designer Jan Folsom selected for Hmong women in the camps patterns and color combinations that would appeal to an international clientele. The level of interest tourists of the refugee camps showed for story cloths led Western relief workers and others to market them in the First World.

Some three decades after their birth, Hmong story cloths may appear formulaic. But the creator(s), the circumstances of production, the marketing, and the eventual ownership of each piece vary. Figure 22 is a piece my wife and I purchased at an arts and crafts fair held at the courthouse in Bloomington, Indiana, in the early or mid-1980s. Both of us were marginally aware of the Hmong plight through *National Geographic;* my wife, prompted by her artistic instinct, insisted on paying what seemed, for international graduate students then, to be an exorbitant price for it. Her connoisseur's eyes paid off, and I have been using this piece in my college teaching consistently. The Hmong artist was Yer Thor of Detroit. She was kind enough to keep up a correspondence for a number of years and even sent us photographs of Hmong women sewing together as well as newspaper clippings on Detroit's Hmong community. After our several moves away from and back to the Midwest, I unfortunately lost her address and photographs. Yer Thor had been reluctant about one thing, though. I was quite adamant that she "sign" her work. She did so eventually, but she sewed her name in turquoise on the lower right corner against a backdrop of grayish blue, her choice of threads so close to the background color that it appears to be a compromise between acceding to the customer's demand and remaining invisible. Signing and thus claiming authorship over a product seemed to her a completely outlandish, even slightly decadent, idea.

Several tiers exist in Yer Thor's piece. The top one arrays two rows of soldiers firing at each other. Those in light green uniform use Soviet-made AK-47s with their crescent-shaped magazine cartridges and suggest the Vietcong, whereas the Hmong army is attired in dark green. Helicopters in the clouds are in the same color as the Hmong unit and can be assumed to be the U.S. aerial support. The second tier is dominated by an airfield where Hmong evacuees with bundles are about to board an airplane. Although critics have long held that the Hmong have no perspective in their story cloths, the diminishing size of the figures in relation to the plane gives depth to this scene. The soaring, pointed mountain peaks surrounding the airstrip recall the evacuation of Long Cheng in May 1975, detailed in Gayle Morrison's *Sky Is Falling* (1999). Morrison maintains, based on the testimony of U.S. pilots and Hmong survivors, that the frantic air evacuation transported 2,500 Hmong to safety in Thai refugee camps, but abandoned the bulk of Hmong refugees in Long Cheng. These refugees were left to their own devices, as is evidenced in the stream of Hmong en route diagonally to reach the Mekong River. This journey on foot is punctuated by scenes of the traditional slash-and-burn agriculture, practiced along the escape route for sustenance, and scenes of temporary shelter, breastfeeding, cooking, and the like. Refugees crossing the Mekong River extend the zigzag line across the piece. With the Vietcong shooting at them from the shore and intercepting them in patrol boats, the refugees rely on makeshift bamboo rafts, inner tubes, and an assortment of buoying devices. There is a lone Hmong male on the river bank firing back at the Vietcong.

That the river-crossing never fails to appear in Hmong story cloths—or in Hmong oral testimony, for that matter—is symptomatic of the indelible trauma left on the refugee psyche.[5] Being highlanders, Hmong were unlikely to have grown accustomed to swimming across strong torrents like the Mekong River. In addition, the Mekong seems to be the final lap before sanctuary, so close to the end of their exodus, yet so fraught with danger and uncertainty. In the river they no longer enjoy the shelter of the dense Southeast Asian jungle; they are exposed to the elements and hostile fire. Their vulnerability culminates at the very moment of delivery, much as the treacherous maneuver through the birth canal. On a more philosophical level, swimming is not a natural mode of existence: we swim in order to reach the other shore to continue our normal life as animals on land. Looking back at their experience, Hmong refugees may feel that they have never quite reached the other shore but have continued to "float" as refugees. Death by drowning is a distinct possibility, not only literally at the bottom of the Mekong River, but also metaphorically at the bottom of the American social hierarchy. Yer Thor's Mekong is a metonymy for the perils of refugees.[6]

The reading of the Mekong as a watershed in the refugee saga is borne out both by the form or design of the story cloth and by its content. The white stitches that formulate the river cut across the piece, dividing two blocks of space. The Hmong's position is shown to be drastically diminished once they reach the bottom half of the piece. They are met by border guards, subsequently interviewed by immigration officers sitting behind a desk, and queued up by a traffic controller before boarding buses. Note that in the refugee camps there are three types of characters in non-black, non-Hmong costume: border patrols with guns, immigration officers with pens and documents, and traffic controllers with batons. The only four individuals resting on seats on the Thai side are the officials, proportionally much larger than the refugees being processed, who raise their left hands in a clear gesture of swearing allegiance. The Hmong used to wield guns and farming tools and control their destiny to a certain extent on the Laotian side of the river. Mekong-crossing leaves them with bundles and backpacks only; even the lone Hmong fighter by the river has vanished. The Hmong loss of power contrasts sharply with the three types of authority figure, embodied in the four figures who, literally, "sit in judgment" over life and death. Nature, nevertheless, continues to thrive throughout their ordeal, from their journey on foot to the refugee camps. The Hmong sensibility to nature never wavers, even in their darkest hours. But the lush vegetation observes the Hmong exile mutely.[7]

Because sewing human figures one inch in height or less is so difficult, story cloths usually feature stylized figures with no detailed facial expression. Yet Yer Thor shows expression by not showing it; she intimates human emotions by hiding the human face. The slightly larger couple in the bottom

Figure 23. Detail of Yer Thor's story cloth. Note the slightly larger couple in the bottom right-hand corner.

right-hand corner (Figure 23) invites special scrutiny. A couple, belongings in hand, follows the crowd to board a bus. The woman covers her face with both her hands, sobbing, while the man turns to gaze at her and puts his arm around her in a gesture of consolation. While her emotions have been held in check throughout the fighting, the escape, the river-crossing, the interrogation by officials, and the languishing at the camps, the woman finds it impossible to withhold any longer the grief of displacement upon exiting the refugee camp and Southeast Asia. Yer Thor's story cloth ends on this note—a relocation signifying safety in the West, but one wonders if this should be the natural end of the Hmong fugue. What are we to hear in the silence enveloping Hmong refugee life in the United States? Is the final note of a musical composition necessarily a well-wrought closure or is it a mere sigh before expiration?

Two other pieces collected in MacDowell's *Stories in Thread* complement Yer Thor's story cloth. These pieces also follow the left-to-right horizontal arrangement, modeled after the style of writing "in Lao, romanized Hmong, and English" (Peterson, "From the Heart and the Mind" 1990, p. 361). Figure 24 displays all the key moments in the Hmong saga: the escape, the crossing of the Mekong, the interview and photographing by immigration officials, the distribution of food and supplies in the refugee camps. The detail in Figure 25 is of the upper right-hand corner, which shows three Hmong

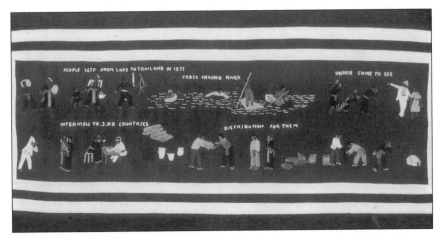

Figure 24. Stages of the Hmong exodus: the escape, crossing the Mekong, the refugee camp. Artist unknown. Michigan State University Museum collection.

Figure 25. Detail of the upper right-hand corner in Figure 24. Note the three Hmong males beseeching visitors from the United Nations High Commissioner of Refugees (UNHCR).

males in various gestures of obsequiousness toward visitors from the United Nations High Commissioner of Refugees (UNHCR). The Hmong fold their hands and bow—one is close to kneeling—whereas the two visitors are turning away, about to leave. The taller male visitor points toward the Hmong, indicating something for the female visitor to see, as if they are tourists on a sight-seeing trip. The bright yellow of the woman's dress and of the man's hat and shirt, coupled with the man's white suit, contrast sharply with the dark,

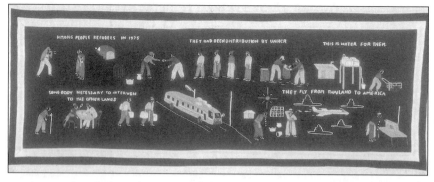

Figure 26. Story cloth on the Hmong plight. Artist unknown. Michigan State University Museum collection.

traditional dress of the three Hmong males as well as with the dark blue background cloth. Such color schemes already make the UNHCR visitors stand out in the somber camp universe, even in the brief moment before their exit, while the three Hmong's costumes submerge them into the background cloth. In fact, not only is the male UNHCR member in a white suit, so are all the other figures of authority—the immigration officials conducting interviews and photographing applicants and the person who distributes supplies to yet another bowing Hmong character. The entire piece finds itself framed as well by two white rectangles, setting the boundaries of Hmong refugee life. Perhaps a subconscious transposition of the power of the "white" race onto the clothes of whites as well as onto the context of Hmong experience, that whiteness emerges whenever there is a symbol of life—a water kettle in their exodus, water buckets in the camp, and the hut that provides the final sanctuary and a closure to the story. The white house is, needless to say, someone else's home for what will be a permanent accommodation of the refugees.[8] Granted that the recurring white stitches may be purely coincidental as a result of the material conditions at the time of manufacturing this piece at Ban Vinai, the largest of Thai refugee camps, the Hmong dependency on outside forces is presented as a deep humiliation.

Figure 26 follows the same pattern of escape and camp experiences. The detail of Figure 27 focuses on the lower right-hand corner, the finale to the story cloth. This proves to be one of the rare instances where life in the United States is portrayed. The caption reads: "They fly from Thailand to America," which is made visual by an airplane in the clouds and the sun. The plane symbolizes the great distance that now separates the Hmong in diaspora. To the left of Figure 27, two people cover their faces, tears dripping in dotted white lines, despite the fact that they are showered in the radiance of the sun. One

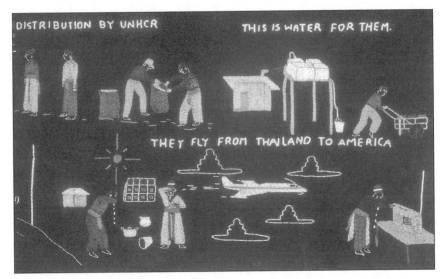

Figure 27. Detail of the lower right-hand corner in Figure 26. Note that the three lower figures are crying.

of the buckets is tipped over, its contents evidently spilled out, intimating the emotional outburst of the two figures. To the right, a figure at the end of the plane ride sobs as he listens to an audio cassette tape sent from the camp. Since the Hmong were preliterate, audio and video cassettes were the only media of communication. It is intriguing that the sun appears in relation to the plane ride and, to a lesser degree, the two weeping figures in camp. The long wait that culminates in the emotional high of the sunny journey sinks into the background murkiness that imprisons the lone crying figure. At the end of the exodus, the lucky survivor graphically turns his back on the Hmong, foreshadowing the unforeseen result of "cultural annihilation." Modern amenities, which are supposed to contribute to a sense of well-being, now manifest in the form of a cassette tape bringing perhaps ill tidings and fueling nostalgia, emptiness, and guilt.

## Contrapuntally...

We await the day when the Hmong and Hmong Americans give us their fugal variations in writing. There are, however, contrapuntal compositions on death by other Southeast Asian refugees. Haing S. Ngor won an Oscar for his role in *The Killing Fields* (1984), a film that depicts Khmer Rouge-occupied Cambodia. Ironically, in 1996, Ngor was shot dead in the driveway of his Los Angeles home. The police investigation determined that he was the victim of a youth crime; three members of the Oriental Lazyboy street gang tried to rob him and shot him when he resisted. More recently, T. C. Huo's *Land of Smiles* (2000) offers a new direction for the Southeast Asian refugee experience, moving from social studies by Western academics to the voices of refugees and their children, from testimonials and oral history scattered throughout miscellaneous projects on refugees to the refugee community writing back. Any ethnic group in the United States evolves through this trajectory, but the Hmong have undergone their vicissitudes in a much more speeded-up fashion in that they were plucked from a traditional lifestyle in the isolated Laotian highlands, thrust into a war, and after horrifying refugee experiences, expected to fit right into modern life in the West.

Much of the refrain elaborated thus far surfaces in Huo's novel as well. The protagonist is Bootakorn, a lowland Loatian boy of Chinese extraction, who swims across the Mekong with his friends to flee from the Pathet Lao. Stranded in a Thai refugee camp, he is eventually joined by his father, who brings the sad news that his mother and younger sister have both drowned in their escape attempt. The novel, in fact, has a refrain of a man singing across the Mekong for his lover, while a corpse of a woman floats by. The lover who apparently has drowned suggests the loss of Bootakorn's mother and sister. And the singer resembles Bootakorn himself longing for a reunion not only with his family but also with his lost childhood and country. In the strictest Freudian sense, the singer Bootakorn yearns for an Oedipal displacement of his father, a powerful drive contributing to his seething resentment against his father. The powerful metaphor of the Mekong River flows from Hmong story cloths into Huo's story.

Inside the camp, residents are plagued by boredom, and Bootakorn takes long walks on the premises to kill time—a habit he continues in the United States, which hints that resettlement is to nothing but a larger, more incomprehensible camp. After roughly two-thirds of the book set in a refugee camp, father and son are admitted to the United States. The book ends with the adult Bootakorn's return to Luang Prabang, Laos, his hometown. During their long stay in the camp and in the United States, Bootakorn paints a most unflattering picture of his refugee father. His father is blamed for the death of the mother and sister; he is said to use his poor English as the excuse not to apply himself and adjust to the United States; he dozes off in English classes and every other time he can as well; he depends on his sister in Ohio and other women; essentially, he regresses from being a father to being an irresponsible child in the United States. However, Bootakorn's father suffers from a set of problems that he shares with the Hmong refugees—inertia, withdrawal, angst, shame. Bootakorn, on the other hand, exhibits confusion and rage typical of refugees and, in particular, the contempt refugee youths feel toward their powerless elders. Unwittingly, Huo has composed apt "captions" to the Hmong story cloths. At this juncture, Hmong refugees, spontaneously and without any orchestration, echo one another in their communal "Death Fugue." The multitudinous threads, like fugal refrains, somehow interweave into a story of cultural demise of infinite sadness. Hope, of course, always resides in the next generation, but what will their song be when Yer Thor's children grow up to be Hmong Americans? Will it still echo a river that they have never seen? If not, and if the Hmong refugees' "Death Fugue" comes to exhaust all variations, we may yet hear the first note in a "Life Fugue" from young Hmong Americans.

# 14 The Fad(k)ing of the 0.5 Generation

## On Taiwanese and Chinese Retirees in the United States

**W. B. Yeats** wrote in 1927, when he was sixty-two years old:

> An aged man is but a paltry thing,
> A tattered coat upon a stick, unless
> Soul clap its hands and sing, and louder sing
> For every tatter in its mortal dress, ...
>     ("Sailing to Byzantium")

As the elderly lose the "appearance" of humanity, they appear to lose its core as well, becoming this "thing-ness" invisible behind "a tattered coat" and "a stick." The sense of alienation deepens with the repetition of the article "a" in the first couplet. While the article "a" could mean a universal condition, the "cloning" of "a" from human to objects veers from the human collectivity toward dehumanization. The gloom and doom of old age, however, is not allowed to saturate the poem; instead, the run-on line signaled by "unless" offers an alternative to the decrepitude of aging. Formally, "unless" stands as part of the ottava rima rhyme scheme, which refuses an early closure on the image of the scarecrow. "Unless" introduces a second couplet in subjunctive mood, leading to the "what if" scenario for soul. "Unless/Soul clap its hands and sing" is not a statement of fact; rather, Yeats creates a Byzantium immortalized by artifice to prevail over the fading of aged men. An imagined core of "soul" is made to enliven the decayed body, interiority made to reenergize exteriority. This is done through art—Yeats's poetry, the soul's singing—through "fabricating." Yeats fakes a Byzantium where the Body is fading. Fading entails a psychic and artistic remake; faking would not be required had there not been a fading. Fading and faking is one. Like the twin images on a hologram, fading and faking remain in close proximity. However dazzlingly Yeats's golden bird and golden bough are in the concluding part of this poem, they arise from the "heart" "sick with desire / And fastened to a dying animal." Yeats may wish to direct our attention to the perfect Byzantium, but his sailing eastward, away from the Western self, resembles escapism into magic inherent in a child's make-believe world. To favor the spiritual transcendence of Byzantium is to ignore the fact that Yeats is merely en route to a paradise, that this paradise is hammered out of worldly materials, and that this paradise is non-Western, out-of-this-world, and imaginary.

In the spirit of Derridean deconstruction, I use fad(k)ing to name the move in Yeats as well as that in other writings on and by the elderly. The "k" parenthetically inserted comes to disrupt and subvert the tragedy of "fading" away, reading into aging power and magic. Fading and faking of power come to merge in specific moments of writings on old age, such as at the turning point of "unless" in "Sailing to Byzantium."

The symbiosis of fad(k)ing suggests that the twin can easily be reversed, i.e., faking exposed as fading. Such a moment of demystification comes to us in the discovery of the wizard's true identity in L. Frank Baum's *The Wizard of Oz* (1900). An American classic popularized by the Judy Garland film, *The Wizard of Oz* is a children's story that has at its—for want of a better term— "rotten core" "a little, old man, with a bald head and a wrinkled face" (p. 151). Oz "the Great and Terrible" turns into a "humbug" when the screen shielding him is tipped over by Dorothy's pet dog Toto. Readers then realize that the giant head, the lady with wings, the beast, and the ball of fire that Dorothy and company have witnessed are mere illusions, conjured up in accordance with their respective psychic longings. Exposed, the wizard confesses that he used to be a ventriloquist and, subsequently, a circus balloonist in his native Omaha. He takes on the role of the wizard in the Emerald City because he fears the neighboring evil witches and because "[h]ow can I help being a humbug ... when all these people [including Dorothy et al.] make me do things that everybody knows can't be done" (p. 161). Magic in this children's fantasy is debunked as an old man's tricks, performed to conceal the wizard's paralysis and to conform to the high expectations of others. Even the most tragic and frightening moment in life—its cessation—is turned into a happy homecoming to Omaha, or Heaven, by way of a balloon ascent. The fanfare of faking in Baum's balloon ride and in Yeats's Byzantium is repeated in the research on and writing by the elderly in the coming pages, in the Asian American social scientists' emphasis on elderly activism as well as in the elderly's black humor and resourcefulness. Yet this faking need not fool us as to the condition of fading that gives rise to the faking in the first place.

Whereas aging is something to be dreaded and veiled in literature and art, gerontology, the study of old age, is perhaps most advanced in medicine and the health care professions for obvious reasons. Social sciences research-ers in the United States are scrambling to understand the aging of America. As President Clinton put it in his State of the Union address on January 19, 1999, "with the number of elderly Americans set to double by 2030, the Baby Boom will become a Senior Boom." However, within the evolution of Asian American studies, gerontology has seldom occupied center stage in the works of sociologists, anthropologists, political scientists, literary scholars, historians, and others: minority struggles seem to belong exclusively to the young. Even in the rare instances where the elderly happen to be the focus, scholars are most likely to feature elderly who have been in the United States for longer periods of time, if not their entire lives.

Before a review of the extant representations of Asian elderly in the United States, I need to define the target group: the 0.5 generation. To under-stand this term, I must begin with the widely accepted term of "1.5 generation" in Asian American studies, a term that denotes youngsters jostled between the first, immigrant generation and the second, American-born generation.[1] These youngsters typically have been born in Asia and arrive in the United States as children or teenagers, with their formative years spent straddling the Pacific Ocean. I have coined the term of "0.5 generation" to describe retirees who have completed their careers in Taiwan and China and are now aging in the United States, particularly in metropolitan areas such as Monterey Park and Los Angeles in California and Flushing, New York. (A group of these elderly persons situated between Taiwanese and Chinese retirees are the Tai-wanese mainlanders, "gypsies" from Mainland China who fled Communist China to Taiwan around 1949 and whose exile extended into old age and then to the New World.) For a variety of reasons, the 0.5 generation, who are now in their sixties or older, have come in droves to join their immigrant children in the United States—often with little or no English, with no skill to oper-ate an automobile, and with declining health. "Fading," the first half of the keyword in the title, brings to attention the sense of isolation and impotence felt by this 0.5 generation, as if their whole existence is a countdown to zero or nothingness. Indeed, the 0.5 generation is perhaps the least studied group within Asian America—part of "The Last Minority" (1986) conceived by Nancy Datan. They have been virtually written off by Asian American schol-ars and even by themselves, due in no small measure to "age-centrism."[2]

In view of the invisibility of these retirees in Asian American and main-stream American literature, film, and other forms of cultural production (with the exception of Ang Lee's protagonist in *Pushing Hands* [1993]), my research focused on the literary pages *(Fu kan)* in the Chinese-language newspaper *The World Journal (Shijie ribao),* a daily affiliated with Taiwan's *The United News*

(*Lianho bao*) and quite popular among retirees. Founded in 1976, *The World Journal* claims to be the largest Chinese daily newspaper in North America and is published in New York, Los Angeles, San Francisco, Chicago, Houston, Vancouver, and Toronto. *The World Journal's* overall circulation number is unavailable, but the New York office reports a circulation of 135,000 for the Eastern region, the Los Angeles office 200,000 for Southern California, and the San Francisco office 65,000 for Northern California. Claiming to publish between 64 and 128 pages daily, the newspaper covers international news and then devotes specific sections to China, Taiwan, Hong Kong, Southeast Asia, and the Chinese communities in North America.

Within the literary pages, there is a "Jiayuan" ("Homestead" or, literally, "Home and Garden") section that occupies a little over half of a single regular-sized newpaper page. Devoted to sketches of immigrants' lives, "Jiayuan" publishes short contributions from retirees on retirees. Longer pieces on retirees appear periodically in the more formal section on literature. "Jiayuan" is perhaps the only site where the voice of the 0.5 generation is regularly heard, and my research concentrated on "Jiayuan" in 1998–1999 to accentuate the millennial, endgame implications of the dilemma of fad(k)ing. This essay captures a slice of "Jiayuan" that has been part of *The World Journal* since I have begun to read it in the mid- to late-1990s and "Jiayuan" is still going strong a decade later.

It is amazing that Asian immigrant culture as exemplified in the 0.5's writings published in *The World Journal* has been totally excluded from Asian American culture. This invisible wall between the 0.5 generation and the rest of Asian America shows itself once we review Asian American efforts to represent the elderly, a section of the population largely ignored. The 0.5 generation appears to be *doubly* "passed over," not only as the elderly but as the *alien* elderly, which makes the present task of attending to the voices of the newly arrived elderly so much more urgent.

Two influential anthologies, *Island* (Lai et al. 1980) and *Songs of Gold Mountain* (Hom, 1987), document the voices of early Chinese immigrants seeking a better life around the turn of the nineteenth to the twentieth century under conditions radically different from the recent elusive phenomenon of the 0.5 generation. *Longtime Californ'* (1972) by Victor and Brett Nee investigates the residents of San Francisco's Chinatown. The Nees identify their informants by name or nickname, age, and profession; the interviewee's age is a prominent factor in their system of classification. Most interviews, especially in Part 1, "The Bachelor Society," and Part 2, "The Refugees," involve the elderly, many of whom the Nees encounter at Portsmouth Square, but these are retirees who completed their careers in the States, if not themselves

American-born, so once again they are very different from the 0.5 generation. The Nees admit that their book may be handicapped by the authors' inability to speak Cantonese, the language of "recent immigrants" (p. xv), but they quickly assure the reader that this poses no obstacle to understanding life in Chinatown, and they supplement the book with interviews through interpreters. While that may have been true for Chinatown of the 1970s, a study of the 0.5 generation of the 1980s and beyond demands facility with a number of Asian languages, without which Asian Americanists, increasingly American-born and in a world with English as its lingua franca, encounter tremendous obstacles. Using methodology similar to that of the Nees two decades ago, Timothy Fong's *The First Suburban Chinatown* (1994) is based on interviews in English only. Without Mandarin, Cantonese, and the other native tongues of the immigrants, the researchers' grasp of the immigrant condition is bound to be piecemeal. Insofar as the 0.5 generation are concerned, a proficiency in at least one Asian language is the first step toward smashing the myth of their alleged silence. This need for the immigrants' mother tongue is likewise keenly felt by a researcher such as Sarah Lamb, in "Intimacy in a Transnational Era" (2002). Despite her subjects' relative fluency in English, Lamb laments that English fails to capture "the nuances of their [the subjects'] feelings and observations" (p. 302).

An intriguing similarity exists among sociological and political science monographs, namely, isolated incidents of politically active elderly are featured. The Nees, for instance, pay special attention to the International Hotel on Kearny Street in San Francisco's Chinatown, home to many "retired Filipino laborers who live on social security and welfare checks" (p. 389). The authors record that starting from 1968, this hotel was the site of an ethnic struggle by community activists and students to resist a move to demolish the building. By the same token, Timothy Fong details at least two marches that retirees engaged in. One was in 1986 when "four hundred people, mostly elderly Chinese" marched to Monterey Park City Hall to protest rejection of a senior housing project (p. 4). Another show of force by senior Chinese took place in the summer of 1991, as "a hundred Chinese American seniors—many of whom did not speak English—marched in front of the Monterey Park City Hall demanding a recall of Judy Chu because she was supposedly 'anti-Chinese'" (p. 150). The highlighting of elderly activism resembles the magic in Yeats's scarecrow and Baum's wizard; social scientists wish to cancel out the impotence of their subjects by a single stroke of engagement.

Assuredly, aging exists in literature, yet literature and gerontology have largely avoided each other. If anything, literary scholars seem to agree with writers like Yeats in that aging is tied to characters "as to a dog's tail," part of a fate to be endured. This blanket stereotyping is explored by Kathleen Woodward in *Aging and Its Discontent* (1991), a title recalling Freud's *Civilization and Its Discontents* (1930) "with its deeply grained pessimism" (Woodward, *Aging and Its Discontent* 1991, p.10). To combat such gerontophobia, fading and faking are deployed in close proximity:

> In a culture which so devalues age, masquerade with respect to the aging body is first and foremost a denial of age, an effort to erase or efface age and to put on youth. Masquerade entails several strategies, among them: the addition of desired body parts (teeth, hair); the removal or covering up of unwanted parts of the body (growths, gray hair, "age spots"); the "lifting" of the face and other parts in an effort to deny the weight of gravity; the molding of the body's shape (exercise, clothing). (p. 148)

Ironically, such a desperate attempt at faking only underlines the fear of fading.

With respect to the sporadic appearances of aging protagonists in Asian American and Asian diaspora literatures, they are not, by the strictest definition, 0.5 generation. Nevertheless, consistent with Woodward's book title, age is invariably presented as barren and bleak. The Taiwanese emigré novelist Chen Jo-hsi chooses to narrate *Erh Hu (The two Hus)* (1985) through the eyes of an uncle and a nephew. The uncle is referred to simply as the old man. The old man's beauty-conscious, anorexic wife commits suicide. The old man's neighbor, Lao Mi, formerly a Xian city government bureaucrat retired at the age of fifty, hangs himself in San Francisco's city park. Lao Mi fails to adjust to life in the United States: he cannot speak English or function as an adult, his wife demands a divorce and custody of their children, he is accused by school officials of child abuse for disciplining his sons, and, as a last straw, he is shamed by the interrogation of police officers following a family dispute. Lao Mi manifests all the symptoms of the 0.5 generation, despite the fact that he is a bit too young in the American context. As Lowell Holmes puts it, the general consensus seems to be that old age "begins at age 65, for that is the usual age of retirement from one's job and the age at which Social Security checks begin to arrive" ("Anthropology and Age" 1980 p. 277). The old man—the uncle Hu—is in his seventies, but he has completed his career in the United States. Neither character fits the profile of the 0.5 generation. Characterization of the old man reflects the culture's ageism or loathing for the elderly. Selfish and manipulative, the old man is far from a sympathetic character, and because the first half of the novel is told from the old man's point of view, the Machiavellian workings of his mind are exposed. Faking in this instance is seen in a most unflattering light, in part as a result of being interpreted by the younger generation.

A recent comedy in Chinese by an amateur Chinese American playwright reflects in a lighthearted way the discontent of the 0.5 generation. Shen Yueh's "A Bushel of Love" (premiered in 1999 in the San Francisco Bay area) opens with the arrival of a retiree, Chou Danian, from Taiwan and proceeds to dramatize visits from a variety of female suitors.[3] The matchmaking in Act 1 resembles Ang Lee's *Pushing Hands* (1992), suggesting the retirees' loneliness, which becomes bitterness in some instances if they perceived that their children neglect and ill-use them. Two of the three female suitors are in their sixties and are introduced in the List of Characters as either "moving from Taiwan to the U.S. to live with her son" or "living by herself." That their living arrangements—with children or alone—is essential to their characterization demonstrates the ultimate concern of 0.5s. Both Chou and his visitors complain profusely of their children, children-in-law, and grandchildren who speak only English. Chou's relationships with his divorced daughter and two grandchildren are far better than those of his female suitors. In fact, his grandchildren seem to speak perfect Mandarin and are comparatively well versed in Chinese tradition. In view of the intended audience—the West Coast Chinese community of a diverse range of age, where the 0.5 quandary is felt keenly but from various perspectives—it makes sense to portray the dilemma of retirees in a humorous rather than bleak manner.

On the other hand, Bienvenido Santos, in his collection of stories *Scent of Apples* (1992), portrays quite lovingly the elderly and their tricks. The fact that a Filipino American text is referred to amidst an essay on Taiwanese and Chinese retirees illustrates the paucity of elderly characters in Asian American and Asian Diaspora literatures. The *manong* (Filipino oldtimer) Alipio in "Immigration Blues" (1977), the first story in *Scent of Apples*, leads a life in the United States fraught with falsehood: dentures, limping, and two "sham" marriages, with Seniang and with Monica. In addition, Mrs. Zafra, Monica's sister, has a sham marriage, which clearly demonstrates a proliferation of schemes to outwit the immigration and naturalization laws. Alipio and other *manongs* with U.S. citizenship often get married to help Filipino women stay in this country. Although such maneuvers may be viewed as cagey and deceitful by mainstream Americans, Alipio and his peers exhibit amazing resourcefulness in devising ways to beat the U.S. system, which is crudely conceived and ethnocentric in the first place. Furthermore, Asian immigrants have historically had to balance on a knife-edge created by the U.S. immigration and naturalization laws; many Chinese in the nineteenth century entered the United States as "paper sons" and assumed stereotypically menial roles for survival. In other words, Asians in diaspora are what Homi Bhabha calls "mimic men," who shun open confrontation. Instead, subservience to hegemony yields occasional moments of counterhegemonic subversion from within "the belly of the beast."

Rather than be content with these rare "sightings" of the elderly in literature, one can, in fact, contextualize the 0.5 within the Chinese diaspora. And here is where the 0.5 generation's writings in *The World Journal* can find their place in the long stream of publications throughout the twentieth century oriented toward overseas Chinese, or *huaqiao* as they continue to be called. This approach tilts the research more toward Asian Diaspora rather than Asian American studies, as the 0.5 generation suddenly becomes part of *huaqiao*. In comparison with the U.S.-centric character of Asian American studies, Asian Diaspora studies adopts a more flexible, fluid, and global approach. Madeline Hsu, in *Dreaming of Gold, Dreaming of Home* (2000), has attempted exactly that. Setting out to "construct bridges between the historically related but as yet critically unlinked fields of Asian American and Asian studies" (p. 4), Hsu accomplishes it in Chapter 5, "Magazines as Marketplaces," where she analyzes *qiaokan* (overseas Chinese magazines) produced in Taishan and Hong Kong during the period of the Chinese Exclusion Act (1882–1943) and distributed worldwide, wherever Taishanese happened to have settled. A nexus of information, *qiaokan* came to forge solidarity for a dispersed community, one which Hsu calls "transnational." Hsu resorts to Asian studies in her detailed study of the impact on Taishan County, Guangdong, exerted by overseas Chinese, a community which has enjoyed a great deal of attention from Chinese scholars. Overseas Chinese, for example, have been euphemistically called "Mothers of the Revolution" (the revolution of 1911 that overthrew the Qing dynasty), due to the fact that Chinese students and sojourners in the United States, Japan, and elsewhere contributed unstintingly to the cause, at times sacrificing their own lives.

Inheriting the tradition of *qiaokan, The World Journal* is likewise a nodal point of the lives of Chinese-speaking immigrants, reflecting a piece of the puzzle that is the massive Asian diaspora to the United States since the Immigration Reform Bill of 1965. My project isolates a tiny fraction of material within the newspaper, a network of information and services on English lessons, laws and codes of conduct, immigration attorneys, physicians, restaurants, jobs, tours and vacations, and whatnot. The short sketches on the elderly are closely related to other pieces in "Jiayuan" on middle-aged professional immigrants as well as those on the young. For instance, almost daily there is a "Tungyen tungyu" (kid's talk) column, a collection of jokes revolving around children's linguistic mistakes, particularly over the mixing of Chinese homonyms. Mandarin, of course, is a language with frustratingly numerous homonyms. Such jokes for the consumption of immigrant readers are ironic in the sense that the ABC (American-born Chinese) children supposedly producing these jokes are likely to grow up as passive speakers of Mandarin, if at all. The unconscious mis-use of the "mother" tongue in childhood gradually lapses into conscious dis-use in adulthood. The bare-bones knowledge of Mandarin natural in a preschooler is frozen and memorialized, as that moment may be the acme of that individual's Chinese-speaking performance. Schooling and Americanization often mean peer pressure to abandon whatever fails to conform to the majority, including language. Sigmund Freud would no doubt read into these innocuous jokes the anxiety of immigrant readers over the next generation. Intertextuality comes into play when "Kid's Talk" is juxtaposed with the retirees' stories. Two polarized groups in terms of age and interest, they resemble each other in the deliberate play on Chinese words. Although "Kid's Talk" produces nervous laughs over the prospect of the abandonment of Chineseness, retirees, faced with increasing dependency in the United States, frequently sneak in, parenthetically, the letter "k" in the narrative of their fading to alleviate somewhat the anguish. A play on words is a strategy of empowerment through which retirees cling to a semblance of dignity and Chinese identity. Their facility with the Chinese language serves to neutralize the ordeal of inhabiting an alien culture.[4]

Motivated by such psychic need, faking in retiree writings consists of an exponential intensification of their dire condition, out of which black humor is distilled.[5] Similar to Freud's coupling of jokes and dreams in *Jokes and Their Relation to the Unconscious* (1905), retirees manifest their repressed disappointment and anger in an explosion of jests. Certain jokes or gallows humor are directed against themselves, but many more satirize or even accuse others. At times, the retirees' black humor locates its unnamed target in the "unfilial" children. A case in point is a piece published on May 15, 1998, entitled "In the Library" by Liu Zhiwen. Liu opens with the wry, self-denigrating comment that the retiree's life in the United States is the life of a *sandeng gungming* (third-rate citizen). (All translations from Chinese to English are mine.) The wordplay centers on the homophone *"deng"* for "rate" or "wait" in Mandarin. The writer proceeds to name three kinds of "waiting": "waiting for newspaper [self-reflexively pointing to *The World Journal*], waiting for meals, and waiting for bedtime." The use of puns is one of many verbal gymnastics performed in retirees' writings, which include composing classical Chinese poems to display their eloquence. Puns are *shuangguanyu* (literally, "double-meaning words") in Chinese, yet *guan* also means "close" or "trap." Linguistic faking eerily doubles back to fading. The last "waiting" alludes perhaps to death. Since such writings are for the public eye, self-censorship may play a role in tempering more gloomy thoughts on the retiree's existence. For similar considerations, a condemnation of those directly responsible for the seniors' sense of entrapment—their children—may be silenced. The grievances publicly displayed in the newspaper may thus be the tip of the iceberg, for traditional Chinese would be too ashamed to air family disagreements. Children's unfilial behavior, after all, springs from the parents' own failure to raise them properly. By examining evidence that we do have—jokes and sarcasm—we begin to discern a pattern, nonetheless, in the drive for some control in life's endgame of those foreign elderly considered to be deaf, dumb, blind, and paralyzed. Such rhetorical flourish appears to defy the English-speaking society in which they are trapped and to taunt their own children.

"In the Library" describes the writer waiting his turn to read the newspaper, flipping through two books, the Chinese classic *Monkey* (*Journey to the West*, an appropriate story for a retiree) and a travel description, *Adventure through the Three Gorges*. Upon discovering some dark gray whiskers hidden in the pages of *Monkey*, Liu imagines them coming from excited readers pulling their whiskers, in subconscious imitation of one of Monkey's seventy-two metamorphoses: Monkey clones himself by extracting his own body hair and blowing on it. Yet neither the previous reader nor the writer is capable of transforming himself in this westward movement, the end of which is *xi tian* ("west sky" or death). When Liu randomly picks up a second book on the scenic Three Gorges, he finds that the illustrations have been ripped out. Instead of the normal reaction of outrage and disgust, the writer speculates that the vandal has pocketed the photographs out of homesickness and sorrow. Underhand and transgressive, this "theft" is legitimized in the name of psychological need; faking is justified, at least if perpetrated by a fellow 0.5, by fading.

The concluding paragraph further magnifies Liu's identification with other retirees. After uncovering the ripped-out book illustrations, Liu observes a library patron clipping the newspaper:

> He took something out of his handbag, and on the newspaper he went twice up and down, twice sideways. He then put his prey in the handbag. And he left as if nothing had happened. I felt like my heart had been slashed a few times. With one hand subconsciously pressing my chest, I fled the library with quickened steps.

Rather than indignation, Liu is besieged by shame. Only someone who identifies with the "thief" will be compelled to flee the "crime" scene. Sympathy for other retirees is established at the outset when Liu adds to the three kinds of waiting a fourth: he waits for the library to open every morning. The snatching of the newspaper article comes to epitomize, eerily, the "ignominious" nature of a 0.5's existence—half human and half thing, somewhat legitimate yet perennially suspect. The ambiguous self-image is reflected in the fact that Liu is both the perpetrator of the theft and the one who is deprived of his rights to read the article, for he departs with a wounded heart. The muddled logic stems from the retirees' entangled condition. A large number of them depend on their children and on the U.S. Social Security and health care systems, such as Medicare and Medicaid, to which they may feel that they are not entirely entitled. After all, the definition of the 0.5 generation presupposes that they worked elsewhere before retiring to the United States. Without having paid into Social Security and the other funds throughout their career, they are nonetheless now drawing from it for medical bills and other necessities. Subconsciously, the 0.5 generation think of themselves as "third-rate citizens," relying on the kindness of children—some estranged—and strangers alike. To read into their dilemma the factor of their children is dictated by the very definition of the 0.5 generation, whose presence in the United States is predicated by a first generation, for without them the U.S. government is not likely to grant visas to the foreign elderly.

Through similar wordplays, "Suiyu er'an" (Easy and comfortable anywhere) by Ho Nian (a name meaning "crane age," which is a euphemism for the elderly, but also a pun for "what year" to die; pen names are a source of endless wordplay, suggesting guises and self-transformations), published on January 16, 1998, attributes unseemly emotions concerning children to a former colleague, Mr. Kerh, in New York. Ho Nien adroitly exploits the various formations of the word *ren* ("people" or "human being"). "I've already retired. I'm no longer a *ren*," confesses Mr. Kerh. "I live at my son's house. People ask[s] me if I am the *zhuren* [host]. No. A *yung-ren* [servant]? No. A *keren* [guest]? No. I am none of the above [*ren*]. I am not a *ren* [human being]." When asked how he entertains himself, Mr. Kerh replies: "I am a *caobao* [grass bag; "*bao*" also meaning "in charge"]. I am a *fantung* [rice pail]." Both *caobao* and *fantung* are common expressions for "good-for-nothing." Mr. Kerh further elaborates: "The grass in the front yard and the back yard is all mowed by me, so I'm a *caobao* [all the grass is my charge]. Both my son and daughter-in-law go to work. I prepare the three meals [*fan* or rice]. So I'm a *fantung*."

Ho Nian's next question underscores Mr. Kerh's affliction: "Do you have any other plan for the remainder of your life?"—surely an offensive way of putting it had it not been the previous dismal confessions. Mr. Kerh responds:

> The only thing I really like is travel. A year ago, I went to Europe and toured France, England, Italy, and some eight countries. Last year, I went back to the Mainland and went on a journey to Mt. Huang and

the Three Gorges of the Yangtze River. This year, I went to Southeast Asia. As long as I can move, I want to travel. And finally, there's the trip to England.

It takes Ho Nian a while to realize that England (pronounced *yinguo* for "yin country" or "realm of the deceased") does not refer to the England Mr. Kerh has toured two years before, but to death. At this point in the narrative, one short paragraph away from the end, the innocent title certainly does not fit with Mr. Kerh's bitter, sardonic remarks. What appears to be self-caricaturing in fact attacks the next generation, who have abandoned the elderly to an empty house and their own devices. This tenor of dejection is softened considerably by the conclusion, when the narrative returns from Mr. Kerh, a mad prophet of sorts, to the ideal retiree of Ho Nian:

> I am very happy. He [Mr. Kerh] remains so optimistic. I should learn from him. The society is different now. The elderly have nothing but surplus value to contribute. I suddenly recall a poem by the Sung dynasty's Xin Qiji: "What am I inclined to do now? Inclined to get intoxicated; inclined to travel; inclined to sleep. I am still in charge of a little something. In charge of bamboos; in charge of mountains; in charge of rivers." This is a fitting motto for old age.

To interpret Mr. Kerh's thinly veiled sarcasm as optimistic requires a willful blindness. In addition, to be in charge of mountains and rivers is a kind of faking for personal satisfaction. Ho Nian's conclusion tempers the Chinese literati tradition of spontaneity and resignation with "surplus value," a Marxist catchphrase, a remnant, perhaps, from a lifetime spent in the Communist bureaucracy. The surplus value of the elderly entails a contentment over small things. What Ho Nian attempts is both an exposé and an amelioration. Just as the piece bares the quandary of retirees, it seeks to distance the pain from himself as well as, in the words of a Sung poet, from pain itself.

Such insulation is at work even in pieces most nakedly charging the next generation. Huang Guping, in "Yanger bu fanglao" (Raising sons won't insure against old age), published on May 11, 1998, cites two examples of elderly women left to fend for themselves. Both women have endured great hardships during the Cultural Revolution prior to joining their children in the United States. The savings of one woman, the author reports, have been stolen by her son while she was hospitalized. She is identified by the surname Chen, and is said to be the daughter of one of the founding fathers of Chinese Communism (most possibly Chen Duxiu). The other lady borrows a proverb to comment on her children's desertion: "Drip drop from the roof tiles—same old story."

The essay's title is a negation of a four-word adage, *yanger fanglao* (raising sons will insure against old age), but the negation is accomplished through hearsay rather than personal experiences. Huang's brief conclusion is equally intriguing: "I remember a few years ago, someone wrote an article on the 'five olds.' I think the most important one of the 'five olds' is 'old capital,' which means one's health and some assets." While the two instances of unfilial children destroy the retiree's happiness, the conclusion, delivered via an intertextual reference, creates a community of the elderly and provides some useful tips. However, the piece on the five olds, said to have come out a couple of years earlier, was, as a matter of fact, written by Yu Zi and published on April 22, 1998, less than a month before. The five olds are "old health," "old companion [spouse]," "old friends," "old pleasures," and "old capital." To integrate health into "old capital" goes against the intention of the original writer.

On February 3, 1999, Fu Hua (the name means "rotting") published "The Imminent Arrival of Old Age," an essay concerning the phenomenon of retirees dying in loneliness. The pen name echoes one example the author uses: the rotting body of a Chinese veteran found dead in his New York apartment. Fu Hua speculates that since the veteran could have been taken to the hospital simply by making a telephone call, he must have sought release in death. Consistent with many retiree writings in "Jiayuan," classical Chinese is employed to voice the sorrow of lonely old age. Specifically, Fu Hua quotes, in its entirety, Li Chingzhao's long *ci* (lyric poem) from the Sung dynasty to illustrate the melancholy of old age—except that Li's *ci* pertains more to forlorn lovers than to single retirees.

Yet of the relevant essays in "Jiayuan," there are far more placid and contented pieces than satirical ones. Wordplay remains prominent in the former, where homophones and classical Chinese rhymes serve to demonstrate, among other things, the writer's mental astuteness, advanced age notwithstanding. Furthermore, publication in the newspaper demands some exhibition of individual talents, which leads to the showing off of mastery of classical or vernacular Chinese. Just as a personal motive may be involved in the preponderance of linguistic acrobatics, the newspaper editor is likewise implicated in shaping the contour of the retiree writings. In any case, the general absence of untoward sentiments may well be the result as much of self-censorship as editorial censorship.

Having said that, I hasten to acknowledge again the overwhelming number of retiree writings on a peaceful and relatively happy retirement in the United States. Some retirees even willingly contribute their "surplus value" to help out with their children's busy professional schedules. "Yusunji," by Pang Shu, published on May 23, 1998, begins: "Two thirds of the Chinese elderly on visitors' visas to the United States donate their 'remaining warmth' to raising the third generation." The key to the more buoyant, positive attitude may lie less in the elderly than in their temporary visas. Strictly speaking, these dedicated babysitters are not the 0.5 generation and their zeal to help might undergo serious challenge were the arrangement permanent. Nonetheless, truly loving relationships surface frequently, such as the piece by Yi Xiao (the name means "one smile"), published on May 2, 1998, where the grandparents not only take care of their tenth-grade grandson but drive around to deliver shoes for their son at work. With regards to the more "happily employed" of the 0.5 generation, they appear to be ingenious do-it-yourselfers. They print and xerox lined paper for their Chinese submissions to *The World Journal* (Run Dan, "Xiegaole," April 14, 1998). They join tours to casinos in Las Vegas (Wang Zhiyi, "Dujing," May 7, 1998). They describe an old people's apartment complex with quite a few retirees from China (Liu Xing, "Laoren gongyu," January 8, 1999). They go apple-picking with a group of elderly Chinese from a Northern Virginia's retirement community, in a piece that even ends with a classical Chinese poem to celebrate the outing (Zhang Xueyi, "Cai pingguo qu," January 10, 1999). An elderly woman, Hu Yun (her pen name means "random mumbling"), pontificates in "Laoma dangziqiang" (The old mom relies on herself), published on January 12, 1999, that old people should be self-sufficient, which is displayed in her writing by the simple English vocabulary such as "Mall," "List," and "Sing" (all capitalized for some reason) that she sprinkles throughout the essay. Even in this uplifting sketch, however, the writer does touch on the retiree's handicap status, which, she says, is "like having only one arm and one leg." Another retiree praises San Francisco as the ideal place, the author having resided in "Dalawar State [sic]," New Jersey, and Minnesota (Ning Shen, "Jiujingshan haodifang," January 20, 1999). If "Dalawar" was printed according to Ning Shen's spelling, it indicates either editorial sophistication in subtly deflating the author's euphoria or editorial sloppiness.

So long as a harmonious relationship exists between the generations, the advice of the young is readily accepted by the old. In "Xingde kunrao" (Troubled by surname), published on May 5, 1998, Tsai Li-li ("Xai" according to *pingyin*, but transliterated in the Wade-Giles system to make obvious all the following derivations of "Tsai") cautions her visiting parents that in the United States, their family name is no longer Tsai. Instead, it is subject to whatever the speaker is proficient in pronouncing. Possibilities include "Sai," "Tai," "Chi-sai" ("valve" in Mandarin), "Tasi," and "Tsia," all hilarious renderings to Chinese speakers. The difference, however, lies in the fact that the parents receive the daughter's instructions with a degree of stoicism rarely seen among retirees. Yet another potentially explosive situation is defused in "Yangnian dianshijie," by Cao Ji (whose pen name means "grass veneration," implying "economized" or "drastically reduced" ancestral worship), published on February 18, 1999. A retiree complains about the three Chinese New Years he and his wife have had in Charlotte (North Carolina?) and recalls nostalgically the festivity in China. On New Year's day, the children leave without tasting the traditional chicken soup with red dates that the parents have stewed. The retirees find themselves in a magnificent yet empty house ("no sound of firecrackers, no sound of drums and gongs, let alone dragon- and lion-dance"), their homesickness soothed somewhat by the New Year party on PRC's Central China TV channel that they receive via their children's satellite dish. Many contributions deal with imminent mortality, ranging from failed plastic surgery to get rid of baggy eyelids (Li Shu, "Yanji jiuyiji," January 6, 1999) and open-heart surgery (Shue Wei, "Sandu kaixin," May 9, 1998) to actual deaths and funerals (Mong Xia [meaning "dream rainbow"], "Yunyian zhishi," April 21, 1998). Like any elegy, the lamentation for oth- ers is performed for the retiree writer as well. Some essays are written by the younger generation about the incapacitated elderly. On January 23, 1999, two sketches ("Shishi duowunai" by Liu Jiayi and "Zhongfeng laoren detong" by Zhou Yutang) describe the condition of stroke survivors, both of whom are bedridden and deprived of speech and movement.

To be sure, the reducing to infancy is inherent in any diasporic experience. The English language and cultural differences cripple and castrate any newly arrived immigrant, whatever the age or background. But the young have a greater capacity than retirees to adapt to a new land and acquire a new identity. After the initial culture shock, most of the young rebound and regain their maturity by learning the language, the culture, and professional skills, whereas retirees, in the worst-case scenario, regress into dependency and resentment.

Given that the Irish poet's vision of old age seems wish-fulfillment, and given that the retiree writings in *The World Journal* are subject to censorship, let me close with a single case study, the unfiltered voice of the Hus.[6] Both Taiwanese mainlanders, they sold their house in Taipei in the late 1980s and purchased a condominium in Los Angeles. Mrs. Hu did this reluctantly, at the urging of her husband, who was in poor health, blind in his left eye after two unsuccessful surgeries for a detached retina, his health ruined by two major medical procedures for kidney stones, and other illnesses. All their children were in the United States, with two permanently settled in Los Ange- les. Recalling their first night in the United States, Mr. Hu described it as trying to stay warm in an ice palace *(binggong)*. Their son offered, as Mr. Hu put it, a single blanket for the night, whereas the Taiwanese are more used to heavy quilts. Other than the differences in lifestyles, the term "ice palace," yet another witty pun typical of 0.5 expression, also implies the cool reception the Hus believed they suffered at their son's house. While most houses of upper-middle-class Los Angeleans would seem impressive to people long crammed into urban apartments, that particular house was freezing cold to the retirees. But note that even this scathing criticism of their son is directed against the house rather than the master of the house, hence accomplishing their attack on him in a roundabout, face-saving fashion. Whether or not only one blanket was actually offered, this story suggests a projection backward onto the beginning of the parents' new life of disappointment accrued from an aging process amidst isolation and incapacitation.

The following is an unedited excerpt from an interview of the Hus conducted on June 25, 1993. It is faithfully translated from Mandarin, in all its rawness and grimness; it deals largely with the purchase of a condominium through their sons. Mrs. Hu speaks:

> If we had moved to Auntie Hao's house [a friend who offered temporary residence before they bought the condo], then *laoda* [her eldest son] could have said his parents had moved out of his house and were renting, then *gungjia* [literally "the public family" or the authorities, in this case, the U.S. Federal Government] would have returned the money to us [the portion of Social Security withheld due to the Hus' living as dependents at their son's house]. People came a few times, asking if we'd like to appeal. But he [the Hus' oldest son] didn't appeal for us. He didn't care at all. And the time expired.
>
> So, you see, for this house, to buy this house, we had a tough time with *laoda*. Why? Because he didn't want to sign. No matter what, he wouldn't sign. If he had signed, I would have put down the money. Dad asked what to do if we couldn't get the house. And I said I'd talk to *laoda*. You, you . . . I'd call him. I called him. He hadn't gone to work yet. Hadn't gone to work yet? Or back from work? And I said: "*Laoda*, the house I'm buying for sure. Whether you sign or not, I'm buying. The house I'm buying for sure. Why is that? If I die, then I wouldn't have you pay for it and drag you down into the water. I'll pay it in two, um, four years. Don't you worry about how I'd pay for it. I'll steal. I'll rob. Don't you worry. So I said whether you sign or not, I'm buying the house. In the end, I'm buying the house." . . . In the end, *laoerh* [her second son] came back and found a friend, a Chen or something, signed something, he's in real estate, tax accountant.

And he said that let *laoerh* come to work for him. As long as he earned over $2,000 monthly, it's okay. Just a letter of proof. For tax purposes, he would give us another letter. So that person wrote the letter, and we bought the house in *laoerh*'s name. It took about five or six months after we came [to the United States] to get this house.

A transcript, and a translated one to boot, fails miserably in registering the rising emotions in the refrain of her resolve: her voice becomes angry and strident. Evident in the maneuver of the closing on the condo, Mrs. Hu continued the magic of faking in financial matters, but her family relationships, recorded during hours of interview, appeared to be in shambles, strung together like Yeats's tattered coat, but with minimum prospect of a redeeming deus ex machina. In winter and spring of 1999, Mrs. Hu underwent radiation treatment for cervical cancer. The birth canal through which all her children had come into this world now suffered from mutated cells. The womb of life had turned against itself. Despite all the magical faking, the half-life of fading always comes to an abrupt halt, a full stop.

# Finis

This book on diaspora does not have one, as Asian bodies keep coming and going. A state of being, even a destiny, diaspora is forever in transit, going somewhere and nowhere. It evokes, ironically, the Chinese ideogram *kun* for "trapped" or "entrapment," with *mu* (wood) framed by a square. Yet it may be the square human mind that imprisons itself in bemoaning the stillness of the tree. A tree, indeed, does not move in space, the conventional meaning of mobility, but it moves in time, seasonal changes in time-lapsed cinematography. Despite a sense of futility over the ultimate destination, being diasporic stands in the flow of time, crucified midstream yet afloat in the flood of tears, a deadwood about to bloom.

—

# Notes

## Establishing Shots

1. P. Quigley discusses the significance of Chinese ideograms to these Westerners in "Eisenstein, Montage, and 'Filmic Writing'" (2004). While focusing on Eisenstein, Quigley creates a "genealogy" that includes thinkers such as Freud and Derrida. Quigley sees Freud comparing "Chinese writing, and pictographic writing in general, to the activity of the dream-work, a comparison Derrida fully approves as 'the writing of dreams exceeds phonetic writing'" (pp. 159–160).

2. See Eisenstein's "Yermolova": montage is "not so much the sequence of segments as their *simultaneity*: in the consciousness of the perceiver" (p. 86). He adds that "various elements are simultaneously seen both as separate *independent units* and as *inseparable parts of a single whole*" (p. 86).

3. David Bordwell traces the etymology of "montage" to the French word meaning "'machine assembly,' in the sense of 'mounting' a motor" (*The Cinema of Eisenstein* 1993, p.120).

4. A more recent case is Charles Frazier's Civil War novel *Cold Mountain* (1997), in which the title and epigraph come from the Tang poet Han Shan, literally, Cold Mountain. See also translations by Gary Snyder and others of Han Shan.

5. See Peter Connor's "The Emptiness of Intelligent Questions" (2000).

6. "Diaspora" is a term coined by academe to manage globalization in the same way "multiculturalism" has been used to manage civil rights movement and ethnic divisions. For a critique of the politics of multiculturalism, see David Palumbo-Liu's "Introduction" to *The Ethnic Canon* (1995).

7. Think of Norman O. Brown's prophetic pronouncement at the conclusion of *Love's Body* (1966): "Everything is a metaphor; there is only poetry" (p. 266).

8. According to Freud, the mind is divided into the tripartite montage of id, ego, and superego, the union of all three becoming the Self that is qualitatively different from any one of the three.

9. See Lavina Dhingra Shankar and Rajini Srikanth's *A Part, Yet Apart* (1998) for a critique of Mukherjee's Brahmin status.

10. Cf. C. T. Hsia's term from *A History of Modern Chinese Fiction* (1961), with David Wang's in Wang's Afterword to *Running Wild* (1994).

## Chapter 1: Anal Apocalypse

1. Ernest Becker likens human beings to mobile digestive systems in *Escape from Evil* (1975).

2. Far more prevalent than wearing the mask on the buttocks is the performance convention of wearing the mask on the back of one's head, a practice found in many cultures, ancient and modern, around the world. In Edward Yang's 2000 film *Yi Yi*, the ingenious boy protagonist captures the back of his subject's head in his photographs. Perhaps Yang should have made his character more outrageous by having him shoot people's bottoms, which are actually about at the boy's height.

3. The Italian version of the golden egg story is entitled "The Ass That Lays Money." See Stith Thompson, *One Hundred Favorite Folktales* (1968), pp. 248–251.

4. Norman O. Brown cites St. Augustine's Latin phrase *"inter urinas et faeces"* to suggest the proximity of reproductive and excretory organs (*Life Against Death* 1959, pp. 187–188).

5. See Judith Kovacs and Christopher Rowland, *Revelation* (2004), pp. 42, 53.

6. Freud's analyses most relevant to anal eroticism are in "Character and Anal Erotism," (1908), "The Predisposition to Obsessional Neurosis" (1913), "On the Transformation of Instincts with Special Reference to Anal Erotism" (1916), and "Anal Erotism and the Castration Complex" (1918).

7. In Chinese slang, the anus is *pigu yan* or *piyan,* literally, the anal eye. Lu Xun's "The Divorce" (1925) inscribes the corrupt, superstitious feudalism in the practice of the anus-stop, a piece of jade inserted into the anus of the dead *(pigu yan)* in ancient Chinese burials to prevent the body from deteriorating.

8. In 1998, the Association of Asian American Studies gave Yamanaka a fiction award for *Blu's Hanging.* The Filipino American caucus protested against the decision and the award was rescinded. The protest took the form of campaigning against Filipino American stereotypes in *Blu's Hanging,* but it is really a politicized language veiling the revulsion over characters associated with anality. To be fair to Yamanaka, certain Japanese American characters are just as anal and deplorable as Paulo the Filipino American in the novel.

9. See also James Clavell's *Tai-Pan* (1966), a novel of Orientalist kitsch on the rise to power of Scottish opium traffickers.

10. A lascar is a sailor or army servant from East Indies, the former Netherlands Indies, which can mean either the entire Malay archipelago or India, Indochina, and the Malay archipelago.

11. In *Dark Paradise* (1982), David Courtwright describes opium use:

> The nature and complexity of opium smoking ... ensured its status as a
> social, rather than private act. ... The opium pipe typically consists of a
> 16-inch to 20-inch bamboo stem, with a ceramic bowl inserted about a
> third of the way down from the stoppered end. Also required is some sort of
> lamp (as a source of heat), a large needle (to manipulate the viscous drug),
> and a knife (to scrape the bowl). The smoker, reclining on a wooden plat-

form, dips the needle into a container of prepared opium, usually purchased from the proprietor of the den. He then holds the globule of opium above the lamp's flame, where it swells and bubbles to several times its original size. Once it is properly 'cooked' and distended, the opium is transferred to the pipe's bowl, where it is rolled into a small 'pill.' This pill is forced into the hole at the center of the bowl and heated, then the needle stuck through and withdrawn, leaving a ring of smoking opium around the hole connecting to the pipe stem. The pipe is tilted, the flame strikes the opium, and the smoker draws in the fume. The whole process begins again" (p. 72).

12. Visual evidence can be observed in the opium den in *Broken Blossoms*. But the best visual example may be N. C. Wyeth's illustration for "A Modern Opium Eater," an alleged report on an opium den written by No. 6606 and published in *The American Magazine,* June 1914. An ape-like Chinaman turns his eyes aside while holding an opium pipe for a Western customer, who is in a stupor, with his eyes closed. The illustration deploys Oriental décor—a dragon on the wall and a divan with many cushions. The right hand that holds the pipe could be either the Chinaman's or the Western man's, except that the long nails give it away.

13. The term "communal bed" comes from Timothy Carens's "Restyling the Secret of the Opium Den" (1995).

14. Beulah Ong Kwoh plays the Mulwrays' maid in *Chinatown*. She has only one line, which she speaks in heavily accented English: "She no here." Henry Yu, in *Thinking Orientals: Migration, Contact, and Exoticism in Modern America* (2001), points out the irony in that Kwoh was "born and raised in Stockton, California, an English literature major with a master's degree in sociology from the University of Chicago" (p. 172).

15. Evelyn is high-strung, becoming almost hysterical whenever the subject of her father comes up in conversation. She even develops a stutter pronouncing "Hollis" and "my f-f-father," a Freudian slip over the f sound (and the f word) denoting an incestuous monstrosity. It turns out that the teenage Evelyn and Noah Cross have had a relationship which has produced Katherine. The name Noah Cross is a deliberate sacrilege of the Christian faith: a reprehensible Noah carrying the cross of sin, siring a bloodline by incest.

16. In celebrating Polanski's powerful conclusion, James Naremore himself succumbs momentarily to Orientalism in his excellent *More than Night: Film Noir in its Context* (1998). Naremore describes the last shot of *Chinatown,* in which the camera rises above a Chinatown street and the theme music plays, predicting that "the only consolation anyone might have [for the bleak and nihilistic ending] would be in opium dreams" (p. 210), an out-of-place, out-of-date return to the Western fantasy about opium.

## Chapter 2: Camp Scatology

1. Out of the 120,000 Japanese Americans, 70,000 had been born in the United States. Of the 21,000 interned and relocated Japanese Canadians, 17,000 were Cana-

dian-born. Whenever this chapter refers to "Japanese Americans," it includes both Japanese Americans and Japanese Canadians, or, simply, Japanese *North* Americans.

2. Sau-ling Cynthia Wong's "Denationalization Reconsidered" (1995) argues for locating Asian American literature squarely within American literary tradition. She reasons that Asian Americans cannot afford to segregate themselves from mainstream American culture, having already been segregated historically. But in regards to the topic at hand—camp scatology—Japanese American representations are such that they situate themselves between the Eastern and Western tradition.

3. Many other social scientists hint at affect as well. David O'Brien and Stephen Fugita, in *The Japanese American Experience* (1991), at first maintain that "the psychological sequelae and life course trajectory effects of the camp experience are difficult to document empirically because they are confounded with so many other historical and developmental changes in the lives of those involved" (p. 75). But they immediately make reference to the internees' emotional scars: one internee compares the camp experience to "rape," another to "incest." Both poignant analogies suggest "the feeling of degradation which makes it difficult to talk about the experience" (p. 76), but this line of argument on internee affect is not pursued further in *The Japanese American Experience*.

4. In "Character and Anal Erotism" (1908) and in a preface entitled "The Excretory Functions in Psychoanalysis and Folklore" (1913), Freud argues that a link exists between excrement and gold. "Excreta," Freud writes in this essay, is "regarded as a part of a child's body and as products of his own organism, have a share in … the narcissistic esteem … with which he regards everything related to his self. Children are proud … of their own excretions and make use of them to help in asserting themselves against adults. Under the influence of education the coprophilic instincts" are repressed and "carried over on to other objects—for instance, from faeces on to money" (p. 221). Freud also discusses lexical opposites in "The Antithetical Sense of Primal Words" (1910). "Visceral" and "crap" fall into this category of primal words, although they are not as "primordial" as Freud's original examples of archaic Egyptian words.

5. Exploring Kogawa's *Obasan* in *Articulate Silences* (1995), King-Kok Cheung restores dignity and value to the concept of *ching* (silence or quiescence) in the Japanese tradition.

6. See the first note to Qian Zhongshu's Preface, included in Yang Jiang's *Six Chapters from My Life "Downunder"* (1983).

7. May Seventh Cadre Schools were first conceived in Mao Zedong's letter to Lin Biao on May 7th, 1966, in which Mao authorized the PLA (the People's Liberation Army) to "participate in the criticism of the capitalist class." A cadre school is not a school but a site where reeducation-through-labor is conducted.

8. René Girard argues in *Scapegoat* (1986) that ancient myths often proffer "persecution texts," where certain individuals or groups are identified as victims by some physical handicap or by the fact of their foreignness.

9. See Despina Kakoudaki, "The Human Machine: Visual Representation and Artificial Intelligence" (2000).

10. The pertinent part of Yeats's "Crazy Jane Talks with the Bishop" reads:

> Fair and foul are near of kin,
> And fair needs foul,
>
> . . .
>
> For nothing can be sole or whole
> That has not been rent.

## Chapter 3: Brush and Blade in East-West Cultures

1. Ruth Benedict's wartime study of the Japanese enemies, *The Chrysanthemum and the Sword* (1946), could easily be renamed "cherry blossom and seppuku," for these are the clichés that populate the public imagination about the Japanese.

2. See Yeats's "A Dialogue of Self and Soul," from *The Collected Poems* (1950).

3. Preceded by a graphic illustration, the entry on "Kali" in the *Encyclopaedia Acephalica* (1995), edited by Georges Bataille, cites Katherine Mayo's *L'Inde avec les Anglais*: "She is black-faced and sticks out an enormous tongue, filthy with blood. Of her four hands, one holds a human head, dripping blood, the second a knife, the third, extended, pours out blood, the fourth, raised in menace, is empty" (p. 55). The entry also describes in gruesome detail temple sacrifices of goats by beheading.

4. An apocalyptic "thingie," rather, since apocalypse always entails an amorphousness that goes beyond words. Destined to be obfuscated, apocalypse finds a perfect medium for self-expression in Orientalism, which is, on the one hand, imprecise and filled with sweeping stereotypes and, on the other, suffused with mysterious otherness.

Buddhism has a tradition of the sword of wisdom, which obliterates all obstacles to enlightenment. Many Buddhist deities have multiple arms, holding various ritual objects, among them the sword for wisdom, the thunder for enlightenment, and human skulls. Gary Snyder translates one poem of the Tang hermit-poet Han Shan (Cold Mountain) as follows:

> There's a naked bug at Cold Mountain
>
> . . .
>
> But he always carries the sword of wisdom:
> He means to cut down senseless craving.

5. Nietzsche's *Thus Spake Zarathustra* (1980), p. 152.

6. See Freud's "Fetishism" (1927) as well as earlier works, such as *Three Essays on the Theory of Sexuality* (1905) and *Gradiva* (1907).

7. See William B. Parsons's *The Enigma of the Oceanic Feeling* (1999), especially Chapter 6, "Mysticism East and West."

8. See David Bordwell's *Planet Hong Kong* (2000): "The alteration of swift attack and abrupt rest is characteristic of the Asian martial arts"—a style Bordwell

attributes to both the tradition of martial arts and that of Beijing Opera, in which movements are punctuated with "moments of pure stasis, the technique of *liang hsiang* (displaying). Often underlined by a cymbal crash" (p. 224) or a clapper *(ban)*.

9. The Chinese media has often taunted Zhang Yimou for his overzealous catering to Western taste in order to be awarded an Oscar. The Oscar craze infects other fifth-generation filmmakers as well, such as Chen Kaige.

10. In "On the Dual Nature of Traditional Chinese Thought" (1991), Li critiques the method of reasoning in traditional Chinese thinking as "a kind of systematic inference (that is, a system that can be inferred from another system) ... different from Western prepositional inference. The Chinese inference is also full of dialectic concepts" (p. 246). Such systematic inference "lacked definite rules and procedures and depended simply on analogous inference," leading to "strained interpretations" (p. 247). Li also faults traditional Chinese thought for its reliance on "mystical intuition," "ambiguous concepts and expressions of infinite capacity" (p. 250). It appears Zhang Yimou is doing no less.

11. See Brecht's "Alienation Effects in Chinese Acting" (1964) and "Alienation Effects in the Narrative Pictures of the Elder Brueghel."

12. Thomas Carlyle's antidemocratic, antievolutionist *On Hero, Hero-Worship, and the Heroic in History* (1841) includes six types of hero: God, Prophet, Poet, Priest, Man of Letters, and King, which is a mix of the brush and the blade.

13. Yamamoto Tsunetomo's *Hagakure: The Book of the Samurai* (1716) is one of the two Eastern books on martial matters often alluded to in Western popular culture. The other one, even more frequently translated and quoted is the Warring States period (403–221 B.C.) Chinese text, *Sun Tzu: The Art of Warfare*.

14. The size of an American football, a device nicknamed the "nuclear football" follows the U.S. President wherever s/he travels. The device contains the mechanism to launch a nuclear strike.

15. The facial features on the three heads in *Spirited Away* resemble those of Yuki-Daruma recorded by Lafcadio Hearn in "Otokichi's Daruma." Japanese make snowmen shaped like Daruma, or Bodhidharma, the twenty-eighth patriarch of Buddhism, who founded Zen in China.

16. Bruce Lee played the Japanese houseboy Kato in the twenty-six episodes of the TV series *The Green Hornet* during the 1966–1967 season. Once he dons a mask, Kato becomes a crimefighter.

17. See Mao Tse-tung's *Talks at the Yenan Forum on Literature and Art* (1942).

18. See Jung's *Psychology and Alchemy* (1953): "The diamond is a carbon crystal. Carbon is black—coal, graphite—but the diamond is 'purest water'" (p. 218).

## Chapter 4: Kung Fu Films in Diaspora

1. Hector Rodriguez argues in "Hong Kong Popular Culture" (1997) that the Huang films of the 1950s are situated at the intersection of "overseas capital," the search for "ethnic identity" of Cantonese emigrants, and the filmmakers' "self-proclaimed goal of promoting patriotism, social responsibility and a sense of ethnic

identity" (p. 2). With some qualifications, Rodriguez's commentaries can be applied to explain my interest in Hong Kong films and that of my fellow expatriates.

2. What Sheldon Hsiao-peng Lu has asserted in "Historical Introduction" (1997) about Chinese Mainland films, particularly Zhang Yimou and Chen Kaige's "art films," is equally valid with respect to King Hu and Ang Lee: "'transnational' films [are] primarily targeted to non-Mainland audiences and international film festivals and are distributed outside of China" (p. 9), and these films are "funded by foreign capital (Hong Kong, Taiwan, Japan, Europe), produced by Chinese labor, distributed in a global network, and consumed by an international audience."

3. In *Hollywood East* (2000) Stephan Hammond makes the same observation that "many of HK's [sic] action heroines like Michelle Yeoh, Cynthia Khan, and Moon Lee were ballet-trained prior to stepping in front of the camera, and many action heroes had Peking opera or acrobatic training" (p. 78); Lenuta Giukin, in "Boy-Girls" (2001), attributes the rise of untrained martial arts performers—Maggie Cheung (Zhang Manyu), Brigitte Lin, Anita Mui—to technology: "Another major feature of the eighties and nineties martial arts movies is the presence of modern technology—such as cars, motor bikes, explosives, guns, and automatic weapons—which, combined with special effects and fast editing techniques, was at the base of a new modality of making and viewing martial arts films" (p. 57).

4. Evidence even links the assassination with Chiang Ching-kuo's second son. For details, visit http://www.taiwandc.org/twcom/tc19-int.pdf .

5. Citing *Swordsman II* (1991) and *The East is Red* (1992), Giukin in "Boy-Girls" (2001) argues that in the fin-de-siècle Hong Kong action movies, "The strong masculinization of the heroine often creates a break with the classical representation of feminine passivity in cinema, a transformation that affects her body representation to a degree that questions the received notion of gender" (p. 55). However, Giukin totally ignores the titillating effect of lesbian love. When a well-known actress like Brigitte Lin is turned into a male, the implied love-making with another actress does not question gender divisions at all. Instead, it strengthens the worst of gender divisions, namely, a pornographic use of gender. More specific to Hu's use of a eunuch antagonist, Giukin believes that "the presence of eunuchs, castrated men in the service of the emperor, prepared society for ... another gender: the neutral. ... In action films, eunuchs are often evil presences" (p. 66).

6. In "Richness through Imperfection" (2000), Bordwell maintains that King Hu "stress[es] certain qualities of these feats—their abruptness, their speed, their mystery. And he chose to do so by treating these feats as only partly visible" (p. 118). To illustrate, Bordwell analyzes Hu's leaping stunts: "Hu gives us only phase 1 or 2 or 3—launch <u>or</u> leap <u>or</u> landing, or only two of them. ... Hu teases us with mere glimpses of the action" (p. 120). Bordwell terms this "constructive editing."

7. In *Hollywood East* (2000), Stephan Hammond notes how Tsui Hark uses the Wong Fei-hong myth: "A turn-of-the-century hero renowned for his abilities as both a martial artist and a herbalist/physician, Wong [Fei-hong]'s defense of Chinese culture against Western encroachment, while opposing internal political corruption,

continues to be seen as an atypical manifestation of Confucian values in a practical, modern setting" (p. 152). Hammond continues to dissect the irony: "A Beijing native [Jet Li] and an American-educated Vietnamese immigrant [Tsui Hark] [come] together on a Hong Kong production about a legendary hero [Wong Fei-hong]" (p. 155).

8. The poet Qu Yuan (343–290 B.C.) wrote in *Zu Ci*: "*Ju qing ming er shu hung xi*." (Leaning against the sky [or the ultimate realm], I arrange a rainbow). "*Qing ming*" signals "the sky" or "the ultimate level one could hope to approach."

9. In *The Sacred Wood* (1920), T. S. Eliot uses "objective correlative" to describe an artistic approach in which a situation or a set of objective materials are presented to evoke a certain affect.

10. The middle-aged Chow Yun-fat, who plays Li, is obviously too heavy for such wirework and looks rather clumsy, especially on landing. Another flaw in the digital manipulation comes when a long shot shows Li and Jen flying on top of the bamboo grove before reaching the boulder by a pool of water. In the distance, they hold their swords in their left hands, only to reemerge from the bamboo grove with their swords in their right hands.

11. In *Death and Sensuality* (1962), Bataille writes that the major cause of transgression is the desire to eliminate a felt discontinuity in life. The erotic form of violation, intercourse, eases the sense of isolation in each individual. Sometimes called "little death," love or lust in consummation, due to the magnitude of the act, propels the participants to a state of temporary cessation of life.

12. For Lo (played by the Taiwanese actor/singer Chang Chen), there is no ambiguity. Jen asks what he wishes for, and Lo replies: "Bring you back to Xinjiang." As Jen leaps into the ravine, Lo can barely hold back his tears. The longing for home is shared by any immigrant or exile, and the feeling increasingly intensifies with the passage of time when there is no way to return home.

### Chapter 5: De/Alienation in Diasporic Dubbing/Rubbing of Maoist China

1. See Bordwell's *Planet Hong Kong* (2000) on "Chop-socky" Hong Kong films: "quickies' disjointed plots, grotesque acting, and otherworldly dubbing, a mixture of snarling delivery, vernacular American vocabulary, and erratically fractured phrasing" (p. 207). But this characteristic grows out of the long tradition of dubbing for audiences of Chinese descent in Malaysia, Singapore, Thailand, Taiwan, and elsewhere, who may be Cantonese, Mandarin, or Taiwanese speakers.

2. By "Maoist" China, I refer to both China under Chairman Mao Zedong and China in the post-Mao era, since post-Mao China continues to operate under his shadow. Maoist China is far better than the abstract and ideological "Communist China" or "PRC" in that it calls attention to the "body" that is being dubbed and rubbed. Most importantly, the diasporic writers reviewed in this chapter describe a China very much in the grip of a totalitarianism best epitomized by Mao and Mao's ghost.

3. This movement from Chinese elegies over Maoist sufferings to diasporic dubbing/rubbing brings to mind what the sinologists see as the shift from "obsession with

China" to "flirtation with China." The former description was coined by C. T. Hsia in *A History of Modern Chinese Fiction* (1961) in reference to early twentieth-century Chinese writers; the latter was expressed by David Wang in 1994 in reference to contemporary Chinese writers. However, native Chinese writers and diasporic writers on Maoist China are contemporaneous.

4. This obsession with sexuality shared by Anchee Min and others is fundamentally different from such a journalistic reportage as Xinran's *The Good Women of China* (2002), which details Chinese women's damaged lives. Originally written in Chinese and translated into English, *The Good Women*, written by a former radio host of programs catering to female listeners in Beijing seems neither to sensationalize, as do the accounts in "Aftersex," nor to flaunt brutality, as happens in the "Afterrape" stories. Rather, it stands as a sincere testimony to Chinese women's sufferings. The title's allusion to Bertolt Brecht and the cover design's play on the Chinese ideogram of "woman" do not diminish its power of exposé.

5. Both *The Lover* and *North China Lover* stem from Duras's experiences as the underage (fifteen-and-a-half-year-old) mistress of a much older, pedophilic Chinese man. This relationship is arranged by Duras's mother as an exchange of sex for money to support the declining French colonist family. See Laure Adler's biography on Duras (1998), especially chapters 3 and 16.

6. In his "Three Essays on Sexuality" (1915), Sigmund Freud outlines five stages of manifestation of the sexual drive. The anal stage is dominated by toilet training, in which children learn to control the environment through bowel movements. Feces can be used as weapon against the outside world, as Shaona does against her teacher, a mother surrogate.

7. See Sau-ling Cynthia Wong in "Sugar Sisterhood" (1995). While Tan's fans are overwhelmingly female, the gender of Ha Jin's following is unclear and awaits further research.

8. In Ha Jin's Third World primitivist charm for the First World, he resembles Mo Yan, whose translations succeed in the American market perhaps for the same reason. From *Red Sorghum* (1993) to the recent translation of *Big Breasts and Wide Hips* (2004), Mo Yan thrives on the earthy and the carnivalesque.

9. Further research is needed to verify this as historical fact or to dispute it as Ha Jin's poetic license. While it is true that many Communist Chinese soldiers who went to Taiwan had anti-Communist slogans tattooed on their forearms to demonstrate their resolve, the reverse is what drives Ha Jin's plot, namely, that such tattoos were to prevent inmates from returning to China.

10. In terms of gothic sensibility, Ha Jin resembles contemporary Chinese writers such as Yu Hua and Su Tong. See David Wang's analysis of "familiarization of the uncanny" in his Afterword to *Running Wild* (1994).

11. See T. S. Eliot's *Four Quartets*. Part II, "East Coker," opens with "In my beginning is my end" and ends with "In my end is my beginning." Beginning and end connect in a circle of life. If only diasporic dubbing/rubbing would spend itself and make way for a new diasporic discourse. . . .

## Chapter 6: Anime's Atom Dialectic

1. The inspiration for skepticism comes in part from Lee Quinby's *Millennial Seduction* (1999), in which she states: "Apocalypse has long been a major confidence game—for over 2,000 years no less" (p. 100).

2. In *Samurai from Outer Space* (1996), Antonia Levi writes: "The use of a single, small symbol to express a greater, universal whole is basic to most traditional Japanese arts" (p. 23).

3. For the 1950s American audience unaccustomed to foreign-language films and with fresh memories of the atomic bombs, Raymond Burr serves, diegetically, as an American amidst Japanese with whom the audience can identify and, ex-diegetically, as an interpretive voice-over to orient an American audience. A cross-cultural bridge at the time perhaps, in retrospect Burr's patronizing role and voice-over totally suppress the Japanese dialogue and fracture the momentum of the film. While Japanese tried to absorb the shock of the atomic bomb in *Godzilla,* Hollywood unleashes the barrel-chested giant Burr to dominate the film. In "Godzilla and the Japanese Nightmare" (1996), Chon Noriega contends that the Japanese Godzilla films "transfer onto Godzilla the role of the United States" (p. 61), further linking Burr to Godzilla.

4. In *Atomic Bomb Cinema* (2002), Shapiro argues that the emperor is "the symbolic head of the rice culture" in Japan and the empress "the head of the silk culture" (p. 279).

5. In *Atomic Bomb Cinema* (2002), Shapiro likens Gojira or Godzilla to a child who misbehaves and ignores the collective. This can be applied to *Akira* as well. Hiruko is the Leech Child in Japanese mythology, the only god excluded from the Japanese pantheon. "Hiruko represents," to Shapiro, "the kid of 'individualistic' personality that is broadly considered disruptive in Japanese society" (p. 280).

6. Brian Ruh, in *Stray Dog of Anime* (2004), points out that "ghost" seems akin to "soul, although it is something physical that can be detected in a computer scan" (p. 123). Ruh also quotes science fiction writer Bruce Sterling about the prevalent cyberpunk themes in Oshii: "prosthetic limbs, implanted circuitry, cosmetic surgery, genetic alteration," even "brain-computer interfaces, artificial intelligence, neurochemistry" (p. 126, qtd. from Sterling, "Preface" to *Mirrorshades* 1986, p. xiii).

7. Shapiro notes that falls are common in Atomic Bomb films as well. See *Atomic Bomb Cinema* (2002), p. 44.

8. In addition to "Techno-Orientalism and Media-Tribalism," Ueno advances the same argument in "Japanimation and Techno-Orientalism" (1996).

9. Yoshitoshi's 1885 woodblock print "The Hag of Adachigahara" deploys a similar technique. A pregnant woman is bound and gagged, a scarf covering half of her face. The hag sharpens her knife and stares at the pregnant woman hanging upside down directly above a fire. Perhaps out of jealousy of the pregnant woman's youth and life, the hag is bent upon murder. Yoshitoshi expresses a male fantasy about women, while subtly transferring male violence to one between women.

10. Yomota Inuhiko, in "Stranger than Tokyo" (2003), disagrees with my argument: "The cities that appear in Oshii ... originate in the peculiarities of a place called Tokyo, shift toward a possible alternative Tokyo, and finally transform into a nationless metropolis that matches nowhere on earth" (p. 80).

11. Roland Barthes's *Empire of Signs* (1982) creates a system of signs that the French philosopher calls Japan, which has little to do with the geographical entity of Japan. Rather, Barthes projects the apocalyptic yearnings of the West into this opposite that is so vacated of meaning that it turns into whatever the philosopher wishes it to be.

12. White Gentleman Toothpaste may be a deliberate play on the racist Black Face Toothpaste popular in Asia for decades. Shapiro refers to it in passing, in *Atom Bomb Cinema* (2002), during a failed attempt at consciousness-raising at the student bookstore at Kyoto University (p. 303).

13. See Chapter 4, "Kung Fu Films in Diaspora."

14. See Eric van den Ing and Robert Schaap's *Beauty and Violence* (1992), p. 131.

## Chapter 7: The O of Han Ju

I dedicate this chapter to my wife, whose absence in April 2004 triggered strong identification on my part with the theme of loss in *Winter Sonata*. She also brought my attention to the red lips of the female Korean stars, the central metaphor of this chapter. I would not have noticed those lips otherwise. Like the gentleman who bought *Playboy* for the articles, I watched *Winter Sonata* for the wintry scenery.

1. A good historical account can be found in Doobo Shim's "The Rise of the Korean Media in Asia and Glocalization" (2003) a published conference paper. Shim's use of glocalization as opposed to globalization calls attention to the local use of global forces. Although Shim focuses on Korean pop music and hybridization, the argument applies equally to Han Ju.

2. While Han Ju VCD and DVD with multiple soundtracks are available, initial broadcast on non-Korean television channels of Han Ju is almost always dubbed. Dubbing, therefore, is crucial to the success of Han Ju across Asia. A multitude of questions evolve from dubbing in the Asian context—its history entangled with Hong Kong kung fu and action films, its perceived low-brow characteristics, its influence on audience reception and on the film and television drama themselves. Western art house productions have long viewed dubbing as corruption to the integrity of art, evident from Renoir's outraged comments quoted in Chapter 5. Mary Ann Doane, in "The Voice in the Cinema" (1999), contends that voice-over is "a *disembodied* voice" (p. 369). Since dubbing involves a suspension of disbelief, an overlooking of slippages between the voice and the lips/bodies, it is related to Doane's notion of "a *disembodied* voice." Chua Beng Huat's "Conceptualizing an East Asian Popular Culture" (2004) gives a nuanced reading of dubbing in the Chinese-speaking viewing context where Mandarin, Cantonese, and Taiwanese intersect, both in dubbing and subtitling; see especially pp. 206, 215–216.

3. Doobo Shim writes that a previous film by *Chunhyang's* director, Im Kwon-Taek, makes use of the Korean folk performance *pansori* even more directly in his 1993 breakthrough film *Sopyonje;* see "The Rise of the Korean Media in Asia and Glocalization" (2003), pp. 3–5.

4. In *Oedipus Unbound* (2004), René Girard views incest as the archetype of hierarchy annihilation. The order of human society based on family is destroyed by incest. A mythic state of oceanic union between Self and Other, incest and its artistic potential has long preoccupied Western romantics. Emily Bronte's *Wuthering Heights* features Heathcliff and Catherine, whose love remains unconsummated due to incest anxiety. The same theme runs through major romantic poets such as Shelley, Byron, and others. *Winter Sonata* subconsciously manifests incest as a romantic impulse for lovers to become one. Hence, the prior generation's thwarted triangular love among Joon Sang's pianist mother, Sang Hyuk's professor father, and Yu Jin's deceased father returns in the trio of Joon Sang, Sang Hyuk, and Yu Jin, except that in this generation the triangular love is further complicated by the mystery of paternity and the possibility of incest.

## Chapter 8: Tradition and/of Bastards in the Korean Wave

1. Rothman writes in his 1993 exegesis of *The Goddess* (1934): "In China, film itself was nontraditional; it entered on the wave of Western influence.... In China, as in Japan and India, film represents a radical discontinuity in traditional culture" (p. 60).

2. For the sake of consistency I have chosen to Anglicize all Korean names, with the given name preceding the surname. This applies to bibliography as well, where Korean filmmakers' last names head the entries on their films. Many of these Korean names in television and films have been sinologized in dubbing and my romanization of these names may sound like mistranslation to Korean readers.

3. See Chapter 7, "The O of Han Ju."

4. Although they are originally in Korean, all titles and character names are romanized according to Mandarin pronunciation, as the bulk of these television serials come dubbed. This dubbing and the attendant sinologizing are intriguing subjects of study. Such translation, linguistic and cultural, may at times commit serious errors, turning into mistranslation. Yet glitches of miscommunication can become productive in creating new meaning. Bilingual, or even multilingual, researchers are needed for this investigation.

5. In addition to the more presentable analogy of sexual arousal, one can liken symbiotic pleasure and pain to the mixed sensations of a Turkish bath, vigorous massage, and even athlete's foot. In the recent Chinese television serial *Shuanxian pao* (Twin cannonballs), a businessman muses about his athlete's foot. "It's been with me for over thirty years. It's unbearable," he continues while kneading his itching feet and issuing a long sigh, "but it sure feels good."

A more concrete example comes from the sole "comic" moment in Kwon-Taek Im's *Sopyonje.* As the traveling troupe of *pansori* is kicked out by the ointment peddler, they traveled along a stone wall across a bleak landscape, having nowhere to go. The father begins singing "Arirang," the famous Korean folksong, then joined by Song-hwa as they near the camera, finally joined by Dong-ha's drum. Thus, steps away from the camera, they perform a comic song and dance, complete with happy gestures and twirling around each other. Yet this comic moment and their fleeting joy are flanked by a humiliating scene when they are "fired" from the only job they can find and by an uncertain future.

6. Invariably, long-running Korean television serials like *Watching* make a mess when they try to conclude, so much so that they seem completely averse to closure. But we viewers find it hard to resist the temptation to rush to the last disk to find out what happened. Still, we dread the emptiness that sets in once the last disk is done, as if life's soothing repetition has finally ceased.

7. See Fredric Jameson's "Third-World Literature in the Era of Multinational Capitalism" (1991).

8. Julian Stringer, in "*Sopyonje* and the Inner Domain of National Culture" (2002), identifies the background music of this scene as "traditional[ly]" Korean with "flute and synthesizer." Perhaps the tune sounds traditional to Stringer, but the synthesizer it is played on is not.

9. Chungmoi Choi advances this claim of rape in "Nationalism and Construction of Gender in Korea" (1998) and in "The Politics of Gender, Aestheticism, and Cultural Nationalism in *Sopyonje* and *The Genealogy*" (2002).

## Chapter 9: Rodgers and Hammerstein's "Chopsticks" Musicals

1. Since I am here concerned with how popular Rodgers and Hammerstein's works were, the Academy Awards of the era are as good an indication as any. *The King and I* garnered five awards in 1956 for Best Actor (Yul Brynner), Best Art Direction-Set Decoration (Color), Best Sound Recording, Best Scoring of a Musical Picture, and Best Costume Design. *The Sound of Music* also received five awards in 1965 for Best Picture, Best Director (Robert Wise), Best Sound, Best Film Editing, and Best Scoring of Music-Adaptation.

2. Landon presents an extreme form of self-transformation: Anna observes that in preparation for the banquet with European guests, the king's Siamese wives are made to look European by having their teeth scraped white after years of chewing betel nut has darkened them and by having their skin painted white (*Anna and the King of Siam* 1944, p. 125).

3. Caren Kaplan, in "Getting to Know You" (1995), examines Anna Leonowens's two-volume autobiography, Landon's *Anna and the King of Siam* (1944), and the two film versions. Kaplan reads these texts through the lens of the nineteenth-century abolitionist and suffragist movements. She finds that Leonowens's autobiography transposes Western antislavery and feminist passions onto Siam, distorting the historical King Mongkut and his Nang Harm harem. Kaplan sees this as a danger to feminist critical discourse. Historians have asserted that the king was, in fact, responsible for many measures to grant slaves and concubines freedom for a fee. Slavery in Siam was viewed as a safety net for people in debt or during a famine.

4. Joan Erdman continues her description of Oriental dance:

Certain features were perceived as essential: fluid boneless arm and
shoulder motion, rhapsodic spirituality, costumes composed of swinging
gossamer drapery and opaque veils, elaborate and wondrously vibrant
jewelry, and hand movements intended to signal more than graceful
positioning. Dancing feet were often bare, women's midriffs were
usually uncovered, and men danced bare chested in draped or bloused
pantaloons.
    Once oriental dance became a genre, created by western devotees with
eastern ideas and values and extended by dancers from places that seemed to
Europeans oriental, the style influenced dancers who arrived in Europe *from*
the Orient, and also dancers *in* the Orient." (p. 288)

5. William G. Hyland reports in *Richard Rodgers* (1998) that Rodgers disliked the
film and called it "awful," "overproduced," and the use of color "atrocious" (p. 189).
6. Andrea Most, in "We Know We Belong to the Land" (1998), argues that "Jewish assimilation into mainstream American culture in the early part of the twentieth
century was largely a theatrical venture" (p. 77). Ethnicity in these performances can be
easily "performed away," which does not preclude taking on attitudes of white racism. In
fact, assimilation entails an eager embracing of racism against blacks in order to shed the
stigma that Jews are a "darker race" in Europe. "Jews (and many other immigrant groups)
found that a powerful strategy for becoming fully American," contends Most, "was to
adopt the prejudices of whites toward blacks" (p. 78). Most then proceeds to analyze Ali
(the Jewish businessman who is trying to assimilate) and Jud (the dark character of evil)
in Rodgers and Hammerstein's *Oklahoma!*
7. In James Michener's original story, Nellie recoils from Emile's children in part
because he has six of them, from three different Polynesian women. Rodgers and Hammerstein have rendered the Southern belle from Little Rock, Arkansas, considerably
more prudish and conservative by decreasing the number of Emile de Becque's wives and
progeny.
8. Hidden in the racial and gender conflicts is, in fact, class conflict. Luther
Billis, a GI, admires Nellie, an ensign, who, in turn, soliloquizes that "probably I'd
bore him [Emile de Becque] / He's a cultured Frenchman— / I'm a little hick."
9. Yul Brynner's mixed heritage can be glimpsed in Rock Brynner's *Yul* (1989).

## Chapter 10: The Nine Lives of *Blackhawk*'s Oriental

1. The Special Collections at the Michigan State University has one of the most
complete runs of *Blackhawk* since its publication in 1941. While most numbers are
in printed form, some are on microform.
2. For discussion of Connie in Milton Caniff's *Terry and the Pirates,* see my *The
Deathly Embrace* (2000), particularly chapter 1 on adventure comic strips.

3. I refer to the comic book itself as *Blackhawk,* in italics, with a capital B. The leader of the group, Blackhawk, appears in roman type, with a capital B. When referring to the entire group, I use blackhawks, in roman type with a lowercase b.

4. As to how soon DC Comics changed Chop Chop's image after it took control of *Blackhawk* in 1955, I cannot say because those crucial numbers in the mid-fifties are missing from the Michigan State University's Special Collections.

5. In my Introduction to *The Deathly Embrace* (2000), I discuss the dragon as an iconographical cliché in Orientalism.

6. The Mark Evanier and Dan Spiegle revival of *Blackhawk* follows the lead of some of the 1960s *Blackhawks* in hyphenating "Chop-Chop." For the sake of consistency, I will continue to refer to the Oriental character without the hyphen, except in direct quotations from Evanier-Spiegle.

## Chapter 11: Asian Immigrants with "Magical" Disabilities

1. Feng Jicai's *The Three-Inch Golden Lotus* is set in his hometown, Tianjin, in the early decades of the twentieth century, when old traditions clashed with the new, Western influence. Bound feet are one of the focal points. The cult of bound feet that Feng documents is based on historical accounts and involves many details, such as the process of binding and its consequences, both physical and social. While the novel describes women's subjugation, the male perspective is evident in that the master of the house tells the story and is an aficionado of bound feet.

2. A versatile comedienne like Margaret Cho, in *Margaret Cho* (2002), caricatures the Korean accent, which she makes vivid with supposedly Korean facial expressions and body language. What Cho has perfected on stage sounds fairly close to the immigrant pidgin in novels by Kingston, Tan, Gish Jen, Frank Chin, David Wong Louie, and others.

## Chapter 12: Dalai Lama Superstar

1. In his memoir, Harrer refers to his homeland for the first time when he pores over old newspapers and states: "The whole world was still simmering, and our country was going through hard times" (p. 129). He follows that with an equally vague comment as he entrusts a message home with a British representative: "We found him an opportune visitor as we very much wanted to send news to our families at home, who must have long given us up for lost" (p. 142). Such is the extent of his allusion to home. The seven years he spent in Tibet is indeed about Tibet, with few backward glances.

2. According to the jacket of David Lewiston's CD on *Tibetan Buddhism* (1972), the Gyuto's chanting style is the so-called "one-voice chording," which means that "each participant produces a chord, which seems to consist of a low bass note (shifting slowly between B and D) and of another note, two octaves and a third higher. However, the structure of the sound is in fact more complex: When the C two octaves below middle C is sounded, the E above middle C is heard clearly. But what the ear does

not easily register is the E an octave higher, which is also present. From time to time, other overtones emerge, giving the impression of augmented fourths, fifths, sixths, sevenths, and ninths."

3. Other Indian body language includes the hand gestures of Siddhartha's father, the king. Bidding farewell to Siddhartha, he raises his right hand straight up, without waving it. At another point, while cleaning his palm of cremated ashes, the king scoops out a bit of water and rubs his thumb, index finger, and middle finger against one another in a way that resembles the Indian way of eating.

4. While Dean Konrad sits "in wake," H. E. Dzongsar Khyentse Rinpoche, the Buddhist consultant to Bertolucci, makes a cameo appearance and provides a "running commentary" on the symbiosis of living and dying. Khyentse Norbu, of course, goes on to make *The Cup* (*Phörpa* 1999), a film about young Tibetan monks in exile and their obsession with soccer.

5. Even the blue house the Konrads have built seems to have its origin in Lama Dorje's wave of a hand. Before his death, a Lama Dorje in blue jeans shows the site where the house is to appear to his disciples. Cinematically, the house plops down from the sky, out of the blue, as fluid as watery reflections. The color on the screen switches from orange to blue once the house is in place.

### Chapter 13: Hmong Refugee's Death Fugue

1. A similar lament is sung by Mai Hang in Nancy Donnelly's *Changing Lives of Refugee Hmong Women* (1994):

> Now we have come over here and the New Year has come.
> But we don't kill the pig, and we don't have a party.
> We have no boars, for we have no land,
> Nowhere to plant our rice and corn.
> Because we have no animals, we cannot have a New Year,
> We cannot invite anybody to come.
> We live on rock. We have no spirit money or incense to burn.
>     . . .
> We have food, we have clothes, but we don't have our country.
> We have clothes, we have food, but our family is homesick.
> (p. 59)

2. In *Changing Lives of Refugee Hmong Women* (1994), Donnelly uses the patron-client relationship to discuss the Southeast Asian refugee existence in the United States: "Refugees enter the United States in a condition of dependency. Clientelism is a fact in the heart and essence of refugee resettlement. Clearly the largest patron is the federal government, and there are many other clientelistic networks" (p. 92).

3. Donnelly points to a joke to suggest the gender instability. She writes that the men say: "When we get on the plane to go back to Laos, the first thing we do is beat

up the women!" This joke has a complicated ironic underlayment of male unhappiness and helplessness, a concatenation of unemployability, sudden economic value placed on women's work, and men's fear of losing power in their families (*Changing Lives of Refugee Hmong Women* 1994, p. 22). The women also laughed at this joke because women are supposed to join in the laughter when a male makes a joke. "In addition, they could easily laugh because they did not expect a plane back to Laos. No Hmong woman has ever told me she wanted to live in Laos again" (p. 22). The last sentence may be a bit too all-inclusive. In Sucheng Chan's *Hmong Means Free* (1994), there are women who said they wished to return.

4. The Michigan State University Museum boasts a large collection of story cloths from refugee camps and from various American cities. The two pieces of story cloth that I analyzed here are housed at MSU and are included in Marsha MacDowell's *Stories In Thread* (1989).

5. Janet Rice, in "Hmong Women's Group Using Traditional Quilting to Recover from Depression and Post-Trauma" (1999), conducted a study of thirteen Hmong women who were using traditional quilting as a way to fight depression and post-traumatic stress. Seven out of the thirteen or so story cloths feature the crossing of the Mekong River. One piece visualizes the Southeast Asian jungle, four depict the rural village, one presents Christmas. Rice and the Hmong chief therapist created pieces dealing with the treatment of the Hmong in Minnesota, a here-and-now distinctly absent in the Hmong pieces, with the exception of one piece that merges the Mekong River with the Mississippi River. This is the one and only depiction of the United States among the thirteen Hmong women.

6. It is ironic that in view of the centrality of the Mekong River in the Hmong refugee experience, the Hmong are mentioned on only one occasion, and that in passing, in Milton Osborne's *The Mekong* (2000). The Hmong's marginality to the history of Southeast Asia is evident in that Osborne alludes to them only in connection with the Central Intelligence Agency operations during the Vietnam War (pp. 203–224).

7. The most dramatic contrast of violence and nature is in Jane Hamilton-Merritt's *Tragic Mountains* (1993), which contains three drawings far more gruesome than Hmong story cloths—they contain scenes of decapitation, stabbing death by a bayonet, bondage and rape, sodomy with a sharp nail, disembowelment, and the crushing of infants on a rice pounder. Each of these drawings is framed by trees, plants, grass, and river. In fact, a naked woman about to be raped or who has obviously just been raped is tied between two luxuriant palm trees. Another outrage takes place amidst flourishing plants, as if nature is totally indifferent to or perhaps silently indicts the unfolding inhumanity. As Hamilton-Merritt does not explain the origins of these three drawings, we can only say that the design is atypical, the content graphic, and the violence overwhelming. The receding mountain and river in one drawing suggests an artist well versed in the Western concept of perspective and depth. It is likely to be the work of, say, one of the few male artists who drew the story cloth's blueprints in the refugee camps.

8. White in many Asian cultures is the color of death. Mourning garb is frequently white, and coffins are often draped in white. But the Hmong culture does not seem to view whiteness in this fashion.

## Chapter 14: The Fad(k)ing of the 0.5 Generation

1. See related research by Larissa Remennick on Israel's 1.5 generation of Russian descent, published in *Diaspora* (2003).

2. Jennie Keith uses the term "age-centrism" to describe what has prevented researchers from investigating the world of old people from old people's perspective ("Old Age and Community Creation" 1980, pp. 170-197).

3. Shen Yueh's amateurishness comes through at a number of places. One particularly crude, thoughtless point concerns an old man's Parkinson's disease, which makes his hands shake involuntarily. This painful symptom is described by Shen Yueh as quite useful in helping to "shake and bake" chickens for dinner. This man in the play, in fact, offers to "shake and bake" chickens for his neighbors. I seriously doubt if patients are ever so blasé about the increasingly debilitating Parkinson's disease.

4. See the last chapter, "Weakness and Power," in Jenny Hockey and Allison James, *Growing Up and Growing Old* (1993). The authors adopt a progressive, sympathetic viewpoint that almost identifies with the elderly. They describe old people's homes in Britain, where a regime of infantilization is imposed on the elderly. In response, the elderly behave like children to disrupt and subvert the institutionalized order, and thus resemble rebelling teens at times. The authors maintain that the elderly offer a critique of the dominant system and expose certain unpleasant truths about life, such as its inherent limitations. The 0.5 generation attempts the same kind of subversion with their public writings.

5. Erdman Palmore cites studies on jokes by the aged in mainstream American society. These studies reveal that "by far the most frequent theme was sex, with one-third placed in that category" ("Attitudes toward Aging Shown by Humor" 1986, p. 112). Why are there no jokes on sex in 0.5's writings in *The World Journal*? Perhaps it is deemed inappropriate among Chinese to joke about sex in a forum as public as the newspaper. Many of the readers of "Chia-yuan" in *The World Journal* are traditional and conservative Chinese. Reader reception plays a role in dictating the content of the newspaper articles.

6. The 1993 interview of Mrs. Hu was conducted under an agreement of confidentiality. All the people in the interview are given pseudonyms.

# Bibliography

*1000 Airplanes on the Roof: A Science Fiction Music-Drama.* Realized by Philip Glass, David Henry Hwang, and Jerome Sirlin. Premiered in Vienna International Airport in 1987. Salt Lake City: Peregrine Smith Books, 1989.

Adler, Laure. *Marguerite Duras: A Life.* Trans. Anne-Marie Glasheen. Chicago: University of Chicago Press, 1998.

Adler, Shelley Ruth. "The Role of the Nightmare in Hmong Sudden Unexpected Nocturnal Death Syndrome: A Folkloristic Study of Belief and Health." PhD diss., University of California, Los Angeles, 1991.

Aho, James. *The Orifice as Sacrificial Site: Culture, Organization, and the Body.* New York: Aldine de Gruyter, 2002.

Althusser, Louis. "Ideology and the Ideological State Apparatuses (Notes towards an Investigation)." In *Lenin and Philosophy and Other Essays,* trans. Ben Brewster, pp. 127–186. New York: Monthly Review Press, 1971.

Anderson, John. Review of *Little Buddha. Newsday.* October 8, 1997: Part II, p. B2.

Ang, Ien. *Watching Dallas: Soap Opera and the Melodramatic Imagination.* London: Methuen, 1985.

*Anna and the King.* Dir. Andy Tennant. Perf. Chow Yun-fat and Jodie Foster. Twentieth Century Fox, 1999.

*Anna and the King of Siam.* Dir. John Cromwell. Perf. Rex Harrison, Irene Dunne, and Linda Darnell. Twentieth Century Fox, 1946.

Annaud, Jean-Jacques, dir. *L'amant (The lover).* Perf. Jane March and Tony Leung. Based on the novel by Marguerite Duras. MGM, 1991.

———, dir. *Seven Years in Tibet.* Perf. Brad Pitt. Columbia, 1997.

Anzaldua, Gloria. *Borderlands/La Frontera: The New Mestiza.* San Francisco: Spinsters/Aunt Lute, 1987.

*Autumn Tale.* Dir. Yun Seok Ho. Perf. Song Seung-heon and Song Hye-gyo. KBS (18 episodes of the Korean television drama). 2000.

Baker, Russell. "View from the Prison Camp." Review of *War Trash,* by Ha Jin. *The New York Times Book Review* 10 Oct. 2004: 1, 8–9.

Bakhtin, M. M. *The Dialogic Imagination.* Ed. Michael Holquist. Trans. Caryl Emerson and Michael Holquist. Austin: University of Texas Press, 1981.

————. *Rabelais and His World*. Trans. Helene Iswolsky. Cambridge, MA: MIT Press, 1968.

Barnes, Elizabeth, ed. *Incest and the Literary Imagination*. Gainesville, FL: University Press of Florida, 2002.

Barthes, Roland. *Empire of Signs*. 1970. Trans. Richard Howard. New York: Hill and Wang, 1982.

Bataille, Georges. *Death and Sensuality: A Study of Eroticism and the Taboo*. 1962. New York: Arno Press, 1977.

————, ed. *Encyclopaedia Acephalica*. London: Atlas, 1995.

————. *The Tears of Eros*. 1961. San Francisco: City Light Books, 1989.

————. *Visions of Excess: Selected Writings, 1027–1030*. Trans. Allan Stoekl, with Carl R. Lovitt and Donald M. Leslie, Jr. Minneapolis: University of Minneapolis Press, 1985.

Bauckham, Richard. *The Theology of the Book of Revelation*. New York: Cambridge University Press, 1993.

Baudrillard, Jean. *Simulacra and Simulation*. Trans. Sheila Faria Glaser. Ann Arbor: University of Michigan Press, 1994.

Baum, L. Frank. *The Wizard of Oz and Who He Was*. 1900. Ed. Martin Gardner and Russell B. Nye. East Lansing, Michigan State University Press, 1994.

Becker, Ernest. *Escape from Evil*. New York: Free Press, 1975.

Bei Dao. *Notes from the City of the Sun: Poems by Bei Dao*. Ed. and trans. Bonnie McDougall. Ithaca, NY: China-Japan Program, Cornell University, 1984.

Benedict, Ruth. *The Chrysanthemum and the Sword: Patterns of Japanese Culture*. New York: Houghton Mifflin, 1946.

Bertolucci, Bernardo. Interview. "Bernardo Bertolucci: Intravenous Cinema." *Sight and Sound* 4, no. 4 (April 1994): 18–21.

————, dir. *The Last Emperor*. Perf. John Lone, Joan Chen, Peter O'Toole, and Ruocheng Ying. Columbia, 1999.

————, dir. *Little Buddha*. Perf. Keanu Reeves, Ruocheng Ying, and Bridget Fonda. Miramax, 1993.

Besser, H. "Internet to Information Superhighway." In *Resisting the Virtual: The Culture and Politics of Information*, eds. J. Brook and I. A. Boal, pp. 59–70. San Francisco: City Light Books, 1995.

Bhabha, Homi K., ed. *Nation and Narration*. New York: Routledge, 1990.

*Blackhawk*. Meriden, CN: Comic Magazine, 1944–1984.

*Blackhawk*. New York: DC Comics, 1989–1990.

Blum, Virginia L. *Flesh Wounds: The Culture of Cosmetic Surgery*. Berkeley: University of California Press, 2003.

Bordwell, David. "Aesthetics in Action: *Kungfu*, Gunplay, and Cinematic Expressivity." In *At Full Speed: Hong Kong Cinema in a Borderless World*, ed. Esther C. M. Yau, pp. 73–93. Minneapolis: University of Minnesota Press, 2001.

————. *The Cinema of Eisenstein*. Cambridge, MA: Harvard University Press, 1993.

————. *Planet Hong Kong: Popular Cinema and the Art of Entertainment*. Cambridge, MA: Harvard University Press, 2000.

————. "Richness through Imperfection: King Hu and the Glimpse." In *The Cinema of Hong Kong: History, Arts, Identity*, eds. Poshek Fu and David Desser, pp. 113–136. Cambridge: Cambridge University Press, 2000.

Braziel, Jana Evans, and Anita Mannur, eds. *Theorizing Diaspora: A Reader*. New York: Blackwell, 2003.

Brecht, Bertolt. "Alienation Effects in Chinese Acting." In *Brecht on Theater*, ed. and trans. John Willett, pp. 91–99. New York: Hill and Wang, 1964.

Bresson, Robert. *Notes on Cinematography*. 1975. Trans. Jonathan Griffin. New York: Urizen, 1977.

Brooks, Peter. *The Melodramatic Imagination: Balzac, Henry James, and the Mode of Excess*. New Haven: Yale University Press, 1976.

Brown, Georgia. Review of *Little Buddha*. *Village Voice*. May 31, 1994: 58.

Brown, Joe. Review of *Little Buddha*. *Washington Post*. May 27, 1994: 42.

Brown, Norman O. *Life Against Death: The Psychological Meaning of History*. Middletown, CT: Wesleyan University Press, 1959.

————. *Love's Body*. New York: Random House, 1966.

Brunsdon, Charlotte. *The Feminist, the Housewife, and the Soap Opera*. New York: Oxford University Press, 2000.

Brynner, Rock. *Yul: The Man Who Would be King: A Memoir of Father and Son*. New York: Simon and Schuster, 1989.

Byun, Hyuk (Daniel H. Byun), dir. *Juhong geulshi (The scarlet letter)*. Perf. Suk-kyu Han, Eun-ju Lee, Hyeon-a Seong, and Ji-won Uhm. L. J. Films, 2004.

Calinescu, Matei. *Five Faces of Modernity: Modernism, Avant-Garde, Decadence, Kitsch, Postmodernism*. Durham: Duke University Press, 1987.

Camus, Albert. *The Stranger*. 1942. Trans. Stuart Gilbert. New York: Vintage, 1954.

Cao Ji. "Yangnian dianshijie" (New Year with TV). *The World Journal (Shijie ribao)*. February 18, 1999: C10.

Capra, Frank, dir. *Lost Horizon*. Perf. Ronald Colman and Jane Wyatt. Columbia, 1937.

Carens, Timothy L. "Restyling the Secret of the Opium Den." In *Reading Wilde, Queering Spaces: An Exhibition Commemorating the 100th Anniversary of the Trials of Oscar Wilde*, pp. 65–76. New York: New York University Press, 1995.

Caruth, Cathy, ed. *Trauma: Explorations in Memory*. Baltimore: The Johns Hopkins University Press, 1995.

————. *Unclaimed Experience: Trauma, Narrative, and History*. Baltimore: The Johns Hopkins University Press, 1996.

Celan, Paul. *Paul Celan: Poem: A Bilingual Edition*. Selected, trans., and intro. by Michael Hamburger. New York: Persea, 1980.

Chan, Sucheng, ed. *Hmong Means Free: Life in Laos and America*. Philadelphia: Temple University Press, 1994.

Chandler, Raymond. *The Raymond Chandler Omnibus*. New York: Knopf, 1976.

Chang, Pang-mei Natasha. *Bound Feet and Western Dress.* New York: Bantam, 1997.

Chaykin, Howard. *Blackhawk.* New York: DC Comics, 1987–1988.

Chen Jo-hsi (Chen Ruoxi). *Erh Hu (The two Hus).* Kaohsiung, Taiwan: Tung-li, 1985.

———. *The Execution of Mayor Yin and Other Stories from the Great Proletarian Cultural Revolution.* 1974–1976. Trans. Nancy Ing and Howard Goldblatt. Bloomington: Indiana University Press, 1979.

Chen, Joan, dir. *Xiu Xiu: The Sent Down Girl.* Image Entertainment Inc., 1998.

Chennault, Anna. *Chennault and the Flying Tigers.* New York: Paul S. Eriksson, 1963.

Chennault, Claire Lee. *Way of a Fighter: The Memoirs of Claire Lee Chennault.* Ed. Robert Hotz. New York: Putnam, 1949.

Cheung, King-Kok. *Articulate Silences: Hisaye Yamamoto, Maxine Hong Kingston, Joy Kogawa.* Ithaca: Cornell University Press, 1993.

Chin, Frank, Jeffrey Paul Chan, Lawson Fusao Inada, and Shawn Wong, eds. *Aiiieeeee! An Anthology of Asian American Writers.* 1974. New York: Mentor, 1991.

Choi, Chungmoo. "The Discourse of Decolonization and Popular Memory: South Korea." In *Formations of Colonial Modernity in East Asia,* ed. Tani E. Barlow, pp. 349–372. Durham, NC: Duke University Press, 1997.

———. "Nationalism and Construction of Gender in Korea." In *Dangerous Women: Gender and Korean Nationalism,* eds. Elaine H. Kim and Chungmoo Choi, pp. 22–23. New York: Routledge, 1998.

———. "The Politics of Gender, Aestheticism, and Cultural Nationalism in *Sopyonje* and *The Genealogy.*" In *Im Kwon-Taek: The Making of a Korean National Cinema,* eds. David. E. James and Kyung Hyun Kim, pp. 107–133. Detroit: Wayne State University Press, 2002.

Chow, Rey. "Nostalgia of the New Wave: Structure in Wong Kai-wai's *Happy Together.*" In *Keyframes: Popular Cinema and Cultural Studies,* eds. Matthew Tinkcom and Amy Villarejo, pp. 228–241. New York: Routledge, 2001.

———. *Primitive Passions: Visuality, Sexuality, Ethnography, and Contemporary Chinese Cinema.* New York: Columbia University Press, 1995.

Chua Beng Huat. "Conceptualizing an East Asian Popular Culture." *Inter-Asia Cultural Studies* 5, no. 2 (2004): 201–221.

Clavell, James. *Shogun.* New York: Knopf, 1975.

———. *Tai-Pan: A Novel of Hong Kong.* New York: Dell, 1966.

Coleridge, Samuel Taylor. "Kubla Khan." 1797 or 1798. In *English Romantic Writers,* ed. David Perkins, pp. 430–431. New York: Harcourt Brace Jovanovich, 1967.

Connors, Peter. "'The Emptiness of Intelligent Questions': Georges Bataille and the Mystical Tradition." In *Trajectories of Mysticism in Theory and Literature,* ed. Philip Leonard, pp. 177–197. New York: St. Martin's Press, 2000.

Conrad, Joseph. *Heart of Darkness.* 1902. New York: Penguin, 1999.

———. *Lord Jim.* Intro. J. Donald Adams. New York: Modern, 1931.

Coppola, Francis Ford, dir. *Apocalypse Now.* Perf. Marlon Brando, Martin Sheen, Robert Duvall. United Artists, 1979.

———, prod. *Koyaanisqatsi*. Dir. Godfrey Reggio. Music by Philip Glass. New Cinema, 1983.

Courtwright, David T. *Dark Paradise: Opiate Addiction in America Before 1940*. Cambridge: Harvard University Press, 1982.

Craig, Mary. *Kundun: A Biography of the Family of the Dalai Lama*. Washington, DC: Counterpoint, 1997.

Crawford, Hubert H. *Crawford's Encyclopedia of Comic Books*. Middle Village, NY: Jonathan David, 1978.

Cvetkovich, Ann, and Douglas Kellner, ed. *Articulating the Global and the Local: Globalization and Cultural Studies*. Boulder, CO: Westview Press, 1997.

Dai, Catherine. *Bound Feet: Taiwanese Collection of Stories*. Taipei: Bookman, 1992.

Dai Sijie. *Balzac and the Little Chinese Seamstress*. 2000. Trans. Ina Rilke. New York: Anchor, 2002.

Dalai Lama XIV, and Howard C. Cutler. *The Art of Happiness: A Handbook for Living*. New York: Riverhead Books, 1998.

Daly, Nicholas. *Literature, Technology, and Modernity, 1860–2000*. New York: Cambridge University Press, 2004.

Datan, Nancy. "The Last Minority: Humor, Old Age, and Marginal Identity." In *Humor and Aging*, eds. Lucille Nahemow, Kathleen A. McCluskey-Fawcett, and Paul E. McGhee, pp. 161–171. New York: Academic Press, 1986.

Davis, Lennard J. *Enforcing Normalcy: Disability, Deafness, and the Body*. New York: Verso, 1995.

De Quincey, Thomas. *Confessions of an English Opium-Eater*. 1821. London: Cressent, 1950.

Demi. *The Dalai Lama: A Biography of the Tibetan Spiritual and Political Leader*. New York: Henry Holt, 1998.

Denby, David. Review of *Little Buddha*. *New York*. June 6, 1994: 52-53.

Derrida, Jacques. *Of Grammatology*. 1967. Trans. Gayatri Chakravorty Spivak. Baltimore: Johns Hopkins University Press, 1976

Dewhurst, C. Kurt, and Marsha MacDowell, eds. *Michigan Hmong Arts: Textiles in Transition*. East Lansing: Michigan State University Museum, 1983.

Dickens, Charles. *The Mystery of Edwin Drood*. 1870. Ed. Margaret Cardwell. London: Oxford University Press, 1972.

Dmytryk, Edward, dir. *Murder, My Sweet*. Perf. Dick Powell and Claire Trevor. RKO, 1944.

Doane, Mary Ann. "The Voice in the Cinema: The Articulation of Body and Space." In *Film Theory and Criticism*, eds. Leo Braudy and Marshall Cohen, pp. 363–375. New York: Oxford University Press, 1999.

Donnelly, Nancy D. *Changing Lives of Refugee Hmong Women*. Seattle: University of Washington Press, 1994.

Douglas, Mary. *Purity and Danger*. London: Routledge and Kegan Paul, 1966.

Doyle, Sir Arthur Conan. *The Complete Sherlock Holmes*. Twickenham, Middlesex: Hamlyn, 1984.

Duras, Marguerite. *The Lover.* 1984. Trans. Barbara Bray. New York: Pantheon, 1985.

————. *North China Lover* 1991. New York: New Press, 1992.

Ebert, Roger. Review of *Little Buddha. Chicago Sun-Times.* May 25, 1994: 49.

Eisenstein, Sergei. "Beyond the Shot." In *S. M. Eisenstein: Selected Works,* ed. Richard Taylor, pp. 138–150. Vol. 1. Bloomington: Indiana University Press, 1988.

————. "Perspectives." In *S. M. Eisenstein: Selected Works,* ed. Richard Taylor, pp. 139–160. Vol. 1. Bloomington: Indiana University Press, 1988.

————. "Yermolova." In *S. M. Eisenstein: Selected Works,* ed. Richard Taylor, pp. 85–105. Vol. 2. Bloomington: Indiana University Press, 1988.

Eliot, T. S. *The Sacred Wood: Essays on Poetry and Criticism.* London: Methuen and Co., 1920.

————. *The Waste Land.* In *The Complete Poems and Plays: 1909–1950,* pp. 37–55. New York: Harcourt, Brace and Co., 1958.

Erdman, Joan L. "Dance Discourses: Rethinking the History of the 'Oriental Dance.'" In *Moving Words: Re-writing Dance,* ed. Gay Morris, pp. 288–305. New York: Routledge, 1996.

Espiritu, Yen Le. *Asian American Panethnicity: Bridging Institutions and Identities.* Philadelphia, PA: Temple University Press, 1992.

*The Face of China As Seen by Photographs and Travelers, 1860–1912.* Pref. L. Carrington Goodrich. Commentary by Nigel Cameron. New York: Aperture, 1978.

Faderman, Lillian, with Ghia Xiong. *I Begin My Life All Over: The Hmong and the American Immigrant Experience.* Boston: Beacon, 1998.

Fadiman, Anne. *The Spirit Catches You and You Fall Down: A Hmong Child, Her American Doctors, and the Collision of Two Cultures.* New York: Noonday, 1997.

Fanon, Frantz. *Black Skin, White Masks.* 1952. Trans. Charles Lam Markma. New York: Grove Press, 1967.

Fass, Simon. "Innovations in the Struggle for Self-Reliance: The Hmong Experience in the United States." *International Migration Review* 20 (1986): 351–380.

Felman, Shoshana, and Dori Laub. *Testimony: Crises of Witnessing in Literature, Psychoanalysis, and History.* New York: Routledge, 1991.

Feng Jicai. *Chrysanthemums and Other Stories.* Trans. Susan Wilf Chen. New York: Harcourt Brace Jovanovich, 1985.

————. *The Three-Inch Golden Lotus.* 1986. Trans. David Wakefield. Honolulu: University of Hawai'i Press, 1994.

Fleischer, Doris Zames, and Freida Zames. *The Disability Rights Movement: From Charity to Confrontation.* Philadelphia: Temple University Press, 2001.

Fleming, Victor, dir. *The Wizard of Oz.* Perf. Judy Garland. Warner Brothers, 1939.

Fong, Timothy. *The First Suburban Chinatown: The Remaking of Monterey Park, California.* Philadelphia: Temple University Press, 1994.

Forster, E. M. *A Passage to India.* 1924. Philadelphia: Open University Press, 1994.

Foster, Hal. "The Art of Fetishism: Notes on Dutch Still Life." In *Fetishism as Cultural Discourse,* eds. Emily Apter and William Pietz, pp. 251–265. Ithaca: Cornell University Press, 1993.

Freidberg, Freda. "*Akira* and the Postnuclear Sublime." In *Hibakusha Cinema: Hiro-shima, Nagasaki and the Nuclear Image in Japanese Film,* ed. Mick Broderick, pp. 91–102. London: Kegan Paul, 1996.

Freud, Sigmund. "Anal Erotism and the Castration Complex." *Collected Papers,* Vol. III: *Case Histories,* pp. 548–567. London: Hogarth Press, 1950.

————. "The Antithetical Sense of Primal Words." 1910. In *Character and Culture,* intro. and ed. by Philip Rieff, pp. 44–50. New York: Collier, 1963.

————. *Beyond the Pleasure Principle.* 1920. Trans. James Strachey. New York: Norton, 1989.

————. "Character and Anal Erotism." 1908. In *Collected Papers,* Vol. II, pp. 45–50. New York: Basic Books, 1959.

————. "The Excretory Functions in Psychoanalysis and Folklore." 1913. In *Character and Culture,* intro. and ed. by Philip Rieff, pp. 219-222. New York: Collier, 1963.

————. "Fetishism." 1927. In *Sexuality and the Psychology of Love,* trans. Joan Riviere, pp. 214–219. New York: Collier, 1963.

————. *Jokes and Their Relation to the Unconscious.* 1905. Trans. James Strachey. London: Routledge, 1960.

————. *Moses and Monotheism.* Trans. Katherine Jones. New York: Vintage, 1939.

————. "A Mythological Parallel to a Visual Obsession." In *Character and Culture,* ed. Philip Rieff, pp. 152–154. New York: Collier, 1963.

————. "On the Transformation of Instincts with Special Reference to Anal Erotism." 1916. In *Collected Papers* Vol. II, pp. 164–171. New York: Basic Books, 1959.

————. *Totem and Taboo: Some Points of Agreement between the Mental Lives of Savages and Neurotics.* Trans. James Strachey. New York: Norton, 1950.

Fu Hua. "Laozhi jiangzhi" (The imminent arrival of old age). *The World Journal (Shijie ribao).* February 3, 1999: C10.

Garner, Dwight. "Somehow I Couldn't Stop." Interview of Ha Jin. *The New York Times Book Review.* 10 Oct. 2004: 9.

Gateward, Frances. "Youth in Crisis: National and Cultural Identity in New South Korean Cinema." In *Multiple Modernities: Cinemas and Popular Media in Transcul-tural East Asia,* ed. Jenny Kwok Wah Lau, pp. 114–127. Philadelphia: Temple University Press, 2003.

Gilman, Sander. *The Jew's Body.* London: Routledge, 1991.

Gilroy, Paul. *The Black Atlantic: Modernity and Double Consciousness.* Cambridge, MA: Harvard University Press, 1993.

Girard, René. *Oedipus Unbound: Selected Writings on Rivalry and Desire.* Edited and with an introduction by Mark R. Anspach. Stanford: Stanford University Press, 2004.

————. *Scapegoat.* Trans. Yvonne Freccero. Baltimore: The Johns Hopkins University Press, 1986.

Giukin, Lenuta. "Boy-Girls: Gender, Body, and Popular Culture in Hong Kong

Action Movies." In *Ladies and Gentlemen, Boys and Girls: Gender in Film at the End of the Twentieth Century,* ed. Murray Pomerance, pp. 55–69. Albany: State University of New York Press, 2001.

Glass, Philip. *Music by Philip Glass.* New York: Harper and Row, 1987.

Goellner, Ellen, and Jacqueline Shea Murphy, eds. *Bodies of the Text: Dance as Theory, Literature as Dance.* New Brunswick: Rutgers University Press, 1995.

Goldstein, Rebecca. "Looking Back at Lot's Wife." In *Out of the Garden: Women Writers on the Bible,* ed. Christina Buchmann and Celina Spiegel, pp. 3–12. New York: Fawcett Columbine, 1994.

Graham, David Crockett. *Songs and Stories of the Ch'uan Miao.* Washington, DC: Smithsonian Institute, 1954.

Griffith, D. W., dir. *Broken Blossoms.* Kino Video. 1919.

Gu Hua. *A Small Town Called Hibiscus.* 1983. Trans. Gladys Yang. Beijing: Panda, 1990.

Guterson, David. *Snow Falling on Cedars.* New York: Vintage, 1995.

Haboush, JaHyun Kim. "In Search of HISTORY in Democratic Korea: The Discourse of Modernity in Contemporary Historical Fiction." In *Constructing Nationhood in Modern East Asia,* eds. Kai-wing Chow, Kevin M. Doak, and Poshek Fu, pp. 189–214. Ann Arbor: University of Michigan Press, 2001.

Hamilton-Merritt, Jane. *Tragic Mountains: The Hmong, the Americans, and the Secret Wars for Laos, 1942–1992.* Bloomington: Indiana University Press, 1993.

Hammond, Stephan. *Hollywood East: Hong Kong Movies and the People Who Make Them.* Lincolnwood, IL: Contemporary, 2000.

Haraway, Donna. *The Haraway Reader.* New York: Routledge, 2004.

Harrer, Heinrich. *Return to Tibet: Tibet After the Chinese Occupation.* 1983. Trans. Ewald Osers. New York: Tarcher/Putnam, 1998.

———. *Seven Years in Tibet.* 1953. Trans. Richard Graves. New York: Tarcher/Putnam, 1996.

Harrison, John R. *The Reactionaries.* London: Gollancz, 1966.

Harvey, David. *The Condition of Modernity.* New York: Blackwell, 1989.

Harvey, Robert C. *The Art of the Funnies: An Aesthetic History.* Jackson, MS: University of Mississippi Press, 1994.

Hawks, Howard, dir. *The Big Sleep.* Perf. Humphrey Bogart and Lauren Bacall. Warner Bros., 1946.

Hayes, Christopher L. "A Study of the Older Hmong Refugees in the United States." PhD diss., The Fielding Institute, Santa Barbara, 1984.

———, and Richard A. Kalish. "Death-Related Experiences and Funerary Practices of the Hmong Refugee in the United States." *Omega: Journal of Death and Dying* 16 (1987–1988): 63–70.

Hearn, Lafcadio. "Otokichi's Daruma." In *The Buddhist Writings of Lafcadio Hearn,* pp. 224–235. Santa Barbara: Ross-Erickson, 1977.

Hearn, Lian. *Across the Nightingale Floor.* New York: Riverhead, 2002.

Hegel, Friedrich. *Lectures on the History of Philosophy.* 1892–1896. Trans. E. S. Haldane. Lincoln: University of Nebraska Press, 1995.

Hemer, Colin F. *The Letters to the Seven Churches of Asia in Their Local Setting.* Grand Rapids, MI: William B. Eerdmans, 2001.

Hesse, Herman. *Siddhartha.* 1951. Trans. Hilda Rosner. New York: New Directions, 1974.

Hiller, J. *Hokusai: Paintings, Drawings and Woodcuts.* New York: Phaidon, 1978.

Hilton, James. *Lost Horizon.* 1933. New York: Pocket Books, 1962.

Ho Nian. "Suiyu er'an" (Easy and comfortable anywhere). *The World Journal (Shijie ribao).* January 16, 1998: C12.

Hockey, Jenny, and Allison James. *Growing Up and Growing Old: Ageing and Dependency in the Life Course.* London: Sage, 1993.

Holmes, Lowell D. "Anthropology and Age: An Assessment." In *Aging in Culture and Society: Comparative Viewpoints and Strategies,* ed. Christine L. Fry, pp. 272–284. New York: Praeger, 1980.

Hom, Marlon K. *Songs of Gold Mountain: Cantonese Rhymes from San Francisco Chinatown.* Berkeley: University of California Press, 1987.

Honda, Inoshiro, and Terry Morse, dir. *Godzilla: King of the Monsters.* Perf. Raymond Burr, Akihiko Hirata, and Takashi Shimura. Toho, 1956. Sony, 2002.

Horkheimer, Max, and Theodor W. Adorno. *Dialectic of Enlightenment.* 1944. Trans. John Cumming. New York: Herder and Herder, 1972.

Houston, Jeanne Wakatsuki, and James D. Houston. *Farewell to Manzanar.* New York: Bantam, 1973.

Howe, Desson. Review of *Little Buddha. Washington Post.* May 25, 1994: p. C1.

Hsia, C. T. *A History of Modern Chinese Fiction, 1917–1957.* New Haven, CT: Yale University Press, 1961.

Hsu, Madeline Y. *Dreaming of Gold, Dreaming of Home: Transnationalism and Migration between the United States and South China, 1882–1943.* Palo Alto, CA: Stanford University Press, 2000.

Hu, King, dir. *Da zui xia (Come drink with me).* Shaw Bros., 1965
———, dir. *Xia nu (A touch of Zen).* International Film Company, 1969.

Hu Yun. "Laoma dangziqiang" (The old mom relies on herself). *The World Journal (Shijie ribao).* January 12, 1999: C12.

Huang Guping. "Yanger bu fanglao" (Raising sons won't insure against old age). *The World Journal (Shijie ribao).* May 11, 1998: C12.

Huo, T. C. *Land of Smiles.* New York: Plume, 2000.

Hwang, Sun-won. *The Book of Masks.* London: Readers International, 1989.

Hyland, William G. *Richard Rodgers.* New Haven: Yale University Press, 1998.

Im, Kwon-Taek, dir. *Chunhyang.* Perf. Hyo-jeong Lee and Seung-woo Cho. Lot 47 Films, 2000.
———, dir. *Sopyonje.* Perf. Myung-gon Kim and Jung-hae Oh. Taeheung Pictures, 1993.

Ing, Eric van den, and Robert Schaap, eds. *Beauty and Violence: Japanese Prints by Yoshitoshi, 1839–1892*. Bergeyk, The Netherlands: Society for Japanese Arts, 1992.

Inuhiko, Yomota. "Stranger than Tokyo: Space and Race in Postnational Japanese Cinema." Trans. Aaron Gerow. In *Multiple Modernities: Cinemas and Popular Media in Transcultural East Asia,* ed. Jenny Kwok Wah Lau, pp. 76–89. Philadelphia: Temple University Press, 2003.

Ishiguro, Kazuo. *The Pale View of Hills*. 1982. New York: Vintage, 1990.

———. *The Unconsoled*. New York: Knopf, 1995.

James, David. E., and Kyung Hyun Kim, eds. *Im Kwon-Taek: The Making of a Korean National Cinema*. Detroit: Wayne State University Press, 2002.

Jameson, Fredric. *Postmodernism, or, The Cultural Logic of Late Capitalism*. Durham: Duke University Press, 1991.

———. "Third-World Literature in the Era of Multinational Capitalism." *Social Text* 15 (1986): 65–88.

Jang, Hyeon-su, dir. *Everyone Has Secrets*. Per. Ji-woo Choi and Byung-hun Lee. Cinema Service, 2004.

Jarmusch, Jim, dir. *Ghost Dog: The Way of the Samurai*. Perf. Forest Whitaker. Artisan Entertainment, 1999.

Jarrott, Charles, dir. *Lost Horizon*. Perf. Peter Finch and Liv Ullmann. Columbia, 1973.

Jin, Ha. *The Bridegroom*. New York: Pantheon, 2000.

———. *The Crazed*. New York: Vintage, 2002.

———. *Waiting*. New York: Vintage, 1999.

———. *War Trash*. New York: Pantheon, 2004.

———. *Wreckage*. Brooklyn, New York: Hanging Loose Press, 2001.

Johnson, Charles. *Myths, Legends and Folk Tales from the Hmong of Laos*. St. Paul, MN: Macalester College, 1985.

Jung, C. G. *The Collected Works of C. G. Jung,* Vol II. Princeton: Princeton University Press, 1967.

———. "Commentary on 'The Secret of the Golden Flower.'" In *Alchemical Studies* from *The Collected Works of C. G. Jung,* Vol. 13, pp. 1–56. Princeton: Princeton University Press, 1967.

———. *Memories, Dreams, Reflections*. Recorded and ed. by Aniela Jaffe. New York: Vintage, 1963.

———. *Psychology and Alchemy*. Trans. R. F. F. Hull. Princeton: Princeton University Press, 1953.

———. "Synchronicity." In *The Essential Jung,* selected and intro. by Anthony Storr, pp. 339–341. Princeton: Princeton University Press, 1983.

Kakoudaki, Despina. "The Human Machine: Visual Representation and Artificial Intelligence." Ph.D. diss., University of California at Berkeley, 2000.

Kang, Je-gyu, dir. *Tae Guk Gi: The Brotherhood of War*. Perf. Jang Dong-Kun and Won Bin. Columbia TriStar, 2004.

Kaplan, Caren. "'Getting to Know You': Travel, Gender, and the Politics of Representation in *Anna and the King of Siam* and *The King and I.*" In *Late Imperial Culture,* eds. Roman De La Campa and E. Ann Kaplan, pp. 33–52. London: Verso, 1995.

Kawajiri, Yoshiaki, dir. *Ninja Scroll.* 1993. Toho, 1995.

Keith, Jennie. "Old Age and Community Creation." In *Aging in Culture and Society: Comparative Viewpoints and Strategies,* ed. Christine L. Fry, pp. 170–197. New York: Praeger, 1980.

Kibria, Nazli. *Becoming Asian-American: Second Generation Chinese and Korean American Identities.* Baltimore: Johns Hopkins University Press, 2002.

Kim, Kichung. "Unheard Voices: The Life of the *Nobi* in O Hwi-mun's *Swaemirok.*" *Korean Studies* 27 (2004): 108–137.

Kim, Kyung Hyun. *The Remasculinization of Korean Cinema.* Durham, NC: Duke University Press, 2005.

Kingston, Maxine Hong. *China Men.* New York: Knopf, 1980.

———. *The Woman Warrior: Memoirs of a Girlhood among Ghosts.* New York: Knopf, 1976.

Kitano, Takeshi, dir. *Dolls.* Perf. Miho Kanno and Hidetoshi Nishijima. Palm Pictures, 2002.

Kogawa, Joy. *Obasan.* Boston: Godine, 1981.

Kovacs, Judith, and Christopher Rowland. *Revelation: The Apocalypse of Jesus Christ.* Malden, MA: Blackwell, 2004.

Kristeva, Julia. *About Chinese Women.* 1974. Trans. Anita Barrows. New York: Marion Boyars, 1993.

———. *Powers of Horror: An Essay on Abjection.* Trans. Leon S. Roudiez. New York: Columbia University Press, 1982.

Kurosawa, Akira, dir. *Kagemusha.* Perf. Tatsuya Nakadai. Twentieth Century Fox, 1980.

———, dir. *Ran.* Perf. Tatsuya Nakadai. Orion Classics, 1992.

———, dir. *Seven Samurai.* Perf. Toshio Mifune. The Criterion Collection, 1954.

Kwak, Jae-young, dir. *Keulraesik. (The classic).* Perf. Ye-jin Son, In-seong Jo, and Seung-woo Cho. Media Suits Ltd., 2003.

Lacan, Jacques. "The Signification of the Phallus." In *Ecrits: A Selection.* 1966. Trans. Alan Sheridan, pp. 281–291. New York: Norton, 1977.

Lai, Him Mark, Genny Lim, and Judy Yung, eds. *Island: Poetry and History of Chinese Immigrants on Angel Island, 1910–1940.* 1980. Seattle: University of Washington Press, 1991.

Lam, Joseph S. C. "Embracing 'Asian American Music' as an Heuristic Device." *Journal of Asian American Studies* 2, no. 1 (1999): 29–60.

Lamb, Sarah. "Intimacy in a Transnational Era: The Remaking of Aging among Indian Americans." *Diaspora: A Journal of Transnational Studies* 11, no. 3 (Winter 2002): 299–330.

Landon, Margaret. *Anna and the King of Siam.* Editor's Note by Elsie Weil. New York: Pocket Cardinal, 1944.

Lao She. *Rickshaw.* 1936–1937. Trans. Jean M. James. Honolulu: University of Hawai'i Press, 1979.

LaRue, Michele. "Stress and Coping of the Indochinese Refugees in a California Community." Ph.D. diss., United States International University, San Diego, 1982.

Lau Kai-leung, dir. *36th Chamber of Shaolin (Master Killer).* Shaw Bros., 1978.

Lee, Ang, dir. *Crouching Tiger, Hidden Dragon.* Columbia TriStar, 2000.

———, dir. *Pushing Hands.* Taipei: Central Motion Picture, 1992.

Lee, C. Y. *Ci-p'ao ku-niang (Cheongsam girl).* Taipei, Taiwan: Chiu-kerh, 1996.

———. *Days of the Tong Wars.* New York: Ballantine, 1974.

———. *The Flower Drum Song.* New York: Dell, 1957.

Lee, Chang-rae. *Aloft.* New York: Riverhead, 2004.

———. *Native Speaker.* New York: Riverhead, 1995.

Lee, Changsoo, ed. *Modernization of Korea and the Impact of the West.* Los Angeles: East Asian Studies Center, University of Southern California, 1981.

Lee, Kwang-hoon, dir. *Ghost in Love (Jaguimo).* Perf. Hee-seon Kim and Sung-jae Lee. Cinema Service, 1998.

Levi, Antonia. *Samurai from Outer Space: Understanding Japanese Animation.* Chicago: Open Court, 1996.

Levi, Primo. *Shema: Collected Poems of Primo Levi.* Trans. Ruth Feldman and Brian Swann. London: The Menard Press, 1976.

Li Shu. "Yanji jiuyiji" (Going to an eye doctor). *The World Journal (Shijie ribao).* January 6, 1999: C12.

Li Zhilin. "On the Dual Nature of Traditional Chinese Thought and Its Modernization." In *Culture and Modernity: East-West Philosophic Perspectives,* ed. Eliot Deutsch, pp. 245–257. Honolulu: University of Hawai'i Press, 1991.

Lin, Angel, Becky Kwan, and Ming Cheung. "The Dilemmas of (Modern) Working Women in (Post-)Confucianist Asia: Women's Use of Korean TV Dramas." International Communication Association (ICA) Annual Conference, New Orleans, USA, 27–31 May 2004.

Liu Jiayi "Shishi duowunai" (Resigned to fate). *The World Journal (Shijie ribao).* January 23, 1999: C10.

Liu Xing. "Laoren gongyu" (Old people's apartment). *The World Journal (Shijie ribao).* January 8, 1999: C10.

Liu Zhiwen. "Tushu guannei" (In the library). *The World Journal (Shijie ribao).* May 15, 1998: C12.

Lo Wei, dir. *Wuhu tulong (Five tigers killing a dragon or Brothers five).* Shaw Bros., 1970.

London, Jack. "Koolau the Leper." In *The House of Pride and Other Tales of Hawaii.* New York, Macmillan and Company, 1912.

Lopez, Donald S., Jr. *Prisoners of Shangri-La: Tibetan Buddhism and the West.* Chicago: University of Chicago Press, 1998.

Lowe, Lisa. *Immigrant Acts: On Asian American Cultural Politics.* Durham, NC: Duke University Press, 1996.

Lu, Sheldon Hsiao-peng. "Historical Introduction: Chinese Cinemas (1896–1996) and Transnational Film Studies." In *Transnational Chinese Cinemas: Identity, Nationhood, Gender,* ed. Sheldon Hsiao-peng Lu, 1–31. Honolulu: University of Hawai'i Press, 1997.

Lu Xun. "The Divorce." In *Selected Stories of Lu Xun,* pp. 216–225. Beijing: Foreign Languages Press, 1960.

———. "The Story of Ah Q." In *Selected Stories of Lu Xun,* pp. 65–112. Beijing: Foreign Languages Press, 1960.

Lucas, George, dir. *Star Wars: Episode II—Attack of the Clones.* Twentieth Century Fox, 2002.

Luciano, Dale. "Comics Past, Comics Present." *The Comics Journal* 77 (Nov 1982): 54–64.

Ma, Sheng-mei. *The Deathly Embrace: Orientalism and Asian American Identity.* Minneapolis: University of Minnesota Press, 2000.

———. *Immigrant Subjectivities in Asian American and Asian Diaspora Literatures.* Albany: State University of New York Press, 1998.

MacDowell, Marsha. *Stories in Thread: Hmong Pictorial Embroidery.* East Lansing: Michigan State University Museum, 1989.

Mao Tse-tung. *Talks at the Yenan Forum on Literature and Art.* 1942. In *Modern Literature from China,* eds. Walter J. and Ruth I. Meserve, 286–314. New York: New York University Press, 1974.

Maugham, W. Somerset. *The Moon and Sixpence.* 1919. New York: Heritage, 1941.

———. *On a Chinese Screen.* 1922. London: Heinemann, 1935.

———. *The Painted Veil.* 1925. New York: Penguin, 1952.

———. *The Razor's Edge.* Philadelphia: Blakiston, 1943.

McConachie, Bruce A. "The 'Oriental' Musicals of Rodgers and Hammerstein and the U.S. War in Southeast Asia." *Theatre Journal* 46 (1994): 385–396.

*Military Comics.* Buffalo, NY: Comic Magazines, 1941–1945.

Min, Anchee. *Katherine.* New York: Riverhead, 1995.

———. *Red Azalea: Life and Love in China.* New York: Pantheon, 1994.

Miyazaki, Hayao, dir. *Nausicaä of the Valley of the Winds.* Walt Disney, 1984.

———, dir. *Princess Mononoke.* Miramax, 1997.

———, dir. *Spirited Away.* Buena Vista Pictures, 2001.

Mo Yan. *Big Breasts and Wide Hips.* Trans. Howard Glodblatt. New York: Arcade, 2004.

———. *Red Sorghum.* Trans. Howard Goldblatt. New York: Viking, 1993.

*Modern Comics.* Buffalo, NY: Comic Magazines, 1945–1950.

Modleski, Tania. *Loving with a Vengeance: Mass-Produced Fantasies for Women.* Hamden, CT: The Shoestring Press, 1982.

Mong Xia. "Yunyian zhishi" (Gone is the cloud). *The World Journal (Shijie ribao).* April 21, 1998: C10.

Moore-Howard, Patricia. *The Hmong—Yesterday and Today.* Sacramento, CA: Patricia Moore-Howard, 1982.

Morrison, Gayle L. *Sky Is Falling: An Oral History of the CIA's Evacuation of the Hmong from Laos*. Jefferson, NC: MacFarland, 1999.

Most, Andrea. "'We Know We Belong to the Land': The Theatricality of Assimilation in Rodgers and Hammerstein's *Oklahoma!*" *PMLA* 113, no. 1 (January 1998): 77–89.

Mukherjee, Bharati. *Jasmine*. New York: Fawcett Crest, 1989.

Mulvey, Laura. *Fetishism and Curiosity*. Bloomington: Indiana University Press, 1996.

Mumford, Laura Stempel. *Love and Ideology in the Afternoon*. Bloomington: Indiana University Press, 1995.

Murayama, Milton. *All I Asking for Is My Body*. Honolulu: University of Hawai'i Press, 1975.

Naremore, James. *More than Night: Film Noir in Its Context*. Berkeley: University of California Press, 1998.

Nee, Victor, and Brett de Bary Nee. *Longtime Californ': A Documentary Study of an American Chinatown*. New York: Pantheon, 1972.

Nguyen, Viet Thanh. *Race and Resistance: Literature and Politics in Asian America*. New York: Oxford University Press, 2002.

Nietzsche, Friedrich Wilhelm. *Thus Spake Zarathustra*. Trans. Walter Kaufmann. New York: Penguin, 1980.

Ning Shen. "Jiujingshan haodifang" (San Francisco is a good place). *The World Journal (Shijie ribao)*. January 20, 1999: C10.

Nolan, Frederick. *The Sound of Their Music: The Story of Rodgers and Hammerstein*. New York: Walker, 1978.

Noriega, Chon A. "Godzilla and the Japanese Nightmare: When *Them* is U.S." In *Hibakusha Cinema: Hiroshima, Nagasaki and the Nuclear Image in Japanese Film*, ed. Mick Broderick, pp. 54–74. London: Kegan Paul, 1996.

O'Brien, David J., and Stephen S. Fugita. *The Japanese American Experience*. Bloomington: Indiana University Press, 1991.

Okada, John. *No-No Boy*. 1957. Seattle: University of Washington Press, 1979.

Okawara, Takao, dir. *Godzilla and Mothra*. Toho, 1992. Columbia TriStar, 1998.

Okubo, Mine. *Citizen 13660*. Seattle: University of Washington Press, 1946.

Orwell, George. *Burmese Days*. 1934. San Diego: Harvest, 1962.

Osborne, Milton. *The Mekong: Turbulent Past, Uncertain Future*. New York: Atlantic Monthly Press, 2000.

Oshii, Mamoru, dir. *Ghost in the Shell*. Anchor Bay Entertainment, 1995.

———, dir. *Ghost in the Shell II: Innocence*. DreamWorks SKG, 2004.

Otomo, Katsuhiro, dir. *Akira*. Twentieth Century Fox, 1988.

Palmore, Erdman B. "Attitudes toward Aging Shown by Humor: A Review." In *Humor and Aging*, eds. Lucille Nahemow, Kathleen A. McCluskey-Fawcett, and Paul E. McGhee, pp. 101–119. New York: Academic Press, 1986.

Palumbo-Liu, David. *Asian/American: Historical Crossings of a Racial Frontier*. Stanford: Stanford University Press, 1999.

————, ed. *The Ethnic Canon: Histories, Institutions, and Interventions.* Minneapolis: University of Minnesota Press, 1995.

Pang Shu. "Yusunji" (Record of raising grandchildren). *The World Journal (Shijie ribao).* May 23, 1998: C10.

Park, Chanwook, dir. *Oldboy.* Perf. Min-sik Choi, Ji-tae Yu, and Hye-jeong Kang. Showeast, 2003.

Parsons, William B. *The Enigma of the Oceanic Feeling: Revisioning the Psychoanalytic Theory of Mysticism.* New York: Oxford University Press, 1999.

Perry, N. *Hyperreality and Global Culture.* London: Routledge, 1998.

Peterson, Sally Nina. "From the Heart and the Mind: Creating Paj Ntaub in the Context of Community." PhD diss., University of Pennsylvania, 1990.

Pfaff, Tim. *Hmong in America: Journey from a Secret War.* Eau Claire, WI: Chippewa Valley Museum Press, 1995.

*Phörpa (The cup).* Dir. Khyentse Norbu. Fine Line Features, 1999.

Polanski, Roman, dir. *Chinatown.* Perf. Jack Nicholson, Faye Dunaway, John Huston. Paramount, 1974.

Porter, Dennis. "Soap Time: Thoughts on a Commodity Art Form." *College English* 38, no. 8 (April 1977): 786.

Pound, Ezra, and Ernest Fenollosa. "The Chinese Written Character as a Medium for Poetry." *Instigations.* 1920. Freeport, NY: Books for Libraries Press, 1967.

Pratt, Ray. *Projecting Paranoia: Conspiratorial Visions in American Film.* Lawrence, KS: University Press of Kansas, 2001.

Quigley, P. "Eisenstein, Montage, and 'Filmic Writing.'" In *The Montage Principle: Eisenstein in New Cultural and Critical Contexts,* ed. Jean Antoine-Dunne with Paula Quigley, pp. 153–169. Amsterdam: Rodopi, 2004.

Quinby, Lee. *Millennial Seduction: A Skeptic Confronts Apocalyptic Culture.* Ithaca: Cornell University Press, 1999.

Quine, Richard, dir. *The World of Suzie Wong.* Perf. William Holden and Nancy Kwan. Paramount, 1960.

Quirke, Stephen. *The Cult of Ra: Sun-Worship in Ancient Egypt.* London: Thames and Hudson, 2001.

Ratner, Brett, dir. *Rush Hour II.* Perf. Jackie Chan and Chris Tucker. New Line Cinema, 2001.

Remennick, Larissa. "The 1.5-Generation of Russian Immigrants in Israel: Between Integration and Socio-Cultural Retention." *Diaspora: A Journal of Transnational Studies* 12, no. 1 (Spring 2003): 39–66.

Renoir, Jean. *My Life and My Films.* New York: Atheneum, 1974.

Rice, Janet. "Hmong Women's Group Using Traditional Quilting to Recover from Depression and Post-Trauma." PhD diss., University of Minnesota, 1999.

Rodgers, Richard. *Musical Stages: An Autobiography.* New York: Random House, 1975.

Rodgers, Richard, and Oscar Hammerstein II. *6 Plays by Rodgers and Hammerstein.* New York: Modern Library, 1959.

————. *Flower Drum Song*. Dir. Henry Koster. Perf. Nancy Kwan, James Shigeta, Miyoshi Umeki, Juanita Hall, Benson Fong, and Jack Soo. Universal Pictures, 1961.

————. *The King and I*. Dir. Walter Lang. Perf. Yul Brynner and Deborah Kerr. Twentieth Century Fox, 1956.

————. *Oklahoma!* Dir. Fred Zinnemann. Perf. Gordon MacRae, Shirley Jones, Eddie Albert, and Rod Steiger. RKO, 1955.

————. *The Sound of Music*. Dir. Robert Wise. Perf. Julie Andrews and Christopher Plummer, 1965.

————. *South Pacific*. Dir. Joshua Logan. Perf. Mitzi Gaynor and Rossano Brazzi. Twentieth Century Fox, 1958.

Rodriguez, Hector. "Hong Kong Popular Culture as an Interpretive Arena: The Huang Feihong Film Series." *Screen* 38, no. 1 (1997): 1–24.

Rosholt, Malcolm. *Flight in the China Air Space, 1910–1950*, Rosholt, WI: Rosholt House, 1984.

Rothman, William. "*The Goddess:* Reflections on Melodrama East and West." In *Melodrama and Asian Cinema*, ed. Wimal Dissanayake, pp. 59–72. New York: Cambridge University Press, 1993.

Rowlandson, Mary. *A True History of the Captivity and Restoration of Mrs. Mary Rowlandson*. 1677. Fairfield, WA: Ye Galleon Press, 2000.

Ruh, Brian. *Stray Dog of Anime: The Films of Mamoru Oshii*. New York: Palgrave, 2004.

Run Dan. "Xiegaole" (The joy of writing). *The World Journal (Shijie ribao)*. April 14, 1998: C12.

Said, Edward. *Orientalism*. New York: Pantheon, 1978.

Santos, Bienvenido N. *Scent of Apples*. Seattle: University of Washington Press, 1992.

Sartre, Jean-Paul. *Nausea*. 1938. Trans. Lloyd Alexander. New York: New Directions, 1964.

Scorsese, Martin, dir. *Kundun*. Buena Vista, 1997.

Scott, George M., Jr. "Migrants without Mountains: The Politics of Sociocultural Adjustment among the Lao Hmong Refugees in San Diego." PhD diss., University of California, San Diego, 1986.

Shankar, Lavina Dhingra, and Rajini Srikanth, eds. *A Part, Yet Apart: South Asians in Asian America*. Philadelphia, PA: Temple University Press, 1998.

Shapiro, Jerome F. *Atomic Bomb Cinema*. New York: Routledge, 2002.

Shim, Doobo. "The Rise of the Korean Media in Asia and Glocalization." Paper presented in the Symposium on Global Challenges and Local Responses, 10–11 October 2003, Asia Research Institute, National University of Singapore.

Shue Wei. "Sandu kaixin" (Three heart surgeries). *The World Journal (Shijie ribao)*. May 9, 1998: C12.

Smith, Adam. *The Wealth of Nations*. 1776. Ed. Andrew Skinner. New York: Penguin, 1979.

Smith, Paul Julian. *The Body Hispanic: Gender and Sexuality in Spanish and Spanish American Literature.* New York: Oxford University Press, 1989.

Sterling, Bruce. "Preface." In *Mirrorshades: The Cyberpunk Anthology,* ed. Bruce Sterling, pp. ix–xvi. New York: Ace Books, 1986.

Sternberg, Josef von, dir. *Macao.* RKO, 1952.

———, dir. *The Shanghai Gesture.* United Artists, 1941.

Stevenson, Robert Louis. *Treasure Island.* 1883. New York: Oxford University Press, 1985.

Stowe, Harriet Beecher. *The Oxford Harriet Beecher Stowe Reader.* Ed. Joan D. Hedrick. New York: Oxford University Press, 1999.

Stringer, Julian. "*Sopyonje* and the Inner Domain of National Culture." In *Im Kwon-Taek: The Making of a Korean National Cinema,* eds. David. E. James and Kyung Hyun Kim, pp. 157–181. Detroit, MI: Wayne State University Press, 2002.

Sun Tzu. *The Art of Warfare.* Trans. Roger T. Ames. New York: Ballantine, 1993.

Suzuki, D. T. *The Zen Doctrine of No-Mind.* Ed. Christmas Humphreys. London: Rider, 1949.

Takezawa, Yasuko I. "Children of Inmates: The Effects of the Redress Movement among Third-Generation Japanese Americans." In *Contemporary Asian America: A Multidisciplinary Reader,* eds. Min Zhou and James V. Gatewood, pp. 299–314. New York: New York University Press, 2000.

Tan, Amy. *The Bonesetter's Daughter.* New York: Ballantine, 2001.

———. *The Joy Luck Club.* New York: Putnam, 1989.

Tarantino, Quentin, dir. *Kill Bill I.* Perf. Uma Thurman and David Carradine. Miramax, 2003.

———, dir. *Kill Bill II.* Perf. Uma Thurman and David Carradine. Miramax, 2005.

Tenhula, John. *Voices from Southeast Asia: The Refugee Experience in the United States.* New York: Holmes and Meier, 1991.

Thompson, Mark. "The Elusive Promise." *Far Eastern Economic Review* 134 (1986): 46–49.

Thompson, Stith. *One Hundred Favorite Folktales.* Bloomington: Indiana University Press, 1968.

*Tibetan Buddhism: Tantras of Gyuto.* Recorded by David Lewiston in 1972 at Gyuto Tantric College at Dalhousie, Himachal Pradesh India. CD. Los Angeles: Elektra/Asylum/Nonesuch Records, 1988.

Tobin, Joseph Jay, and Joan Friedman. "Spirits, Shamans, and Nightmare Death: Survivor Stress in a Hmong Refugee." *American Journal of Orthopsychology* 53 (1983): 439–448.

Turan, Kenneth. "'Kundun' Lacks a Certain Presence." Review of *Kundun. Los Angeles Times.* December 24, 1997: 6.

Tsai Li-li. "Xingde kunrao" (Troubled by surname). *The World Journal (Shijie ribao).* May 5, 1998: C10.

Tsui Hark, dir. *Once Upon a Time in China (Wong fei-hong), I.* Columbia TriStar, 1991.

————, dir. *Once Upon a Time in China (Wong fei-hong), II*. Columbia TriStar, 1992.

————, dir. *Once Upon a Time in China (Wong fei-hong), III*. Columbia TriStar, 1993.

————, dir. *Peking Opera Blues (Dao ma dan)*. Gordon's Films, 1986.

Tsunetomo, Yamamoto. *Hagakure: The Book of the Samurai*. 1716. Trans. William Scott Wilson. New York: Kodansha, 1979.

Ueno, Toshiya. "Japanimation and Techno-Orientalism: Japan as the Sub-Empire of Signs." *Documentary Box* 9 (December 31, 1996): 1–5. http://www.t0.or.at/ueno/japan.htm

————. "Techno-Orientalism and Media-Tribalism: On Japanese Animation and Rave Culture." *Third Text* 47 (Summer 1999): 95–106.

United States. Cong. Senate. S. 933. Americans with Disabilities Act of 1990. http://www.usdoj.gov/crt/ada/pubs/ada.txt

Vang, Lue, and Judy Lewis. *Grandmother's Path, Grandfather's Way: Oral Lore, Generation to Generation*. Rancho Cordova, CA: Vang and Lewis, 1990.

Walker-Moffat, Wendy. *The Other Side of the Asian American Success Story*. San Francisco: Jossey-Bass, 1995.

Wang, David Der-wei, and Jeanne Tai, eds. *Running Wild: New Chinese Writers*. New York: Columbia University Press, 1994.

Wang Ping. *Aching for Beauty: Footbinding in China*. Minneapolis: University of Minnesota Press, 2000.

————. *American Visa*. Minneapolis, MN: Coffee House Press, 1994.

Wang Zhiyi. "Dujing" (The tao of gambling). *The World Journal (Shijie ribao)*. May 7, 1998: C12.

Weber, Max. *The Protestant Ethic and the Spirit of Capitalism*. 1904–1905. Trans. Talcott Parsons. New York: Charles Scribner's Sons, 1958.

Welles, Orson, dir. *The Lady from Shanghai*. Perf. Orson Welles, Rita Hayworth. Columbia Pictures, 1948.

————, dir. *A Touch of Evil*. Perf. Orson Welles, Janet Leigh, Charlton Heston. Universal Pictures, 1959.

Wilde, Oscar. *The Picture of Dorian Gray*. 1891. New York: Oxford University Press, 1981.

Wiles, Timothy J. *The Theater Event: Modern Theories of Performance*. Chicago: University of Chicago Press, 1980.

*Winter Sonata*. Dir. Yun Seok Ho. Perf. Choi Ji Woo and Bae Yong Joon. KBS (20 episodes of the Korean television drama). 2002.

Wong, Sau-ling Cynthia. "Denationalization Reconsidered: Asian American Cultural Criticism at a Theoretical Crossroads." *Amerasia Journal: Double Issue on Thinking Theory in Asian American Studies* 21, nos. 1–2 (1995): 1–27.

————. *Reading Asian American Literature: From Necessity to Extravagance*. Princeton: Princeton University Press, 1993.

————. "'Sugar Sisterhood': Situating the Amy Tan Phenomenon." In *The Ethnic Canon*, ed. David Palumbo-Liu, pp. 172–210. Minneapolis: University of Minnesota Press, 1995.

Woodward, Kathleen. *Aging and Its Discontents: Freud and Other Fictions*. Bloomington: Indiana University Press, 1991.

Xinran. *The Good Women of China: Hidden Voices*. Trans. Esther Tyldesley. New York: Anchor, 2002.

Yamada, Mitsuye. *Camp Notes and Other Poems*. 1976. Latham, NY: Kitchen Table, 1992.

Yamamoto, Hisaye. *Seventeen Syllables and Other Stories*. Latham, NY: Kitchen Table, 1988.

Yamanaka, Lois-Ann. *Blu's Hanging*. New York: Avon, 1997.

Yamauchi, Wakako. *Songs My Mother Taught Me: Stories, Plays, and Memoir*. New York: The Feminist Press, 1994.

Yang, Edward, dir. *Yi Yi*. Perf. Nien-Jen Wu and Elaine Jin. Criterion, 2000.

Yang Jiang. *Six Chapters from My Life "Downunder."* 1981. Trans. Howard Goldblatt. Seattle: University of Washington Press, 1983.

————. *Womensa*. Taipei: Shibao wenhua, 2003.

Yeats, W. B. *The Collected Poems of W. B. Yeats*. New York: Macmillan, 1950.

Yep, Laurence. *Ribbons*. New York: PaperStar, 1992.

Yi Xiao. "Pixie fengpo" (All about shoes). *The World Journal (Shijie ribao)*. May 2, 1998: C12.

Yu, Henry. *Thinking Orientals: Migration, Contact, and Exoticism in Modern America*. New York: Oxford University Press, 2001.

Yu Zi. "Laole zhenhao" (It's wonderful to be old). *The World Journal (Shijie ribao)*. April 22, 1998: C12.

Yun, Heung-gil. *The House of Twilight*. London: Readers International, 1989.

Zhang Che, dir. *One-Armed Swordsman*. Perf. Wang Yu. Intercontinental Video, 1967.

Zhang Xianliang. *Getting Used to Dying*. New York: HarperCollins, 1991.

————. *Half of Man is Woman*. Trans. Martha Avery. New York: W. W. Norton, 1988.

Zhang, Xinyan, dir. *Shao si (The Shaolin temple)*. Perf. Jet Li. World Video, 1979.

Zhang Xueyi. "Cai pingguo qu" (Let's go apple-picking). *The World Journal (Shijie ribao)*. January 10, 1999: C12.

Zhang Yimou, dir. *Hero*. Perf. Jet Li. Universal Pictures, 2002.

————, dir. *Raise the Red Lantern*. Perf. Gong Li. Orion Classics, 1991.

————, dir. *Red Sorghum*. Perf. Gong Li and Jiang Wen. New York Films, 1987.

Zhou Yutang. "Zhongfeng laoren detong" (The pain of the elderly stroke victim). *The World Journal (Shijie ribao)*. January 23, 1999: C10.

Zwick, Edward, dir. *The Last Samurai*. Perf. Tom Cruise. Warner Bros., 2003.

# Index

body, the, xxii–xxiii
body as waste in Japanese American
    internment literature, 22–36;
    amputees, 32–36; disability
    and deformity, 22–23, 32–33;
    existential puke, 23–25, 28; Maoist
    manure, 23, 28–31; shit, Japanese,
    23–31
bound feet, 191–196, 199–200
Brecht, Bertolt, 10
Bresson, Robert, 79, 80
*Broken Blossoms*, 17
Brooks, Peter, 129
Brown, Norman O., xxii, 3, 5
brush and blade, dichotomy and
    attraction of, 39–42
Burchett, Rick, 180, 182

camp scatology. *See* body as waste in
    Japanese American internment
    literature
Camus, Albert, 24
Caniff, Milton, 159, 160, 184
cannibalism, 54
Capra, Frank, 204, 206, 207
Celan, Paul, 217
Chandler, Raymond, 18, 19
Chang, Pang-Mei Natasha, 199
Chang Xiong, 228
Chan, Jackie, 60, 61, 75
Chaykin, Howard, 178, 181, 184
Chen Chi-Li, 65
Chen Duxiu, 249
Chen, Joan, 81, 82, 95
Chen Jo-hsi, 29, 82, 83–84, 89,
    243–244
Cheung, Ming, 115
Chia Kua Xiong, 226
Chiang Kai-shek, 159
Chiba, Sonny, 109
*Chinatown*, 20–21
Chinatown in film: *Flower Drum Song*,
    143, 144, 147, 148, 150–151;
    Godzilla movies, 105; Japanese
    anime, 105–107; w/hole of Asia and
    Christian West, 17–21

Chin, Frank, xx, 189
Cho, Margaret, 271n2
Chop Chop. *See Blackhawk* comics
"chopsticks" musicals, 143–156;
    East-West spatial relationships
    in, 147–151; English teacher
    characters, 144–147; *Flower
    Drum Song*, 143, 144, 147, 148,
    150–151, 153–155; *The King and
    I*, 143–149, 151, 155; mixed-race
    stars employed in, 153–154; music
    of, 154–156; "mutt" teases in,
    151–154; predecessors of, 155–156;
    *South Pacific*, 143–147, 149–152,
    155
Chow, Rey, 9, 53
Chow, Stephen, 46
Chow Yun-Fat, 61, 70, 73, 75
Chow Yun-fat, 144
Christianity. *See* Bible; w/hole of Asia
    and Christian West
Chua Ben Huat, 120, 127
Chu, Judy, 242
*Chunhyang*, 118, 134
Clavell, James, 47, 48, 49
Coleridge, Samuel Taylor, 13
colonial acephalism and swordplay,
    39–42, 49, 51–59
Conrad, Joseph, 39, 48, 51, 54, 56, 57,
    145, 189, 212
Coppola, Francis Ford, 7, 56–57, 145,
    205
cosmetic surgery of actors in Korean
    Wave, 125–126, 130
Craig, Mary, 208, 209
*Crouching Tiger, Hidden Dragon*, 40, 45,
    60, 70–75, 115

*Dae Jang Kum*, 133–134
Dai, Catherine, 199
Dai Sijie, 81, 82, 88
Dalai Lama, xxiii, 144–145, 202–203,
    205, 207–210
*Dances with Wolves*, 47, 48
death and feces, 5–6
death of a thousand cuts, 58–59

decapitation and swordplay, 39–42, 49, 51–59

Demi, 203

De Quincy, Thomas, 13–14

Derrida, Jacques, xi, 9, 41, 239

Descartes, René, xiii, 11

diaspora, concept of, xvi–xxii, 245

Dickens, Charles, 14

disabilities studies, 32, 36; Americans with Disabilities Act (ADA), 189–190; body as waste in Japanese American internment literature, 22–23, 32–36; Western literature, disability and deformity in, 22–23, 32–33. *See also* immigrant Asians with "magical" disabilities

Donnelly, Nancy, 221, 272–273nn1–3

Douglass, Mary, 4

Doyle, Arthur Conan, 15–16

dubbing, 79–80, 267n2

Duras, Marguerite, 6, 86, 204

East-West montage, xi–xxiii; Asian diaspora, concept of, xvi–xxii, 245; the body, xxii–xxiii; from classical to modern era, xiii–xv; fluid concepts of East and West, xiii–xiv; montage theory and Asian ideograms, xi–xiii, 10, 40; reflection, concept of, xv–xvi, 18

Eisenstein, Sergei, xi–xiii, xiv, 10

elderly. *See* retirees, Taiwanese and Chinese, in US

Eliot, T. S., xiv, 7, 40, 42, 264n10, 265n11

English teacher characters, 144–147

Espiritu, Yen Le, xix

Euripides, xiii

Evanier, Mark, 172, 177, 178

excrement. *See* body as waste in Japanese American internment literature

executions, public, 51–54, 58–59

existential puke, 23–25, 28

face and facial features: anus and face/mouth, resemblance between, 3–4; cosmetic surgery of actors in Korean Wave, 125–126, 130; fetishization of face in Korean Wave, 120–122; (over)painted lips in Korean Wave, 114, 115–119, 120; stylized Western features in Japanese anime, 98, 102–103

Faderman, Lillian, 217–218, 226–227

Fadiman, Anne, 218, 223

Far, Sui Sin, xix

Faulkner, William, 18

feces. *See* body as waste in Japanese American internment literature

feminist theory. *See* gender studies

Feng Jicai, 82, 83, 84, 89, 193, 195, 271n1

fetishism, concept of, 192

*Flower Drum Song,* 143, 144, 147, 148, 150–151, 153–155

Fong, Timothy, 242

foot binding, 191–196, 199–200

Forster, E. M., 39, 51, 54, 55–56

Freud, Sigmund, and Freudian psychoanalysis, xi, xiii; body as waste, 25; the elderly and, 246; Hmong refugees and, 219–220; Korean Wave and, 114, 119, 120, 123, 137; kung fu films, 72; "magical" disabilities, 191; swordplay, 41, 49; Tibet, Western interest in, 204; w/hole of Asia and Christian West, 6, 7, 9, 10, 260n4

gender studies: *Blackhawk* comics, 180–181; bound feet, 191–196; diaspora and, xvii; Japanese anime, female bodies in, 102–105; Korean Wave, 114–115, 138–139; polygamy, 193–195

*Ghost Dog,* 46, 47, 48–49

*Ghost in Love,* 119

*Ghost in the Shell I* and *II,* 98, 100–102, 104, 105, 107, 108

Glass, Philip, 204–205, 209–210

global postmodernism and swordplay, 42–51

sexuality: anus and sexual organs,
proximity of, 6; in *Blackhawk* comics,
181–185; of bound feet, 191–195,
199; existentialist puke and, 24;
Japanese anime, female bodies in,
102–105; in kung fu films, 6,
70–75; "mutt" teases in "chopsticks"
musicals, 151–154. *See also* Maoist
China; Korean Wave
Shakespeare, William, 11–12, 22–23,
32–33, 43, 49
*Shan dao,* 116–118, 131–132
*Shangri-La,* 204, 205–207
Shapiro, Jerome, 97, 99–100, 102
Shen Yueh, 244
Shim, Doobo, 113
shit. *See* body as waste in Japanese
American internment literature
*sibuxiang,* xxi
*Singin' in the Rain,* 79
Smith, Adam, xi, xiii
solar anus, 3, 11–12
Sophocles, 22–23
*Sopyonje,* 134–137
*South Pacific,* 143–147, 149–152, 155
Spiegle, Dan, 172, 177, 178
*Spirited Away,* 49, 98
*Star Wars,* 63
Stevenson, Robert Louis, 33
story cloths of Hmong refugees,
227–235
Stowe, Harriet Beecher, 146, 149
Stringer, Julian, 131, 136
Sucheng Chan, 228
Sudden Unexpected Nocturnal Death
Syndrome (SUNDS), 219–226
Sun Yat-Sen, 69
survivor guilt among Hmong refugees,
223
Su Tong, 194
Suzuki, D. T., 48
swordplay and swordplay films, 39–59;
brush and blade, dichotomy and
attraction of, 39–42; colonial
acephalism, 39–42, 49, 51–59;
with disabled fighters, 36; global

postmodernism and, 42–51; kung fu
films and, 61, 67–68, 70; naming of
swords, 40, 41; phallic fetish, sword
as, 41–42; public executions, 42–51

Takezawa, Yasuko, 23
Tan, Amy, xix, 87, 91, 191, 197–198,
201
Tarantino, Quentin, 46–51, 107–109
Tenhula, John, 223, 224
*Terry and the Pirates,* 159, 160, 184
thousand cuts, death of a, 58–59
Tibet, Western films and narratives
about, 202–214; Dalai Lama, xxiii,
144–145, 202–203, 205,
207–210; *Kundun,* 204, 208–210,
213; *Little Buddha,* 203–204,
210–214; *Seven Years in Tibet,* 144,
204, 207–208; *Shangri-La,* 204,
205–207
*Touch of Zen, A,* 60, 67, 71, 75
Tsui Hark, 46, 60, 62, 63, 67–70

Ueno, Toshia, 103

Vang Xiong, 224–226
vomit, 23–25, 28
von Sternberg, Josef, 17–18

Wachowski brothers, 10, 48, 107, 109
Wang, David, xxii
Wang Dulu, 70
Wang Ping, 81, 87–88, 89, 199
Watana, Onoto, xix
Welles, Orson, 18–20
w/hole of Asia and Christian West,
3–21; Biblical apocalypses, 3–9;
Chinatown in film noir, 17–21;
oneness and unity, 9–10; opium dens,
12–17, 258n11
Wilde, Oscar, 14–15
*Winter Sonata,* 113, 118, 119–125, 138
women. *See* gender studies; sexuality
Wong, Sau-Ling Cynthia, xix, xx, xxii,
260n2
Woo, John, 61, 62, 64, 75

## About the Author

**Sheng-mei Ma** is professor of English at Michigan State University, specializing in Asian Diaspora/Asian American studies and East-West comparative studies. His publications include *The Deathly Embrace: Orientalism and Asian American Identity* (University of Minnesota Press, 2000), *Immigrant Subjectivities in Asian American and Asian Diaspora Literatures* (State University of New York Press, 1998), *Chenmo de shanhen (Silent scars: History of sexual slavery by the Japanese military—A pictorial book)* bilingual edition (Shanzhou, 2005), *San-shi zuoyou (Thirty, left and right),* a collection of Ma's Chinese poetry (Shulin, 1989), and numerous articles and book chapters.

**Production Notes for**

*Ma East-West Montage*

Cover designed by Santos Barbasa, Jr.

Interior designed by Lucille C. Aono in
Bernhard Modern Std, with display type in Bauhaus

Composition by Lucille C. Aono

Printing and binding by Edwards Brothers, Inc.

Printed on 50 lb. EB Opaque, 606 ppi